W9-CEN-726

THE MAKING OF THE
AMERICAN CONSERVATIVE
MIND

THE MAKING OF THE
AMERICAN
CONSERVATIVE
MIND

National Review

AND ITS TIMES

JEFFREY HART

ISI BOOKS

Wilmington, Delaware

Copyright © 2005, 2007 ISI Books

All rights reserved. No part of this publication may be reproduced or transmitted in any form or by any means, electronic or mechanical, including photocopy, or any information storage and retrieval system now known or to be invented, without permission in writing from the publisher, except by a reviewer who wishes to quote brief passages in connection with a review written for inclusion in a magazine, newspaper, or broadcast.

All photos used by permission of the Intercollegiate Studies Institute, Inc., and National Review, Inc.; all rights reserved.

Hart, Jeffrey Peter, 1930–

      The making of the American conservative mind : National review and its times / Jeffrey Hart. — [2nd ed.]. — Wilmington, Del. : ISI Books, 2006, c2005.

          p. ; cm.
          ISBN-13: 978-1-933859-13-2
          ISBN-10: 1-933859-13-X
          Includes bibliographical references and index.

          1. Conservatism—United States—History—20th century.
2. Political culture—United States—History—20th century.
3. Conservatives—United States—History—20th century. 4. United States—Politics and government—20th century. 5. National review—History. 6. Buckley, William F. (William Frank), 1925– I. Title.
II. National review and its times.

JC573.2.U6 H37 2006   2006933804
320.52/0973—dc22   0610

Book design by Claudia Henrie

Published in the United States by:

      ISI Books
      Intercollegiate Studies Institute
      Post Office Box 4431
      Wilmington, DE 19807-0431
      www.isibooks.org

This book is dedicated to my wife Nancy,
whose love every day makes
everything possible.

Fifty Years

They who were are not, and
These who are were not.
See how they go, now they are here.
Now not, O Palinur . . .
but here, in the stillness, here,
And the house echoes, echoes
As the leaf falls near the cataract and the
New thrush sings in the pines.

—JH (with WS and WW)

Table of Contents

Acknowledgments

Without William F. Buckley Jr., *National Review* would not have existed. His cooperation has also been invaluable in the writing of this book. Yet this history of *National Review* during its first half-century is in no sense an official history, as will be more than evident to the reader. Throughout, the evaluations and judgments are my own, and they come from a conservative perspective I would characterize as Burkean, yet interpreted for the American situation. I confess to a fondness for gossip, which, indeed, is a conservative genre. Gossips do not want to change the world; they want to enjoy it.

The learned help of my editor at ISI, Mark Henrie, has been enormously useful. He is a stylist, a scholar, and a political theorist; he has focused my mind on important issues such as theology, abortion, and political philosophy and otherwise has been a valuable guide. But my conclusions are not necessarily his. I have known Mark since his undergraduate days at Dartmouth and am not surprised by his brilliance now. Priscilla Buckley had the idea for this book; she and Linda Bridges have helped immensely with their inside knowledge of the history of the magazine. Rich Lowry, current editor of *National Review*, has been forthcoming with information, not only about the magazine since the Clinton years—Clinton being the subject of his fine history, *Legacy*—but helpful also about the current editorial positions of the magazine.

As well as serving as a senior editor at *National Review*, I am de facto poetry editor, that feature having been reestablished in 2002 after a long hiatus since Hugh Kenner handled it in *National Review*'s earliest days; Books editor Mike Potemra has been splendidly cooperative there. John Virtes, research director at *National Review*, has been ever willing to provide valuable help. Ed Capano, publisher of the magazine, maintains an expert eye on its entire operation and has been generous with his time and knowledge of its operations, circulation, and many other matters. My thanks to all.

Jeffrey Hart
Lyme, New Hampshire
August 2005

Preface

The history of *National Review* represents a Quest Narrative: the quest for a politically viable and thoughtful American conservatism. The journey is difficult, because it involves the search not merely for political positions—which are, after all, ephemeral—but for the underlying basis upon which such positions ought to be derived: which is to say, abiding principles. This history of *National Review* is thus, in one sense, a course in how to think, which is much more important than transitory advocacy, in which one might be correct by chance, or by echo.

The journey recorded here is far from tranquil, since it has sometimes involved throwing much overboard, and this entails a continuing struggle to discipline desire with a sense of changing social, economic, and scientific actuality. As the historian here, I have been educated myself, first as a reader of the magazine since 1955, then as a senior editor beginning in 1969, and most recently as a reader of the entire corpus of the magazine in its very heavy forty-nine bound volumes. I have sometimes felt more like a foreman than a writer. To come to my judgments, I have compared what *National Review* said on a given occasion with what the relevant historians now can tell us about it. Hell for opinion journalists must consist of the perpetual re-reading of last year's editorials.

Throughout the history of *National Review* we find a struggle going on, in diverse ways, between Idea and Actuality. Success is sometimes achieved, as Idea adjusts to Actuality, but sometimes there is a lurch back toward the Idea at odds with Actuality: utopianism. A nonnegotiable maxim emerges from a fixed Idea, or many fixed Ideas, often parading as "principles," but when these are excessively abstract they become *ideology*, the lethal enemy of thought. To think, as in another connection the great West Point football coach Earl "Red" Blaik once said, means "You have to pay the price"—that is, the price in pain and sorrow as favorite notions go overboard when contradicted by the facts. Reading the books that have lasted acclimates one to a sense of changing, surprising, disappointing, and joyful Actuality—a vale of laughs as much as a vale of tears—and also requires a sense of readiness and flexibility in the face of changing circumstances. Change is part of Actuality, and the struggle against Actuality is an uneven contest.

When Idea becomes divorced from Actuality, the result is fanaticism, the wings of discourse beating in a void. Over the entrance to the first of the three kingdoms in Dante's *Divine Comedy* stands this forbidding notice:

> Abandon all hope, you who enter here.

Fortunately, the journey the reader is about to take with this book will not be as arduous as that of the pilgrim Dante in that great poem, because *National Review* has pioneered the journey already. The historian who tells this story of *National Review*'s quest has himself been shaped in good measure by reading the magazine from November 1955 through the present. So what judgments are passed along the way amount to *National Review* examining itself. In this narrative, the pilgrim magazine followed the guide James Burnham for much of the way, as the pilgrim Dante followed the guide Virgil, who brought the pilgrim much of the way up the cleansing Mountain, but unfortunately dropped away before the journey ended. Similarly, the guide Burnham leaves part of the way through the journey, even as the helmsman Palinurus does in Virgil's earlier epic.

So, reader, let us now take the journey together through the refining fire, the sign above our first gate reading:

Abandon hope—but not quite all hope—all you fanatics, dogmatists, single-issue obsessives, all you wild-eyed apparitions with straws in your hair, all you who have forgotten that man is neither angel nor brute, and through the disciplines of the great historians, lasting books, and alertness to experience, learn prudence, measured skepticism, and other sober virtues, which in politics translate into consensus government through the deliberate sense of the governed. For some, the way will be hard, but fare forward, voyagers! and avoid the whirlpools of nonsense and the fever swamps of prefabricated thought.

Introduction to Paperback Edition

In *The Making of the American Conservative Mind*, my method is to use the work of our best historians to establish the facts about successive administrations beginning with Eisenhower, and then to give an account of what *National Review* had to say when the history was happening. I hope that what the historians have discovered will be as interesting to readers as it was to me. Sometimes, a great disconnect appears between what *seemed* to be true about public figures and what actually *was* true. Thus, Princeton historian Fred I. Greenstein in *The Hidden Hand Presidency* showed that Eisenhower was not really who we had thought, the genial, avuncular "Ike" with the lopsided American grin and jumbled syntax. Rather, he was ruthless, lucid, a fine administrator, and completely realistic. "Ike" was a deliberately achieved persona, a mask. Stephen Ambrose, in *Eisenhower the President,* confirmed this portrait and added to it. In 1960, everyone thought Jack Kennedy was young, vigorous, and athletic. In *An Unfinished Life,* Robert Dalleck, the first historian to see Kennedy's complete medical records, showed that he suffered from multiple disabling ailments and was the sickest man ever to be elected president. In January 1969, when he came to the presidency, Richard Nixon knew the Vietnam war could not be won. His job, as he saw it, was to get America out; he also knew he could not admit this publicly.

Based on the evidence, Eisenhower and Reagan emerge as the great presidents of the postwar period. They both confronted and dealt successfully with the problems they faced, both were prudent realists, and both were reelected by landslides. Franklin Roosevelt joins them as the third great president of the twentieth century, a man who was successful in peace and world war and was elected four times.

The Making of the American Conservative Mind ends with the narrow reelection of George W. Bush in 2004, and the final chapter discusses twelve items in the constellation of ideas that in combinations constitute the American conservative mind. I deliberately use the word "combinations" in its plural form because the relative importance of the ideas can change with time. These ideas are not to be applied mechanically but with tact. Thus, free-market economics is valid, but it must be modified by what Burke called "the unbought grace of life," that is, by other values of civilization. Not everything is for sale.

Measured against those twelve ideas, George W. Bush—as everyone saw when this book first appeared—did not score well, though *National Review* has continued to admire him, Richard Lowry even characterizing him as "neo-Reagan," despite the manifest success of the Reagan presidency and a gathering consensus among historians that Reagan was indeed a great president, while it seems clear that George W. Bush is in various kinds of serious trouble.[1] Nevertheless, I have heard at *National Review* the thought that Bush is "even better than Reagan," and one writer for the magazine has even compared Bush to Lincoln.

Now, in the latter half of 2006, it is time for another provisional assessment of the Bush administration from a conservative perspective, with an account of *National Review*'s ongoing response to the central issues of this presidency. It must be provisional because we lack access to archival material, oral histories, and other evidence that eventually will be available to historians, and so we necessarily depend on journalists of various kinds and books as they come off the presses. Still, a great deal is emerging and judgments are forming, as Bush's approval rating hovers around 30 percent—a lot better even there than Dick Cheney's, which as I write stands at about 18 percent.

In the June 5, 2006, *National Review*, Ramesh Ponnuru published an article wondering why, with the economy relatively strong, Bush's approval rating remained so low. In answering Pommuru's question I am tempted to echo Elizabeth Barrett Browning's famous sonnet and say "Let me count the ways," that is, the ways in which Bush has sunk so low in the nation's estimation. I can think of nine major reasons:

1. The Iraq War
2. The response to Hurricane Katrina
3. Bush's proposal to privatize Social Security
4. The Terri Schiavo case
5. Embryonic stem-cell research
6. The Bush administration's contempt for, perhaps ignorance of, science
7. The administration's overall fiscal mismanagement
8. The Jack Abramoff scandal and the corruption it revealed
9. The indictment of Lewis I. Libby in the Joseph Wilson case, and what the indictment of the vice president's chief of staff implies for the claims about weapons of mass destruction in Iraq

The Iraq invasion looms as the largest factor, since it is often said to be the centerpiece of Bush's presidency. George W. Bush bet his reputation and historical standing on the Iraq gamble. In this outline it will be taken up last. There are many other important reasons for Bush's slide into disfavor.

The response of the Bush administration to the damage done by Hurricane Katrina indicated to many that the administration did not know how to administrate, and persuaded people that the federal government could not evacuate even a medium-sized city if required to do so by a terrorist attack. Michael Brown, direction of FEMA, had no relevant experience for his post, though Bush absurdly said he'd "done a heck of a job." Bush's nomination of Harriet Miers to the Supreme Court reinforced the impression that qualifications—and competence—counted little for Bush. Following Katrina, Bush's approval rating dropped to 2 percent among American blacks. Jefferson Davis might have scored higher.

Soon after his narrow reelection in 2004, Bush invested what he called his "political capital" in a radical idea. He proposed to privatize Social Security, one of the most successful New Deal Programs. Instead of direct payments, people would establish personal accounts and invest in the stock market. White House polls indicated that at first this sounded like an appealing idea; but soon it dropped like a stone, since it seemed to make the social safety net depend on the value of Enron or Worldcom stock. The Bush plan looked less and less attractive the more people thought about it.

National Review said editorially that it admired Bush for his "heavy lifting" on Social Security and Iraq. Social Security proved too heavy for Bush to lift, and the same looks true of Iraq.

THE TERRI SCHIAVO CASE was particularly important, certainly for the individuals involved, but also for what it revealed: the poisonous effect the radical Christian right has had on the Bush administration, and through it on the entire nation. As *National Review* editor Richard Lowry correctly said in his syndicated column of February 23, 2004, evangelical Christians continue to form the indispensable political base of the Bush administration. But their passionate dogmatism overwhelms common sense and their policy preferences turn out to be rejected by the majority of Americans. Often such policy preferences have nothing to do with scripture or the teachings of Jesus, even though "faith" energizes the politics of the Christian right. Conservative columnist Andrew Sullivan coined the term "Christianist" to describe this politics, seeing it as related to Christianity in the same way that Islamist ideology is to the religion of Islam. On one occasion Bush provided educational leadership by declaring that Intelligent Design should be taught "along with" evolution in biology classes.

This Christian right base was fully mobilized in a well-financed effort to "save Terri," who had long been in a permanently vegetative coma.[2] The Bush administration spearheaded the effort to prevent the removal of her feeding tube, which had sustained her for eight years. This proved to be a public opinion disaster. On whether the feeding tube should be removed, the American people said yes by almost a two-to-one majority (a Fox News Channel poll showed that 61% of respondents favored removal of the tube, while a CNN/*USA Today*/Gallup poll put the same number at 80%; other polls fell somewhere in between).

No doubt existed regarding Terri's condition. On the early morning of February 25, 1990, Terri collapsed in her apartment. Her husband Michael Schiavo called 911. By the time the paramedics arrived, her heart had stopped beating for several minutes, depriving her brain of oxygen. There was no doubt about the result. Neurological tests and CT scans showed that her cerebral cortex had become liquid spinal fluid. Cognition was completely impossible. Any physical movement by Terri was stimulated by her autonomic nervous system, her brain stem. Existing in an irreversible vegetative state, she was kept alive by the feeding tube that sent nutrients directly to her digestive system and was incontinent. (Her eventual autopsy showed that her brain was half its normal size.)

On June 1, 1990, a judge appointed Michael Schiavo as Terri's legal guardian. Devastated by her condition, he took nursing lessons so he could participate in her hospital care. He also took her to California for experimental therapy, including the implantation of a thalamic stimulator into her brain. It didn't work. Years elapsed. Michael developed a relationship with another woman; they had a child. Terri's parents, Bob and Mary Schindler, agreed that this is what Terri would have wanted. Their own daily visits to Terri's bedside had become important events in their lives.

In May, 1998, more than eight years after the accident, Michael petitioned the court for authorization to remove the feeding tube, claiming that Terri had explicitly said she would not want to persist in such a degraded state. There was specific corroborating testimony. Florida judge George Greer granted his request. There then transpired an astonishing sequence of events, lasting until March 31, 2005, when the feeding tube was finally removed and Terri died. The events are difficult to summarize briefly. Suffice to say, by the end Congress had passed legislation designed to "save

Terri," and President Bush had flown on Air Force One to Washington from Crawford, Texas, to sign the bill, conspicuously hoping to save precious time.

Throughout, the constitutional issue concerned the separation of powers, legislative and judicial. But on this issue, at least, the Constitution did not concern the religious right. As the denouement approached in early 2005, noisy crowds gathered outside Terri's hospice. Michael Schiavo received death threats from crusaders for life. Under pressure from the religious right, Governor Jeb Bush almost sent Florida state law enforcement personnel to seize Terri and save her, despite the determination of local police to enforce the law.

In Washington during this feverish period, politicians said strange things. According to majority whip Tom DeLay, "Terri Schiavo is not brain-dead. She talks, she laughs, and she expresses happiness and discomfort." Senate majority leader Bill Frist, heretofore a respected physician, gave everyone a reason to question his integrity. Without examining Terri and basing his opinion on a highly edited videotape, he said Terri's diagnosis might be wrong. This was irresponsible. Editorially, *National Review* expressed the opinion that Terri might be capable of some cognition, apparently unaware of the evidence available to the contrary about her cerebral cortex. On March 31, 2005, the feeding tube was removed and Terri died painlessly, completely unaware. President Bush said that "we need judges who understand that our rights derive from God," thus offering a religious condemnation of judges who had upheld the Constitution and the independence of the judiciary from the legislative branch. The legal right of Michael Schiavo to speak for Terri as determined by the courts apparently did not occur to Bush. He had rewarded his indispensable base but lost the confidence of the majority of Americans.

Not surprisingly, the Terri Schiavo case caused a large spike in "living wills." In a *National Review* article, Ramesh Ponnuru took the extreme position that such living wills should be invalidated—by the courts?—since they amounted to suicide. One can imagine the unpopularity of such a position. In fact, it is absurd.

Another absurd position taken by the Bush administration concerns the therapeutic use of embryonic stem cells, an issue that has simmered since the president for all practical purposes blocked federal funding for such research in August 2001. Again, a large majority of the public supports the research, and it was a marginal issue in the 2004 elections when a California initiative authorized $30 billion for it. Embryonic stem cells hold out the promise of curing devastating diseases. Bush frames his opposition this way: "It is wrong to destroy life in order to save life." In that sentence, his first use of the word "life" refers to an almost microscopic clump of fertilized cells, most of them now frozen in fertility clinics and doomed anyway. His second use of "life" refers to anyone from a baby with deadly Type I diabetes to an adult with Parkinson's, Alzheimer's, or countless other diseases. *National Review* agrees with Bush. Editorially, the magazine has said that a fertilized cell "must not be destroyed no matter how noble the cause." That absolutist prohibition does not survive a moment's reflection. I believe that Dartmouth Professor of Medicine and Biochemistry Lee A. Witters demonstrates genuine moral imagination when he puts it this way: "If you had a child with Type I diabetes [life threatening], and I told you that I had a few cells that would cure her, would you turn this down?" Almost everyone would say no. Bush's position is nonsense, and most people know it. For all practical purposes, the argument about embryonic stem cells is over.

BUSH INHERITED a budgetary surplus from Clinton and his treasury secretaries Lloyd Bentsen and Robert Rubin. By spending massively and at the same time cutting taxes, Bush has run up federal indebtedness to unprecedented heights, the debt financed mostly by China. In 2005, Reagan economic advisor Bruce Bartlett published *Impostor,* a comprehensive criticism of Bush's budgetary policies. As he wrote in a *Los Angeles Times* op-ed column (March 12, 2006):

> As a lifelong conservative, I have to be honest: George W. Bush is not one of us and never has been. There can be no denying that he has enacted polices contrary to conservative principles on too many occasions. In my view, his

greatest failing has been a total lack of control over federal spending—to the point where liberal Democrat Bill Clinton is looking more and more like the "good old days."

Bartlett believes that Bush's successor is going to have to enact large tax increases to clean up the mess Bush will leave behind. It is not the only mess Bush's successor will have to deal with. For Bush decided to go to war with Iraq soon after he came to office in early 2001, long before 9/11.[3] Two reasons were given: 1) the threat to the United States posed by Saddam's weapons of mass destruction, chemical, biological, and nuclear; and 2) the idea of spreading democracy through the Middle East, on the view that democracies do not start wars. The threat of weapons of mass destruction sold the American people on the war. As it turned out, Iraq had none at all. There are now serious reasons to believe that the claims about WMD by the Bush administration had a very weak basis. Intelligence expert Thomas Powers has used the work "fabricated" about some of the administration's claims. A particularly effective case has been made in support of that charge by the report of the minority staff of the House Judiciary Committee. Titled *The Constitution in Crisis*, it is readily available online.[4] Bush's defenders shy away from the evidence here, evidently for partisan reasons. Historian Robert Dallek has called this report "devastating." I have compiled a bibliography of recent work tending to support the "devastating" claims of the report.[5]

Chapter 25 of *The Making of the American Conservative Mind* includes an important statement by Bush outlining his theoretical basis for attempting to spread democracy in the Middle East, first by achieving it in Iraq. Speaking before the American Enterprise Institute on February 26, 2003, Bush put forth the following theory of human behavior:

> Human cultures can be vastly different. Yet the human heart desires the same good things, everywhere on earth. In our desire to be safe from brutal and bullying oppression, human beings are the same. For these fundamental reasons, freedom and democracy will always and everywhere have greater appeal than the slogans of hatred and the tactics of terror.

Much of this is refuted by history and individual experience. The people going to work in the World Trade Center on the morning of 9/11 did not want the same things as Mohammed Atta. Holiness, conquest, and national glory—just to name a few things—may have greater appeal than freedom and democracy. But Bush's belief in the convergence of human interests and the superficiality of conflicting goals is apparently unshakable. On April 24, 2006, he repeated this theory in a speech delivered in Irvine, California:

> I based a lot of my foreign policy decisions on some things that I think are true. One, I believe there's an Almighty, and secondly, I believe one of the great gifts of the Almighty is the desire in everybody's soul, regardless of what you look like or where you live, to be free. I believe liberty is universal. I believe people want to be free. And I know that the best way to defeat the enemy, the best way to defeat their ability to exploit hopelessness and despair, is the ability to give people a chance to live in a free society.

Free societies are a relatively new thing in human history, and are still far from the norm in this world. The work of the Almighty has certainly taken its time in being accomplished. Dick Cheney differed sharply with Bush's theory about the harmony of human goals:

> Once you get into Baghdad, it's not clear what you do with it. It's not clear what kind of government you put in place of the one that's there now. Is it going to be a Shia regime, a Sunni regime? Or one that tilts toward the Baathists, or one that tilts toward Islamic fundamentalism? How much credibility is that going to have is it's set up by the American military there? How long does the American military have to stay there to protect the people that sign on for that government, and what happens when we leave?

But Cheney said that in 1991 when he was secretary of defense under George H. W. Bush.

The Bush invasion and occupation of Iraq was meant to overthrow Saddam and establish a beacon of democracy and freedom that would inspire the Islamic world. Speaking at Whitehall on November 19, 2003, Bush said: "The establishment of a free Iraq in the heart of the Middle East will be a watershed event in the global expansion of democracy . . . as the alternative to instability and hatred and terror." Professor Andrew Bacevich of Boston University, a conservative strategic thinker, has marveled at Bush's "[f]usion of breathtaking utopianism with hardly disguised *machtpolitik*. It reads as if it were the product not of sober, ostensibly conservative Republicans but of an unlikely collaboration of Woodrow Wilson and the elder Field Marshall von Moltke."

From the beginning (see pp. 352*ff.*) *National Review* supported the invasion of Iraq as part of the renovation of the Middle East and, while admitting difficulties and setbacks, ran articles supporting the war with cover headlines such as "Arab Spring" (March 28, 2005) and "We're Winning" (May 9, 2005). Meanwhile, other conservatives saw it differently. *National Review*'s founder William F. Buckley Jr. wrote in a syndicated column that "the American war in Iraq has failed," and conservative writers from George Will to Andrew Sullivan to Francis Fukuyama have all agreed.

Under the weight of his multiple policy failures, Bush's approval rating had dropped to 31 percent by the time of the 2006 elections. More than half of the nation regarded Bush as dishonest and untrustworthy. With a gian of six seats in the Senate and twenty-eight in the House, the Democrats captured Congress. Now, the minority on the House Judiciary Committee that compiled the "devastating" report on Bush's WMD claims will be the majority, and the basis of the administration's claims, which sold the war to Congress, will be examined in public hearings. Things could get ugly. Where will *National Review,* and conservatism, go from here? The future, fortunately, is always open.

Jeffrey Hart
November 2006

1

William F. Buckley Jr.: Present at the Creation

"To a very considerable degree," writes George Nash, "the history of reflective conservatism in America after 1955 is the history of individuals who collaborated in—or were discovered by—the magazine William F. Buckley founded."[1] A similar observation was made recently by Niels Bjerre-Poulsen in *Right Face: Organizing the American Conservative Movement, 1945–65*. Buckley, "more than any single figure, made conservatism a respectable force in American life."[2] Before the New Deal, conservative assumptions were not felt to need much articulation or defense. Then, during the Depression and Franklin Roosevelt's ascendancy, the defeat of conservative assumptions seemed complete, their spokesmen few, and the universities captured by liberalism. A profound creative work needed to be undertaken, though scattered recent materials were beginning to become visible again after the war. To quote Bjerre-Poulsen, Buckley "personally seemed to be able to embody most of the apparent contradictions and incoherence of American conservatism. . . . Despite Buckley's considerable diplomatic skills and firm intent to defuse the various ideological controversies, the relationship between the various factions in the magazine was not always one of 'peaceful coexistence.'"[3]

John Leonard, at the time of the following interview (July 6, 1973) the liberal editor of the *New York Times Book Review,* talks with Neal Freeman, a longtime *National Review* contributor, and describes the atmosphere that made collegiality possible:

> FREEMAN: Garry Wills has referred to the "open secret" that the [*Times Book Review*] owes a large debt to *National Review.* Could you describe that debt, if there is one?

> LEONARD: Not exactly a secret: I wrote a letter that *NR* uses as a promotional piece talking about the writers Bill Buckley discovered in *NR* that I've begged, borrowed, or stolen. On a deeper level, I'm indebted to the atmosphere Bill created at *NR* while I was there. The pick-up picnics that substituted for staff meetings; the encouraging of the staff to enter into the decision-making at every level of assignment and production; the sense that everybody working for you knows *why* you are doing something, and feels free to argue against it; the blending of office life into social life—I've adapted all these aspects to TBR procedure as it is now, with happy results. It wasn't that way before I became editor; and it wouldn't be that way now if I hadn't enjoyed the *NR* stint.

One of Buckley's strengths as an editor was a remarkable magnanimity. He enjoyed disputations involving principle, as between libertarian and traditionalist, enjoyed them for their own sake, and because he had both positions in his own makeup. He was also an impresario, orchestrating a magazine for an audience containing many variations within the conservative spectrum: which in turn meant that he would have to define what was outside that spectrum, or beyond the pale altogether.

National Review would prove the foundation for a career that was to make Buckley the most important journalist since Walter Lippmann. In fact, Buckley's career was more impressive. Lippmann had been the ultimate insider, an explainer of things already in process. To a considerable degree, Buckley, coming from the outside, played a central role in *creating* the politics of which he would also be the principal interpreter.

NO ENTIRELY SATISFACTORY biography of Buckley has yet been written, and while the odds against one appearing are steep, surprise is always

possible. To succeed, a writer would have to combine political and historical acumen with a visual and auditory imagination, psychological insight,
and literary skill. Gibbon with Henry James. A biographer of Buckley would
have to communicate so many things, and in particular the relationship
between Buckley and James Burnham, a key to the whole enterprise, and
through it to American conservatism. As Alexander Pope said of
Bolingbroke, Burnham was Buckley's "guide, philosopher and friend." He
and Buckley undertook the journey together, and both were shaped by the
experience.

What I can offer here are only a few notes toward a portrait of, and
understanding of, Buckley, such as might contribute to an understanding
of the creation of *National Review*. In conversation, and publicly on the
speaker's platform or on television, Buckley's voice was so distinctive that
it amounted to a dramatic event in itself. Willmoore Kendall once said
that Buckley could do as much with his voice as Laurence Olivier. Perhaps the effect was produced by the multiple linguistic environments in
which he grew up. His first language was Spanish. His father, William
Sr., was a successful oil entrepreneur in Mexico, Venezuela, and Canada,
and he surrounded his family with Spanish-speaking nannies. (He still
has Spanish-speaking servants.) Buckley also had a French governess. His
education was also unusual. The ten children were taught at home by
tutors. The family lived extensively in Europe, where the children either
attended schools or were tutored. Surprisingly, Buckley learned to speak
English at a day school in England when he was seven years old. His first
regular grade school was in Paris, where he picked up workable French.
Reaching prep school age, he attended an English Catholic boarding
school, St. John's Beaumont, and British English became part of his linguistic mix. He found his Catholicism deepened by the experience.

The Buckleys had a large estate in Camden, South Carolina, located in
the middle of that most southern of states. Charleston, social and spiritual
capital of the old Confederacy, had the harbor where Confederate artillery
opened up on Fort Sumter. Camden, famed for horses and hunting, also
was the site of the estate of Mary Chesnut, whose luminous diary recounted
the life of Charleston in the days of Jefferson Davis and the Confederate

aristocracy. A Southern drawl hides somewhere in Bill Buckley's voice, re-flecting also his mother's Louisiana background. The South became part of the amalgam that constituted the early *National Review*, with such con-tributors as Richard Weaver and James Jackson Kilpatrick, and, through the Agrarians, was part of Russell Kirk's self-creation.

I record here an anecdote about Camden, a brief moment after the 1972 Democratic convention in Miami that nominated George McGovern, a wild happening surrounded outside the Convention Center by beards, beads, bongos, and, as young women nursed infants, the sweet smells of the counter-culture at play. Late in the convention, Buckley, Garry Wills, a few of Bill's old friends, and I left Miami and sailed from Coral Gables headed for Connecticut on Buckley's yacht "Cyrano."

On the Gulf Stream, pausing to swim, admiring the colorful, sinister Portuguese Men of War with their gelatin sails and poisonous tentacles, we eventually reached Charleston; with supplies running low, we docked. Bill proposed we rent a plane and fly to Camden for lunch, and at once the decision was made.

On the Buckley estate, near the main house, there stood a classical struc-ture, which had been the elder William Buckley's office when in residence. He had lived in Sharon, Connecticut, during the summer and fall, until he died of a stroke in 1958. At the door of the main house, Negro servants greeted us, immensely dignified, slow of speech and movement. These were among the sounds with which Buckley grew up, the Carolina drawls of both whites and blacks. By the time he reached the last three years of prep school—at the Millbrook School, in Millbrook, New York, not far from Sharon—his combination of American English, Carolina English, and Brit-ish English, with possible tinctures of Spanish and French, produced what now everyone knows: a diction American and, not surprisingly, not quite American.

I mentioned Sharon, the site of the main Buckley home, Great Elm, on a large tract of land. Its venerable Elm, the tallest in the state of Connecticut, was there until it succumbed to Dutch Elm Disease in 1954. On the week-end of September 9, 1960, about ninety students showed up at Great Elm for the founding of Young Americans for Freedom, an offshoot of the multiple Buckley operations. A student there is said to have observed: "Now I know what Russell Kirk means by 'the permanent things.'" To express things of even more permanence, Buckley in 1955 founded *National Review* and made it into the arbiter and educator of the American conservative mind.

BUCKLEY IN SO MANY ways stood apart from mainstream American culture, stood apart when he graduated from the Millbrook School and, after two uncomfortable years in the Army, stood apart when he entered Yale in 1946. As an undergraduate, he only irregularly saw football games. Once, at a *National Review* editorial meeting, he had to be gently corrected when using the baseball term "stealing a base" to mean something crooked. Similarly, when his brother Senator James Buckley was asked at a press conference what the death of coach Vince Lombardi meant to America, he answered, "New Year's Eve will never be the same again." It took the reporters a while to figure out that he was confusing coach Lombardi with Guy Lombardo, of "Auld Lange Syne" fame. To some extent, the brothers were separated from mainstream America by their unusual childhoods.

Throughout Buckley's adult life there persisted a tension in his politics. On the one hand was an aristocratic conservatism, influenced by his early admiration for family friend and prose stylist Alfred Jay Nock, author of *Memoirs of a Superfluous Man*, a conservatism that was pessimistic and felt doom to be near at hand. But that kind of conservatism collided with a rival pull, toward the necessities of practical reform under American democratic conditions. Buckley once expressed his intermittent populism when he said that he would rather be governed by the first two thousand names in the Boston telephone directory than by the faculty of Harvard University. But he contradictorily admired Ortega y Gasset's Nietzschean-aristocratic *Revolt of the Masses*, and at one point contemplated a book to be titled *Revolt Against the Masses*.

At Yale, his institutional social life centered on the Fence fraternity, the Whiffenpoofs, and Skull and Bones. At that time, the names of those annually selected as Bonesmen were listed in the *New York Herald-Tribune*. One can see many things in his Yale experience that were important for Buckley: experience in journalism, for example, as editor of the *Yale Daily*

News, and his assessment of the Yale curriculum, about which he wrote his first book, *God and Man at Yale* (1951). Indeed, Buckley's particular experience of undergraduate life, which included teaching Spanish, was a period about which he remains cheerful and anecdotal.

Especially important was Professor of Political Science Willmoore Kendall, a man of penetrating and original intelligence, who later followed Buckley to the new *National Review* as a senior editor. Kendall had come to Yale with an enormous reputation in political theory, based on his published work and especially his 1941 study *John Locke and the Doctrine of Majority Rule*. A tall man with blue eyes and graying hair parted in the middle, speaking sometimes with an Oklahoma accent and sometimes in clipped British tones left over from his Rhodes Scholarship and Pembroke College, Oxford, Kendall was a charismatic teacher. But at Yale, and almost everywhere else, he could be the most difficult personality either Buckley or I have ever met. Though a conservative and a patriot, his temperament was that of a revolutionary, which in a sense he was, against the then-dominant liberalism.

At Yale Buckley also became notable for his talents as a debater, afterwards to be displayed on public platforms and on TV's *Firing Line*. He and his best friend Brent Bozell, a tall, red-haired Merchant Marine veteran from Omaha, were the stars of the undefeated Yale Debating Team.

It is said famously that Bozell began at Yale a Protestant and liberal World Federalist, but soon became a conservative and zealous Roman Catholic, one who got into trouble in Spain by questioning Franco's orthodoxy. He married Buckley's sister Patricia. After a productive senior editorship at *National Review*, he left to found his own rival magazine. In *Triumph*, Bozell broke with *National Review* philosophically and politically, becoming theocratic, indeed anti-American. This was a losing proposition for a magazine hoping to find a readership among American Catholics, a conspicuously patriotic group. *Triumph* was useful to me, since it published several of my longer essays, later to appear in my volume *Acts of Recovery* (1989). Several of these were written in Sacramento, when I was there as a writer for Governor Reagan. In 1968, however, I ceased publishing in *Triumph* after it editorially endorsed the black riots in Washington, D.C., as a rebellion against "materialism." Strange, on TV the rioters I saw were shattering store windows and stealing all they could carry away. The absence in Buckley of any temptation toward theocracy and political dogmatism and his embrace of constitutional "deliberate sense" politics made him a pariah to *Triumph*: Buckley was heretically American.

AN IMMEDIATE RESULT of Buckley's college experience, *God and Man at Yale* became a best-selling scandal. People outside an Ivy League university always want to know what is going on inside it. This early work still commands an interest of various kinds. Yale's religion had become a liberalized Protestantism tending toward secularism, its politics liberal, and its economics Keynesian–New Deal. There was poignancy in the fact that Buckley, a firm Catholic, tried in this book to recall the elite of Protestant Yale to their roots in Christianity and to their institutional debt to capitalism. The Yale administration was scandalized, however, and had the book denounced wherever its influence reached.

When Buckley graduated with the Class of 1950, he had been admitted to Yale Law School and also to Yale's Graduate School for further work in political science. His father advised the latter and more study with Kendall, but that was not the path Buckley chose to take. His mind was acute, very quick to grasp an argument, but disinclined to work patiently at theory. The Korean War had broken out in June; Kendall recommended the CIA and referred his student to James Burnham, then a consultant to the Office of Policy Coordination, the CIA covert action wing. At Burnham's Washington apartment Buckley met E. Howard Hunt, a Brown graduate, author of popular espionage novels, and about to take over covert action in Mexico City. Buckley's fluent Spanish, obvious intelligence, and anticommunist convictions impressed Hunt, and so Buckley went to Mexico City. Hunt had yet to star in the best real-life espionage novel of all, the Watergate break-in, coauthored with G. Gordon Liddy, and ending with the destruction of a presidency.

Buckley wanted to have a more direct impact than academic life offered, and he had his Yale experience in journalism to draw upon. In the phrase of Richard Weaver, he believed that ideas have consequences, and when he surveyed the magazine field it was clear that a gap existed for a new conservative journal. He considered that the success of New Deal liberalism as a collection of ideas had been greatly fostered by the *New Republic* and the *Nation*, magazines which reached the educated classes, especially through the 1930s and the 1940s, and which had published important journalists and literary figures. These magazines were read in the academy, in Washington, and by a wider literate audience.

There existed no comparable conservative outlet. The existing conservative magazines were variously inadequate, including the *American Mercury*, the monthly once made famous by H. L. Mencken. Buckley worked for it, but only for a few months, and withdrew to write a book with L. Brent Bozell, now his brother-in-law, *McCarthy and His Enemies* (1954), a mildly critical defense of the anticommunist muckraker. Here again we see one of the contradictions in Buckley, and derivatively in *National Review*: the contradiction between elite sensibility and populist power, now represented by McCarthy. Dwight Macdonald hit off the contradiction vividly when he wrote in *Partisan Review* that *McCarthy and His Enemies* defended "a coarse demagogue in an elegantly academic style replete with nice discriminations and pedantic hair-splittings, giving the general effect of a brief by Cadwalader, Wickersham and Taft on behalf of a pickpocket arrested in a subway men's room."

Burnham, Max Eastman, and Whittaker Chambers all were wary of McCarthy, Chambers writing to Buckley,

> McCarthy divides the ranks of the right. . . . He is a man fighting almost wholly by instinct and intuition against forces for the most part coldly conscious of their ways, means and ends. In other words, he scarcely knows what he is doing. He knows that somebody threw a tomato at him and the general direction from whence it came.[4]

IN 1954, BUCKLEY MET William Schlamm, who provided the catalyst for a new conservative journal of opinion. Schlamm was an intelligent and stereotypical European intellectual and former Communist who had fled the Nazis and ended up with Henry Luce at Time-Life. Now fifty, swarthy, and with black hair combed straight back, he was a virtuoso conversationalist who could talk a hole in a cement wall—about politics, culture, or almost anything else. He also envisioned a new conservative journal with an educated audience, and meeting Buckley, agreed to join with him in such an enterprise.

Aware of the political feuding between Taft and Eisenhower backers that in 1952 had brought about the meltdown of the *Freeman*, Buckley and Schlamm decided to establish a more stable corporate structure, with two kinds of stock. Stock A would be put on the market, but have no voting rights; one hundred percent of Stock B would belong to the editor-in-chief, Buckley himself, and would possess all the voting rights. In practice, this was a strategic and stabilizing arrangement, allowing Buckley to settle differences of opinion that sometimes became extreme. And Buckley turned out to be quite talented at this, usually effecting a truce without using his plenary powers, though sometimes individuals self-destructed. Very likely, with his age and professional experience, Schlamm believed that he might prevail at the magazine intellectually, with Buckley in the background. As it happens, the ingenious stock mechanism that Schlamm had helped devise eventually jumped up and bit him. Before that crisis, however, he contributed valuably, especially on cultural subjects. And over the years, the stock arrangement held the magazine together amid several fractious disagreements that conceivably could have wrecked it.

Despite the efforts of Buckley and Schlamm to raise the substantial funds needed to go to press, the amount on hand fell well short of their goal. Still, Schlamm argued that the existence of the magazine would itself raise the necessary money, and they decided to push ahead. *National Review*'s first number appeared during the second week of November 1955, with a print run of 7,500 copies and a readership no doubt considerably less. During these perilous days of dubious financial viability, a small group of backers came forward to sustain *NR*, their generosity probably saving the shaky venture. Ten years later, by 1965, the magazine had 100,000 subscribers. At its fifty-year mark, it would reach 170,000. An accepted way of calculating readership for this and comparable magazines is to multiply by 2.5. Clearly there had been an opening for a new conservative magazine. Considered only in terms of the history of publishing, *National Review* was a phenomenon.

THE IMMEDIATE RESPONSE to *NR* was probably predictable. The magazine did have its shortcomings, including matters of tone, and it also displayed some amateurishness. In the January 1956 issue of *Harper's*, the editor John Fischer devoted his "Easy Chair"—that is, the entire editorial section—to *National Review*. He warned his readers that the magazine "exhibits all the stigmata of extremist journalism" and was "dedicated to the Conspiracy Theory of politics." Mr. Fischer concluded, more in sorrow than in anger, that *National Review* was "the very opposite of conservative."

There might have been a bit of truth in that. Republican Senate majority leader William Knowland and Joe McCarthy, both of whom appeared on early covers, were hardly conservatives. Dwight Macdonald boiled over with rage and contempt in the April issue of *Commentary*, charging *National Review* with being a refuge for "the lumpen bourgeoisie, the half-educated, half-successful, provincials." Macdonald seemed to be losing control, this characterization inaccurate and even wild.

In the *Progressive*, Murray Kempton argued that the very idea of trying to publish a conservative magazine was absurd, since the conservative position exists only in a ghostly sense. It was his opinion that "The New American Right is most conspicuous these days for its advanced state of wither," the implication being that *National Review* was at best a hopeless endeavor; what's more, feeling "no compulsion to re-write," the magazine was an "affront to literary sensibilities"; what's still more, *NR* erred morally by refusing to "look into the faces" of those it attacked. The language used in all this, surely excessive, expressed a deep desire that the magazine not exist at all. Yet Burnham also knew from a professional point of view that the magazine needed some polish and maturity of style or it would not reach the kind of audience Buckley desired. He pushed, with some success, to change the manners of the magazine—its style, appearance, tone—all to seek the mainstream. Burnham had the British *Economist* in mind as a model.

What early critics failed to recognize was the fact that a considerable body of knowledge underpinned the new magazine. For example, by 1955 there existed the Austrian and Chicago schools of free-market economists, associated with such names as Hayek, Mises, and Friedman. Also prominent in the *National Review* mind was an awareness of the special threat of communism: that although "materialist" in its basis, it had a powerful quasi-religious appeal in promising a transformed human future, something to live and die (and kill) for. This Communist vision had been inspiring to many, including many sensitive intellectuals—had given meaning to their lives and kept back an enclosing nihilism, as with Whittaker Chambers. Because of the power of the Communist ideal, Chambers had believed that in joining the anticommunists he was joining History's losing side. But there had also emerged, under assault by communism, a renewed sense of the West and its central components. Chambers, Burnham, Kendall, Russell Kirk, Leo Strauss, Richard Weaver, and many others had written important books on these matters, and these were, as much as the work of the free-market economists, part of *National Review's* patrimony. *National Review* would have an important elite and cerebral aspect, always pulling in that direction amid the political coverage.

In November 1955, when the first issue of *National Review* appeared, President Dwight Eisenhower, recently ill from a heart attack but a revered figure with global prestige, faced the decision of whether to run for reelection. *National Review* had to settle the question of its position on this world-hero, who was closely connected to the liberal Eastern Establishment. Discussions ensued about whether the magazine should go ahead and endorse for president the California senator William Knowland, Republican leader in the Senate. Knowland was well known for strongly supporting the Republic of China on Taiwan and was otherwise reliably right-wing. For *National Review* to endorse Knowland now would make a sharp, self-defining statement in its first appearance. A Knowland endorsement would be a slap both at Eisenhower and at Vice President Richard Nixon, with whose apparent policy of accommodation with New Deal liberalism at home and the Soviet Union abroad *National Review* had serious quarrels.

James Burnham liked the idea of endorsing Knowland. This seems surprising in light of the way Burnham subsequently defined himself at *National Review*: he disliked right-wing provincialism. But now, given his experience with marginal magazines, he probably was enticed by the attention such an endorsement would receive.

But in September 1955 Buckley and Schlamm paid a visit to Whittaker Chambers at his Maryland farm and received a dose of emphatic skepticism. Readers of *Witness* are likely to think of Chambers as morose and pessimistic—sitting, he tells the reader, while a Columbia undergraduate, on a campus bench and pondering whether he should commit suicide or join the Communist Party. Here, Chambers was an extremist figure out of Dostoyevsky, overwhelmed by nihilism. But *Witness* is the autobiography of Chambers's soul; the portly daylight Chambers had a jolly and also a practical side. His discussion with Buckley and Schlamm provided an example of his political thinking, which usually would ally him with Burnham at *National Review*. The magazine would steer overall, with occasional lurches toward purist ideology, in the "strategic" direction favored by Chambers and Burnham: toward the conservative side of mainstream American politics.

Naturally, Chambers had a favorable opinion of Vice President Nixon, deriving from their cooperation on the Hiss case. On that occasion, the defenders of Hiss had been the usual liberal suspects, while Chambers and Nixon won the grinding battle. Chambers had a low opinion of Knowland's intelligence and, more fundamentally, of the idea of endorsing him. Chambers sensed a whiff of right-wing Jacobinism, an unwillingness to accept the situation for what it was: Knowland was not, repeat *not*, going to move into the White House. Advocating his nomination amounted to right-wing escapism, as Chambers called it, and this separated him from *National Review* as it seemed at that moment to be tending. Chambers delayed signing up for the masthead.

The issue raised by Chambers would be central to the evolution of *National Review*, and it would deeply engage Burnham. It might be framed as the choice between ideal right-wing Paradigm and realistic Possibility. But at this time, did Knowland represent even a paradigm? He was hardly distinguished for intellectual powers or any other notable qualities.

So, while Burnham continued to favor an endorsement of Knowland, Buckley and Schlamm backed away and settled for a lead article by the senator in the maiden issue: it would be called "Peace with Honor" and was critical of arms reduction negotiations.

To the surprise of everyone at *National Review*, Burnham attended the

Republican Convention and then voted for Eisenhower, even though he considered Ike's version of Truman and George Kennan's "containment" policy too passive. In *National Review*, Buckley made the case for boycotting the election, and he followed his own advice.

Reflecting on the Knowland episode, we see some important points for the future of the magazine. Chambers would say that his own politics was "dialectical." This meant that he would assess a political situation as accurately as he could, and react to it in a corrective direction. He could not play with cards that were not on the table. His action thus would form one part of the dialectic, with the result a synthesis, more conservative than it otherwise would have been. That result might represent only a small gain, and if so emotionally unsatisfying: yet still a gain compared with nothing. Over the years, Burnham would embody that strategy, gradually prevailing over Buckley's "ideal" impulses. Both Chambers and Burnham had a sense of the intractability of actual circumstances, and neither took pleasure in idealist acts of political self-expression.

As we look down the years at the development of *National Review*, Burnham's cumulative effect was to move his friend Buckley, his superior at the magazine, toward this kind of realism—and the magazine toward greater effectiveness. Over the years, however, the appeal of idealism and political illusion would persist, surfacing at intervals with predictable results. For example, in one of the first issues (December 28, 1955) there appeared none other than Joseph McCarthy, who by then had all but been ruined by Senate censure. As if by way of deliberate insult, he reviewed a new book by the elegant Dean Acheson, *A Democrat Looks at His Party*. Acheson, in fact, had been a principal architect of the systems put in place to block postwar Soviet expansion: NATO, the Marshall Plan, the Truman Doctrine in Greece and Turkey, German rearmament. At *National Review*, prudential conservatism was not yet in charge.

A CONTRADICTION, HOWEVER, is emerging. Did Buckley want to *reform* the Eastern Establishment, or did he want to *destroy and displace* it? In *God and Man at Yale* he had identified and attacked the inculcation of what he saw was destroying the old Eastern elite from within—its liberalism, secularism, quasi-socialism. Would the destruction of the old Yale elite involve Pareto's classic "circulation of the elites" (such circulation an important analytical idea for Burnham)? If so, with what results? A circulation of that sort cannot be an innocent thing; even if without violence, its results are seldom pretty.

In his words to the fortieth reunion of the Yale Class of 1950 titled "A Distinctive Gentility: Four Decades Later" (June, 1, 1990), Buckley recalled "a genetic attribute of Yale, and this was a distinctive sense of gentility. . . . [I]t is an ineffaceable part of the memory of four years at Yale: the very idea of institutional courtesy. We have never been quite the same after those four years."[5] Buckley himself in every respect—taste, prose style, manners, yachting, wines, piano, and harpsichord—never ceased to embody such distinctive gentility, and there was not a shred of populist kitsch in his being.

To reach out toward an educated elite was the goal of *National Review*. Its "Books, Arts and Manners" section would pursue that direction, though in tone and a certain raggedness the magazine still had improvements to make. The covers of the first issues of *National Review*, featuring Knowland and McCarthy, offered an unmistakable pointer in the direction of populist defiance.

Revolving around this elite/populist contradiction, but united in anti-communism, a commitment to Western civilization, and a presumption for the free market, *National Review* sailed forward toward the election of 1956, congratulating its political foe Eisenhower on his recovery from his heart attack:

> By a coincidence that is unqualifiedly happy for us, our first issue leaves the printshop on the day that the President, his health fully recovering, quits the Denver hospital. In days to come, and even in this first issue, we shall be critical, sometimes sharply so, of those Administration policies with which we disagree—that, after all, will be part of our business. But no disagreement will lessen our whole-hearted wish for the personal well-being and happiness of the man who is the elected head of our country and its government.

The author of that graceful paragraph was James Burnham. It exhibits his characteristic good manners, the manners, in fact, of the Eastern Establishment. But the destructive hand of history would leave little unchanged, including Burnham's Cold War liberation strategy against a Soviet Union just recently gone nuclear.

2

James Burnham: Power

When I saw him in that vast desert,
"Have mercy on me, whatever you are,"
I cried, "whether shade or living man."
        —Pilgrim Dante meets Virgil, *Inferno* I

From the beginning, James Burnham was absolutely central to *National Review* and remained increasingly so until, troubled by failing eyesight, he retired in 1978 after a serious stroke. His role was second only to that of Buckley. Though he had an important career before joining *NR,* his work there over the years might be judged the best he ever did. He helped create the magazine, and it in turn developed the best in him.

His political focus throughout was on strategy in what is generally called the Cold War—"cold," though hundreds of thousands, perhaps millions, died in that conflict. He himself, accurate as usual, called this prolonged event or series of events the "Third World War."

At the same time he paid scrupulous attention to every aspect of the *NR* operation. In the beginning he strenuously sought financial support to launch it. He worried about paying writers enough, and sought to recruit Raymond Aron and his friend André Malraux, a measure of his ambitions for *National Review.* He worried a bit about the magazine's Ivy League aura, and had thoughts about the design of the format—favoring a chic, uneven right-hand margin, for example—and he was choosy about type-face, paper, and illustrations. His ideal for style was cosmopolitan, and he denounced any hint of vulgarity or even doubtful taste, since his goal was to steer away from anything that suggested amateurism. Though he was pas-sionate about these matters, he led gently, without direct criticism let alone condescension. He was also useful and diplomatic in dealing with flare-ups among sensitive egos and good at coaching new writers and making them better. It is often said that no one is indispensable. That is almost always true. But Burnham was indispensable.

Let us begin with the first masthead, top of the page, November 19, 1955. Here, beneath Buckley, who is listed as editor and publisher, we see five names, arranged like this:

James Burnham   Willmoore Kendall

Suzanne La Follette   Jonathan Mitchell

William Schlamm

Most important for the future of the magazine were the two senior editors listed first: Burnham and Kendall. In addition to much else, Burnham contributed his "Third World War" column and Kendall his "Liberal Line," satirizing liberal predictability. Buckley, who personified the magazine for the public, wrote the regular "From the Ivory Tower," no doubt alluding to his recent graduation from Yale and notoriety there. His column would comment on the academy but also range more widely. Kendall, it turned out temporarily, edited "Books, Arts and Manners," the back of the book, with Schlamm a cultural commentator on arts and manners. Brent Bozell, not yet a senior editor, would contribute "National Trends," on politics, and Russell Kirk, remaining off the masthead, added "From the Academy." Suzanne La Follette, a feisty Taft Republican and an experienced journalist, had come over from the old *Freeman*. She functioned as managing editor.

A little more than a year later, by the end of 1957, the top of the mast-head looked like this:

L. Brent Bozell   James Burnham

John Chamberlain   Whittaker Chambers

Willmoore Kendall   Suzanne La Follette

The *annus mirabilis* of 1956 had changed the world, and in the process brought about changes at the magazine. Khrushchev denounced Stalin and Stalinism, bloody uprisings took place within the Soviet empire, especially violent in Hungary, the British had been thrown out of Suez and the once-great European empires were on the rocks, Eisenhower and Nixon easily defeated Stevenson and Kefauver, and *National Review*'s own orientation had changed in important ways. Brent Bozell handled the Washington beat. Schlamm, there with Buckley at the beginning a year earlier, had disagreed with Burnham's reaction to Hungary and emotionally launched a power struggle against him which he could only lose. He departed in the direction of West Germany, to go into journalism there.

I STARTED COMING TO the office regularly in early 1969 as a senior editor, having been a speechwriter temporarily, first for Reagan, then for Nixon in the 1968 campaign. Though I had known Burnham's work well, especially in *Partisan Review*, I had never met him. I arranged my classes at Dartmouth so as to fly to New York for the regular Monday morning editorial conference, where the editors sat around the large table in the conference room and suggested what events and topics might be written about in "The Week" editorial section. The conference began as soon as Burnham arrived from the train at Grand Central, which he had boarded at Kent, Connecticut, where he and his wife Marcia owned a Revolutionary Era house. Buckley sat at the head of the table making a list of topics; Burnham always spoke first, then the other editors went in clockwise fashion back around to Buckley.

Often the discussion was lively, educating—sometimes with undercurrents of disagreement, which left Burnham serene. Soon after the meeting broke up, Buckley sent his assignments around, and the four or five senior editors who normally came to the meeting adjourned for lunch at Paone's on 34th Street, an excellent Italian place and a sort of *National Review* clubhouse. The table talk concerned the editorial issues raised, but much else too.

Burnham—we called him Jim—was a tall man with thinning white hair and a strong, blunt nose that seemed to search for smells. Exquisitely polite and soft-spoken, he dressed in dark suits, often pin-striped. He never relaxed to the extent of a sports jacket. I knew that he had been a professor of philosophy at New York University back in the 1930s, a friend and colleague of Sidney Hook, and friends of mine had taken his famous course on Thomas Aquinas. He did not dress like a professor at NYU, rumpled urban, let alone tweedy Princeton, where he had been an undergraduate. He looked perhaps like a diplomat who would have been at home in the corridors of power, at the Quai d'Orsay, for example, or in the plush offices at Whitehall. Burnham, indeed, had been in the "operations"—covert activity—branch of the CIA in Washington from 1949 to 1953. Style spoke to and through Burnham, the ultimate anti-bohemian. Around the *National Review* office I heard the story that once, when a new young staffer arrived, he had made a terrible impression on Burnham, who soon had a low opinion of his work and a lower opinion of his attire, actually coming to work in a sweater, no tie. The sweater or sweaters, Burnham had said, looked to be part of a Sears shipment that had been lost thirty years earlier in the backwoods of Manitoba.[1]

Burnham's CIA work greatly contributed to his value at *National Review* in that he had contacts in London, Paris, Athens, and Rome, was friends with people like Arthur Koestler and André Malraux, and knew what to look for in the foreign press. Later on, in 1975, when Buckley and the editorial staff were planning to spend Christmas in Moscow, Burnham, though he liked to travel, begged off on Russia. "They might have to ask me some things, and I might have to answer." Those things, I gathered, involved some CIA/military action in Yugoslavia timed to coordinate with uprisings within the Soviet empire, not the sort of subject for a friendly interrogation by the KGB.

If you have concluded here that Burnham was reserved, perhaps I have even understated the matter. His self-presentation suggested pure analytical intellect. Willmoore Kendall once remarked to me that Jim was so solicitous of the formidable instrument in his skull that he limited himself to a single weak martini before dinner, a marvel to Kendall. Burnham's approach to political matters was one of insistent, disciplined rationality. Opinion, emotion, prejudice, ideology: these were worse than useless. In considering editorial matters with editors his junior he was patient and pedagogical. He spoke in calm and slightly rasping tones, without regional accent, always introducing into their writing, which was likely to be passionate, such terms as "usually" and "it may be that." He never rebuked or scolded, never said a writer was "wrong," which would have been *ad hominum* or, worse, a moral judgment. He was himself a moral and civilized man, but he did not want that to interfere with analysis. Rather than "wrong," he would say, considering fact and analysis, that a conclusion or an inference was "incorrect." Burnham could be pushed but seldom bent. I might come forward with a political event I considered unacceptable and outrageous. That was not his language. His comment about the same event might be something like: "That's fascinating." He approached it much as a botanist might regard a strangely colored and probably poisonous mushroom. Sometimes I thought of Burnham as resembling Paul Valéry's great rationalist M. Teste, all head.

THE ONLY PROBLEM WITH that interpretation was that everything I knew about Burnham's tumultuous life contradicted it. After Balliol College, Oxford, and in response to the 1929 Crash and the Great Depression, he had veered into revolutionary politics and organizations that had less chance than Little Orphan Annie of seizing power. His reaction to what he regarded as Eisenhower's failure in 1956 in Hungary was extreme. He talked of "lost honor," not a rational idea, became depressed, and advocated a wild scheme to neutralize Germany. His actual behavior sometimes proved far from rational, analytical, and prudent. His insistence on fact and analysis might best be seen as a method for disciplining powerful and turbulent emotions.

Before arriving at *National Review* in 1955, Burnham's career stretched back through the CIA and *Partisan Review*, where he had been a contributor and member of the advisory board, to the radical 1930s when, instead of becoming a prudent New Deal reformer, such as Adolf Berle and other young men who joined the parade to Washington, he had taught philosophy at NYU and, somewhat incongruously, been involved with revolutionary politics of a Trotskyist character.[2] Born into the family of a vice president in James J. Hill's railroad conglomerate, he grew up in the new suburb of Kenilworth, a wealthy enclave on the shore of Lake Michigan embellished with Walter Scott gothic homes. His mother was a devout Catholic and he went East to a Catholic boarding school in Milford, Connecticut, where he graduated first in his class, then went to Princeton where he again graduated at the head of the Class of 1927. At Princeton he majored in English and took what philosophy was offered. A young gentleman of his time and place, he was popular and enjoyed tennis and the social life of what was still Scott Fitzgerald's Princeton—the golden haze of the Coolidge boom and the world of John Held Jr., short skirts, jazz, and ukuleles, when, as the hit song went, "It Ain't Gonna Rain No More."

From Princeton it was on to Balliol and more outstanding work in literature and the philosophy then in vogue, this last shaping a permanent feature of his mind. What it amounted to was the systematic empiricism of the Vienna School. One gets the impression that on dates students argued about Russell and Wittgenstein, referents and pseudo-statements. This kind of empiricism held any statement that could not be verified empirically to be meaningless, a "pseudo-statement." Such an approach disposes of most of the products of human reflection, starting with Plato, and empties all metaphor and symbol of cognitive meaning—and of course, regards metaphysics and all religion as illusions, altogether simplifying the history of thought. Later, as a professor at NYU, Burnham counseled his students to read Russell and Whitehead's *Principia Mathematica*, a heavy assignment. That great work operates at a huge distance from experience.

The adult Burnham later would consider religions and ideologies as masks for the reality of *power*. But along with these exclusionary severities, and powerful since his Princeton days, there existed in Burnham a strong aesthetic dimension. While at New York University he published professionally on aesthetics, taught a course on Dante along with his course on Aquinas, and was drawn to the modernist movement in the arts, especially admiring Picasso, Matisse, Eliot, and Yeats. As one regards him in these earlier days, he was a model of the upper-caste, educated gentleman, a paragon of the breed. But I think his emotional and aesthetic side found little or no philosophical support in Balliol's radical empiricism.

The Depression knocked the foundations out from under his custom-ary world and constituted for him, as for millions of others, an unmitigated catastrophe. The older post–Civil War patrician business class, hit hard financially, suddenly became discredited, and a world of meanings disap-peared. Burnham must have despaired, because he responded much more drastically than almost all of his peers. He became, without ceasing to be an aristocrat, an aristocratic revolutionary. He saw the Communist Party, whether Moscow or deviant, as the disciplined replacement for the bank-rupt—financially and morally—old patriciate. His *Managerial Revolution: What is Happening to the World* (1941) amounts to a *summa* of his thinking during this period. It is essentially Marxist, except that power passes not to the party but to a new managerial class, which does not own corporate property but rather manages it. Adolf Berle and Gardner Means, among others, were pursuing similar lines of thought, and in less schematic ways what they and Burnham describe was actually taking place. The political side of things, for Burnham, would be handled by a disciplined political party.

Even as he made his way through radical politics, becoming a Trotskyist Communist and editor of the *New International* newspaper, this second and consuming existence, remarkably, went on while Burnham was teach-ing Aristotle, Aquinas, and Dante, and, with Philip Wheelwright, editing a series of journals called *Symposium*, a predecessor of *Partisan Review*. That there was comedy in Burnham's situation was not lost on his friend and colleague Sidney Hook, a brilliant urban-savvy graduate of City College. In his autobiography *Out of Step* (1987), Hook recalls in a fine vignette that

> Burnham's [Trotskyist] comrades were proud of his growing reputation, but were puzzled by his mode of life, which was strictly separate from his political activity. He did not socialize with his comrades but with his old college and family friends, all of whom were well-to-do and regarded his involvement in sectarian Communist politics as a quaint eccentricity, living on Sutton Place which even in the 1930s no one could mistake for a working class neighbor-hood. His wife (Marcia) was often distressed by the appearance of seedy-looking members of the Socialist Workers Party bringing copies or urgent telegrams Burnham had received from Trotsky or other affiliates of the Fourth

International, or waving proofs that had to be read before *The New International* went to press. The embarrassment was mutual, for more often these messengers would find Burnham in formal dress together with his friends at the table or in the midst of bibulous party-going. Burnham would excuse himself, have a hurried conversation with his comrades, and then return to his dinner parties.

What Burnham must have admired in the Communist movement was its discipline, appearance of tough-mindedness, and hard-boiled sense of purpose.

Moreover, the Communist Party did not consist entirely of intellectuals—far from it. It commanded the services of numerous goons and even gangster types from the labor movement, who were up to doing what was required. Marxism, aside from its "metaphysical" properties carried over from Hegel, also had a tough-minded quality. It recognized real conflict, and in fact made conflict the mainspring of its view of history. Fascism had Darwinism, communism had continuing class struggle. Humphrey Bogartism appealed aesthetically to this tough-guy side of communism. In addition, the basis of Marxism was material, hard not flimsy, and Communists despised softness. Marxism might be thought to "look like" the world we were living in. Along with Burnham's gentility, this aesthetic-power aspect of communism undoubtedly appealed to him.

Nevertheless, is there not something extraordinary and hardly consistent with facts and analysis about Burnham's behavior during the 1930s? It must have been the powerful emotional jolt of the Crash and sense of dispossession that propelled him from the shade trees and stately residences of Kenilworth, from Princeton and Balliol, all the way to his intense participation in these tiny and hopeless revolutionary groups. The Trotskyists, after all, were a tiny faction of a tiny faction: a faction of the regular Communist Party USA, itself a faction in American politics.

And what was Trotskyism, beyond the feeling of its leader that he, rather than Stalin, was the legitimate heir to Lenin? Nothing in Trotsky's writing or behavior gives any indication that his leadership would have led to anything but Communist tyranny. Burnham's entire Communist entanglement, to put it bluntly, was absurd. To have become a New Dealer would have made more sense. When he finally joined tiny *National Review* in 1955, he at least associated himself with established Western traditions of thought reaching very far back beyond the present, beyond the nineteenth century, to the very beginnings of the West. This represented a genuine body of thought in contrast to the nineteenth-century philosophical shards of Trotsky, way out there in far political space. *National Review* was undertaking a long march toward the centers of power in the government of the most powerful nation on earth, which would win the Third World War in 1989, the bicentennial of the fall of the Bastille, when the Berlin Wall came down.

BY 1945, IN FACT, Burnham was ready to condemn communism in any form. As a contributor to *Partisan Review* he published an essay titled "Lenin's Heir" (1945), which argued that the enmity of communism toward the West was implacable and would continue even if it softened from time to time for tactical reasons. The essay also argued that Stalin had not stolen and corrupted communism after the death of a beneficent Lenin. No, said Burnham, communism is communism and Stalin is what you get. This view demythologized Lenin and also constituted the core of Burnham's work throughout his *National Review* career. The first group it antagonized were those who were "optimists" about the nature and likely course of Soviet policy. The second group it antagonized were the Trotskyists and Trotskyoids still present at *Partisan Review*. This struck at the original foundations of the magazine, which, interestingly for a while, had sought to fuse revolutionary (Trotskyist anti-Stalin) politics with the modernist revolution in the arts—a problem, since modernism was so individualistic.

In 1948 Burnham developed a friendship with André Malraux, both a man of action and an intellectual, famous as a pilot on the Loyalist side in Spain, a traveler in revolutionary Asia, author of *Man's Fate* (about Spain) and *Man's Hope* (about China), as well as a writer on many subjects, including art. Burnham and Malraux were close enough that he and Burnham discussed exchanging sons for a year of education abroad. In Paris during a spring break from teaching at NYU, Burnham interviewed Malraux at length, Burnham doing most of the talking. The text appeared in *Partisan Review*, and also as a book, *The Case for De Gaulle*, seeing the war hero as anticommunist and capable of rallying French patriotism. A close advisor to De Gaulle, Malraux was playing a role Burnham savored, a man of intellect and action, aesthetics and politics. When Malraux died in December 1976, Burnham wrote the *National Review* obituary, which read in vivid part:

> [Though] his career was of the twentieth century, his essence sprung out of the nineteenth. Like D'Annunzio, T. E. Lawrence, or Antoine de Saint-Exupéry, with all of whom he recognized kinship, Malraux's person—or, rather, more accurately perhaps, persona—was nineteenth century: of the nineteenth century's romantic genius-type. . . . He kept death's blackness close: his hair was black; he wore black clothes, and drove in a black Citroën with a driver in a black uniform. His eyes seemed so dark as to be black—though deep in their blackness you could see mesmerizing fire that held you immobile as he talked—his eternal cigarette drooping, his dark face twisting in its strange nervous tics.

There, indeed, we have the truth about Burnham himself: a romantic, disguised as cold and rational, but passionately committed, knowing dark things and familiar with international violence.

His break with *Partisan Review* came over Joseph McCarthy, who had attained the height of his notoriety and therefore political power during the early 1950s. Burnham's position on McCarthy was that Stalin and American fellow-travelers were much more dangerous than the senator, and in that respect the furor over McCarthy was a distraction. He also disliked the mob psychology of the anti-McCarthyites. Burnham was "anti-anti-McCarthy," and so he refused to sign a collective *Partisan Review* letter of condemnation. This refusal aroused so much fury among staff and readers that the editors asked Burnham to resign from the masthead, which he did, calmly.

But that was not the worst. Burnham was ostracized by New York liberals and leftists. As Philip Rahv, the coeditor of *Partisan Review*, candidly observed, "The Liberals now dominate all the cultural channels in this country. If you break completely with this dominant atmosphere, you're a dead duck. James Burnham has committed suicide."[3]

As the 1940s spun past, Burnham left Marxism and worked on a new comprehensive theory. He developed this line of thought in two books, *The Managerial Revolution* (1941), already mentioned, and *The Machiavellians* (1943), also important for his work at *National Review*, and probably his best book. It performed an imaginative service by bringing together four political philosophers in an original way and setting forth as complementary their separate doctrines: Georges Sorel, Robert Michels, Gaetano Mosca, and Vilfredo Pareto.

They all are "Machiavellian" in their focus on *power*. What Burnham distills from them is a theory of the circulation of elites in pursuit of power, and the role of beliefs, ideologies, ideals, religions, and other ideas, or pseudo-ideas, in that pursuit. These enabling elements are not themselves verifiable. They are useful, functioning as rationalizations for the universal pursuit, and as "masks" for what lies "behind" them. This "masking" of the "real" reality is familiar in Marx, Freud, Levi-Strauss, and other such unmaskers. Power thus is the real business of politics, the real business behind all the masks and rationalizations. "The recurring pattern of change," writes Burnham, "expresses the more or less permanent core of human nature as it functions politically. The instability of all governments and political forms follows in part from the limitless appetite for power." Following his four theorists, Burnham holds that power is characteristically exercised by elites, and that a governing elite rises, prevails for a time, and then is replaced by another elite. Burnham had seen the older business elite fall from power with the Depression, to be replaced by the new liberal elite, and he views the characteristic set of liberal beliefs as *its* enabling myth: heredity less important than environment, malleable human nature, a human core essentially tending toward goodness, a general coincidence of shared goals and so the prospect of a "brotherhood of man," the great utility of reason and discussion, the nonexistence or non-importance of racial differences, the near certainty of progress. Burnham notices the absence of verifiability here, which does not, apparently, damage the utility of these myths in the pursuit of power. In fact, some or all of them seem to be contradicted by experience. This makes no difference to believers. One gathers that Burnham even regards the liberal myth as inferior among other facilitating myths applied by rival elites in their own struggle to gain or hold power.

A case study for the application of Burnham's theory, derived from his *Machiavellians*, might be the fifty-year circulation of elites described by *National Review* between 1955 and 2005: the replacement of the Eastern elite by an emerging elite from the South and Southwest, with the facilitating "myth" that accompanied this. To what extent did *National Review* understand itself in Burnham's terms as playing a role in the circulation?

Abundant evidence suggests that Burnham regarded the passing of the older Eastern elite, with its manners and manifest attractions, as a tragedy and perhaps unnecessary. Hence his unremitting hopes for Nelson Rockefeller, whom he regarded as suitably tough-minded—hopes not shared, to say the least, by his colleagues at *National Review*.

OF COURSE, BURNHAM could not always be the cold analyst of power. Morality kept breaking in. Joseph Sobran has recalled, as part of a September 11, 1987, memorial tribute to Burnham, his response to a buffoonish use of part of the liberal myth as rationalization for outrage and a downward "circulation of elites":

> Jim Burnham was so refined that I nearly fainted the first (of two) times I ever heard a vulgar word [from him]. A State Department official had just announced, with moral pomp, that the United States was withdrawing recognition from Rhodesia. I found Jim alone in his office on a quiet summer day. He commented, "Sometimes you have to throw your friends to the wolves. But you don't have to talk a lot of shit about democracy while you do it."

Yes, that is what the official was talking, as we turned prosperous Rhodesia over to Robert Mugabe, chaos, corruption, hunger, and murder; these still rule "Zimbabwe." But something striking is going on here: Burnham's anger, his use of the vulgar word. Fact and analysis would merely have observed that the myth of democracy and the myth of liberation were being used to make U.S. policy palatable. Perhaps anger might be a response when intelligence is insulted by the poor quality of the myth. But is there not more: "throw your friends to the wolves"? A sardonic smile would seem more suitable for a "Machiavellian."

Again and again Burnham does employ "mythic" language—"cold," "conscienceless," "dishonorable," "unthinkable," "devilish"—in connection with atrocities in Algeria or the "betrayal" of the 1956 Hungarian Revolution by Eisenhower's *Realpolitik*. Those modes of language were more suited to Burnham's Dante course at NYU than to the philosophy of Balliol or to the world of the Machiavellians.

BUT BURNHAM'S HARDHEADED skepticism may be very useful in political analysis, especially in a period when sentimental illusion prevails. There, Machiavelli may well be a better guide than liberal idealism, toughness better than dreamy escapism.

Burnham seems at times to imagine himself an "advisor to the Prince" in a brutal, revolutionary world, where simplified theories of knowledge may be called for. Burnham's first "Prince" was Leon Trotsky; later he looked with favor on Nelson Rockefeller. Burnham's great success was as an advisor to Buckley, and through *National Review*, to some extent to Ronald Reagan.

The ongoing process of Burnham changing in response to world events, in effect being educated by them and having to respond in detail, under the pressure of deadlines, and at the same time helping to shape *National Review*, more often than not moving it his direction, was one of the main things that made it intellectually exciting to work at the magazine. Quietly, he was a pervasive influence and educator.

I will close this introduction to Burnham with an ongoing dispute, representative of the overall tendency he urged, which Burnham only partially won, but which became legendary. Frank Meyer dissented from it vociferously. Early in 1956, he replaced Kendall as "Books, Arts and Manners" editor. Burnham in general wanted *National Review* to be smoother and more professional, eliminating undergraduate touches, expressions like "*grrrr*" and other slapstick. He also wanted it less conspicuously right-wing, appealing beyond its core readers to a general audience. He wanted less ideology, less "sectarianism," as he called it. With that in mind, he had his eye on Meyer's section.

At every quarterly senior editors' meeting he inevitably urged that the reviews be shorter, descriptive, less partisan. His models, he said, were the short reviews in the *Economist*. At this awaited moment, Meyer would erupt as if Burnham had touched off an electric jolt in his back pocket, jumping out of his chair, arms flailing, hand clawing at his gray brush-cut. The book *reviews*, he shouted, *had to be the length they were*. The *entire* magazine had a mission. Was he supposed to work for an *Atlantic Monthly*? Book reviews had to be exciting, *political*. He used them to bring new writers to the magazine—Joan Didion, Guy Davenport—and they came because the magazine was *conservative* and gave them a chance to *write*. With his force of personality, because the editors valued him, and because they probably agreed with him, Meyer always had his way on this point. But Burnham always came back at the next meeting, smiling his little smile. And eventually the magazine did move a bit in his direction, "dialectically," as Chambers would put it.

If Burnham had succeeded completely in taming the magazine, *National Review* very likely would not have succeeded. The *Economist* spoke to and for an existing British establishment. *National Review* was trying to shape a new conservative one. There, it seemed, was a bit of a confusion. Did Buckley, did Burnham, want to educate or destroy the liberal Eastern Establishment?

Burnham's repeated feints toward Nelson Rockefeller might suggest that he wanted to educate, indeed join, the Eastern Establishment, serving as its rightward edge. Just what, if it occurred in America, would Burnham's, and Pareto's, circulation of elites look like? Burnham had in view a governing elite. There still were many fights to be waged.

3

Willmoore Kendall:
Perhaps Too, Too . . .

Like James Burnham, Willmoore Kendall came to *National Review* trailing clouds of intellectual glory, even intimations of genius. Also like Burnham, he was a senior editor from the start. Unlike Burnham, however, he was erratic in his productivity, sometimes ego-explosive, and—though often instructive—also troubling. This kind of personality is far from rare among original thinkers; one thinks of Thorstein Veblen or C. S. Peirce, both impossible in the academy.

But remembered in prose and song, Kendall belongs in the magazine's Pantheon, and he remains a remembered influence. He had been a child prodigy in Oklahoma, graduating from college at sixteen; after that, a Rhodes Scholar at Pembroke College, Oxford, Dr. Johnson's college. His *John Locke and Majority Rule* (1941) had been widely acclaimed, Leo Strauss writing that "I do not know of any other theoretical study by a man born and trained in your generation in the U.S. in your or my generation which equals your work on Locke."[1] At Yale he had been a charismatic teacher, a tall, intense professor who challenged and influenced a number of the best students, including William Buckley and Brent Bozell. In seminars he used the question-and-answer Socratic form, of which he was a master. He wrote out his lectures in green ink, and they were the product of concentrated care. He carried the green ink over to his editorial duties at *National Review*. He figures prominently in Buckley's novel *Red Hunter* and in Saul Bellow's novella *Mosby's Memoirs*. Many good storytellers appreciate an original when one comes to hand. With Kendall, no imagination need be added.

He was an original teacher and writer with an ability to make the United States Constitution and its tradition shine afresh, always with Leo Strauss's rule in mind—to read a text as the author intended it to be read. And, as he wrote to Leo Strauss, "my ultimate modern master is Burke."[2] He was a profound student of Burke, uncovering his universal content and reinterpreting him as relevant to America. He disdained Russell Kirk's sense of Burke, saying it had "nothing to do with America." A master of American prose, his style was unique. It combined some vernacular words and phrases with a mandarin's baroque syntax. This reflected his interpretation of the Constitution: the "We the People" of the preamble filtered through the delaying and refining process of constitutional forms, democratic instincts and experience combined with high political theory. Nothing could go wrong with such a man.

Or could it? At *National Review* it was said that he was always on speaking terms with one person, but that this was not always the same person. Nevertheless, he sparkled brilliantly from the beginning, swooping down from New Haven and dispensing informal teaching on political theory— though Priscilla Buckley remembers him as sometimes grandstanding at Monday editorial meetings. For a short time he ran the "Books, Arts and Manners" section, until it passed to Frank Meyer. Kendall had been considered inattentive and given to academicism.

Like James Burnham, he articulated a comprehensive political theory, and he agreed with Burnham on many important matters. For example, like Burnham and Whittaker Chambers, he accepted some form of the welfare state, given the conditions of a populous industrial democracy. And like them he was not absolutist about free-market economics. He did not believe that the United States is or was founded as an open society, everything political always "up for gabs," as he characteristically put it. As a result of his experience working as a journalist in Spain during the Civil War, he was a committed anticommunist, considering communism utterly alien to the American tradition. But, more comprehensively, he thought that a great many political possibilities had already been definitively excluded by Americans and that advocates of such rejected positions could and should pay a price for their beliefs: Fascists, Communists, monarchists, anarchists, polygamists, and many others that can be imagined. He liked to point out, mischievously, that thousands of Tories had "emigrated" after the Revolution.

To *National Review* he contributed a regular column titled "The Liberal Line." This rested on the comic assumption that liberals, like Communists, were a conscious, centrally directed conspiracy. Of course Kendall and everyone else knew that this was not so, that the liberal subculture obeyed no such central direction, that in fact, the *New York Times* was not, functionally, *Pravda*, exactly. But everyone also knew that there was a high degree of uniformity in liberal opinion, often extending to details, as was seen in the reaction to *God and Man at Yale.* So the analogy with a central political directorate had some purchase on experience, and could also be funny. As Henri Bergson had said, one version of the comic is produced by the spectacle of life behaving mechanically, as in some clown acts where the clowns move stiffly, resembling marionettes, or as in a Dickens comic character who constantly repeats a tag line: "Barkis is willin'." Since liberals are advertised as independent thinkers, and since in practice there is such pervasive uniformity in their thought, that aspect of liberal behavior was ripe for comic treatment. Thus, someone coined the phrase "herd of independent minds," and it stuck. Therefore, "The Liberal Line."

Soon after the first number of *National Review* appeared, for example, readers found a "Liberal Line" beginning with a directive:

TO: All Echelons
FROM: Content Committee: Liberal Propaganda Machine.

In this satirical instruction we read:

When *National Review* was first announced, this committee asked Mr. John Fischer of *Harper's* to keep it under observation, and to make recommendations concerning the propaganda policy we should adopt toward it. Despite his heavy responsibilities in other directions (among them that of occupying

Harper's editorial "Easy Chair"), this committee regarded him as peculiarly qualified for this assignment, which he has executed with his usual thoroughness and courage. . . .

Operatives will note, and, as opportunity affords, echo Mr. Fischer's overarching "we-are-bitterly-disappointed-in-*National-Review*" theme, and will note also his daring skillful use of our recently neglected "the-conservatives-dominate-the-mass-communications" theme. Our tack: we always wanted the kind of magazine *National Review could* have been; the nation *needs* a magazine that will express the philosophy of modern American conservatism. . . .

Operatives are reminded of our general rule that only upper echelons are authorized to make statements about output that cannot be documented, and that such statements must be so formulated that they are incapable of documentary refutation. Note especially Mr. Fischer's charges that there are "heavy clerical overtones" in *National Review*; that the magazine wishes to "leap back to 1928." [T]hese statements are, in the enemy's peculiar sense of the term, "false" (that is, intentionally inaccurate). But statements that we wish to be true whether they are or not, they clearly fall under our White Lies dispensation.

This is in the straight-faced comic-persona genre, its comic quality depending upon its hint of plausibility.

BY THE TIME KENDALL WAS writing these columns in the early *National Review*, I was teaching in the English Department at Columbia, and beginning the Ph.D. program there. I looked forward to "The Liberal Line," finding it funny and refreshing. Kendall seemed to me to be tweaking the set of opinions that were rituals of conformity among liberals; his columns were instruments for disciplining the mind.

Another "Liberal Line" column, this in the mid-1950s, depends on the liberal supposition that we were living through a Reign of Terror in the United States. As a fact of experience, where civil liberties are concerned, I did not feel threatened, and I did not know anyone who was or had been threatened, in the largely liberal community of Columbia University. Of course my experience was limited by place and age. Still, I think I would have known *someone* who, though innocent, had heard the "knock on the door." "The Liberal Line" had some fun with the supposed *grande peur*:

Two of the Liberal propaganda machine's continuing long-term missions—and two it works away at most noisily—are:

1. The waging of psychological warfare against those forces in American society that are bent on "undermining" our "civil liberties."

2. Keeping the American people "informed" as to the "state" of our civil liberties; or, to put this a little differently, issuing theater-level communiqués that tell the target audiences at home how the battle against the underminers of our civil liberties is progressing. . . .

The liberal line in connection with Operation Two has for a long time now been that, despite heroic and Herculean efforts by our boys, things are going badly. For one thing, there's the Terror, which has assumed such proportions that during the long hours of the night one lies and wonders when—the security police having discovered another subscriber to *The Nation*, or another chap whose wife's first cousin's grandmother lives next door to a Communist and sometimes lends him her power lawnmower—they'll come knocking at the door and carry one off to the Senate caucus room.

These mockeries were funny because there really were big puffy balloons out there that needed puncturing, and Kendall was good with a needle.

Kendall could also be funny in the editorial section:

The attempted assassination of Sukarno has all the look of an "operation" by the Central Intelligence Agency: everyone got killed except the appointed victim.

Nikita Khrushchev has challenged the U.S. to compete with Soviet Russia "in the peaceful things" such as the production of radios and televisions and vacuum cleaners, any kind of cleaners. Knowing the Soviet ability to surfeit its own population and those of its satellites with all manner of high-grade consumers' goods, we would not be surprised to hear tomorrow that one of the Barnum & Bailey midgets had challenged Ted Williams to a home-run hitting contest. Or, as the mouse shouted after his third cocktail, "Bring on that goddam cat."

Kendall could also write things for *National Review* that drew on his special field of political philosophy (in contrast, notice, to the Yale Political

Science Department). On November 16, 1957, taking a vacation from "The Liberal Line," he discussed the important fissure then opening up in the university teaching of politics. One way to describe it would be as between statisticians and philosophers. Kendall identifies the former as associated with the prominent Harold Lasswell, and then goes on to describe the "new breed" of the 1950s:

> The new breed has its roots, by sharp contrast, in Plato and Aristotle and Thomas Aquinas. . . . [The] new breed are still *rara avis*, and come, for the most part, from a single institution, namely, the University of Chicago, for a good reason: most of them are pupils of one of the two or three great teachers of politics of our day, Professor Leo Strauss, who communicates to them, as if by magic, his own love of learning, his own sense of the gravity of the great problems of politics, and his own habit of thinking deeply about a problem before rushing into print. The old breed are riding high, and make and un-make reputations for professional achievement; the new breed are unlikely, for a good while anyhow, to cut much ice in the political science profession's exalted counsels. But they may well do something far more important, namely, to revive the habit of political thought in the United States, to set standards for it that the old breed, because of the patent inadequacy of their training, cannot live up to, *and* bring under challenge the Liberal orthodoxy that is the main burden of our current political science literature.

Kendall then goes on to discuss a recent book by Walter Berns, *Freedom, Virtue and the First Amendment* (1957), which he calls "the first full-dress book we have had from the new breed that addresses itself to a traditional problem of American politics." Shrewdly, Kendall calls attention to the word "virtue" in Berns's title. This word would not exist in the vocabulary of a "political science" statistician.

In this column, Kendall was describing a development of the first importance. He gave deserved credit to the teaching and published work of Leo Strauss as having had an enormous influence on the discussion of political theory, where Kendall excelled. About Strauss then and now there has been a great deal of misunderstanding. He was not a liberal or a conservative in the sense ordinarily used. A striking thing about him is that his students do not turn out to be mere replicas of their teacher and are variously liberals and conservatives on current matters. What they have in common is a careful or deep reading of major texts of political philosophy. Professor Roger Masters of Dartmouth came away from Strauss a liberal; Walter Berns came away a conservative, in current political usage. Yet I have even heard Strauss accused of being responsible for the 2003 invasion of Iraq. This is like asking whether Heraclitus would have voted for Adlai Stevenson.

In a longer *National Review* essay, Kendall tried for analytical depth. "Three on the Line" sets out to answer the question of what conservatism in America *is*, a question under constant discussion. He rules out preserving the status quo. And he rules out trying to define conservatism by reference to supposedly "conservative" politicians. Pick a "conservative" senator, and he is almost always conservative on some things, not on others. Nor are our political parties sharply divided ideologically. Perforce, they must be coalitions. And he dismisses the contention of Louis Hartz and a great many others that the American tradition itself is uniformly liberal.

Then he makes his central point: We hear about *liberalism* so much, and liberals keep proposing one thing after another, because *the American people* keep *resisting* liberal proposals, at least until they have been around for a long time and gained credibility in practice. Here he articulates what later he would call, in his major works, the idea of the "virtuous people," a civic concept that has nothing to do with individual virtue. In his constitutional theory, the "virtuous people" acts as an anchor.

> The American political tradition is a profoundly Conservative tradition, with a profoundly conservative content; *but precisely for that reason American politics tend to be about Liberalism.* The basic inertia of our politics is a forward Conservative inertia: when American society "changes" it changes for the most part—as Conservatives wish it to—in the proper direction; that is, in the direction in which it must change in order to become more and more like itself at its best. Changes in that direction—the various steps in the evolution of our present party system are conspicuous examples—tend, however, to take place quietly, unobtrusively, and without becoming sharp political issues.
>
> Of late, to be sure, our politics have tended to by very noisy indeed; but the reason is that the Liberals, here as everywhere rebels against Tradition,

do not wish American society to become more like itself. They are, there-fore, constantly putting forward proposals for making it over in their image of what a society should be like—proposals born of their distinctive dislike for the American way of life and for the basic political and social principles presupposed in it, and certain to run up against vigorous and uninterrupted Conservative resistance.

Kendall notices that the various conservative leaders who arise to fight off one or another liberal proposal almost inevitably disagree with one an-other on a range of other issues. On anticommunism, conservatives agree—but Joe McCarthy supported an entire list of midwestern populist mea-sures. Hence the difficulty, or impossibility, of identifying conservatism with practicing politicians.

Kendall trusts the instincts of his "virtuous people." By that term he means that Americans, in their aggregate, possess a sense of what America is and is not, and also a sense of political restraint. Kendall very much dis-trusts, for example, the John Stuart Mill of the essay *On Liberty*. His model American conservative, he writes,

> views with horror the thesis of Mill's essay *On Liberty*, according to which a man can hold and publicly defend any opinion, however repugnant to moral-ity, and still be regarded as a good—or even acceptable—citizen. And—to come to the main point—he regards the present determination of the Ameri-can people not to permit the emergence of a Communist minority in their midst—their determination, as I like to put it, to place the price of being a Communist so high that no American is likely to pay it—as a manifestation that he can only applaud.
>
> In a word: if by an open society is meant a society built on an unlimited right to think and say what you please, with impunity and without let or hindrance, then Conservatives hold that American society is *not* such a so-ciety and must not become such a society.

OF COURSE, THIS CONVICTION, that the American people *know* what American society actually *is* as lived in daily existence, underlies Kendall's strenuous defense of the original "deliberate sense" mechanism of the Con-stitution—and his loathing of derailment through plebiscites, that is temporary majorities, or by improbable judicial "interpretations" of one or another clause in the Constitution. Kendall's views here may seem Panglossian. Little seems to restrain the Supreme Court, at least in recent years, from self-constituting itself as a legislature and ruling directly through "interpretation." Still, in support of his argument, could one really win in an American election, or hold a responsible civic post as, say, a school principal, as an advocate of polygamy, communism, open marriage, fascism, or any number of other "un-American" opinions? Kendall thought that there are such things as "un-American" opinions, and that the vast majority of Americans know what these are through their daily experience of American life, which is not a permanent seminar. America is not an open society, and the Constitution was not written by Walt Whitman. Kendall articulated this view in *National Review* and also more systematically in "Conservatism and the Open Society" in *The Conservative Affirmation* (1963).

Naturally, discordant views such as this were part of the reason for Kendall's troubles at Yale. Among liberals and among academics, to an extent overlapping categories, the very idea that some things are *un-American* was and is scandalous, certainly not admissible to the free discussion of ideas, even as applied to political theory. To be sure—as if confirming Kendall despite themselves—colleges and universities have their own orthodoxy and impose their own penalties. But these contentions were far from Kendall's only problem at Yale. Strauss, after all, had flourished at Chicago.

Institutionally, Kendall had been impossible, though in all accounts a great teacher. Dwight Macdonald, hardly a lodestar of accuracy, described Kendall in a 1955 *Commentary* article as "a wild Yale don of extreme, eccentric, and very abstract views who could get a conversation into the shouting stage faster than anyone within memory." That is colorful, but impressionistic. In fact, as I think the views I have described here show, his ideas were anything but abstract, eccentric, or extreme. He wanted to define a constitutional orthodoxy based on common sense, American experience, and the founding texts, closely read. It seems likely, however, that he did get conversations quickly into the shouting stage through his confrontational style of argument. Before long he was on poisonous terms with everyone in his department at Yale.

WITHIN DAYS OF HIS ARRIVAL in New Haven he had been present at one of those tame academic affairs at which a colleague, this time the chairman of his department, delivers a small paper on something or other and answers a few questions preparatory to tea and sherry. But now, when the chairman had finished, Kendall immediately tore everything he had said to shreds. His usual mode of argument was to force things back quickly to first principles, then to argue first principles. At this he was a master and could be devastating. His students loved this; the faculty did not. That day, within his first few days on the Yale campus, the ivy on the walls of that Gothic building must have shriveled.

One other thing that must have made him intellectual enemies in his department was his insistence that "deliberate sense" topped "rights" in the American constitutional system. The goal of the Constitution, he held, was to effect the six purposes listed in the preamble: form a more perfect union, establish justice, insure domestic tranquility, provide for the common defense, promote the general welfare, and secure the blessings of liberty to ourselves and our posterity. The enforcement of a "right" is nowhere among these six. And which of the six goals takes precedence at any time is up to the deliberate sense of the people as expressed through the constitutional process. During the Civil War, Lincoln suspended *habeas corpus* in Maryland, for example. By withholding impeachment, among other sanctions available to it, Congress expressed acceptance. The survival of the nation, implicit throughout the preamble, took precedence over *habeas corpus* and everything else in the Constitution. After all: no nation, no Constitution. This kind of thing from Kendall was "heretical," at odds with the "usual [academic] books," as Kendall called them, and evoked varying degrees of outrage, no doubt intensified by his vehemence. Before long, Yale was giving him every other year off with pay, so that the other members of the department could repair their nerves before he returned to his New Haven cauldron.

EVERYWHERE WILLMOORE KENDALL went he carried turbulence with him. Unusual behavior. Outrages. The geometrical opposite of the decorous, diplomatic, and elegant James Burnham.

At *National Review* there remains to this day a leather couch known as

"The Willmoore Kendall Memorial Couch." One evening, after hours, an editor returned to the premises and surprised Kendall on this piece of furniture *in flagrante* with an employee. Bill Buckley, hearing of this, wondered why he could not have found a hotel room. The business-hours occupant of that office was appalled that he had used her couch for this purpose.

A former Books editor at *National Review* remembers the following about a drive through New Jersey with Willmoore at the wheel: "We were stopped for speeding, requested to 'follow me' to a headquarters building where a State Police sergeant or captain was sitting behind an ordinary desk. This officer requested Professor Kendall to show him his driver's license. Kendall said he didn't have one, and then added, rather gratuitously I thought, 'I don't believe in them.' A look of blank disbelief crossed the officer's face. He started to speak, paused, peered intently at Kendall, and finally in a quiet voice asked, 'What do you do?' 'I'm an associate professor in the Political Science Department at Yale University,' Kendall replied. The officer looked at Kendall again, started to nod his head up and down, and said, 'Oh, I see.' What he saw I don't know, but I'm here to attest that he allowed Professor Kendall to continue on his way, unticketed and unlectured, simply demanding, after asking for and being shown my driver's license, that I drive the car at least until we had passed beyond his jurisdiction." Weird. Willmoore.

Though Kendall had been granted tenure by Yale on the basis of his publication and professional reputation as a political philosopher, he was eventually given to understand that he would not receive the normal next promotion to full professor. Beyond Yale, his professional reputation remained formidable, and, thinking about teaching elsewhere, he accepted a position as visiting associate professor at Stanford for the academic year 1958–59, with every expectation that it would lead to a permanent post as full tenured professor. But three weeks into his first term he was arrested for driving drunk and against the traffic flow on a California freeway. The state police jailed him for the night. This got into the Stanford student newspaper, and that was the end of his Stanford opportunity. He wrote to Leo Strauss explaining that he had been drinking a bit of bourbon for a cold and some snoop had smelled it on his breath.

His Yale career ended in a unique, that is Kendallian, way. Somehow he prevailed upon Bill Buckley, as a friend, to find out why Yale was refusing to promote him to full professor. Buckley profoundly disliked the whole idea of becoming involved in this.[3] Universities usually insist upon holding such decisions closely, for many good reasons, including the professional reputation of the candidate. But Buckley did make an appointment to see President Charles Seymour, who was direct and said the reason was lack of publication while at Yale.[4] That is a perfectly valid reason. Yale had every right to demand more than Kendall had produced. He had published essays and reviews. But his last book had been *John Locke and Majority Rule* (1941), which earned him his reputation, his Yale post, and Stanford's interest. That book was almost twenty years old. Two more important works came along, *The Basic Symbols of the American Political Tradition* and his edition of Rousseau's *The Government of Poland*; but those were published posthumously, years later, in 1972. Yale might have been justified in promoting him on the basis of his teaching, but that would have been rare for a research university and would have required institutional goodwill, which was absent.

Since he was inspired by important ideas, what was the explanation for his lack of publication? In addition to his disorderly private life, the evidence suggests a profligate scattering of energy on nonprofessional matters. He wrote letters of gargantuan length, enough prose and enough articulation of ideas for several books, a singular phenomenon. Perhaps a *Selected Letters* may yet be published. In addition, with a construction project in hand on his New Haven property, he wasted time driving hundreds of miles for cheaper bricks, nonsensically in that the sum saved was trivial.

Then, naturally, his Yale career ended in an extraordinary manner. Kendallian. While he was in Madrid on one of his therapeutic leaves from Yale, so the Kendall oral tradition goes, he phoned President Seymour and, probably drunk, said something like, "You sonofabitch. I know you hate my guts. I'll tell you what. You can buy back my tenure." The deal was struck, a check arrived immediately for $42,500. That was a lot of money in 1961, about five times his annual salary.

After his departure from Yale, he remained a senior editor at *National Review*, contributing valuably, as we will see, until 1963. I spent some time with him later in Europe. This proved in its entirety a bittersweet experience, also an education in political theory. It was a week memorable, strange, and leading to a bad ending. But what else could have been expected?

4

Russell Kirk vs. Frank Meyer

It was a minor tragedy for *National Review* that Frank Meyer and Russell Kirk not only disagreed with each other but despised each other, at least in the early years. In 1955, Kirk gladly joined the new *National Review*, agreeing to write a regular column, "From the Academy," but refused to become a senior editor because he did not want so close an association with any enterprise that included Meyer. The tragedy was that the differences between them, essentially about the relationship between the individual and society, could have amounted to a creative tension in the magazine. Indeed, later a somewhat similar disagreement between Meyer and Brent Bozell, about the individual and the obligation of society to foster virtue, produced one of the most valuable internal debates ever conducted in the pages of *National Review*. But in 1955 Meyer and Kirk were so at odds that sustained civil discourse was simply impossible.

Few people reading *National Review* during the early weeks of 1956 would have sensed this from two articles that now appeared. Kirk knew exactly what he was doing when, in the January 26, 1956, issue he published "Mill's *On Liberty* Reconsidered." Meyer recognized this as a direct attack on him and replied with "In Defense of John Stuart Mill" on March 28.

The original source of the enmity was Meyer's attack on Kirk's *The Conservative Mind* in the July 5, 1955, *Freeman,* aggressively titled "Collectivism Rebaptized." There, Meyer said that Kirk's major work, an astonishing critical and publishing success, amounted to little more than a thinly disguised tract in favor of the "collectivist" welfare-state status quo. He attacked Kirk as setting forth no discernible political *principle*, of espousing mere attitude and sentiment, of articulating no standard by which to judge the slide into omni-competent government, and no way, in his account of "tradition," to discriminate between good and bad traditions. At about the same time, well-received books by Clinton Rossiter and Peter Viereck were being praised as articulating a "New Conservatism." Meyer included these in his condemnation of Kirk as merely putting forth, in archaic costume, the "spirit of the age."

In 1955, when this *Freeman* blast appeared, Kirk was trying to launch a new conservative quarterly, *Modern Age.* He must have been outraged by this characterization, especially as he sought to interest backers for his project. So his January 1956 article "reconsidering" Mill's *On Liberty* was one form of response to Meyer. When Meyer's *In Defense of Freedom: A Conservative Credo* (1962) later appeared, Kirk hit it hard in the April-June 1964 *Sewanee Review*, matching Meyer in venom and unfairness. Kirk titled his attack, "An Ideologue of Liberty." He called Meyer's book a "political pamphlet," used such language as "zealous," "abstract," "weary liberalism of the nineteenth century," an "attempt to erect an ideology with slogans and dogmas." He accused Meyer of isolating freedom from all other human goods, of idolizing it, of advocating a condition in which no human being could possibly exist. But Kirk did not give Meyer credit for attempting—with some success—to set forth a practical, if in political theory not entirely successful, platform on which existing libertarians and traditionalists could work together.

Oddly, Meyer and Kirk actually had some things in common. Both were eccentric, bookish conservatives, enormously isolated in their personal lives, and colorful personalities with large followings. Kirk's Man is the Man of the Church, the university, the library, the community, Aristotle's Man of the *Polis*. Meyer's Man is Man against the Sky, creating himself in perpetual acts of choosing. Both of these conceptions were rooted in the lived experience of these two colorful men. In that sense, both were "existentialists"—though Kirk would have loathed that neologism. Jaspers used it in the precise sense of "philosophizing from one's own situation." All three men spoke from within the drama of the twentieth century, a period of radical ideologies and revolutions, when the moon had fallen from the skies and all the signs had been removed. Luther had said, "A mighty fortress is our God." Kirk might say, "A mighty fortress is my library." Meyer might reply, "A mighty fortress is my mind and my conscience."

If, as Matthew Arnold said, the Protestant principle is individual choice, then both Kirk and Meyer were Protestants—though, as it happened, both eventually chose the Catholic Church, Kirk in the middle of his journey, Meyer at the very end of his, still arguing on his death-bed with the priest over the moral admissibility of suicide. Of both it could be said, as Milton said of *Paradise Lost*, that in deciding on his theme he had been "long choosing, and beginning late."

What we can say at once about the argument between Kirk and Meyer is that each man was a learned proponent and example of contrasting themes within the emerging conservative movement. Each was an icon to his many followers, traditionalist or libertarian, no doubt because each expressed and embodied such tendencies so purely. More generally, almost everyone is, most of the time, something of each. But upon just what basis can Meyer possibly announce that, "I assert the right of individual freedom not on the grounds of utility but on the grounds of the very nature of man"?

The short answer is that, as he often said to me but never in print, so far as I know, he considered Hegel's *Phenomenology of Mind* to be, as he put it, a "holy book." This may be the most difficult of Hegel's characteristically difficult works, but I have no doubt that Meyer's copy was dog-eared and much underlined; and Hegel, after all, is a much more formidable figure than Mill. Hegel's books and his university lectures had the power to change students' lives, teaching that human history, examined from archaic times through Hegel's Germany, consists of the actualization of the Idea of Freedom. Hegel sees setbacks, of course, but he sees this process as inevitable. Gazed upon from a very great distance, inevitability may be true of history, though actual people with free will and engaged in daily conflicts cannot know that. Still, it does seem as though human beings, acting in history, do seek more freedom, since that is inherent in the human mind.

Meyer's emphasis on freedom and the individual mind might well have found theoretical support in Hegel, but it certainly also had special force for Meyer because the defining moment of his life had been his break with the Communist Party in 1945, a break achieved, it seemed to him, at the risk of his life.

I FIRST MET MEYER IN 1963, initially over the phone of course, when he called to ask me to review my first book for *National Review*. At the magazine, I found, the joke was that an emergency call from Frank was one that interrupted the second hour of his call to Brent Bozell. In person, he combined physical and intellectual energy to a degree that could be over-whelming: wiry, in motion, pacing and talking, smoking and drinking bour-bon in the book-packed living room of his isolated home up a mountain road near Woodstock, New York. By then his brush-cut was gray. He had a sallow complexion, a long thin nose, and a wide mouth. He had inherited from the period of his break with the Communist Party his eccentric mode of life. Like Whittaker Chambers under similar circumstances, he had feared assassination, and so, in order always to have someone awake in the house, he worked at night, his wife Elsie during the day—Elsie very much a part of his life as Books editor and *NR* columnist.

From his time in the party he also carried over an intense cultivation both of theory and *praxis*, energetic as a speaker all over the country, an organizer of Young Americans for Freedom, the New York Conservative Party, and the Goldwater for President movement. In his energy, his pros-elytizing, and his organizing activities, he sometimes reminded me of Saint Paul, who had been active all over the Middle East and around the Medi-terranean to Rome, theorizing, orating, organizing, writing. On the public platform Meyer had a booming voice, at first surprising from such a small man.

The earlier part of his life bore some similarities to that of James Burnham. He was born in 1909 and his Newark, New Jersey, family was well-off enough to send him to good schools and to Princeton in 1925. But unlike Burnham, he was obscure and unhappy there, and he left after two years.[1] His parents could afford education abroad, so after some private tutoring he sailed for England and enrolled for a B.A. at Balliol, where Burnham, the more glamorous figure, had preceded him again. Meyer was drawn both to the famous Martin D'Arcy, who tutored him in Catholic theology, and to the works of Marx.

It was Marx who provided a principle of structure for him in an economy shattered by the Depression. He joined the Communist Party and, urged to do so by the party, entered the London School of Economics in 1932, where he became an agitator and student organizer. His work impressed the party, and on his return to the United States in 1934 he was assigned to the Chicago area, enrolled as a graduate student at the University of Chicago, and again was successful enough as an agitator that the party appointed him education director of its Illinois-Indiana district.

Deeply involved with party activities, he met another young Communist, Elsie Brown, a Radcliffe graduate from a wealthy and, it seems, anti-Semitic family. She had become a Communist in college and had married a Communist soon after. That marriage did not work out. Making her way to Chicago, she enrolled at the Communist Workers School where Meyer was teaching. She soon married him. With the coming of war, Meyer volunteered for the Army, was sent to Officer's Training, but was medically discharged for bad feet, which had to be operated on after his discharge.

During his recuperation he had a chance to reflect deeply, and it was then that doubts began to accumulate about Marxism and the Communist Party. His Army experience had given him a sense of "the masses" as actual Americans, and of America as something other than a Marxist diagram. Audaciously, he wrote a long letter to Earl Browder, chairman of the American Communist Party, expressing his reservations about party organization and practices and speculating about the possibility of de-Bolshevising the party structure, i.e., making it more democratic.

Browder himself, unknown to Meyer, had been moving in the same direction. In 1944, Browder dissolved the old party structure and announced the formation of a new and voluntary "Communist Political Association."

Meyer was sent to teach at the party's Jefferson School in New York, where his doubts increased as he argued with colleagues and students and did some writing for the *New Masses*. His break came at the end of 1945, when Stalin purged Browder and the American Communist Party reverted to Stalinist orthodoxy.

THAT MEYER HAD REFLECTED his way out of Marxism and Leninism was fundamental to his thought as it crystallized in *National Review*, his books, and his later conservative recruitment and organizing activities. He had re-made himself inside his own mind. Now, with Moscow clamping down, the robotic party proceeded with its expected vilification of Browder and Browderism internationally. Danger vibrated in the leftist air. Meyer, alone now with his wife, had a proven, lethal enemy in Stalin: Meyer against the empire. Everyone was aware of what had happened to Trotsky in 1940. He and Elsie had a small income, enough to buy the modest house near Woodstock. A great deal of thinking remained, to be undertaken alone. The sky was empty and the branches were bare. It is not surprising that he would say, in response to Kirk's reconsideration of Mill, "I assert the right of individual freedom not on the grounds of utility but on the grounds of the very nature of man."

Meyer's experience led directly to his radical emphasis on the individual in his social thought, and to his lasting contribution to knowledge based on his own experience of communism, *The Moulding of Communists* (1961), reviewed by Gerhart Niemeyer in the January 26, 1961, *National Review*:

> [The book] is a testimony offered from personal experience, a probing search into what went and goes on in the minds of people who, like the author, spent the formative years of their lives under Communist Party discipline. . . . It is "belief in ideology"? To some extent, emphatically yes . . . in the sense that an almighty History permeates the whole being of a Communist. But Communists are moulded primarily not so much by acceptance of beliefs as by the incessant training. Training here must not be understood in the analogy of Western formal education in courses. There are, of course, formal schools, but training goes on through continuous discussions, criticism, correction, clarification concerning not merely Communist Party actions but every aspect of

the Party member's personal life. "Every Party meeting, from the unit level to the level of national and international conventions, committees and bureaus, is treated as an occasion for 'theoretical' analysis and discussion. . . . Unguarded expressions in ordinary conversations, sometimes on the most trivial subjects, are regarded as highly significant signs of "weakness of understanding" and can become the subject of long campaigns of "education."

The Moulding of Comunists was a powerful book indeed, not at the level of high theory, but down in the trenches. Like Burnham, Meyer brought much with him to *National Review*.

WHEN *THE CONSERVATIVE MIND* came out in 1953, its publisher, Henry Regnery, called its sales "beyond all expectation."[2] Robert Nisbet said that it had broken "the cake of intellectual opposition to the conservative tradition in the United States." T. S. Eliot pronounced himself "very much impressed" by it. It received a laudatory review in the *New York Times*, while *Time* magazine devoted its entire July 6, 1953, book section to it. With such a reception in those important organs, reviews of the book spread across the country. It would have been surprising if it had not received criticism from liberals, who vehemently reasserted the essentials of liberal thought against it.

In part, its impact was due to the convergence of a book with a moment. New Deal liberalism had become tired and tiresome; communism was clearly an enemy and alien to the West; and the new president Dwight Eisenhower was widely regarded as conservative. The "end of ideology" was supposed to be at hand. *The Conservative Mind* appeared, and rebutted Mill's assertion that the conservatives were "the stupid party." It exhibited not just one powerful conservative mind, but a galaxy of brilliant ones. Many college students looked up with a wild surprise from Louis Hartz and Keynes and R. H. Tawney and Ruth Benedict and the *New York Times*. The liberals seemed to shrink alongside Kirk's *dramatis personae*, not only in mind, but in style.

In addition, utopia had acquired a bad reputation. During the same period, a stream of powerful anticommunist works appeared, led by *Nine-*

teen Eighty-Four, Witness, The Captive Mind, The God That Failed, Darkness at Noon, Animal Farm. But more: T. S. Eliot was the laureate of the age, a Christian. His *Cocktail Party* and Graham Greene's *Potting Shed*, both Christian plays, spoke to large audiences on Broadway. Reinhold Niebuhr had recovered original sin, Evelyn Waugh celebrated aristocratic Catholicism in *Brideshead Revisited*, Bishop Fulton Sheen starred on TV, in full regalia, with serious sermons, and C. S. Lewis's popular and often profound books on Christianity were read everywhere. Bliss it was in that dawn to be alive. There could not have been a better moment for *The Conservative Mind* to arrive on the scene. Burke remains a presence throughout, standing as Kirk's exemplary conservative, Kirk extracting from Burke his own love for old and quaint things, crenellated walls, ancestral mansions, yews, winding paths, even graceful decay.

Like his *National Review* colleague and foe up that mountain road near Woodstock, Kirk lived isolated, his aerie the large Victorian house thought to be haunted, which he had purchased in rural Mecosta, Michigan, near where he had been born in 1918. But Meyer did not hate the modern world, while Kirk hated most of it. He almost never visited New York City, never responded to its particular poetry, or to the poetry of other great cities: he preferred Gothic ruins. As a result, he very seldom visited the *National Review* offices. But when he did, the staff met a plump fellow with a kindly face wearing a cape, a black, wide-brimmed, floppy felt hat, a gold stick-pin in his necktie, and carrying a sword cane. The staff at *National Review* believed him to be a confirmed bachelor on the traditional English-eccentric model until he astonished everyone by marrying the beautiful, dark-haired Annette, a devout Catholic from suburban Long Island, with whom he raised a large family in the haunted home in Mecosta, where he once threw a television set out of a second-story window in a fury against its invasion of his household.

KIRK GREW UP IN RURAL Michigan, the son of a railroad engineer, and he regretted the advance of all the aspects of modern machine culture into the small towns of that rolling landscape.[3] He received a B.A. from Michigan State College and did graduate work in history at Duke, where he wrote a Master's thesis later published as his first book, *Randolph of Roanoke* (1951). In it he much admired the aristocratic John Randolph, Southern localism and states' rights, strict constructionism, and agrarian economy. Kirk's conservatism is not properly understood without recognizing its connection to his idea of the antebellum South as a conservative society. While at Duke and working on Randolph he had discovered his affinity for the Southern writers of the manifesto *I'll Take My Stand* (1930): Tate, Warren, Ransom, Davidson, Lytle, and the rest. Their myth of the Old Confederacy powerfully informed their verse and energized their social criticism. It is this element that Kirk admires in T. S. Eliot, whose social criticism owes much to the Agrarians—though Kirk did not much care about Eliot's achievement in revolutionary modernist verse. Still, it remains this perspective that gives imaginative strength to his criticism, often valid, of the huge university, big labor, big business, big bureaucracy, and big crowds.

His sensibility did not have its first roots in the lyrical Agrarian vision of the South, but in the Midwest of his early youth, the much less poetic small-town conservatism of Ohio's senator Robert Taft.[3] It must have seemed like a bad dream in retrospect, but in 1941 Kirk actually worked at the colossal Ford River Rouge plant, which was in the early stages of winning World War II, the epitome of modern assembly-line production. In the summer of 1942, drafted into the Army, bigness and bureaucracy choked him once again, and he loathed the experience. After the war he taught the history of civilization at Michigan State University, the despised Behemoth University of his *National Review* "From the Academy" columns, and also pursued a doctorate at St. Andrew's, Scotland, where he forever touched holy ground. In his "From the Academy" column of August 25, 1956, he reported on a visit to his profoundly loved ancient university, and it is a glorious piece of writing. I wish I could reproduce this entire object—it is Kirk absolutely to perfection—but excerpts will have to do. Here we can put no greater distance between us and the awful Ford River Rouge plant, the U.S. Army, and Michigan State:

So far as I know, I am the only living American who holds the St. Andrews doctor of letters; and I feel quite sure that I am the only person who has been capped with the cap of John Knox (literally) and hooded with the hood of St. Ignatius of Loyola—this last, I add, not at St. Andrew's but at Boston University. . . .

The town of St. Andrews is far older than the university; it goes back to the time of the Culdees, and scraps of tombs and architecture of every age from that dim Christian dawn to the present are scattered about the little old gray city, on its cliffs above the sea. Of the ancient buildings of the university, two medieval chapels and some Renaissance halls and lodgings survive.

I wonder if the evidence at St. Andrews of the destruction wrought by John Knox's Reformation there helped make Kirk a Catholic. This was worse than Appomattox.

Again and again in his long career as a columnist and general advisor at *National Review*, Kirk's highly distinctive, his entirely self-invented personality makes itself felt. Here he is, as again and again, on Behemoth University:

Michigan State University (formerly College) at East Lansing has a beautiful campus—or had, until most of it got covered with "modified college Gothic" buildings in recent years. . . . Michigan State is only one of hundreds of agricultural schools, technical colleges, and teachers' colleges in the process of growth into something quite different from their original condition. Does such a university, on assuming the name university, take on the traditional responsibilities of university education?

In column after column, book after book, Kirk makes it clear that the business of a university is the perfection of the soul and the understanding of the world. He knows all too well that, as Wordsworth said, the world is too much with us; getting and spending, we lay waste our powers.

Russell Kirk remained a mainstay of *National Review*. He wrote a widely syndicated column, spoke all over the nation and abroad, wrote a great number of books, and was a campus favorite.

I CAN TESTIFY FROM MY OWN experience that as a visitor to campuses and lecturer to twentieth-century college students, Kirk was a marvel. I once brought him to Dartmouth, where he spoke in the congenial setting of a finely appointed, dark-paneled room full of antique furniture in the Georgian English Department building. Kirk was a self-invented work of art, prodigiously learned: he came as a delight to the students and as a change from the banalities of their ordinary world of do-good deans and predictable professors. Kirk to them was a *rebel*, enacting the *J'Accuse!* against the shopworn liberalism that met them from the moment they woke up in the morning. He had read one hundred times as many, one thousand times as many, books as anyone they had ever met, including plenty of Latin, quotations from which, in the original, punctuated his talk.

He stood before them in that sumptuous, paneled Ivy League lounge, filling his pin-striped, three-piece suit, his floppy black felt hat near him on a chair, and he spoke very quickly and not very audibly on the subject of "character." Citing numerous classical and Renaissance authorities, he advised the students that character is chiefly the product of old and distinguished families, to which a young man looks up with awe and a desire to imitate.

This was amazing stuff. He was talking about *noble ancestry*. Probably not one of these students was anything but an American meritocrat, an ace of the Scholastic Aptitude Test, offspring of, at best, nice professional-class parents. But they loved Russell Kirk. He was more rebellious than Che Guevara and Malcolm X combined. What would the hockey coach think?

The chief motive in building character, they heard, is an unwillingness to disgrace one's ancestors. From the dark walls around them, oil portraits of old Calvinist Dartmouth patriarchs frowned down. To the listening students, Kirk embodied the romance of learning, a fabulous figure, in a wholly unexpected sense a rare example of the freedom of the individual. Gorgeous. I cannot imagine what his father, the old Michigan railroad engineer, would have thought of him. Was *he* a noble ancestor? God knows, maybe he was.

It is too bad Russell Kirk never became personally familiar with Frank Meyer. I think he might have treasured him as an aesthetic experience, another original, like himself. What each contributed to *National Review* and to the making of the American conservative mind were necessary parts of that mind, which is not either/or, tradition or individualism, but both/ and. Very few conservatives are all one or the other. Russell Kirk was a fantastic individualist—in his own way, of course.

5

Arriving Talent

In its first year of publication, the most important job for *National Review* was to establish a team of distinctive writers—the senior editors and regular contributors, but others as well, writers often unknown to the magazine's management at the outset. A generally acknowledged principle, articulated by Buckley, holds that the very purpose of politics is the sustaining of civilization and that aesthetic and intellectual pleasure, beyond quotidian well-being, constitutes the high achievement of civilization. Thus, culture matters; style matters. From the beginning, *National Review* held that in mind, and at once it was well started on the way to the high pleasure described by William Rickenbacker, a former senior editor, looking back in 1980:

> Besides paying extraordinary attention to matters of style, the 35th Street crew worked a profound change in the use of language in journalism. Gone was the Strunk and White stricture against the use of foreign phrases. Down the memory hole went the fear of long words, unusual words, difficult words, and weird words. "Oxymoron," considered dead for centuries, took on new life on East 35th Street and has now passed into the Elysian Fields of television commentators, standup comedians and newspaper editorialists. Other exhumations—"exiguous" and "eximious" come to mind—haven't caught on

quite so quickly. Latin phrases appeared with dismaying frequency, and an aristocratic refusal to translate and explain, driving the egalitarians, populists, and yahoos to paroxysms of helpless rage.[1]

Thus Bill Rickenbacker, economist, fierce libertarian, concert pianist, Harvard man, amateur pilot, and son of Captain Eddie Rickenbacker, whom he worshipped. This passage displays the energy, the tone, the defiant vocabulary of an embattled but joyous band.

At the outset, only a few of *National Review*'s writers were known to a generally educated audience: Buckley, Burnham, Kirk, Chambers, John Chamberlain, Max Eastman. But the magazine soon brought forward other writers, all of special excellence, many of them young and previously unknown. They made high spirits their signature, in line with Buckley's project of making *National Review*, and with it American conservatism, more aware of its rich intellectual resources. The magazine was always willing to publish material of a more than usual scholarly voltage.

Sometimes it was only a smile that made the difference. In the following three sentences from James Burnham's review of former president Truman's *Memoirs*, the first two sentences set up the smile in the third:

> A third of the text of ex-President Truman's *Memoirs* consists of official documents, speeches, memoranda and letters. The remainder, in which a flat syntax links one cliché to the next, lacks every literary quality. Nevertheless, if we stick through the 1200 pages of the two volumes, we become in some degree acquainted with the author, or perhaps the foreman, of this work.

That is actually friendly compared with the magazine's treatment of President Eisenhower's syntax, and very likely Harry Truman would have laughed.

National Review characteristically *enjoyed* the spectacle of politics, cherishing to a degree even Eleanor Roosevelt's unique goofiness, among many examples the following editorial paragraph, quoting the former First Lady:

> The establishment of this new regime [in China] seems to have cost 800,000 lives, according to the admission of the present government. This does not seem to be a happy way to inaugurate reform.

Helen Hockinson presides again. To many, Eleanor Roosevelt was a saint, and possibly she was, but she was also absurd, and such remarks are aesthetic marvels entirely apart from skewed political content.

NATIONAL REVIEW HAD A previously unknown cartoonist named John Kreuttner who possessed a talent for expressionist illustration of balmy states of mind, and many of his erratic-line illustrations were striking originals. Mr. Kreuttner's relationship with *National Review* became turbulent during the later collision of the magazine with the John Birch Society, which came to a climax in the 1960s. Mr. Kreuttner, believing the position of the magazine too rigorous and considering that there were good conservatives within the society, ceased to contribute. He later returned when the fevers subsided, but perhaps like many artists he savored outrageousness.

In those innocent early days of American conservatism, many a *rara avis* flew in through the window, some of them a bit too *rara*. One of the most brilliant was Revilo Oliver.[2] A professor of linguistics at the University of Illinois, he entered weekly journalism through *National Review* and was one of the most remarkable people ever connected with the magazine. He would never have seen the light of day in any of the existing weeklies, though there was nothing bizarre about his contributions; as a writer he was a mainstream conservative. The name Revilo Oliver may seem odd. His father, himself fascinated with linguistics, had given him a palindrome for a name, that is, a combination of letters that reads the same forward or backward, like the name of the statesman Lon Nol. Interesting father.

In Oliver's study at home he had a large U-shaped desk arrangement on which sat a dozen typewriters, each with a different typeface: Latin, Classical Greek, Modern Greek, Egyptian, Arabic, Italian, French, German, Spanish, etc. Professor Oliver was a genius in his field, also a perfectionist. He wrote some remarkable things—for example, on the cultural function of grammar—and he could bring his erudition to bear on a variety of fields, often with a touch of humor. Here is an example from a mini-review of Reuben Levy's *Social Structure of Islam* (1957):

Exhaustive erudition, precise discrimination, and lucid exposition make this book a model of what a sociological study should be and rarely is. One will find in it not even a trace of the tendentious gibberish that now so commonly passes for "sociology." Instead, we get a comprehensive and compendious account of fundamental concepts, attitudes and customs that shape Islamic society. Mr. Levy writes with complete objectivity. Here and there, perhaps, he could have permitted himself a discreet smile. Next to the Koran, the basis of Islamic law is the vast body of traditional aphorisms (*ahadith*) attributed to Mohammed by later writers. It might have been interesting to note that one of the aphorisms thus put into the Prophet's mouth is: "If you come across a fine saying, don't hesitate to attribute it to me. I must have said it."

Professor Oliver was a gifted generalist and a crisp writer, as is shown by two paragraphs from one of his frequent reviews, this one of a book about Saint-Simon, sometimes known as the founder of sociology, and also as the most important precursor of Marx:

It's a pity that the forty-seven volumes of Saint-Simon's collected works are seldom taken from the shelves these days, for our Liberal friends would find it interesting to open the oyster from which came so many of the pearls of wisdom that they now wear with pride. Everyone now knows, of course, that Saint-Simon invented plebiscites and the Wilsonian doctrine of the "self-determination of peoples." He denounced colonialism, and thought prosperous nations should provide the technological and financial assistance necessary to industrialize the whole world. He was a vociferous advocate of a United Nations that would infallibly prevent war and insure "world cooperation." It was he who discovered how easy it is to abolish poverty everywhere by applying science to the twin problems of raising everyone's standard of living and organizing mankind. He was, furthermore, sentimental about the "workers," and he devised the now popular "New Christianity" in which religion is replaced by a blind faith in the miracles to be wrought by Progress.

Professor Oliver here is being sardonic about a linear, comprehensive, and, as it were, redeeming doctrine of progress, the redemption offered being infinitely postponable, as when Anthony Lewis would later write in the *New York Times* that at least the Khmer Rouge and Pol Pot were "building a new society."

Assuming that all this Saint-Simonian enlightenment might be too much to bear, and drawing on the book he is reviewing, Oliver shares some fun with his reader by offering a portrait of "what manner of man he was." He also excuses the reader from plunging into Saint-Simon's own forty-seven volumes:

> He was, to put it briefly, a liar who cannot be trusted to report veraciously the simplest details of his own life. He lived under every government in France from the *ancien regime* to the Restoration, and, more agile in conscience that the Vicar of Bray, he promptly discovered that each new government was the realization of his long-cherished ideals. He was a conceited *halluciné* who enjoyed conversations with his ancestor Charlemagne, who obligingly informed him that he was destined to be the great philosopher of the modern world. He was a *debauché* who made his vices odious by pretending that his sensuality was a high-minded urge to apply the empirical methods of science to human relationships. He was a scoundrel who attempted to blackmail even the wife of a benefactor from whom he was receiving an annual subsidy. He had, in short, a highly developed social consciousness.

Professor Oliver has the goods on Saint-Simon but, alas, he proved to be the biter bit. With material like this, Oliver would have been welcome to write for *National Review* as long as he wished. He continued to contribute excellent prose as a book reviewer and essayist until it was discovered that . . . he was an official of the John Birch Society. *National Review* drew the line against an organization the Maximum Leader of which viewed Dwight Eisenhower and George Marshall as being under Communist Party discipline. And as it happened, in a long post–*NR* career publishing in evermore-obscure journals, it seems that Oliver himself went off the rails, further and further into the fever swamps.

PROFESSOR RICHARD WEAVER of the University of Chicago was another classicist, far less abstract in temper than Revilo Oliver, though equally homemade. From the beginning of *National Review* he was a regular contributor. He was, to put it one way, a theoretician of Southern-ness, finding in his Idea of the South a metaphor for Western civilization as a whole.

However, he was not a Confederate, and he differed from the Vanderbilt group of Agrarians and Fugitives in several respects.[3] Born in the small town of Weaverville, in the mountains of North Carolina, in 1910, he can be called a "Mountain Whig." He graduated from the University of Kentucky, taught at Texas A&M, and pursued graduate work at Vanderbilt, where he was deeply impressed by the Agrarians, especially John Crowe Ransom. There, he began working on a dissertation which would be posthumously published in 1968 as *The Southern Tradition at Bay: A History of Post-Bellum Thought*.

His central insight was philosophical. That is, for Southern values to survive the great defeat of 1865 and the Reconstruction that followed, those values must have been metaphysically rooted. Weaver considered the South to be the last nonmaterialist culture in the West. But his heroes were Plato and Lincoln, the latter *persona non grata* to the Vanderbilt writers. Thus, though offered a teaching position at Vanderbilt, he chose to take a post at the University of Chicago instead. A solitary by temperament, he lived alone in a Chicago hotel room and never married, enduring the winds off Lake Michigan by wearing two overcoats. Familiar around the university with his bulldog jaw and furrowed brow, he once was named Teacher of the Year.

His intellectual quest was a classical one, and Weaver had the special virtue of a man who deals with students—the virtue of making this quest both vivid and lucid. Following Plato under modern conditions, he sought principles of lasting philosophical order. In 1948 he had published *Ideas Have Consequences*, a book that became an early conservative classic. Willmoore Kendall thought the book earned him the nomination for "the captaincy of the antiliberal team." Yet the book divided liberals, drawing praise from, for example, Paul Tillich and Reinhold Niebuhr, but severe attack from liberal empiricists and pragmatists. It was by no means unusual to trace the effacing of traditional order to the triumph of empiricism, which operates with its effective focus on the sensory world but in so doing turns away from general principles and laws. Most intellectual historians trace the operational triumph of empiricism to John Locke and the founding of the Royal Society, but tracing the philosophy is a different matter, and you could go all the way back, not surprisingly, to Empiricus.

It is characteristic of the homemade character of Weaver's thought that he traces the modern victory of empiricism back to the fourteenth-century philosopher William of Ockham, whose "Ockham's razor," as it is sometimes called, separated empirical fact from philosophical universals. There is something gorgeous about Weaver pinning the tail on Ockham. And it was Weaver's own particular experience that brought him to locate the idealist philosophical tradition in the practice of the antebellum South. The South, however, was only his local experiment in the wider tradition of the West.

Superbly qualified, a deeply reflective conservative, Weaver proved to be a practical and productive contributor of reviews and articles to *National Review*. He would have continued as a major contributor had he not died very prematurely at age fifty-three in 1963. It was a great loss, as can be judged by his published contributions. In an early review of Robert Maynard Hutchins's *Great Books: The Foundation of Liberal Education* (1956), for example, one would expect Weaver to find a kindred spirit in the sometime president of his university. Weaver certainly wanted us to read the classics. But he found in Hutchins a serious weakness that, without its being mentioned, defined one of Weaver's great strengths: Hutchins was too abstractly Aristotelian, in other words too *rationalistic* rather than rational:

> Mr. Hutchins has always been disarmingly candid about his own lack of education, and he has in fact written *The Autobiography of an Uneducated Man*. I do not feel, however, that he has told us where the deficiencies of his education really lie. He has no education in common life. Despite his earnest concern for the salvation of the average man through liberal education, I see no evidence that he has understood him. Santayana once wrote that if John Stuart Mill had ever learned in what the common man, who was the object of his solicitude, found his happiness, he would have been chilled to the bone. I think Mr. Hutchins would be chilled to the marrow.

Professor Weaver was a better classicist than Hutchins. Indeed, Hutchins the Aristotelian lacked the sense of experience that is one of the foundations of Aristotle's work.

Richard Weaver had the capability of handling intricate but important topics with ease, making him nearly unique in weekly journalism. Of particular interest in these early days was a review Weaver wrote of a collection of essays titled *Speculative Instruments* by I. A. Richards, the literary critic and philosopher. In a review of a mere hundred words, Weaver defines the essence and the difficulty of the humanities as contrasted with the sciences. He cites Richards to the effect that "language is inescapably normative," and continues about his "general defense of humanities education":

> I have yet to encounter a better formulation of the goal of humanistic training than his phrase "the discernment of relevancies." As soon as value-bearing terms are introduced, the user of language is finding his relevancies with reference to a "hierarchical organization of choices." With that admission, metaphor, myth and religion are again established in the real world.

Other things follow from that, matters ever more important. Francis Bacon held that once the scientific method was established, even mediocre people could make genuine contributions to knowledge. The humble worker in the lab with his beaker and Bunsen burner may in some small degree advance the collective project. In his review of Richards's book, Weaver sees that,

> today quite ordinary intellects *can* teach most branches of science, and carry forward research on some level. It is otherwise with literature and philosophy. In teaching the humanities, as in writing poetry, one is not permitted to be second-rate. . . . *Speculative Instruments* thus throws light on some special aspects of the cultural crisis of our time.

Excellence in the humanities sets the bar high; teaching the humanities is something of a different order from more utilitarian specialties. The passage of fifty years has rendered Weaver's—and Richards's—words only more urgent.

HERE WE HAVE APPRECIATED only two of the early contributors to *National Review,* highly distinctive writers. Both were more academic, yet important and intelligible, than almost anything then seen in weekly journalism. Of course Buckley, Burnham, Meyer, Kendall, Bozell, and Chamberlain were well known by 1955 and wrote regularly, Chambers more sporadically. And there were many others, each excellent in different modes.

They included, to mention only a few: Gerhart Niemeyer, political philosopher, Notre Dame professor, an explicator of Eric Voegelin, and at one point, with Burnham, a crucial shaper of *National Review*'s understanding of communism; Hugh Kenner, premier writer on modernism, Pound, Joyce, Beckett, and others; Guy Davenport, writer of *avant garde* stories but brilliantly lucid in reviews; Robert Phelps, an aspiring novelist; Garry Wills; Joan Didion; and John Leonard.

Davenport, an exquisitely cultivated writer, came to the magazine through Hugh Kenner. John Leonard came directly from Harvard to a junior editorial position, and his liberalism led to the resignation of Suzanne La Follette. Garry Wills had been training in a Jesuit seminary, was disengaging himself from that, and sent a parody of *Times*-style to the magazine. On the basis of that initial contribution Buckley engaged him to write cultural material for *National Review*. Joan Didion had come east from California. She had a position at *Vogue* and was discovered by Meyer. At the time, she was an admirer of William Knowland, a shocking conservative to her friends in the Village. Her reviews for Meyer showed her critical taste and professional ambition. She had not yet achieved the sensibility that looked at mushrooms and found every one of them a toadstool. Robert Phelps had secreted himself up in the Catskills—Meyer country—about a hundred miles from New York City, and was trying to write a novel. His critical reviews on modern literature were as good as they come.

Though Meyer had developed a rigorous philosophy based on individualism and strong anticommunism, he was surprisingly hospitable to a great variety of political views among his contributors. His rule was informed good taste, his achievement impressive, and he was highly regarded by some of the most discerning—Hugh Kenner for example—and by those as well who later veered away from *National Review* politically, such as John Leonard and Garry Wills. Meyer did his best for conservative readers likely to prefer Longfellow to Eliot or Yeats, instructing them to look again at the modernists' achievement and even their essential antiliberalism.

A reader of *National Review* in those first years was correct in sensing that something quite new had now come into existence in American weekly journalism, writers seen nowhere else in the magazines, because not part of "the sole intellectual tradition in America," and producing work of a sustained high quality, which was also new.

DURING THE SUMMER OF 1957, Buckley brought William Rusher to *National Review* as publisher, a post Buckley himself had filled, to give full attention to the job and to straighten out the financial side of the magazine. Rusher would thenceforth become one of the most important senior editors. Beyond the magazine, he would become known as a public speaker, television performer, and political organizer, notably in the 1964 Draft Goldwater effort. Rusher was a midwesterner, had graduated from Princeton and Harvard Law School, had served with the Army in Asia, and had been active in the New York Young Republicans when Governor Thomas E. Dewey managed the state for the party. He shared some traits with Dewey. He was impeccable sartorially, formal in manner, and highly organized—though I never caught him, like Dewey, wiping off every doorknob before using it. He was ruthlessly efficient—*National Review* badly needed this—and astonishingly precise. And at the magazine he was a beloved character, whom Buckley described this way at a 1969 banquet in his honor at the Plaza Hotel in New York:

> [It] strikes anyone who views him coming jauntily to his office every morning, not sooner than nor later than two minutes to ten, that he could not be other than the president or vice president of a prosperous house of usury; well cast in that the first person he will encounter on entering his office is an irate creditor; and the second, his secretary, giving notice.
>
> Our friend is a man of most meticulous habits, and it is a miracle, of the kind that providence less and less frequently vouchsafes us, that he should have endured for so long the disorderly habits of his colleagues. . . .
>
> To this end he began his famous graphs. We have graphs at *National Review* charting every quiver in the organization's metabolism. We have graphs that show us how we are doing in circulation, in promotion expenses, in political influence. . . . Our late friend and colleague, the late Willmoore Kendall, once dumbfounded Bill Rusher by telling him, "Bill, there is no proposition so simple that it cannot be rendered unintelligible to me by putting it on a graph. . . .

Occasionally his admirers show their envy of him, as when, while he was away on a lecture tour, we traipsed into his office and exactly reversed every reversible physical accoutrement. Thus the picture of Lincoln hung now, at our mischievous hands, where the picture of Washington had hung from time immemorial, and the picture of Washington hung where the picture of Lincoln had hung. Thus when he pressed Button One, instead of his secretary, the bookkeeper would answer, and when he depressed Button Two, instead of the bookkeeper, his secretary would answer. When he turned over the leaves of his calendar, he would find himself moving not towards the end of the month but toward the beginning of the month; and when he opened the drawer were his graphs were kept he would find not his graph but his pills. . . .[4]

Politically, Rusher had a distinctive position to advance at *National Review*. Despite, or perhaps because of, his experiences at Princeton and Harvard, he urged a populist instead of an elite political strategy. This frequently made for arguments with Burnham, in which Burnham would listen patiently and respond gently, always with his little smile. Rusher sometimes detected in Burnham a creeping centrism, as in the latter's more than tolerant attitude toward Nelson Rockefeller, and Rusher strongly objected when, much later, *National Review* Washington Correspondent George Will relentlessly criticized Richard Nixon during Watergate and dealt unforgivingly with Spiro Agnew as corruption charges caught up with him.

Rusher could be a rough character in these internal arguments, and in public debate he could be slashingly take-no-prisoners—very effective, as I can confirm on the basis of having heard him discomfit the formidable debater Michael Harrington in the basement of a Greenwich Village left-wing church. I have heard him called "the Protestant Buckley." A midwesterner at heart, he had no sympathy for the Eastern liberal establishment, gleefully watched as the Goldwaterites, with his help, hijacked the Republican Party from them, and even contemplated the possibility of a third, and populist, political party.

One other important addition was made to the staff in the first year of the magazine. Bill Buckley asked his sister Priscilla, with some urgency, to join the magazine soon after it was launched. She had graduated from Smith

College in 1943, worked for United Press International until 1951, then briefly for the CIA in Washington, then, bliss for her, as a reporter in Paris. She recalled those Paris days in *String of Pearls*, an exquisite memoir published in 2002.

National Review had writers but badly needed an experienced professional journalist. Installed as managing editor and sharing a front office with James Burnham, Priscilla proved to be everything *National Review* needed—indeed, a professional who believed in getting a writing assignment done pronto, and who could handle almost any topic. Since she possessed no neuroses whatsoever, she would have reduced Freud to silence. Cheery and capable, a skier, golfer, and traveler extraordinary, she exhibited a great enjoyment of life and did not need to rebuke ego tantrums and funk since they seemed merely ridiculous in her presence. So too did fanaticism. She and James Burnham became good friends and an outstanding professional team. In all respects the magazine remained steady-as-you-go. *National Review* moved with confidence and *esprit* through its discontents with Eisenhower's second term.

6

1956:
NR's *Education Begins*

Scholarship has now made clear just how inaccurate was most people's understanding and assessment of Dwight Eisenhower during his two highly successful terms in the White House, despite the fact that he was one of the most famous men in the world when he became president in 1953. This absence of an accurate sense of the man was not accidental. For public purposes, Eisenhower deliberately adopted a mask—that of the kind, old general with the avuncular American grin, immensely reassuring and "normal." Thus did "Ike" appear to *National Review*, as he did to the Kennedy campaign in 1960: stodgy, not sufficiently mobilized against communism, and inert as the economy briefly stagnated. One might think that a moment's reflection on his career would have given pause. He had lost only one battle during the Second World War, at the Kasserine Pass, where his tanks had been outgunned by Rommel's 88s. After that, Eisenhower's leadership proved a total success. As Supreme Allied Commander in Europe he had managed an especially difficult band of personalities: Churchill, De Gaulle, the Poles, Montgomery, George Patton. He always seemed to win.

Only recently have historians been able, with access to the archives, to show us the truth about Eisenhower. He was a grand-scale realist, an unsentimental, icy, and even ruthless leader who saw the world as it was. His thought was highly organized and, when he desired, he could sum up his points in crisp and lucid sentences. The key book here has been Fred I. Greenstein's *The Hidden Hand Presidency: Eisenhower as Leader* (1982). During the Hungarian crisis and with Suez in 1956, he seemed to *National Review* to be unforgivably weak. Yet we now know that Ike seriously considered destroying—yes, destroying—the Soviet Union with nuclear weapons when, during the Suez crisis, he received intelligence reports that Soviet "volunteers" were on their way to the Middle East. Fortunately, the reports proved incorrect.

When Eisenhower came to the presidency in January 1953, the apparently fuzzy old general ended the fighting in Korea with a covert threat to Beijing through New Delhi. Unless the fighting ended, he would launch a new assault "unrestricted as to weapons." He meant nuclear. Mao did not like the sound of that, coming from the man who had chased the *Wehrmacht* right across the Rhine. Shooting stopped and talks began. Yet in 1956 Ike refused to do anything dramatic about the Hungarian uprising: Berlin was too vulnerable and too strategic; Hungary had no coastline and was surrounded by preponderant Soviet forces; the Soviets also had the Bomb. Risking an American city or two was a prohibitive price for saving Budapest.

In addition to that, and knowing that the British and French empires were washed up, Eisenhower refused to intervene to support the French in Vietnam, or to back up the French, British, and Israelis in their attack on Egypt during the 1956 Suez crisis. At roughly the same time, he waited for the right moment and engineered the downfall of Senator Joseph McCarthy. On the economy, he presided over three years of budgetary surpluses, an economic boom with low inflation, and launched the Interstate Highway project. Had he been able to run for a third term, historians now judge that he would have won easily.

His famously jumbled syntax and wandering logic turn out to have been elements of his mask. To all appearances he seemed to be "good ole Ike," the man from Abilene, and this proved immensely effective politically. The American people had only a few years before fought and won a world war; they were now enjoying economic prosperity and were wary of bellicosity in light of the Bomb. He talked of "peace" too often for *National Review*, but he knew the people wanted just such reassurance. He pushed the nuclear submarine program and with it the development of the revolutionary Polaris missiles, fired from the bottom of the sea. He launched the U-2 flights over the Soviet Union, capable of comprehensive high-altitude photography. He was prepared to use force when prudent, and even the Bomb if necessary.

His close associates were not deceived by the mask. He advised Nixon not to answer a question from the press too promptly, even if he had answered the same question a hundred times. Instead, Nixon should hesitate and pretend thoughtfulness. When Eisenhower, ready to go before the press about a delicate diplomatic problem, perceived that his press secretary Jim Hagerty seemed nervous, he calmed him: "Don't worry," he said. "When I'm through, they won't know what I said." Outwardly "like all of us," he came from the Heartland, a regular guy, married to a woman named Mamie. But he was cold, intelligent, meticulous, and very tough.

As THE YEAR 1956 BEGAN, *National Review* had only just begun to publish, yet it was soon confronted by a sequence of events that required the careful application of its leading assumptions. Accordingly, it judged and condemned what it saw as the unforgivable weakness of Eisenhower as president, his inadequacy in response to the Soviet threat and, as a creature of the Eastern Republican Establishment, his domestic me-tooism, illustrated by his legitimizing and even extension of the New Deal welfare state. *National Review* would sum up all this discontent in a major editorial when Eisenhower left office in 1960.

National Review's guide in foreign policy, James Burnham, had advocated liberation rather than containment. In *Suicide of the West* (1963), Burnham argued that the territorial shrinkage of the West with the loss of the European empires signaled a fatal weakness. Yet on Hungary, Eisenhower gave Burnham a lesson in the cruelties sometimes entailed by *Realpolitik.* And Suez also instructed *National Review* that the old empires could not be held: they had been lost on the Somme through dissipation of the power that sustained them. The United States and the Soviet Union were the major powers now, not Britain and France.

If the presidential election season of 1956 lacked suspense, it amounted to a referendum on Eisenhower, an opportunity for a national assessment and, derivatively, an opportunity to judge the attraction or vulnerability of the probable 1960 Republican candidate, Vice President Richard Nixon. Where Nixon was concerned, *National Review* had behaved all along almost as if he did not exist, despite his valuable role in the Hiss case. So jaundiced was the magazine's estimate of Nixon that John Chamberlain felt obliged to publish an article defensively titled "What's Wrong with Nixon?" He saw the vice president as an unshakable anticommunist and knowledgeable about Communist tactics, as attracting enemies who themselves constituted a strong recommendation, and on domestic policy as tending in suitable directions, though flexible. The article understood reservations about Nixon's personality—to put this mildly—but bravely concluded:

> The points of view that emphasize Nixon's prosecutor background and his undoubted ambition are certainly relevant, for the tone of a society is affected by the personal flavor of its leadership. But they are interesting to me at the moment for quite another reason. Taken altogether, they make mincemeat of the particular theory pushed by the intellectuals, that Nixon is a cunningly devious man who a) hides his true opinions or b) changes them periodically to suit the prevailing winds. I find Nixon four-square even in his errors, which is one reason I like him.

Chamberlain thus was mildly enthusiastic about Nixon—Whittaker Chambers and Ralph de Toledano much more so—but *National Review*, throughout Nixon's entire career, remained wary. In this the magazine agreed with Eisenhower, who largely ignored Nixon and did not invite him to Gettysburg, thus inflicting some of Nixon's many painfully felt wounds. Stephen Ambrose has uncovered what I have not seen elsewhere: that Eisenhower seriously considered replacing Nixon with Tom Dewey on the 1956 Republican ticket. In conversations with press spokesman Jim Hagerty and chief-of-staff Sherman Adams, he proposed the idea several times. Hagerty eventually vetoed it, saying that if Eisenhower tried to foist Dewey on the Republican Party one more time the right wing would revolt and nominate Knowland. "I guess you're right," Eisenhower sighed.[1]

This might have been one of those great missed opportunities in history. Nixon stuck like a limpet, but the idea of Dewey remains interesting. Surely, even if Eisenhower had "dumped" Nixon, the Republican Party would not have nominated Knowland instead of the certain winner Eisenhower. A Vice President Dewey would have been loyal to NATO and Europe; he supported a strong containment policy; and he had none of Nixon's psychological baggage, which increased with Eisenhower's snubs. Dewey probably would have gone on to win in 1960. He was part of the Eastern Establishment, but no liberal: rather, a center-right Republican, like Eisenhower. He was, as Eisen-hower had demanded of Nixon during a 1952 scandal, "as clean as a hound's tooth." The might-have-beens loom. Most obviously, there might have been no Watergate, a baroquely Nixonian scandal, postponing the hopes of a center-right establishment.

THROUGHOUT THE SPRING and summer of 1956, the coverage of Eisenhower by *National Review* was entirely negative, suggesting that Ike's first term had been unsatisfactory. Eisenhower, who had been convalescing from a heart attack, recovered by the spring and soon was rolling toward a landslide, as Sam Jones found in traveling around the country:

> There are many Republicans who feel that Ike lacks the qualities which his office demands, but they will vote for him against nobody. Traveling across the continent I found this: "With Eisenhower we have peace and prosperity. Why change it? What have the Democrats got to offer that is better? Ike looks good because of the quality of his competition. . . . Mr. Stevenson is literate, perceptive . . . [but to] the voters he is supercilious. Not since 1928 has the Democratic Party been so bankrupt of presidential possibilities.

That summer, James Burnham attended the Republican Convention in San Francisco and reported to Buckley that the only anti-Eisenhower manifestations were those of right-wing kooks. Both Burnham and Buckley were aware of this disreputable company, which included racists, anti-Semites, neo-Nazis, and Birchers, the last crazily claiming Eisenhower to be under Communist Party discipline.

Buckley decided it was time for a symposium in the magazine to see whether a corporate position on a candidate could emerge. This had many advantages, including that of giving *NR* readers, who undoubtedly were divided and perhaps divided several ways, the opportunity of seeing their views articulated by intelligent conservatives. Furthermore, it would help define by exclusion views that were beyond the pale. Thus, in the October 20, 1956, issue, for example, James Burnham argued for an Eisenhower vote, William Schlamm opposed. These arguments have importance because they set forth contrasting positions that will emerge again and again in the history of the magazine, and in different contexts: the flexible and strategic option versus the ideological and intransigent option.

Burnham leads off. He argues that the American two-party system functions differently from the European parliamentary system in that American majority coalitions form before the election rather than afterwards. European parties are more likely to be pure in an ideological sense before the election, waiting to make their compromises to achieve parliamentary power only when the voting is over; in America the reverse is true. Therefore, in America a principled conservative must vote for the candidate who has formed the more conservative coalition, despite deviations from ideological purity. Burnham named the groups backing Stevenson, and found them well to the left of the Republicans.

If one pauses to analyze Burnham in 1956, what he wants begins to become clear—that *National Review* represent the anticommunist, conservative wing of a transformed American Establishment, with liberals becoming a minority faction instead of dominant. Such "Wise Men" as Acheson, Bohlen, and Kennan were certainly unwavering anticommunists—though Kennan, the theorist of containment, was also a melancholy Hamlet. Burnham, in fact, even could look with some approval on Nelson Rockefeller, and he exerted continuing influence to bring Buckley along to a more "strategic" or realistic position, while recognizing as legitimate the "principled" opposition to his efforts at the magazine.

William Schlamm answered for the opposition, which represented a majority of *NR*'s senior staff. His overall argument maintains that we now have two liberal candidates, Eisenhower and Stevenson, and so the result of the election will be a liberal victory in either case. For the conservative position to flourish, let alone prevail in the United States, we need at least one party that is essentially conservative. Therefore the necessity this year is that Eisenhower be defeated:

> Mr. Dwight Eisenhower, an inconsistent Liberal, is in firm control of the
> Republican Party. For conservatives, the strategic job in this year's election is
> to break that control. It can be broken only by defeating Mr. Eisenhower.
> This campaign, everybody agrees, is cleansed of the smallest shred of an issue.
> Why? Because both parties are trying to elect a Liberal President.

Schlamm supposes that "Should two or three million Americans who in 1952 felt obliged to vote for Mr. Eisenhower draw the same conclusion, Mr. Eisenhowever [sic] will be defeated. The nation will then suffer through a Stevenson administration and then will have returned to the muscular toughness of the two-party system." If the election results in an Eisenhower victory, "his second administration will be even more recklessly Liberal than his first; with hardly bearable humility, he will claim the halo of a popular mandate."

There are some telling differences between these two presentations. One is struck, for example, by the specificity of Burnham's analysis of the interest groups and leaders in the Stevenson camp, markedly to the left of anything in Eisenhower's. It is also doubtful that two or three million conservatives would be found to abstain, much less vote *against* Eisenhower, in a triumph of theoretical logic over common sense.

Still, the Schlamm argument no doubt did reflect the disaffection of many conservatives from the administration. What seems most important in this exchange, however, is the overall direction of Burnham's political thought, away from alienation and toward engagement and centrality. What might have been at stake for conservatives in all of this was not the prospect of a liberal victory in 1956—certainly Eisenhower would win—but the kind of conservatism that would eventually emerge from the crucible. Would it be coalition conservatism, or right-wing populism—a grim prospect? In the end, Buckley abstained from voting. Yet in 1956 Buckley was already moving in the direction of Burnham's position: as he later formulated it, he would prefer "the most conservative electable candidate." In that world of actuality, Stevenson obviously was the weaker candidate: Dean Acheson reportedly said of him that he had "a third-rate mind that he cannot make up."

FAR BEYOND THE OFFICES of *National Review*, events were convulsing the international landscape and redefining Burnham's Third World War. On the meaning of Nikita Khrushchev's January 1956 "secret" de-Stalinization speech, *National Review* editors disagreed, though all were strongly anticommunist and all were steeped in the details of Russo-Soviet history. James Burnham, in his column for April 11, 1956, viewed the speech as a swerve in party policy for which there was ample historical precedent, but which, for the noncommunist world, did not signify any great change. The celebrated "thaw" was "window-dressing."

Frank Meyer had also been thoroughly schooled in Communist Party affairs as a ranking member and official ideologue from 1931 to 1945. The voice of experience speaks in his July 11, 1956, regular column, "Principles and Heresies":

> There is, if I read the signs aright, great danger that, as we view the spectacle of the devaluation of Stalin and speculate about the motivations and inner power-struggles involved in it, that we shall speculate about everything but the substance of the matter, and ask every question but the serious one. That question is the one the Communists themselves always address to developments of importance: what is the objective historical meaning of these events?

Meyer regards the devaluation of Stalin as the symbol not of the relaxation of the world-revolutionary project of the Soviet Union but of its intensification:

> The shift underway was already indicated in Stalin's last work, *Economic Problems of Socialism in the USSR*. It breathes through every section of Khrushchev's main political report to the 20th Congress. It is the belief that the balance of world power has shifted decisively to world Communism; that the period of "capitalist encirclement" is ended and the period of "socialist encirclement" is at hand.

Neither Burnham nor Meyer interprets the Khrushchev speech as a sign of the mellowing of Soviet communism. In fact, Khrushchev would develop his "envelopment" thought along lines similar to those set forth by Meyer, seeing the possibility of outflanking the West by way of Soviet influence and strategic allies in the Third World. Stalin had built the internal strength of the Soviet Union, "socialism in one country." Now, dialectically, the success of that industrialization and modernization must lead, by Communist logic, to the *denunciation* of Stalin, its author, and the expansion of the Soviet strategic opportunity, the erstwhile but premature policy of the long-since purged and murdered Trotsky. The formerly hard-line Stalinists would now become Trotskyites, because the time was ripe. The "dialectic" had a magical quality, as patriots became traitors, and formerly purged deviationists now became orthodox.

Yet on August 12, in his "Third World War" column, Burnham shifted his view that little had changed. The "thaw" was real. It was not a sign of increased strength but of the unwilling loosening of Moscow's grip on its European empire:

> The thaw is modest in degree. It is a February thaw, turning the surface to slush rather than the start of the spring break-up of the ice. Nevertheless, it is real, and its reality is indirectly proved by the fact that it is different in depth from nation to nation. It has scarcely touched Albania; and Bulgaria and Rumania, only a little. It has been felt noticeably in Czechoslovakia, more in Hungary, most of all in Poland.

Burnham saw the possibility of explosions in Poland and Hungary, which in fact took place within a matter of weeks. The uprisings in Poland and Hungary broke out successively in 1956, Poland that spring, Hungary in the fall, erupting with revolutionary violence and a potential for igniting far-reaching change in the empire. In *The Struggle for the World* (1947), Burnham had foreseen what seemed to be happening now, and his statement in that book is central to his thinking in 1956, especially in its sweeping and dramatic formulation:

The reality is that the alternative to the Communist World Empire is an American Empire which will be, if not literally world-wide in formal boundaries, capable of exercising decisive world control. Nothing less than this can be the positive, or offensive, phase of a rational United States policy.

Hungary in 1956 also resembled a scenario set forth by Burnham in *Containment or Liberation?* (1953):

What if in a captive nation a broad mass uprising against the regime began? Or what if one of the Communist governments, supported by a majority of the people, decided against Moscow? And, in either case, what if help were then asked from the free world? . . . Would not passivity under such circumstances be *a final proof of the irreversibility of Communist world victory?* [italics added]

Burnham in 1956 continued to advocate a forward strategy in Europe, as demonstrated by his positional editorial in the November 10 issue. It concluded that, "after specifying escalating kinds of pressure, and as a last step, an ultimatum should be given to the Soviets to withdraw their troops from East Europe." The editorial pointed to the necessity of those troops for the maintenance of the Soviet empire, such "Red Army units . . . acting as occupying forces to ensure the subordination of the local governments to Moscow and to Communism." Without them, the East European nations would move away from communism itself—not necessarily at once, having native Communists to consider, but over a period of time:

If the Soviet troops remain, and are perhaps reinforced, this evolution, or revolution, could be stopped by the brute weight of overpowering force. The withdrawal of the Soviet troops could be made more likely if the Western powers maintained unrelenting pressure for it. Withdrawal from all the satellites, not merely from Hungary, should be the first demand in all contexts. It could be properly made a condition to Moscow on any subject.

That very tough editorial, written by Burnham in November 1956, represented the corporate judgment of *National Review*.

On November 2, Soviet troops withdrawing from the vicinity of Budapest paused, then turned around to march back and crush the uprising in heavy street fighting. While that editorial appeared, the fighting was going on. The Hungarians *were* calling for help. Were we indifferent? Eisenhower, aware of the strategic situation, was a block of ice. The situation was exactly as described by Burnham in *Containment or Liberation?* The West did nothing at all, not even the measures recommended by Burnham short of an ultimatum.

In that same passage from *Containment or Liberation?* Burnham said analytically that inaction would be "final proof of the irreversibility of a Communist world victory." That formulation is excessively colorful. But the inaction of the West over Hungary was in fact defining. Henceforth, we would not directly challenge Soviet rule in Eastern Europe. The Soviets would not, supposedly, threaten our presence in West Berlin. This by no means indicated pacifism on Eisenhower's part, but rather an estimate of Soviet determination, especially since the Soviet Union not only possessed nuclear weapons but had announced a fusion explosion. Yet even the lesser kinds of pressure had not been put on the Soviet Eastern empire. The status quo would prevail, for the time being.

Burnham now declared that the United States had lost its "honor" in failing the Hungarian rebels. The word "honor" comes from a very different realm of discourse from "fact and analysis." Burnham biographer Daniel Kelly cites Buckley to the effect that Burnham was in agony, and could not bear to be in the same room with a representative of the East bloc.[2] Burnham seemed furious, emotionally fragile, and depressed. He had said, after all, that such inaction would lead to the actual defeat of the West, because it had demonstrated lack of will. What he next proposed at *National Review* can perhaps best be explained as a product of almost terminal despair.

Only a week following his November "ultimatum" editorial, he published a flabbergasting proposal in his November 17 "Third World War" column, which he would elaborate further in a major January 19, 1957, article. The proposal was that East and West Germany, and the satellite nations, be neutralized on the Austrian model, and that a thousand-mile demilitarized zone be created in the middle of Europe, including Germany, eastern France, and western Poland. The single thing to be gained by this plan would be the removal of the Soviet army from Germany and Eastern Europe.

Had Burnham been jolted loose from strategic rationality by the Hungarian tragedy? Perhaps, since the fate of Germany was the central issue of the Third World War: who controlled Germany, with its resources, industry, geostrategic position, and population, won the war. Replies from Burnham's *National Review* colleagues began to appear beginning in January, with an editorial on the 5th rejecting it, and with replies continuing through February 1957, from Schlamm, Bozell, Meyer, and Buckley. Burnham's fellow editors were unanimously opposed to his position, no one on the fence.

On February 23, Buckley wrote a substantial article summarizing the criticisms of the Burnham Plan and rejecting it with about as much decisiveness as he cared to manage, given his loyalty to Burnham, and given that Burnham had proved emotionally fragile in the wake of Budapest. And in fact, not only did the resistance of the West *not* collapse after Hungary, it did not even *come close* to doing so. Eisenhower 1, Burnham 0.

Burnham's German neutralization proposal had the side effect of preparing the exit from *National Review* of William Schlamm, who seems to have regarded it not only as a serious error, but as an opportunity to displace Burnham from his pinnacle of authority. Jealous of Burnham and reaching for power, Schlamm became emotionally roiled, schemed against his adversary, and agitated the magazine's offices. Both Burnham and Buckley characteristically tried forbearance, but the inevitable happened. Schlamm discovered the hard way Burnham's value to the magazine. With Schlamm's departure, *National Review* sustained a loss in its coverage of the theater and other cultural matters, but before long this gap was filled by the arrival of young Garry Wills.

ANOTHER MAJOR DISAPPOINTMENT for *NR* occurred almost simultaneously when Eisenhower refused to intervene in support of the British, French, and Israelis when they attacked Egypt in response to Nasser's seizure of the Suez Canal. Yet by the time of Suez, the British empire was exhausted, becoming, in Kipling's terms in "Recessional," one with Nineveh and Tyre. The Captains and the Kings had departed, forever.

Eisenhower had refused to support the French in Vietnam, and he refused to support the British and French here. In general, *National Review* had illusions about the former European colonies, a *summa* of which appears at the beginning of Burnham's *Suicide of the West* (1963), certainly his weakest book. There, under the influence of the old-fashioned global strategist Halford Mackinder, he gazes at a map of the world and sees, with the loss of the nineteenth-century colonies, the power of the West contracting (suicidally). No, the power of the West was not shrinking; it was merely being reconfigured, passing to the United States. Eisenhower was not about to pick up a lot of useless baggage in this process. We would defend only what should be defended, and we were fortunate that Eisenhower did not have one molecule of Churchillian poetry in his body or his mind. It is almost inconceivable that Eisenhower would have made Kennedy's decision to put substantial American forces into Vietnam. Lesson: *What a president does* not *do can be as important as what he does do*. Eisenhower 2, Burnham 0.

Why was Eisenhower's record so impressive? At the beginning of this chapter, I referred to the work of professional historians, meaning principally Fred I. Greenstein of Princeton in his *Hidden-Hand Presidency: Eisenhower as a Leader* (1982). Very briefly, I will try to summarize their conclusions, which have created a new historical consensus.

1) Why did Eisenhower choose to run in 1952? Greenstein writes in *The Hidden-Hand Presidency*:

> Just before leaving to command NATO in January 1951, Eisenhower met with Taft privately at the Pentagon. Eisenhower brought to this meeting a prepared statement in which Taft was to commit himself to international principles of foreign policy and Eisenhower would renounce a candidacy. But when he and Taft could not agree, Eisenhower destroyed the document and left himself in position to accept the nomination on grounds that keeping open the nomination was the only weapon against the selection by the Republicans of an isolationist candidate.[3]

2) What were Eisenhower's own political views? Greenstein:

In fact, they were to the right of Robert Taft. While President of Columbia, he admired the right-wing *New York Sun*, considered the welfare state a "gravy train," Socialism and Communism and all paternalism as eating into the marrow of initiative.[4] He disliked Taft's "leftist" domestic initiatives, such as his aid to education bill, which, he explained to Rep. Clarence Brown of Ohio after Taft's death, were "far more liberal and radical than anything to which I could agree."[5] He condemned Taft's advocacy of public housing.

3) Then why did Eisenhower as president appear to be a liberal-lite Republican? Greenstein:

> [His] assessment of what realism required if the Republicans were to prosper led him to deliberately temper his private conservatism. In justifying his maintenance of new Deal social reforms to his fervently right-wing brother Edgar, he bluntly admonished: "Should any political party attempt to abolish Social Security and eliminate labor laws and farm laws and programs you would not hear of that party again in our political history."[6]

Accordingly, his contempt for Senator William Knowland was complete: "In his case," Eisenhower wrote in his diary, "there seems to be no final answer to the question, 'How stupid can you get?'"[7]

4) What about Eisenhower's syntax and often confusing answers to questions in public? Greenstein:

> Eisenhower found it natural to express himself straightforwardly and incisively, arraying facts and rigorously justifying his policies and actions. He could do that using precisely etched prose and he took pride in his ability to do so. He was, however, willing to replace reasoned discourse with alternative ways of expressing himself when they better served his purposes. Neither pride in his ability nor his natural predilection for clarity kept him from deliberately turning to language that was emotive or inspirational or purposely ambiguous. Verbal expression was his instrument; he refused to indulge his obvious pleasure in analytic thought as an end in itself.
>
> I say that clear expression was natural to him because it is the manner he adopted in private conversations. The personal diary entries he used for self-clarification and that he never released for publication are lucidly written, as

are his innumerable pre-presidential and presidential memoranda to aides
and associates, as well as letters to his most confidential correspondents.[8]

Greenstein presents abundant evidence here. Eisenhower often had no
intention of clarifying his motives or goals at press conferences and purpose-
fully rambled and mused.

5) What did Eisenhower intend that the public see? Greenstein:

> [Eisenhower's effectiveness involved] a shrewd use of political art and craft
> masked by a non-politician's façade. The hard evidence began piling up in
> the mid-1970s in the form of countless secret documents showing a fasci-
> nating leader. . . .[9]
>
> His mask was that of the simple farmer boy turned soldier . . . rather
> than of a politician whose operations were deliberately shielded from his
> contemporaries other than his immediate associates. . . . As a thinker, the
> public saw a folksy, common-sense replica of the man in the street. The
> confidential records show a man with extraordinary capacities for detached,
> orderly examination of problems and personalities. In public he seemed to
> be removed from the arena. But the inner Eisenhower reasoned about po-
> litical contingencies with greater rigor and readiness than many political
> professionals.[10]

6) Nuclear weapons? Greenstein:

> When Eisenhower entered the White House, he was convinced that the
> Chinese forces were so well entrenched that a negotiated settlement was
> the best course of action. The alternatives were bloody fighting for limited
> gains or a major assault on the mainland that at worst could escalate into
> a global war and at best might unify Korea, thus leaving the United States
> with unwanted control of North Korea, which seemed to him to be wholly
> inappropriate. But truce talks were stalled and no obvious advantage was
> to be gained in reopening them. After considering the possibility of using
> tactical nuclear weapons on North Korean troop concentrations and be-
> ing persuaded that such a course of action would be repugnant to the NATO
> allies, Eisenhower records that he conveyed an unpublicized message to
> the Chinese through indirect channels. Proceeding on the premise that

China would not relish nuclear devastation of its industrial and military concentrations and would expect a new American regime to be more bellicose than Truman's, he acted in a way calculated not to arouse NATO fears of an expanded war, but also to create among the Chinese the expectation that if they did not negotiate a settlement they would bear unacceptable losses. As he put it: "In India and the Formosa Straits area, and at the truce negotiations at Panmunjon, we dropped the word, discreetly, of our intention to move decisively without inhibition in our use of weapons, and . . . no longer be responsible for confining hostilities to the Korean peninsula. . . . We felt sure that it would reach Soviet and Chinese ears."[11]

A truce settlement followed.

On nuclear matters, Stephen Ambrose writes:

> Not long before the 1956 election, Eisenhower received intelligence reports that the Soviets were planning to send half a million "volunteers" to the Middle East. At the same time, the situation in Budapest was reaching a crisis. Eisenhower at a meeting thought out loud: "[We] have to be clear in our every step. And if these fellows start something we may have to hit 'em—and, if necessary, with *everything* in the bucket." [italics added] He also wondered just what we would do with a Soviet Union that had suffered enormous casualties in a nuclear assault and had its government and infrastructure completely burned out.[12]

7) With regard to Senator Joseph McCarthy, Greenstein shows that while declining to "get down into the gutter" with him, and while publicly announcing general and unexceptionable principles, Eisenhower nonetheless plotted to destroy him politically as soon as his hubris got out of control. Ike operated through subordinates, carefully intervening in the complex events involving Fort Monmouth, the demand by Roy Cohn for special favors for Private David Schine, McCarthy's invitation to all government employees to bring him derogatory information, and McCarthy's ferocious questioning of General Zwicker, a war hero. The result was the televised Army-McCarthy hearings, which ruined McCarthy politically and were a cause of his death. Vice President Nixon was Eisenhower's main cat's paw.

James Burnham had written *The Machiavellians*, referring to four philosophers. Eisenhower was a Machiavellian in expert practice.

AT THE CONCLUSION of his *Eisenhower: Soldier and President* (1990), Stephen Ambrose offers this assessment:

> Soon after Eisenhower left office, a national poll of academic American historians placed him nearly at the bottom of the list of Presidents. By the early 1980s a new poll placed him ninth. His reputation is almost certain to rise. . . .
>
> In attempting to assess the Eisenhower Presidency, certain comparisons must be made. Since Andrew Jackson's day, only five men have served eight consecutive years or more in the White House—Grant, Wilson, Franklin Roosevelt, Eisenhower, and Ronald Reagan. . . . Of the five, only three—Eisenhower, Roosevelt, and Reagan—were more popular when they left office than when they entered. . . .
>
> Eisenhower is unique in another way. In contrast to his Democratic predecessors and successors, Eisenhower kept the peace; in contrast to his Republican successors, Eisenhower both balanced the budget and stopped inflation. . . . Eisenhower gave the nation eight years of peace and prosperity. No other President in the twentieth century could make that claim. No wonder that millions of Americans felt the country was damned lucky to have him.

If *National Review* was fooled by Eisenhower, that was not the magazine's fault. So was almost everyone else outside his inner circle. Eisenhower wanted it that way. What we can say is that, in his time and place, given his real-world options, and based on his overall record, Eisenhower was a model of political prudence yet courageous when courage was called for. Foreign leaders took no liberties with him. He was a solid example of a conservative Republican.

The most successful presidents are coalition builders, and during the twentieth century, these included Roosevelt, Eisenhower, and Reagan. Roosevelt was center-left, as his times required, Eisenhower and Reagan center-right, in response to different exigencies. Both Eisenhower and Reagan were prudent, resolute, trustworthy. They both inspired broadly based confidence, and won reelection by landslides. Both used force reluctantly; and when they did so they did so overwhelmingly and unanswerably. In the second half of the twentieth century, Eisenhower and Reagan have gained recognition by historians as the great presidents of the era.

National Review saw Eisenhower as drifting without principle, refusing to define himself in terms of *ideas* against the ideas of international communism. His refusal to engage in principled argument with Marshal Zhukov, for example, became a scandal from that point of view. But if we can make an abstraction of Eisenhower's animating "idea," it would be *Americanism*. Eisenhower did not think he had to talk about it: because he *was* it.

7

McCarthy:
National Review's *Populist Agon*

Viewed within the context of the magazine's history, *National Review*'s defense of Senator Joseph McCarthy represented another of its recurrent struggles between wish and reality, what it would like to be true and what in fact was true. James Burnham, *National Review*'s guide concerning realism and power, had learned his own hard lessons in 1956 from Eisenhower about both liberation in Hungary and the continuing viability of the British and French empires. To the projects both of liberation and of saving the empires it would have been appropriate to comment, as Jake Barnes says to Brett Ashley at the end of *The Sun Also Rises*: "Isn't it pretty to think so."

National Review supported McCarthy from its beginning in November 1955, and continued to support him after his censure. Brent Bozell worked for McCarthy part time beginning in 1954. Nevertheless, McCarthy's flamboyant carelessness had been evident in the speech that made him famous, in Wheeling, West Virginia, on February 9, 1950. McCarthy's populism also might have been expected to cause problems at a magazine hoping to form and instruct a conservative opinion-making readership. Its Ivy League–tuned wit, learning, and general manner were part of its appeal, and these also were expressed in Buckley's public persona. All this was considerably at odds with McCarthy's populism.

In 1954, Buckley and Brent Bozell published *McCarthy and his Enemies*, a careful defense of the senator, and still well worth reading for its analysis of federal security lapses persisting into the late 1940s and for its general analysis of the issues that stirred politics at that time. On the cover of *NR*'s December 28, 1955, issue, well after McCarthy had been censured by the Senate, *National Review* featured a review by Joseph McCarthy himself of Dean Acheson's *A Democrat Looks at His Party*. The review was in fact written by Brent Bozell—as a joke of sorts, since McCarthy and Acheson had been archenemies. Perhaps this was not the wisest of jokes, however, since when Buckley approached T. S. Eliot to write for *National Review*, Eliot replied that he was not disposed to write for a magazine that published book reviews by Joe McCarthy. Cross off the most influential poet of the twentieth century and a huge audience for whatever Eliot might have written.

Looking back, it is possible now to forget that McCarthy in private was not at all the boor the cartoonists depicted; in fact he was very good company. Bozell and Buckley regarded him as a friend, and he was close to the Kennedy family, sometimes a guest at Hyannisport. Robert Kennedy served as Democratic counsel on his committee. There was, indeed, a considerable band-of-brothers sense at *National Review* in supporting McCarthy, the excitement of defying the media and the Eastern Establishment. This generated a strong esprit de corps within the new and still small magazine, especially, it should not be forgotten, because the so-called "witches" out there in the haunted wood of the postwar years often were quite real and active Communist agents, and often protected by the big trees around them.

IN 1955, MOST SENIOR people at *National Review* had long been McCarthy supporters. After his emergence in 1949, Burnham considered him correct in some allegations, and a useful sounder of the alarm: without McCarthy's impetus, Burnham thought, many fellow travelers and Communist front organizations would have been whitewashed by the media.[1] There can be little doubt that this was correct, given the temper of the times. The Popular Front mentality was far from exhausted. However, as Whittaker Chambers would write to Buckley,

> McCarthy divides the right. . . . He is a man fighting almost wholly by in-
> stinct and intuition, against forces for the most part coldly conscious of their
> ways, means and ends. In other words, he scarcely knows what he is doing. He
> simply knows that somebody threw a tomato and the general direction from
> which it came.[2]

Chambers drew back, however, from a frontal attack against McCarthy because of the fierce partisan nature of the controversy.

At *National Review* in 1955, Buckley, Meyer, Bozell, and Schlamm were McCarthy partisans, as was Kendall, who added a political-theory dimension to his support.[3] Like his mentor Leo Strauss, Kendall thought that a nation must have a "public orthodoxy," its very essence excluding other options. He developed this idea at length in his theoretical writing. Representative government, he argued, does not mean that all questions are "open." He thought a people had the privilege, if not the duty, to enforce such an established fact by a variety of means, including legal, political, and social penalties. He was willing to support McCarthy as penalizing the deservedly excluded Communists. Buckley and Bozell had been Kendall's students at Yale, and *McCarthy and His Enemies* shows the influence of his theory of a "public orthodoxy." Yet whatever its considerable merits, such a theory requires accurate definitions of the unacceptable and necessarily excludes McCarthy's epic inability to make necessary distinctions.

Years later, in 1999, Buckley would publish his novel *Redhunter*, a valuable portrait of the senator. It describes McCarthy's friendliness, humor, loyalty, and other generally attractive qualities, difficult for people who did not know him to reconcile with the frequent bullying and demagogy of his public behavior. Of course, McCarthy's anticommunist passion is prominent in Buckley's novel, also his carelessness. At the end of *Redhunter* stands a letter from Chambers to Buckley, written at the height of the furor, and condemning McCarthy. Its position there in 1999 implies Buckley's concluding judgment that "Whittaker, you were right":

Tell your friend Professor [Kendall], who you tell me is outspoken at Yale on the McCarthy question, that I think it would be a mistake to perpetuate the myth of McCarthy as something he really was not. For the Left will have no trouble in shredding a myth which does not stand on reality. I am urging a decent prudence, unstinting but firm, because I believe that the tighter the Right clings to a myth which does not justify itself, the farther and faster it will be swung away from reality; will be carrying not a banner but a burden. Give this man, as a fighter, his due and more than his due. Hamlet has noted the penalties in giving anybody more than his due. But let the Right also know where and when to stop. Of course, time and deliberation will take care of this.

IN ITS MAY 18, 1957, issue, after McCarthy's death from despair and alcoholism, *National Review* published a number of retrospective comments. Before the articles about McCarthy as a fallen hero, however, the lead editorial expresses some doubts, and such an editorial must be taken as a statement of official *National Review* policy. It begins by surveying the political landscape burned out by McCarthy's brief career and his flaming crash. It has much of value to say about his career that remains of interest, but the following paragraph deserves special attention:

In the same week that Senator McCarthy fell fatally ill, the Penguin Book publishing company brought out a "Dictionary of Politics," by two Oxford scholars, which defines "McCarthyism" as the "intolerance of liberalism." The book was laid to rest by Mr. William Schlamm in our issue of May 4. It is certainly believable, on Mr. Schlamm's showing, that its authors are Communists; and if that is the case, the perverted definition is neither here nor there. Such a definition of the movement to which Senator McCarthy gave his name is, however, accepted by men who are not Communist or insane, and *there is the awful truth* [italics added]. The Labor Party of Great Britain is not Communist, but its mouthpiece, the *Daily Herald*, identified Senator McCarthy last week as the man who had "used his position to hound men whose only crime was love of freedom of thought." There are no Communists or, that we know of, neurotics on the Conservative *Daily Sketch*, which last week wrote that it was *with justice* that "McCarthy became the world's most hated man" [emphasis added again]. The *Liberal News Chronicle* was not moved by the

Communist's bloodlust to conclude its obituary notice by saying that "America was the cleaner by his fall, and is the cleaner by his death."

Thus, despite the fact that the authors of the article in the *Dictionary of Politics* were likely Communists, their judgment of McCarthyism was supported by journals that could not be suspected of communism. McCarthy had failed to distinguish between communism and liberalism. This editorial, veering in the direction of Chambers, counsels skepticism and second thoughts. Analytically, the phrase "intolerance of liberalism" should be held in mind here.

After this May 1957 editorial there followed passionate articles by Bozell, Meyer, and Schlamm honoring the heroism of McCarthy in facing down a host of enemies and in fighting the good fight. Burnham's "Third World War" column, in this context conspicuously, avoids the subject of McCarthy altogether and discusses the kind of military organization suitable to the nuclear era. If *National Review* could be said at this time to be at all divided because of the hint of disagreement in the editorial just cited, what held the two sides together was a shared perception of the profound evil of communism. All saw it not as an "adversary" but as an *enemy.* The senior people at the magazine knew what Koestler and Orwell knew, and what Solzhenitsyn would make plain to the world in *The Gulag Archipelago.* Chambers, we know from *Witness,* had experienced the deepest pit spiritually, but he wanted to fight intelligently and prudently, gathering allies, and he was no populist, much less a populist swinging wildly.

McCarthy had emerged from obscurity as a junior senator from Wisconsin, becoming a national and international figure in a way that gave ample warning of his recklessness, first visible in the claims he made in the speech delivered on February 9, 1950, to a Lincoln Day audience of the Republican Women's Club of Wheeling, West Virginia.[4]

In this thirteen-page speech, the paragraph that sent up rockets included the statement that there were 205 Communists, known to the Truman administration, who were still employed by the government. That statement went out as the news item. By the time it attracted attention, no transcript of the original speech existed, and in the version McCarthy placed in the *Congressional Record* the figure was fifty-seven Communists. But reporters and guests in the audience insisted it had been 205. Soon, where the figure of 205 had come from became reasonably clear. It was contained in a letter dated July 26, 1946, from Secretary of State James F. Byrnes in answer to questions from Rep. Adolph Sabath of Illinois. Byrnes stated that of 3,000 State Department employees who had been screened under the Truman loyalty-security program, 285 had been described as *unsuitable* for permanent employment, and seventy-nine had been separated from the service, twenty-six of them because they were not citizens and therefore ineligible for employment. Apparently McCarthy or an aide had subtracted seventy-nine from 285 and gotten 205, but in the Byrne letter these were not identified as Communists at all, but as various "security risks" under the Truman loyalty-security legislation. Soon, the furor made McCarthy famous, even a world figure.

This happened because McCarthy had thrown a grenade into a fuel dump. No cool historical account can fully convey the anxieties, justified in large part, of that period. The Soviets, now in possession of half of Europe, had detonated their first nuclear device in 1949, well ahead of schedule, breaking the American monopoly, while in England the physicist Klaus Fuchs confessed to stealing the details of the Bomb and passing them to the Soviets. On January 21, 1950, Alger Hiss, only recently in a high post at the State Department, had been convicted of perjury in his espionage trial and was now in Lewisburg prison. Polls showed that 10 percent of the American people thought Communists controlled the American government, while 35 percent believed the membership of the party was growing and that its members occupied key positions in the government. Moderately well-informed people knew that the Communists regularly received 25 percent of the vote in France and Italy. The summer after McCarthy's Wheeling speech, Julius and Ethel Rosenberg were arrested as nuclear spies, and it soon became evident that Julius had recruited an extensive and effective espionage ring. By 1949, Mao Zedong had won the civil war in China, and Chiang Kai-shek with his remaining forces had escaped to Taiwan. Chiang had been so favorably publicized during the war that the public was astonished by his defeat and ready to suspect betrayal. On June 25, 1950, Communist North Korean forces invaded South Korea. Liberal magazines such as the *Nation* continued to dispute the conviction of Hiss, indeed did so for years, as did much liberal opinion, reinforcing the impression of liberal "softness on communism." In domestic politics, the Republicans had not won a presidential election since 1928, and were ready to use almost any political weapon against the Truman administration. Truman, in growing disrepute because of scandal and the Korean war, had only narrowly upset Thomas E. Dewey in the 1948 election, and seemed ripe for defeat in 1952.

Under these conditions, McCarthy, with his Wheeling speech, suddenly became a political force, a populist power from the Wisconsin "Heartland," a foe of the Eastern Establishment. Many conservative intellectuals, and certainly *National Review*, were more than willing to cut him some slack because of his good intentions and political value.

IT IS IMPORTANT TO RECOGNIZE, too, that the probably Communist authors of the article on McCarthyism in the *Dictionary of Politics* were right in saying that McCarthy had been attacking *liberals.* McCarthy may have been doing this only through intuition and a failure to make distinctions, but *National Review* was capable of making such distinctions. So too were our professional counterintelligence services capable of making distinctions, yet they also saw continuities between liberalism and communism. Those continuities were the salient fact in this entire furor, and though the matter is complex, it should be understood. In this way we get at the meaning of "McCarthyism."

National Review, while making the appropriate distinctions, also saw that philosophically, communism and liberalism were both products of the Enlightenment. Both emphasized equality, Communists through force, liberals as a political goal. Though communism could be called "hard" socialism, liberals, or many of them, were simply "soft" socialists.

The American counterintelligence agencies focused on the relationship of liberalism to communism, and in fact, that very overlapping of communism and liberal culture proved to be the undoing of Soviet espionage in the United States. The complexity of this matter is not to be underestimated, and has been best explained by intelligence historian Thomas Powers in an important 2004 article.[5] Using the metaphor of concentric circles, Powers shows how difficult it was during the 1930s and 1940s to discern the shades of difference among individuals on the American Left.

In Powers's diagram of concentric circles, the solid red one at the center represents the organized Communist Party USA. Moving outward from that center, "progressives" range from darker hues of red near the center to the light pink of the outmost circle: mild fellow-travelers there. Between the 1920s and into the wartime 1940s, Powers says, professional Soviet agents recruited spies from within the party, but U.S. investigators, following their trail, also moved outward through the inner circles to the lighter-reds and on to pink, observing how Soviet agents recruited among progressives—who often had friends, lovers, and such, in the lighter shades of red. This proved lethal to Soviet intelligence because the Communist Party itself had been heavily infiltrated by the FBI, whose agents then could trace outward through the circles the associates of the party members they knew, in that way running down the spies. Guilt by association indeed, but often enough guilty in fact.

Powers quotes Stalin's KGB spy chief Lavrenti Beria warning Soviet intelligence officers in the American networks about "members of the Communist Party organizations who were known to authorities of that country for their progressive activity." Of the interlocking relations among the concentric circles, says Powers, it "would be hard to have designed a pattern better suited to help the FBI, once aroused, to roll up entire networks."

Here then is the issue regarding "McCarthyism": If the availability of potential agents among noncommunist progressives had made recruitment easy, it also guaranteed that innocent progressives, who had enough contacts within the deeper shades of red circles, were vulnerable to false charges of "guilt by association." They became the "witches" of liberal rhetoric—witches, of course, understood to be nonexistent. The liberals during the "McCarthy era" thus had a point when they said that innocent progressive activity had been "chilled." The insight, a correct one, that complex linkages existed among and between leftist groupings and active Communist agents, was agreed upon by well-informed conservatives at *National Review*, including Chambers and Burnham, who could make the distinctions. But McCarthy did not make distinctions.

Still, McCarthy sometimes could smoke out a real witch. He was the one who called attention to the influential Institute for Pacific Relations, and in view of the extensive evidence, no one can now deny that the IPR was indeed a Communist front—though many of its members undoubtedly were unaware of that fact. The multivolume report of the McCarran Committee, summing up a meticulous investigation, leaves no doubt about the IPR.[6]

PERHAPS THE MOST BAROQUE episode of McCarthy's wild career involved someone who would become a frequent contributor to *National Review*, Forrest Davis, an old-time journalist and good friend of senior editor John Chamberlain. On the afternoon of June 14, 1951, approaching the pinnacle of his power, McCarthy, lugging a fat briefcase, rose in the Senate to deliver an anticipated major speech. He proceeded to begin reading a 60,000-word text—yes, *60,000* words—attacking George C. Marshall. As General of the Army in World War II, Marshall had directed the reorganization of the United States military; he was responsible for supervising weapons procurement and top personnel recruitment, even promoting Eisenhower through the officer ranks to his wartime European command. As secretary of state under Truman, Marshall had been the moving force in organizing the anticommunist Marshall Plan for European Recovery, as well as NATO. His anticommunism seemed certain.

But by 1951, Marshall had his detractors. Admirers of General Douglas MacArthur correctly held Marshall, then Truman's secretary of defense, responsible for MacArthur's dismissal. MacArthur had repeatedly been insubordinate over policy in Korea, but Republicans saw the general as a hero treated unjustly.[7] Marshall, as Truman's special emissary to Chiang Kai-shek, was even held by some to have sold out the Nationalist cause to Mao Zedong's Communists.

It is difficult to believe, but McCarthy apparently had not even read the massive document he began to deliver to the Senate, sometimes having difficulty with sentence constructions more complicated than he was used to and containing arcane allusions alien to his populist manner. McCarthy accused Marshall of selling out China to the Communists and of "marching side by side" with Stalin. Marshall had stood "at FDR's elbow" at Yalta, supposedly giving away Eastern Europe. The logic of the manuscript was supposed to establish a "pattern" which justified the following passage:

> How can we account for our present situation unless we believe that men high in this Government are concerting to deliver us to disaster? This must be the product of a great conspiracy, a conspiracy so immense as to dwarf any previous such venture in the history of man. A conspiracy of infamy so black that, when it is finally exposed, its principals shall be forever deserving of the malediction of all honest men. What can be made of this unbroken series of decisions and acts contributing to the strategy of defeat? They cannot be attributed to incompetence. If Marshall were merely stupid, the laws of probability would dictate that part of his decisions would serve his country's interest.[8]

Senators began to leave the chamber long before McCarthy could stumble through this massive document, and he quit after a while, entering the whole text in the *Congressional Record*.

McCarthy had called Marshall a conspirator and a traitor, no doubt about it. The phrase "a conspiracy so immense" became a basis for anti-McCarthy humor. But his speech, when its contents were absorbed, caused a shock yet more immense—amazement that a senator would employ such far-out theorizing in accusing Marshall of treason. The author, in fact, had not been McCarthy at all, but a journalist, a colorful character indeed, and later a contributor to *National Review*: Forrest Davis.

Davis had covered the Scopes "Monkey Trial" (1925) and was a companion of Bryan and Darrow; he rode in the Chicago police cruiser with Leopold and Loeb when they confessed to the murder of Bobby Franks; on the night of the Lindbergh kidnapping, he was, coincidentally, having dinner with the Morrows, parents of Lindbergh's wife; when the Dionne quintuplets were born in Callendar, Ontario, he was there, and when asked in what capacity, he replied, "Well, certainly not as the distraught, bewitched, bewildered father."[9]

Now in his sixties and coeditor of the *Freeman,* a fortnightly, Davis had been commissioned by that magazine to write an article on Marshall's "retreat from victory," and when turning that piece into a book-length manuscript, he had accepted advances for it, based on an outline, of $3,000 from Putnam and $5,000 from Doubleday. However, he volunteered the manuscript to McCarthy at a cocktail party.

In *Redhunter,* Buckley describes this scene as a convivial gathering of anticommunists, including publisher Henry Regnery; frequent contributor Ralph de Toledano; Freda Utley, a journalist who had written the exposé on the 1949 loss of China, *The China Story;* Frank Hanighen, editor and publisher of *Human Events;* and Ben Mandel, a former Communist official who had written out the party card in 1925 for the twenty-four-year-old Whittaker Chambers. Buckley recreates the scene as Davis hands the manuscript to McCarthy:

> "I want to make what I think will be an important contribution to your fight. I want to give you my story on George Marshall."
>
> "I know you're working on a book, Forrest, but what are you suggesting, a speech based on your material?"
>
> Davis drew himself back. He looked now, with his goatee raised slightly, his eyes drawn down, his hands raised to his waist, like a Chinese emperor bequeathing a whole province to one of his sons.
>
> "I propose to give you the whole thing. The entire manuscript. As if you or your staff had written it. It is dynamite, Joe, an explanation of the person primarily responsible for our problems, from Yalta to the present."

The gravamen of the charge by Davis and many hard-line anticommunists at the time was that Acheson, as Truman's secretary of state, and Marshall, as former secretary of state and then special emissary to Chiang Kai-shek, both perhaps manipulated by the Communist front Institute of Pacific Relations, had sold out the Chinese Nationalists and were responsible for the victory of Mao Zedong's Communists in October 1949; and further, that it was the weak performance of Acheson and Marshall that had led to the invasion of South Korea by the North a year later in June 1950. Despite the fact that the IPR was in fact a Communist front, no serious historian today considers the defeat of the Nationalists to have been the result of American betrayal. Chiang's administration was inept, his army out-fought, and Mao had a program that appealed to many peasants.[10]

McCarthy and His Enemies listed seventeen decisions or proposals by Marshall that might be construed as favorable to the Communists, such as urging an earlier second front in Europe, which Stalin also desperately demanded. Without analyzing these in detail here, it is not difficult to account for each of them as reflecting realistic judgment. For example:

- *Marshall advocated a second front in Europe in 1942.* This would have helped the Soviets, true, but the prospect of Russian collapse, leaving the British and Americans facing the Nazis alone, surely warranted such a proposal.

- *Marshall's mission to Chiang Kai-shek in 1945 undermined the Nationalists and guaranteed Mao's victory.* In fact, the Chinese Nationalists were corrupt and politically weak; Marshall was playing a weak hand when he cobbled together a Nationalist-Communist coalition in Manchuria, and his goal had been the containment of Soviet expansion in Asia.

- *Marshall (and Alger Hiss) had been present at Yalta, and so gave away Eastern Europe to the Soviets.* In fact, nothing was given away at Yalta by Roosevelt and Churchill. Stalin's armies controlled East Europe, the key geostrategic fact. And with Roosevelt's death, it was Marshall who presided over the reconstruction of Western Europe and the organization of "containment."

In retrospect, it is difficult to see Marshall as anything other than an American patriot and one of the most effective anticommunists of his time.[11]

Davis's manuscript came out in 1951, some months after McCarthy's speech, as *America's Retreat from Victory: The Story of George Catlett Marshall* by Joseph R. McCarthy. Apparently Putnam and Doubleday swallowed their $8,000 loss on advances to Davis. In his obituary of Davis in the May

22, 1962, *National Review*, Davis's friend John Chamberlain asserted, without documentation, that the text had been much altered in McCarthy's office.

Davis joined *National Review* when it was founded and was a regular contributor until his death, not once showing a taste for fantasies. The speech of course was McCarthy's responsibility, since he delivered it on the Senate floor and put it into the *Congressional Record* in his own name.

INEVITABLY, THE CURTAIN WAS beginning to drop on McCarthy, not to somber Wagnerian strains but to catcalls, boos, and curses. The last act involved Eisenhower springing the trap with the aid of Nixon, as McCarthy commenced an investigation into Fort Monmouth, New Jersey, over the Army's supposed breaches of security there. At the center of the scandal, however, was the homosexual passion of McCarthy's assistant Roy Cohn for David Schine, another young assistant, who was straight. When Schine was drafted into the Army, Cohn made feverish and threatening attempts to force the Army to give him special leaves from his duties at Fort Monmouth. These demands were wiretapped and recorded as Nixon orchestrated the case against McCarthy. In another move, especially outrageous to Eisenhower, McCarthy issued an invitation to federal employees to furnish him with information about wrongdoing, thus skipping the intermediate institutions.

Cohn's behavior, plus his own numerous extravagances, doomed McCarthy. In the televised hearings, McCarthy appeared dark, unshaven, and villainous, Cohn sulky and sinister. The Senate censured McCarthy that December. He might have fought back with a counterattack and retained much of his following, but he was exhausted and he died two years later of despairing alcoholism. Cohn died many years later of AIDS.

8

National Review
and the Black Revolution

The forbears of many black Americans arrived in the Virginia Colony in 1619, a year before the *Mayflower* colonists made it to what was first called Plymouth Plantation. If priority of arrival confers status, those earlier black arrivals have the edge. Still, the history of blacks in America has been distinctive from that of every other major ethnic group; it is a troubling history, with convulsive episodes.

The 1954 *Brown v. Board* school desegregation decision, implemented by court order, began a period of sometimes violent controversy over integration. Broader racial controversy has been continuously present in America—sometimes explosively, with riot, murder, and assassination, most destructively during the 1960s and early 1970s, and more sullenly later, despite the emergence of a successful black middle class. As in Faulkner's mythical Yoknapatawpha epic, the continuing black presence runs as a special, sometimes wise and lyrical stream through American history. Perhaps James Burnham was in an excessively pessimistic mood when he remarked to me once that the black problem "probably will ruin the country."

From its beginning in 1955, *National Review* stood in principled opposition to *Brown* and related rulings, on both constitutional grounds and on a conservative and historically based sense of desirable social change. It did so in full knowledge that *Brown* was being hailed in nearly all quarters as "historic," "a landmark," "trailblazing," and as "Gideon's trumpet," blowing down the walls of segregation.

A 1962 editorial illustrated the *National Review* gradualist case, using as a foil the tumultuous scene at the University of Mississippi, where the Kennedy administration had sent 15,000 troops to protect James Meredith as he tried to register as a student:

> The degrading spectacle at Oxford followed inescapably from the acts of judicial usurpation of "rights reserved to the states respectively" that began with the Supreme Court's 1954 decision; from the assumption of legislative and executive power over the nation's school system by a judicial body not equipped to act in such capacity in such a field; from the centralizing, totalist obsession shared by the Court and the federal executive and, apparently, the majority in Congress.

This view—that the Supreme Court had assumed powers properly and explicitly assigned to the state legislatures—has recently received powerful support within the legal profession, and explicitly on the grounds *National Review* had advanced. For example, Paul D. Carrington in *Stewards of Democracy: Law as a Public Profession* (1999) argues that national judicial action during the 1950s should have addressed blacks' voting rights, since voting is the bedrock of democracy—and that school desegregation in time would have reflected electoral realities. Carrington believes the command that desegregation proceed "'with all deliberate speed' has been appraised and found a disaster."[1] Carrington, by no means opposed to desegregation as such, holds that it should have been the result of a political and not a judicial process. Thus, *Brown*

> and its progeny surely made a contribution to the demise of public schools. . . . On that account the federal courts have substantially but belatedly abandoned the goal of racial integration of school children as one that is both unattainable and counterproductive. In the extensions of its application, *Brown* has indeed been overruled.[2]

Carrington sums up his demonstration this way:

> It is perhaps too harsh to declare extended school desegregation [and similar issues] . . . were all failed heroics. There were benign consequences. But a significant price was paid in thrusting the Court and the Constitution into the political cockpits where they do not belong, jeopardizing the independence of the Court and the integrity of the Constitution. And in different ways and to different degrees, all of these heroic initiatives at social reform backfired in precisely the ways that Cooley, Brandeis, Freund, and Hand foretold.[3]

Carrington concludes that the Court too often has derived its decisions arbitrarily, on the basis of shaky interpretations, and without regard to the citizens' "right to self-government." He considers that the law schools have fostered a culture that encourages its students to regard themselves as philosopher-kings, and that they are further encouraged by the publicity given to "impact decisions." In a review of Carrington's book in the *Journal of Law and Politics*, Jeffrey O'Connell, Professor of Law at the University of Virginia, notices with a touch of amazement that "Carrington is politically incorrect enough to argue boldly and at length that *Roe vs. Wade* was a decision that should not have been made in court." He notes that "[s]ome of the Court's resisters practiced defiance, while others took to the streets and became violent. Those violent reactions have no counterpart in the politics of other nations, even predominantly Catholic ones in which abortion rights have been established by parliamentary means."[4] Not surprisingly, Carrington identifies Justice William Brennan as a prominent figure in what Willmoore Kendall frequently called the judicial "derailment" of the Constitution:

> Perhaps the leading practitioner of twentieth-century constitutional law-making in disregard of the rights of citizens to govern themselves was William Brennan. . . .
>   Unlike Cooley or Brandeis, Brennan seldom if ever gave weight to the political judgment of elected officials, perhaps especially at the state or local levels. Frankfurter only somewhat unjustly described the Brennan Court as animated by "self-willed, self-righteous power-lust." Whether lustful or not,

the Court embraced the belief that anything the legislature could do it could do better. . . .[5]

Professor O'Connell sums up: "Carrington's unarticulated question pervades his book: 'Who are now our stewards of democracy?'" It should be emphasized here that O'Connell agrees with Carrington that the problem lies in the culture of directive liberalism, sometimes called "prophetic," that pervades the major law schools.

These same concerns informed *National Review*, having been made central in the political thought of Willmoore Kendall, who stressed the democratic "deliberate sense of the people" nature of the American political system and the prime importance of the first three words of the Constitution: "We the People." Again and again, *National Review* articulated this perspective on the Court's "heroic advances," as in this editorial, worthy of partial but extended quotation:

> In June 1954 relations between Whites and Negroes in the United States, and racial relations generally, were in a more amicable and promising condition than ever before in the nation's history.
>
> Then a Supreme Court obsessed with an egalitarian ideology rendered its decision in *Brown v. Board of Education*. What has happened, what is happening, was predicted. Every observer, whatever his views, concurs in the finding that Negro-White relations in the South, and in many northern cities also, have catastrophically worsened. (Even the rate of integration in the schools is actually slower than during the five years prior to 1954.) From this poisonous cauldron the fumes of anti-Semitism, too, begin to spread, both because the racist impulse tends to be non-selective, and because organized Jewish groups have noisily egged on the Court, and called for immediate implementation of its decisions. Now comes the shutting down of Southern schools, the dynamiting of homes, schools, and Jewish temples. And it will be worse. A viciousness has been released that is not easily brought back to kennel. The Court, in *Brown* and the successor decisions, was "obsessed": the word is carefully chosen. Obsessed in that it acted from abstract imperatives of a monolithic dogma, without reference to the real situation of real men in the real world. It is easy enough for Earl Warren and Felix Frankfurter, at the turn of an ideological spigot, to lecture their 175 million countrymen about instant

and total obedience to "the law of the land," but platitudes from the bench—
that so plainly exempts itself from the restraints of judicial precedent and
tradition—will not, overnight, transmute the ingrained sentiments and convictions of self-reliant communities. Tragically, the resistance by self-reliant
and decent men to what they deem the usurpations of the Court and the
despotism of the central government tends to promote a general atmosphere
of civil disobedience, and disrespect not only for the Warren Court but for the
law; in which *the dregs of society break through to the surface.* [italics added]

Notably, at the time of *Brown*, Hannah Arendt created a minor scandal
by opposing the ruling not on constitutional grounds but on the grounds
that Court integration had made *children* the spearhead of the supposed
solution. Her essay appeared, in, of all places, the socialist magazine *Dissent*, but she had a point.

The larger part of *National Review*'s editorial certainly appears sound
and resembles the substance of Carrington's *Stewards of Democracy*. Its last
clause (italicized above) adds some domestic prophecy. Tocqueville had
observed, apropos of the Revolution of 1848 in Paris, that in the revolutionary atmosphere, violent and hitherto unknown individuals, often bizarre in appearance, came forth as if from nowhere, out of alleyways and
cellars, greatly adding to the frenzy in the boulevards. It seems intuitively
likely that the law-breaking, mass demonstrations, and threats of the Black
Revolution exerted a synergy on the wider violence of the Sixties, which
reached its dizzy climax in that *annus horribilis* 1968, making thinkable the
escalating murder and civic outrage that stalked the streets. Violence became a token of sincerity.

RICHARD WHALEN, FROM NEW YORK, was a reporter in Virginia
during the early 1960s. Later he wrote some excellent books: *Founding Father* (1964), a biography of patriarch Joseph Kennedy, and *Catch the Falling
Flag* (1972), a negative assessment of the then-current Nixon administration. For *National Review* he added shrewdly observed social fact in support of the editorial position on *Brown*. So did James Jackson Kilpatrick, a
fine journalist, then writing from a quasi-anti-integrationist point of view,

which he later repudiated. Whalen did have a far-reaching criticism to make about the behavior of the native white Southerners:

> [But] what of the growing Negro middle class? The Negro white-collar worker, who has achieved middle-class rank by great exertion, is excluded as ruthlessly from white schools and society as the shiftless Negro field hand. The Negro middle class is the key to future race relations in the South—and the North as well. Negro leaders, if they see the wall of white resistance transformed into a gate of acceptance, may assert themselves more effectively in dealing with the social and moral problems of the Negro community.

Richard Weaver, always and refreshingly seeing matters from his own angle, wrote as a southerner and resisted the kind of federal action that was in the offing. He did not participate in the segregation fight as a partisan but as a philosopher and Carolinian admirer of Lincoln who discerned features of permanent and universal value in the persistence of southern culture. As Weaver wrote in "The Regime of the South" (March 14, 1959):

> In the national controversy raging over segregated schooling, we often hear of "the Southern way of life." I suggest that this phrase is used with too little understanding, both by those who use it and those who hurl it in attack. It is true that the South has a "way of life," but the point that is missed is that a way of life is a normal social phenomenon.

We have seen earlier that Weaver inferred permanent bases for that "way of life" in the fact that it had survived Appomattox, Reconstruction, and even some industrialization—together, enough to have devastated any other *modus vivendi*. He inferred from this that the southern way of life must possess a metaphysical basis, and in fact was the only such culture in the modern West. The South, he writes:

> has a society more unified by imponderables, more conscious of self-definition, more homogeneous in outlook than any other region. All of these are strong barriers against anomie. The idea of transcendence is the real source of symbolization in life, which persuades men that they have lived and are living for something more than things of the moment.

This was the same insight that Weaver had offered in *Ideas Have Consequences*, and his introduction of the word "symbolization" shows the influence of Voegelin. *National Review* had such exploratory thinkers writing commentary during its early and middle years, shapers of the modern American conservative mind, interpreting the flux of current controversy in terms of permanent political principle. In the absence of such principles, opinion becomes mere assertion.

Weaver's essay is impressive and persuasive about the Burkean-Platonic basis of the southern way of life, but for all that, a regime's self-definition should not rest on the subordination of people because of color, or on the basis of traits that are transitory. The fact that a metaphysics can be deduced from its practice does not exclude the fact that a metaphysics can be flawed. Yet Weaver writes as a philosopher of culture, and not as a segregationist.

A March 1960 unsigned editorial (and therefore a corporate *National Review* statement) unfortunately contains much that seems ill thought-out:

> We offer the following on the crisis in the Senate and the South: 1) In the Deep South the Negroes are, by comparison with the Whites, retarded ("unadvanced," the National Association for the Advancement of Colored People might put it). Any effort to ignore the fact is sentimentalism or demagoguery. Leadership in the South, then, quite properly, rests in White hands. Upon the White population this fact imposes moral obligations of paternalism, patience, protection, devotion, sacrifice. 2) Those who want segregation must be prepared to pay its economic cost. In Montgomery, Alabama, a few years ago it became clear that although the white population wanted separate seating in the buses, it did not want separate seating enough to pay the costs of separate buses and segregation ensued. If those who patronize Woolworth's, et al., do not want integrated lunch counters, they and the managers must be prepared to accept the costs of a Negro boycott. The boycott is a classic and wholly defensible instrument of voluntary protest. 3) The filibuster, which we are being urged from all sides to hold in horror, is a valuable political device which can be put to honorably political use on those occasions when the majority wants to smash the minority. The filibuster is a living remnant of the great doctrine of the concurrent majority defined by John C. Calhoun. It survived the Civil War. One hopes that it will survive the displeasure of *The New York Times*. 4) Nobody knows

what is the solution to the Negro problem, or whether there is a "solution." It certainly does not lie in the Omnibus Bill of 1960.

Even if the bill were to go through Congress, the problem in the South would be no less acute; indeed, very possibly it would worsen. In the Deep South there is room for give and take, but the essential relationship is organic, and the attempt to hand over to the Negro the raw political power with which to alter it is hardly a solution. It is a call to upheaval, which ensues when reality and unbridled abstractions meet head-on.

Everyone has a bad day. This wanders off into the tall grass. The use of "retarded" is insulting. The whole proposal remains so abstract, so far from the concrete matters at stake, that it makes Harry Blackmun look positively Burkean. The matter is certainly not economic, whether the whites will buy separate buses or pay for separate lunch counters. The legitimacy of boycotts and filibusters is well known and to defend them here is irrelevant. So is the mention of Calhoun. The issue at bottom is on what basis these two historically separate groups will live together as amicably as possible. There is no way of keeping so large a segment of the population subordinate indefinitely, even if they are "retarded" socially and even if the whites are paternal, patient, protective, devoted, and sacrificial. To say that such a fanciful situation is "organic" is laughable. It looks as if the sentence, "Leadership in the South very properly rests in White hands," means denying blacks the right to vote. One must conclude that "to hand over to the Negroes raw political power" is a characterization of the right to vote. As a constitutionalist such as Carrington recognizes, the vote is the foundation of our deliberate-sense system. But this editorial does not advocate the right to vote for blacks.

Before long this position went into the *Untenable* file. Buckley and others recognized that what amounted to the position of the Southern Agrarians was impossible—paternalism, patience, protection, and so on notwithstanding.

The Agrarians, along with the Vanderbilt group of poets, novelists, and critics, might use the Old South as a poetic myth. You really can make fine poetry by filtering *Gone With the Wind* through the modern verse techniques of T. S. Eliot, as in Tate's "Ode to the Confederate Dead":

> *You shift your sea-space blindly*
> *Heaving, turning like the blind crab . . .*
>
> *Dazed by the wind, only the wind*
> *The leaves flying, plunge.*

That comes from *The Waste Land*, via the Confederacy.

Yet *National Review* could not put the myth of the Lost Cause forward as a political recommendation, not if it were to live up to its name as a national and not a sectarian magazine—and as a guide in the development of a strong American conservatism. It had set forth already the legitimate and historically orthodox theory of deliberate sense, of "We the People" and judicial restraint, which entailed the right to vote. It would have to let the magnolias go. Deliberate sense constitutionalism was enough for the actual evolving American South, which was moving in the direction of the Republicans. *National Review* and Buckley continued to be works in progress. The Black Revolution also continued.

In fact, the magazine's critique of *Brown* was soon at least partially validated by what everyone could see. *Brown* plus "all deliberate speed" destroyed the once excellent public school systems, especially in the metropolises of the North, whites and their tax money fleeing to the suburbs beyond the reach of "busing." *Brown* was tacitly shelved as unenforceable, but not before the destruction of the public schools. *Brown* had made a desert and called it peace.

FAR BEYOND *BROWN* IN 1954 and its immediate results, the Black Revolution rolled along, perhaps both creative and destructive, the latter sometimes at *National Review*. Garry Wills—so brilliant at *NR* in his writing on Newman, on Augustine, on ancient authors, so sharply aware of the tragedy of human limitations, so valuable as an exemplary philosophical conservative—lurched into a kind of utopianism. He seems to have been profoundly shaken, indeed transformed, by the black turmoil and also by the Kids' counter-culture. Little could have been more surprising than this development.

These changes first appeared in the turbulence and opacity of Wills's May 21, 1963, review of James Baldwin's *The Fire Next Time*. This proved to be the beginning of changes that altered permanently his relationship with *National Review*. They would show most clearly in his long *National Review* essay "Convention in the Streets," about the hordes of Kids who created the chaos outside the 1968 Democratic Convention.

The publication of Wills's review—titled "What Color Is God?"—was resisted by some editors, most emphatically by Frank Meyer. It perhaps merited publication, however, as a strange, sometimes discerning and at other times gullible and, when analyzed, baffling piece of prose. Wills, usually an intelligent writer, allows Baldwin to lie, fake, vulgarize his own prose, and make preposterous historical assertions—and then professes himself tremendously impressed. Perhaps it reflects Wills's own confusion. Not least, it gives the attentive reader a workout.

Earlier, in his celebrated essay "Everybody's Protest Novel," Baldwin himself had castigated the coarseness of protest prose, as in Richard Wright's writing. At that time he considered such prose to amount to mere propaganda. He had shown in this essay, collected with others in *Notes of a Native Son*, that he himself could write with a Henry Jamesian refinement, and he had been widely admired for that. Baldwin was not a mere *protest* writer, he proclaimed, but an artist.

In *The Fire Next Time*, however, he commits obvious vulgarities of protest prose, as if he were daring us to point them out.

With his alternating modes of refined language and vulgarity, Baldwin seems, on one possible interpretation, to be enacting a public self-crucifixion as an artist, as if saying, "Look, white man, at what you have done to me. I can't even write any more." Garry Wills, a man of some discernment, must have seen this. And he also must have seen Baldwin's transparent lies, pretending throughout that his suffering is due to his *blackness*. Not so. Any reader of Baldwin's novel knows that his suffering had other causes, among them the neurotic sadism of his father, a minister, who abused Baldwin and ultimately starved himself to death. As his novels show, Baldwin had his own homosexual rage as well. But in *The Fire Next Time*, we are supposed to trace his rage, suffering, bad writing, everything—to Whitey.

Wills's "What Color Is God?" amounts to a long, turbulent, baffling, alarming, and hopeless piece of prose. In the end, Wills wants to say that at least for our time, the suffering and crucified black man can redeem sinful white people. And Wills's essay does possess a sort of drama, whether tragic or comical. He writes of Baldwin here:

> He makes no effort to soften the hard lines of inconsistency that extrude everywhere in his piece—saying in one breath that it is too late for us to convince the Negro of our good faith, since the growth of black power in the world makes any gesture on our part look like an effort to buy off our future conquerors; then with a change of mood, but no answer to the former argument, singing that our nation is the one best equipped to lead the world into a new era of racial love.

That is, we are to admire this writing of Baldwin's, mess though it is, and plunge along to promised rewards of the promised land, glory hallelujah.

But Wills is too shrewd a reader not to know how awful much of *The Fire Next Time* really is:

> The last part [of the essay] is mechanically protreptic [*sic*: "designed to instruct"! Why not just say "pedagogical"?] to a degree that is startling in Baldwin. He parades all the liberal clichés in their pristine naïveté—the wave of history, the courage to change, and the need to export our revolution.

Baldwin is ruining his prose, as Wills at moments seems to know—may perhaps be consciously ruining his prose as a dramatic illustration of his own suffering. This, then, might be Baldwin's broken oratorio of black suffering, an example of expressive form: "Come, watch me suffer. Because of *you*."

Could be. But read soberly, *The Fire Next Time* is anti-writing, hopeless as prose. Maybe that's simply the way Baldwin in fact now writes in 1963. In a famous essay published in the *New Republic*, black critic Henry Louis Gates, chairman of Harvard's Black Studies Department, argued that the contemporary black movement put Baldwin under tremendous pressure, ruining him as an artist and turning him into a propagandist. But a real artist, such as the author of *Notes of a Native Son*, would have told any such movement to get lost.

Amazingly, Wills sees what is happening here to Baldwin's prose—and still decides that Baldwin *wins*: "And yet he can give the game away and still win." Wills cannot help but remember other days:

> He who, in *Notes of a Native Son*, wrote, "I am not one of the people who believes that oppression imbues a people with wisdom or insight or sweet charity" here becomes "one of the people who." The Negro, we are told, has been forced "to look beneath appearances, to take nothing for granted, to hear the meaning beneath the words."

And yet, dammit, Baldwin, becoming one of "the people who," does win. Wills takes it all as a powerful statement with "a seismic effect":

> Yet, despite the manifesto prose about "changing the world," the contrived effects, the unexpected stridency, *it is intensely moving; it has had a seismic effect, whose tremors are not even beginning to subside*. [italics added]

This must be taken as Wills's considered judgment. But how can this be? In the end, Wills lets Baldwin get away with everything, Wills crucifying his own intelligence, one guesses, for what?

Wills, who was not and is not simple-minded, lets Baldwin get away with anything, even with calling Jesus a "sunbaked, disreputable Hebrew," the sort of statement that might be found scrawled on a wall, and enough to make any educated person, certainly including Baldwin, want to throw this essay back in its author's teeth—that "sunbaked disreputable Hebrew" who had deepened Moses with the Sermon on the Mount. Wills lets Baldwin get away with junk thought, Baldwin even demanding "immediate secession from our civilization," the "transcendence of color, and of nations and of altars"—that is, for a rejection of the profoundly *actual*. Jump, white man, jump. Wills knows that we should respond to this kind of disgraceful performance by a black man by getting angry with him—that is, we should treat him as an equal. Yet Wills voluntarily accepts nonsense.

What are we to make of Wills's performance? Literary criticism throws up its hands. Apparently, he had been utterly disoriented by the black revolution.

Soon enough came Wills's *The Second Civil War: Arming for Armageddon* (1968), with its astounding sympathy for the black "revolutionaries," or Black Panthers. This led to his break with *National Review*, Buckley telling *Time* that Wills "had gone over to the militants."[6]

9

National Review *and Religion*

National Review has always been certain that religion must be an important part of the American conservative mind. The Christian religion had been a leading constituent of Western civilization from the beginning, and from the beginning Catholicism had been a presence in the magazine. Buckley and his sister Priscilla were Catholics, also the converts Kendall and Bozell, and later Kirk. Prominent Catholic contributors included Hugh Kenner, Erik von Kuehnelt-Leddihn, Thomas Molnar, and Frederick Wilhelmsen. Ernest van den Haag showed in his book *The Fabric of Society* that social structures require some kind of religious basis, but he was, if a Catholic, not a declared one until shortly before his death in 2002. Perhaps his Catholicism resided in his pronounced Europeanness; as Belloc had said, "Europe is the Faith and the Faith is Europe."

Somehow, Belloc's aperçu may be true: in the manners, the art, the memories, the monuments, the civilization. The church might be seen as latent in Europe, as perhaps it seemed to van den Haag. It was difficult to tell. Whittaker Chambers, on the evidence of *Witness*, was some kind of Kierkegaardian Protestant, his faith a chime heard in the midnight of nihilism—though he called himself a Quaker. Russell Kirk gave religion a prominent place in his *Conservative Mind*, and in mid-course he became a Catholic, while Meyer had a death-bed conversion, though it was the product of long reflection. Burnham had been born a Catholic, but no longer seemed to be one. He even felt that the Catholic presence at *National Review* might be too strong to suit a national magazine, and he sought to moderate the Romanist element.

Some contributors were conservative Protestants, and Will Herberg, a scholarly Jewish professor and admirer of Reinhold Niebuhr, became Religion editor in 1961. His *Catholic–Protestant–Jew* (1954) sketched the American amalgam empirically, and also critically. Herberg's guide Niebuhr was a sort of ambassador to Judaism. A Protestant minister as well as professor at Union Theological Seminary, in his many influential works Niebuhr characteristically speaks not of Jesus of Nazareth but of "biblical religion." Herberg's inclusion in the magazine foreshadowed a friendly relationship, much later, between *National Review* and those who came to be known as the neoconservatives, many of whom were Jewish.

Buckley, though devout, could be flippantly serious about papal encyclicals, as in the famous "*Mater, Sí, Magistra, No!*" editorial reacting to John XIII's *Pacem in Terris*, which had muted any criticisms of communism. Such criticism by the magazine of the liberal encyclical and papal obiter dicta evoked a comical furor, especially against Buckley, by liberal Catholics at *America* and *Commonweal*, who suddenly discovered their own deep devotion to papal authority. *National Review* later criticized *Humanae Vitae* (1968)—the stricture against artificial birth control—issued by Paul VI, viewing it as a desperate effort to shore up his authority against modernity by creating a saving remnant. This rejection of the fact of modernity was desperate and hopeless. All in all, these editorials on Catholic questions suggested a reliance on experience, a version of the politics of actuality.

SOONER OR LATER THE QUESTION had to arise of whether it was possible to be a conservative *without* being religious. The senior people at *National Review* knew that George Santayana had been an atheist and also a conservative, and so had been David Hume, a thoroughgoing skeptic. Russell Kirk had included Santayana in his model of the "conservative mind." Still, *National Review* had not faced the problem of defining on what principle religion could be understood as central to the West while still allowing atheists to be understood as conservative. This problem had to be faced with Max Eastman, a senior editor, a follower of John Dewey philosophically and an anticommunist advocate of the free market.

Eastman pushed the question forward with his January 28, 1964, article titled, "Am I a Conservative?" His philosophical skills had evidently atrophied since his Columbia days with Dewey, for here he was little more than a nineteenth-century village atheist. His performance, to say the least, was at odds with the history of philosophy, from the pre-Socratics through the present. The serious thinker, on the historical evidence, often tries to push into the semi-knowable and even the unknowable through a variety of methods: Eastman was stuck in a crude facticity, contemptuous of faith. Eastman's challenge led to Buckley's formulation that *a conservative need not be religious, but a conservative cannot despise religion*, which here Eastman manifestly did. His departure from *National Review* was cordial. But Buckley's formulation in response to the Eastman episode had been merely negative. What about eccentric faiths, such as Mormonism? Christian Science? Or the repeated Great Awakenings, with their wild, homemade variations of fundamentalism? At the time, this was not a salient issue, but it would emerge later with the Republican Party's increasing reliance on an electoral base of evangelicals.

IN 1997, BUCKLEY OPENED up the religious question in *Nearer My God: An Autobiography of Faith*, telling his own history of inherited Catholicism, but also sending some of his colleagues, including several Catholic converts, a questionnaire in the hopes of achieving clarity. Their answers were highly individual and woven throughout Buckley's text. But before we come to that, a word about *the* central problem might be raised.

All Christian religions, including Catholicism—and Judaism, as well— are implicitly or explicitly metaphysical, having to do with realities beyond *physis*, or the reality known to the empiricism of the five senses. Of course, all of us are born empiricists. Not to believe in the evidence of the senses would be suicidal: you could hardly take a few steps without walking into a wall. But if empiricism reveals the *only* reality, then the claims of religion to other kinds of knowledge are nonsense. Some of the so-called pre-Socratics tried to push beyond the five senses. Then, Socrates and Plato considered that they had done so.[1] Empiricism had been called in doubt; and again, in the twentieth century, the possibilities of philosophy opened up once more, pulling away from the empiricism-materialism of the nineteenth century.

A more radical philosophical criticism of empiricism than Plato's, because based upon empiricism itself, came from Ludwig Wittgenstein. A star of the "Vienna school" of radical logical-empiricists, Wittgenstein went ahead and refined, refined away, pushing on logically in a technical and disciplined way toward his conclusion. To illustrate the problem of empiricism, Wittgenstein's simple metaphor is useful. You have to get Wittgenstein's fly out of the bottle, its glass walls representing the limits of what the five senses can report.

Wittgenstein thought through the problem in his *Tractatus* (1921), operating only with the tools of logic. He had been an advanced student at Cambridge under no less a logician than Bertrand Russell; with Alfred Lord North Whitehead, Russell had written the formidable *Principia Mathematica* (1913), which Burnham had assigned to his classes at NYU. In the *Tractatus*, employing the logical empiricist method, Wittgenstein pushed the method to the walls of the bottle, and there knew that *there is more*, which he called *das Mystiches* and *Hocheres*. Wittgenstein had bumped into the limits of empiricism, and knew there must be *something* beyond the empirical senses, for which empiricism has no language. If Wittgenstein were correct, there was something beyond.

Ordinary language is the language of experience. Such radical departures as represented in the *Tractatus* often come through several disciplines. In astronomy, scientists at the Bell Laboratories pushed to the edge of time, measuring the age of the radiation from the Big Bang, the beginning of the universe, finding the universe to be some 17.5 billion years old,[2] and the Hubble Telescope saw to the edge of time. But what was there *before* that? Empiricism, obviously, could not say. Meanwhile, quantum physicists were finding that within the atom, particles are not material at all, but could be in two places at the same time: the ultimate reality might be more like *light* than *matter*. Philosopical materialism was dead[3] and the universe had a beginning. Yet, *something cannot come from nothing.* Why then is there something, rather than nothing? Beyond the wall of Wittgenstein's bottle there must be *something.*

THIS RETURNS US TO *NEARER MY GOD*, a notably attractive book. In chapter seven, Buckley reports on two basic questions he addressed to colleagues, introducing his questionnaire this way:

> I thought immediately to dwell on two broad questions. The first, what *about* Jesus of Nazareth? The second, do you believe his miracles were conclusively documented? I held back on the crowning event, the Resurrection. I wished to pay special attention to it. I was not here conducting a plebiscite. Yes, everybody believed Jesus of Nazareth was a historical figure, but I savor the way in which each answered that question, and the one that came immediately after, about the miracles.

Buckley's book asked large and important questions. What follows establishes a kind of benchmark for evaluating developments to follow at *National Review.*

In his autobiography *The Sword of Imagination* (1995), Russell Kirk explains that he became a Catholic during his middle years after marrying Annette, a devout Catholic. Kirk said that he had been of a religious inclination for a long time, which we could adduce from his traditionalism. He here responds directly to Buckley's two questions. First, regarding Jesus' existence in history, which nineteenth-century biblical scholars have tended to doubt, Kirk replied:

> Nothing in the ancient world is better established than the life of Jesus of Nazareth. We have four separate accounts by four witnesses, contemporaries; also the Epistles of St. Paul, a brief account by the historian Josephus, and several mentions of Jesus and his followers by Greek and Roman writers. By contrast, of Socrates, we have accounts by only two ancient writers, Plato and Xenophon, who knew him; and of some of the great men included in Plutarch's *Lives of the Noble Greeks and Romans* we have inherited no account except Plutarch's own. It has been pointed out that it would be no more absurd to

maintain that Napoleon Bonaparte was a figure merely of myth than to argue that a real Jesus never walked the earth. We even have the Shroud of Turin, Jesus' burial garment, with its scientifically inexplicable image (like a photographic negative) on the linen.

It could be added that recent practitioners of the historical-critical method have themselves discredited much of the work of their nineteenth-century German predecessors.

We move on here to Kirk's view of miracles and of the Resurrection:

> For Jesus' Great Works, we have chiefly, of course, the four Gospels and certain traditions recorded in Eusebius's history and lesser gospels of the early centuries. Astounding wonders appear to have been worked. That nobody works such wonders near the end of the twentieth century of the Christian era is no need for disbelief: by definition, miracles are rare exceptions to the ordinary operation of the laws of nature. See C. S. Lewis's little book *Miracles*.
>
> If the Word became flesh for a second time, presumably such miracles as the Great Works could be worked again. It is said that faith works miracles, and that miracles are worked in order to rouse faith. Were miracles worked in medieval times at the shrine of St. Thomas a Becket in Canterbury Cathedral, or at the shrine of the bones of St. Andrew, at his cathedral in Scotland? And, if so, why did those miracles cease to occur well before the coming of the Reformation? Is it perfect faith that conjures up the miracle?
>
> Why is it that no miracles have been recorded at the splendid shrine of the most wondrous of all relics, the Shroud of Turin, but a good many are said to have come to pass at the shrine of the girl-saint Bernadette Soubirous? Are miracles like beauty, in the eye of the beholder? I do not doubt that Jesus worked his miracles, yet how long the results thereof endured, and whether what the witnesses beheld was physically "real," we have no way of knowing. Oh for a revelation!

Among contributors to *National Review*, Buckley also includes Ernest van den Haag, noting his response as "laconic"—which indeed it was, excusing himself from answering. He was very late in avowing Catholicism, as I have mentioned; he may have wished not to get into philosophy and metaphysics. Both Frank Meyer and Willmoore Kendall, converts to Catholicism, had died before 1997 when Buckley sent out his questionnaire.

In *Nearer My God*, Buckley comes last to me, quoting my response to the question of the historicity of Jesus:

> I certainly consider that the historical presence of Jesus Christ has been estab-
> lished beyond a reasonable doubt. I know nineteenth-century and earlier twen-
> tieth-century biblical criticism cast doubt upon the "historical Jesus." Albert
> Schweitzer provided a good account of this in his *The Quest for the Historical
> Jesus*, which ended up concluding that the historical Jesus is difficult to estab-
> lish and represents a vanishing point. At the same time, the theology of Karl
> Barth and his many followers made a sort of virtue of these negative conclu-
> sions, in that he pushed the "faith" dimension of Protestantism to its extreme
> conclusion. Historical arguments, for Barth, were beside the point. What
> mattered was the encounter with the transcendent God, who would always be
> Other. Meanwhile, Rudolph Bultmann was "demythologizing" the Scriptures,
> that is, bringing them into line with nineteenth-century presuppositions about
> what is possible in the cosmos. . . . [M]ore recent serious work has pointed in
> a different direction. . . . Stephen Neill concludes that the biblical narratives
> are worth far more as history than earlier scholars thought, and that we know
> more—historically—about Jesus than about other figures in the ancient world.
> . . . Archaeology is now constantly turning up confirmation of sites and events
> in the Old Testament. (The existence of Troy was doubted by scholars until a
> German businessman named Schliemann, using Homer as a guide, found it.)
>   It is very difficult for skeptics about Jesus to get around I Corinthians 15.
> Paul there is speaking to an audience that agrees with him on the nature of
> historical fact. Corinth was not some backwoods, but well within the Hel-
> lenic ambience. He appeals to witnesses, "Most of whom are alive to this
> day—that is, you can check it with them, and he uses a blatantly historical
> argument for the life, death, *and* resurrection of Jesus.

Buckley comments: "Once more, a ringing affirmation, done by a scholar trained in the science of evaluating data. Jeff Hart edges into the critical question of the Resurrection."

He then quotes my response to the question of miracles:

> The Gospels include narrative accounts of His miracles, but usually do not
> provide evidence. The Resurrection of course is a miracle. Therefore I regard
> the Gospel accounts as derivatively credible, on the argument that the spiri-

tual force that could accomplish the Resurrection could certainly accomplish lesser miracles. The Resurrection I take to be an expression of the original divine energy that made the universe in the first place. David Hume's comment on miracles has always been something of a puzzle to me, and I notice that Robert Foegelin, in his book of essays, devotes one to this argument. Briefly, Hume, as I understand him, argues that if someone reports a miracle, it is more probable that a) he is lying or deluded than b) the miracle occurred. That is a good approach to ask of some extraordinary report—for example, that Eisenhower was an atomic spy. But it does not seem to touch the question of miracles. No one said that miracles are probable. Actually, Hume is very tricky. In his famous *Dialogues Concerning Natural Religion*, the skeptical position defeats the argument from design too easily, I think, but does not touch the argument from faith (Demea). The dialogue in effect concedes that there may at least be a realm to which the probabilities of the phenomenal world may not apply.

Buckley comments: "I heard from Jeff Hart what I hadn't thought I would so much welcome, namely the *plausibility* of miracles. If a movement that would absorb the Western world was launched by a few dozen men and women all of whom thought themselves witnesses to miracles, isn't the burden of disbelief harder?" To that I would add that it is possible to historicize disbelief; that is, see disbelief as part of a cultural desire to focus on mastery of this world, something very exciting in its beginnings, as in Locke's *Essay Concerning Human Understanding* (1690), which reads like the dawn of a fresh world. That newly seen world also shines in the human and worldly details of Renaissance art, as it emerges from medieval stylization. Not surprisingly, this historical impulse led to the Western mastery of *this* world beyond that of other cultures and civilizations. Unlike some conservatives, I find it impossible to regret the Enlightenment, at least in its moderate expressions.

I have mentioned I Corinthians 15 and the testimony of the narratives. Paul in Corinthians is being *empirical*, calling on witnesses who have seen the risen Jesus. There, Paul is as empirical as you or I might be, or as one might plead before a jury. If Jesus had been raised after three days in the tomb, it had to have happened and not been illusion or myth. A movie camera would have caught it, despite "theologians" who consider it only a "spiritual" event.

BUCKLEY DOES NOT GIVE his own answers to the questions he asks, except in his comments on the replies. It is, to be sure, interesting to hear from Kirk and others, and the book is also an important part of *National Review* history. One must infer from the rest of the narrative in *Nearer My God* the reasons for Buckley's Catholicism: the strict faith of his parents, his education at the English Catholic school St. John's Beaumont, particularly his experience of the Latin Mass (universal once). One must conclude that he *trusts* the church—especially on its metaphysics, not a bad idea.

Not brought up a Catholic, or in any religion, I had to make my way differently. Buckley's questions did not admit of a complete answer, or anything like it, though Catholicism as such was then so important to *National Review*; so I will give, briefly, my more extended answer now. My elaborated answer goes beyond Buckley's questions about what then interested him, and it is traditional, reasoned, and not based on "faith," which properly appears when scholarship and reason have done their work.

To start with, who and what was Jesus? We can compare the language spoken by Jesus in the Gospel narratives with that of the "background" language of the narrators. None of them speaks with anything like the eloquence almost routinely characteristic of Jesus, indeed uniquely his own. It soars far above their humdrum factual narrative. These men surely did not have the power to invent his speeches as a novelist might. Only the first chapter of John rises to anything like such heights, and there the narration derives in part from Greek philosophy, John associating Jesus with the *Logos*, meaning the fundamental principle, or Idea, of Things Seen and Unseen. But John here assimilated that to the Hebrew creating "Word." There, the door opened to theology (the "study of God"). Without the penetration of the Greek language and Greek thought throughout the literate world of the New Testament, there would be no way of "talking about" God, or Jesus, in an intelligible way, but only as a narrative of events that must speak only for themselves. Remarkably, just about everything Jesus says has become part of civilizational memory. Furthermore, we have had many great writers—Homer, Dante, and Shakespeare perhaps preeminent—but what they said does not have the power to change lives, as the language of Jesus does. His language itself is a presence, as he himself must have been when he said to the fisherman, "Drop your nets and follow me."

Jesus of Nazareth could be said to be a credible genius, rare in any literature. The Socrates of the Platonic dialogues may be one, perhaps Prince Hamlet is another, and perhaps Thomas Mann's composer Adrian Leverkuhn in *Doctor Faustus* yet another. Jesus towers above them all from sentence to sentence.

One trait of genius has been precocious mastery. Thus we have the story of the child Jesus (Luke 2:41–51), where the twelve year-old (scholar's guess) disputes with the great rabbis in the Temple at Jerusalem. This dialogue would have involved citing passages from the Hebrew Bible, and evidently he had absorbed those texts by an early age. Indeed, to put it one way, he lived his entire mental life *within* those scriptures, finding there the deep presence of the mind of God. The learned teachers in the Temple must have been amazed. Was he already correcting Moses? His last words on the Cross, the only words not in Greek throughout the New Testament, were in Aramaic: *Eloi, Eloi, lama sabachthani*, or, "My God, my God, why have you forsaken me?"—these, the opening words of Psalm 22. But he was not alone, not forsaken. His learned followers must have heard there a call forward through the suffering in Psalm 22, toward Psalm 23. At that moment, as he dies, the opening of Psalm 23 must have reverberated in the minds of those around him, becoming a kind of prayer:

> *Shepherd, I shall not want . . .*
> *Though I walk through the valley of the shadow of death,*
> *I will fear no evil, because you are with me.*

Jesus had been very familiar with God: in his Lord's Prayer, astonishingly, he addresses God as *Abba*, a familiar vocative, perhaps "papa." This must have been outrageous to the rabbis in the Temple. As a rabbi, or teacher, Jesus corrects Moses and the Prophets, seeing more deeply into the total meaning of the scriptures, and transforming into the soul's goals the teachings of the Ten Commandments and the Prophets. Of course you should not commit adultery; but he who looks at a woman with lust has sinned in his heart. Jesus wants a holy interior, a holy direction of the soul, not a whited sepulcher, a tomb whitewashed outside but corrupt within. He believes the scriptures seek holiness, the vector of the soul toward God, not only external conformity to the rules. These are severe teachings: "If your eye offend you, pluck it out." At least, turn away. Holiness is a pearl beyond price.

The careful reader, attending to the text of the four Gospels, notices certain details, many of them in fact not germane to the surrounding incidents. For example, when Jesus is about to repeal or reinterpret the Mosaic law in the case of the woman caught in adultery (John 8), we hear: "Jesus bent down, and started to write on the ground with his finger." The narrator does not explain this peculiar behavior. It must be there because that is the way it happened.

THE ORIGINAL QUESTIONNAIRE did not broach the question of why (given the answers to the two questions) one would choose the Catholic Church, as distinguished from other churches. My answers to the two questions posed did not result from "faith," but rather from reason. As C. S. Lewis remarks in *Mere Christianity*, in a disbelieving age it requires reason to cut through shared assumptions. Mere emotion is not enough, and proves nothing. As regards the question of "what church?" my short answer would be that the Catholic Church has been successful in guarding its long-perfected metaphysics, or doctrine about God, while Protestant churches have failed through what Dryden called a "downhill Reformation." Individuals cannot do the work that has taken centuries to complete. In the Catholic Church, the monarchical structure—bad popes or good ones—has protected the metaphysics. The Catholic Church has also worked out, also over centuries, both ritual and language that bring its metaphysics forward into to the world. That is, it has evolved ways of talking about metaphysics in appropriate representational modes. The metaphysics of religion is a complex matter, a difficult structure of thought.

Without Greek philosophy, this would have been impossible. John opens the door with his *Logos*. Paul, in Acts, talks to the Greeks, in Greek, at the Areopagus in Athens (Acts 17). I have long been haunted by that woman in verse 32, who heard Paul and believed him: Damaris, immortal though that single mention. Why Damaris? She is one tiny but large figure in history. I would like to talk with her. Formulations about Things Unseen become possible through logic, beginning with the facts of scripture.

One titanic battle occurred during the second half of the third century between Clement of Alexandria on the one side and the "fundamentalist" Tertullian on the other. Tertullian famously said, "What, indeed, has Athens to do with Jerusalem?" The ecclesiastical party of Clement won, however, making way for the Christian assimilation of Greek thought, implicitly of philosophy and science.[4] The tension between Things Seen and Things Unseen, forever present, was contained in the West, and the claims of both recognized. One fateful consequence was that science and philosophy were institutionalized in the great medieval universities. Within Islam, clergy continued to have a monopoly, the intellectual heirs of Tertullian. Mohammed did not know that the question had been settled by Clement, very unfortunately for Islam. Using Aristotelian logic, Aquinas later refuted the Latin followers of the Islamic philosopher Averroes, who mistakenly thought he had advocated a "double truth," one truth in religion and another truth in science. No, said Aquinas in *Summa Contra Gentiles*, a thing cannot be true and false at the same time. Paul had known that, in I Corinthians 15: "If Christ has not been raised, our preaching is vain, and so is your faith."

CLEARLY, WHEN WITTGENSTEIN reached the wall of his bottle, what he lacked was a language with which to talk about his *Mystiches* and *Hocheres*. For him, there was nothing but silence out there. Perhaps we can say that the roots of the religious crisis of our age lie in the absence now of a shared representation of what lies outside the bottle. Empiricism is natural to us; and what we cannot talk about through representation remains unreal, difficult to conceive. Still, that about which we cannot speak may be the most important thing of all.

Outside of its theology, the West developed a great many ways of representing Things Unseen, in all the branches of Art. The great figures in Renaissance religious painting—the Creation, for example—are representations of the unseeable. As are the major figures in *Paradise Lost*, and everything in Dante's vast *Commedia* beyond the first few lines. People once were accustomed to analogy and representation as portals to the Unseen.

The representations in the Apostles Creed took hundreds of years to develop fully, every word important and precise, the process beginning very early, tradition attributing it to the Twelve Apostles themselves. The ordinary parishioner, reciting it regularly, may internalize it as a kind of prayer, but should realize what a grand crystallization of metaphysics it represents:

> I believe in God, the Father Almighty,
> > the Creator of heaven and earth,
> > and in Jesus Christ, His only Son, our Lord:
> Who was conceived of the Holy Spirit,
> > born of the Virgin Mary,
> > suffered under Pontius Pilate,
> > was crucified, died, and was buried.
> He descended into hell.
> The third day He arose again from the dead.
> He ascended into heaven
> > and sits at the right hand of God the Father Almighty,
> > whence He shall come to judge the living and the dead.
> I believe in the Holy Spirit, the holy catholic church,
> > the communion of saints,
> > the forgiveness of sins,
> > the resurrection of the body,
> > and the life everlasting.
> Amen.

It would be valuable if the ordinary worshipper knew what an enormous effort it has taken to put this in final form, based on scripture or logical derivations from scripture. The worshipper would realize how firmly based the faith articulated there really is, the extent to which the Catholic is not naked before the winds of empiricism and fashion. The "faith" is not based on, and is not shaken by, emotion. Of course, no individual can do all the work of reference and derivation alone; and the long process of refining the form of the creed would make many plots for a novel, as set forth here.[5]

The ritual of the Mass constitutes another form of representation, the Eucharist bringing together the Seen and the Unseen.

During the seventeenth century, the Church of England possessed a comparable theology, ritual, and representation, as set forth in Hooker's *Laws of Ecclesiastical Polity.*[6] But the Church of England lacked a central authority, provided by even the worst Popes, to preserve the results of centuries of theology. Within Protestantism, as Matthew Arnold said, the final authority is "individual judgment," that is, a utopian hope that the individual will do the work of two millennia of thought.

TRAGEDY ALWAYS LURKS, however, and the Catholic Church has sometimes crashed into the rocks when it addressed the realm of Things Seen. Evidence of this was shown by *National Review*'s comments on the faulty natural law foundation of *Humanae Vitae*. Since the early Renaissance the church has tried, and failed, to crystallize permanent rules in the realm of Things Seen, as well as Unseen. But in the realm of time and space *change* is the rule. Scientific discovery and advances in technology interact with social and economic change to create the environments in which people make choices. Some general tendencies are universal: pride goes before a fall (Proverbs), and those who would be angels end as beasts (Pascal). The Ten Commandments are transcultural: who can suppose a society functioning otherwise. But historically, efforts to achieve fixed rules in the always-changing realm of time and space have produced intellectual scandal after scandal for the church, defying as it repeatedly did the standards of truth and experience.

It seems clear in considering church ethical teaching that the ethics of the present and past seem "natural," while the new seems "unnatural." The early Renaissance church disapproved of interest-taking, thus taking its bearing from landed wealth. But interest-taking was essential for banking, investment, and a spreading new capitalism. The church created a false analogy: material money cannot grow like an organic form. But money is number, not organic, more like arithmetic than cell growth, and can be added, multiplied, squared, and so on.

The church also preferred the old Ptolemaic astronomy, which had provided a comfortable system of analogies, everything revolving around the earth, God's creation, as in the state everything revolved around the monarch. The church resisted one requirement for medical progress after another—cadaver dissection, hobbling an understanding of the body; smallpox vaccine, which was condemned as "unnatural"; and today, embryonic stem cell research. It developed a "just war" doctrine irrelevant to modern warfare, where the distinction between soldier and civilian collapses because of the role of assembly-line and laboratory. We would have assassinated Heisenberg if we could have done so: he might have given Hitler the Bomb. In "postmodern," asymmetrical warfare, civilians become a shield or constitute recruiting pools for terrorists. Of course "civilians" become targets—because they are no longer civilians.

With his encyclical *Humanae Vitae*, Pope Paul VI condemned artificial birth control, on the natural law theory that the purpose of sex is reproduction. *National Review*'s editorial (August 13, 1968) was especially severe on this, and rightly so:

> His arguments are all made from the philosophy of natural law; and from a particularly circumscribed statement of natural law . . . "the mission of generating life is not to be exposed to the arbitrary will of men." This is a view not only opposed by most modern schools of philosophy (including some Catholic natural law philosophers), but contrary to all modern experience. . . . The Pope seems almost to despair of the world, and to call, through the darkness, for a small remnant of the just to give witness with him before they go under.

The premise that reproduction is the purpose of sex is contradicted by all experience, not especially or only modern—though the reproductive function was once especially urgent under conditions of high infant mortality.

Sex has to do with many purposes, none of which is frustrated by birth control: intimacy, shared pleasure, pleasing the loved one, mutual approval, and a myriad more. The Pope seems to think mankind sunk in sexual profligacy, and shows no confidence in human judgment, nor in natural reason—which may not be perfect, but also which traditional Catholic philosophy did not deny. Rather than enhancing or even shoring up papal authority, *Humanae Vitae* further diminished it, surveys showing that the behavior of Catholics on birth control differed from that of other groups not by religion but according to social class and education. Many priests refuse to hear about birth control in confession.

In its sex-related pronouncements, the church has seemed acutely unaware of the social shift in the position of women toward greater independence. As Diana Trilling once said, the women's revolution has been the only successful twentieth-century revolution. Modern women do not live in extended rural families, self-sustaining through family labor, but enter the professions, business, and the military.

Of course the church opposes abortion, even the destruction of a single fertilized cell. But while most women recoil from abortion with varying degrees of regret and remorse, it seems safe to say that the church's absolute condemnation would never command a deliberate-sense majority of Americans, as based on experience. It does not do so even in Catholic nations.

During the Cold War, *National Review* was constantly at odds with the Vatican and the American Catholic bishops, running editorials with such titles as "Bishops Take a Dive," "Catholic Bishops a Great Problem," and "The Treason of the Clerics." Favored by many bishops, the "nuclear freeze" would not have restrained the Soviets at all.

It may be that instead of seeking a static natural law analogy, let alone a foolish harmony with political fashion, as the American bishops too often seemed to do, a sounder guide to morality might be William James's philosophy of experience, suitable for the changing landscape of Things Seen and lived in—an emphasis on experience, which is implicitly the foundation of American deliberate-sense government. The validity of a principle of behavior would be tested by its effects.

For example, to be a Don Giovanni must require an extraordinary hardness of heart, an anaesthetizing of the capacity really to *see* an individual woman, and thus such behavior becomes a form of self-damnation for a man who is not already a zombie. The proud, angry, lazy, gluttonous, and the avaricious are self-punished, the worst punishment being when they do not recognize their self-distortions. Blindly, they lose the world, at least to varying degrees. This amounts to the spiritual mechanics of Dante's *Inferno* and, indeed, of all the greatest literature.

Basic to all ethics must be the question of what kind of person I want to be—Henry V or Iago? Portia or Shylock? Lear at the beginning, or when he knows Cordelia at the end? I myself am certain that the hidden voice of Shakespeare can be heard throughout his great plays, heard, to use Eliot's phrase, "in the stillness between two waves of the sea." It is the voice, as Ben Jonson said in his famous elegy, of "gentle Will." The innermost being of the person can pursue modes of seeing—the actual woman herself, or as an object lied to or lied about, or some other object, stolen from or sneered at. The pursuit of really seeing the world with a clear lens, a pursuit of perfection, as the Sermon on the Mount knew, is bound to fall short, but is always available in some version, and available for everyone. Nor does it rule out law enforcement, or war, as prudence requires, when all else fails.

10

JFK: The Nightingale's Song

> *"Thou wast not born for death, immortal Bird! . . .*
> *Fled is that music:—Do I wake or sleep?"*
>   —John Keats, "Ode to a Nightingale"

We now know from Thurston Clarke's luminous *Ask Not* (2004) that John F. Kennedy's inaugural address, usually attributed to his speechwriter Ted Sorensen, was in its most important parts written by Kennedy himself. He contributed a great deal to the speech during a flight from Washington to Palm Beach ten days before he delivered it, as demonstrated by the shorthand notes taken by his secretary Evelyn Lincoln. The well-remembered passages reflected his own experience and that of his generation. Among his own words are these:

> Let the word go forth to friend and foe alike that the torch has passed to a new generation of Americans—born in this century, tempered in war, disciplined by a hard and bitter peace, proud of our ancient and bitter heritage."

This reflects Kennedy's experience in the Pacific, the death in Europe of his old-er brother, his visit to a ruined Berlin in 1945. The experience of his generation also shines through in the often imitated "And so, my fellow Americans, ask not what your country can do for you; ask what you can do for your country."

In 1960, Kennedy ran not only against Nixon, but against Eisenhower, a president from an earlier generation; Kennedy, young and vigorous, would "get the country moving again." *National Review* appreciated John F. Kennedy's charm, his eloquence, his self-confidence, the overall style of the Kennedy phenomenon. Yet *NR* also cast a critical eye on his achievements, especially in foreign policy. With Kennedy, the style rises far above any concrete accomplishments. So much of what people remember about Kennedy was an illusion: the health and vigor he projected in the 1960 campaign, the soaring rhetoric of that hour of hope. "Let the torch pass to a new generation. . . ." This was all rhetoric, the reality very different.

Delivering a lecture at Dartmouth during the summer of 2004, historian Robert Dallek observed that the Kennedy myth far outruns the reality: the heroic young president, the beautiful wife, the lovely family, the too-early death by assassination. One might add that the myth has been symbolized by the perpetual Pentecostal flame over his grave at Arlington. Yet with the power of imagination, the myth has become a reality, a presence: Keats's Nightingale. "Thou wast not born for death, immortal Bird!"

National Review itself, especially James Burnham, a former professor of philosophy and aesthetics, sometimes rose toward lyrical prose in contemplating Kennedy's aesthetic dimension. But that prose almost always contained, importantly, hints of skepticism.

"THE PRESS GOT IT wrong again—President-elect Kennedy did not call on Vice President Nixon at Key Biscayne to congratulate him on the Campaign he had made but to thank him for it." So commented *National Review* in its lead editorial paragraph for December 2, 1960. Nixon's campaign had a multitude of flaws, Nixon himself being one, another being the Republican Party, at least as he conceived it. Nixon often mused aloud, "You can't win without the conservatives. But you can't win with just the conservatives." His solution was ambiguity, but leaning liberal. This made him appear devious, especially since he practiced ambiguity badly—that is, too visibly. Nixon also remained in awe of the New Deal coalition, even though by 1948 it had shown early signs of disintegration.

In *National Review* Richard Whalen considered Nixon's autobiographical *Six Crises* (1962) and produced from it many examples of Nixon's trademark radiation of phoniness. Whalen cites, for example, a scene between Nixon and his favorite daughter Julie that one hopes is bad fiction. Nixon had just lost his narrow race to Kennedy, had been up until 4 a.m. election morning, and had slept for only two hours. Julie talks with him at breakfast. She mentions the thought that religion had played a role in her father's defeat. The reader of course knows that religion did play an important role, in a close election probably electing Kennedy. Decency might have impelled a father to discuss this truth. But, as Mr. Whalen remarks, "Nixon wouldn't consider disparagement of democracy and countered by invoking the names and faiths of Julie's best friends." Yes, we are supposed to think that Julie's "best friends" exhibit a variety of religions, pleasant thought. Whalen quotes from the book:

> "So you see, Julie," I said, "it isn't a question of a man's religion when he decides to vote for you or against you. It is whether he believes in you and respects you as an individual."
>
> She did not answer for a moment after I had finished. Finally she said, "I think I understand, Daddy," then, "Well, maybe we didn't win in the election, but we won in the hearts of the people."

With that, Nixon writes, he "wept manfully, telling Julie it was hay fever." Beyond satire, this is Nixon in his Dick-Do-Right mode. Of course, Nixon knew very well how the Catholic issue had counted doubly against him: one, you could vote for Kennedy as a fellow Catholic, but two, if you voted against him because he was a Catholic, you were a bigot. What he probably did not know was that this point had been made in a memo circulated by Kennedy's men in favor of his nomination.

National Review in 1960 could not swallow its comprehensive distaste for Nixon and so endorsed neither candidate. Still, Burnham and others on the masthead voted for him. Nixon remembered that 1960 *National Review* neutrality in October 1965 when he let slip the remark to columnists

Evans and Novak that "the Birchers could be handled but the real menace to the Republican Party came from the Buckleyites." His young aide Patrick Buchanan had to hurry to damage control.[1]

KENNEDY'S CHARISMA, a kinetic and no doubt erotic as well as aristocratic charm, brought women screaming to his motorcades and gave him a huge personal appeal beyond anything Nixon could offer. Nixon was aware of, and resented, that unearned personal attractiveness, the showy youthfulness and vigor, the inbred self-assurance that was smilingly allowed to touch arrogance. Kennedy's assets began to come to wide attention in the first televised debate and the contrast was devastating to Nixon, one commentator saying that Nixon had looked like a sinister chipmunk.

During the summer of 1963, while Kennedy was making a glamorous tour of Europe, James Burnham celebrated just those qualities which seemed so impressive, so *right*:

> Kennedy was setting forth not to negotiate with other heads of government, but to make a grand campaign tour in his contest with President De Gaulle. It is the sort of thing Mr. Kennedy likes to do, and what he does best.

Do not discount the cool Burnham smile in "what he does best." He continues:

> And the President's public performance [N.B.], the lines as well as the gestures, were four-star. At Frankfurt he delivered a splendid speech on the independence of the Atlantic world and the unity of the West. In Berlin his mere presence was compelling enough to pull Khrushchev right out of his Kremlin to the other side of the Wall. The busy pulse-takers were able to report that along the Boulevards, in every airport, square and hall, he outdrew his lofty opponent.

Here we see the use of nouns, not so much for verisimilitude as for suggestion of sweep and power: "along the Boulevards, in every airport, square and hall." But then comes a dose of assessment: "Can anyone show that a single significant change in the course of events has been brought about by one, or all, of these traveling circuses?" The rise-and-fall movement there is beautiful.

Upon Kennedy's assassination in November 1963, Burnham returned editorially to the president's glamour and attractiveness, and did so not merely to reinforce his expression of genuine grief:

> The grief was spontaneous, and, in most cases, wholly sincere. Not because Mr. Kennedy's policies were universally beloved, but because he was a man so intensely charming, whose personal vigor and robust enjoyment of life so invigorated almost all who beheld him. The metabolism of the whole nation rose on account of the fairyland quality of the First Family. After all, no divine typecaster could have done better than to get JFK to play JFK, Jackie to play First Lady, and the children to play themselves.

The language of theater, of divine director and casting, was wholly appropriate. Of course, much politics *is* theater and appearance, but the Kennedy performance brought it to a new perfection, concealing as it did the truth about his medical condition and much else. Eisenhower had used a mask of paternal benevolence to conceal his intimidating strength and steely core; Kennedy used his youth and "vigor" to mask excruciating and life-threatening illnesses.

Both Robert Dallek and Richard Reeves have shown only recently that Kennedy was born with a vertebrae deformation that caused him intense pain throughout his life, was considered too dangerous for surgery, and sometimes required him to be laced into a supporting corset in order to walk or otherwise function. He often needed crutches and used a special rocking chair in the Oval Office. This orthopedic calamity was passed off as a war injury. He had also long suffered from a life-threatening adrenal deficiency called Addison's disease, requiring several injections each day. The disease and the injections, containing cortisone, swelled his face and turned it yellowish. This was explained as residual malaria from the war. These vital medicines were reserved for him at prearranged locations, to be always available during his extensive travels. His venereal disease, contracted as an adolescent, with which he frequently reinfected himself, produced renal problems. No sicker man had ever served as president.[2]

Thomas C. Reeves shows that beginning in 1960, the year of his campaigning on themes of youth, health, and vigor, he began treatment with a doctor, Max Jacobson of New York, a quack who had lost his license and who had a celebrity clientele among whom he was known as "Dr. Feelgood." Jacobson's potions, which involved large cortisone and amphetamine doses, had almost killed Truman Capote. Jacobson treated Kennedy in the White House and accompanied him to the June 1961 summit in Vienna with Khrushchev. Robert Kennedy became concerned about these dosages and had them analyzed by government experts, but when he told his brother that they were dangerous, Jack replied, "I don't care if it's horse piss. It works."[3]

Through the 1960 campaign and the ensuing presidency, Kennedy's seemingly idyllic marriage and family life proved a substantial political asset, yet his marriage was cursed by his frantic philandering. Like his woman-chasing father, he was most at home in Hollywood, Las Vegas, West Palm Beach, and other glitzy spas. And wherever he went, including in the residence at the White House, women were clandestinely made available. For security reasons, J. Edgar Hoover warned him off Judith Campbell Exner, a courtesan he was sharing with a Chicago Mafioso named Sam Giancana, later murdered in a mob killing. The Sinatra Rat Pack supplied Kennedy with women on the West Coast and in Las Vegas. The broken-down actor Peter Lawford, who had married into the Kennedy family, pimped for him in Hollywood. Camelot, indeed—though it is doubtful that when Jacqueline promoted the idea with Theodore White she was the least bit insincere. Still, if she had seen the musical she must have possessed a tincture of irony, since there the court of King Arthur is disgraced and ruined by sexual corruption. In a nice metaphor expressing the contradiction between appearance and reality in the Kennedy phenomenon, the music in "Camelot" is often very charming.

In fact, as Dallek makes plain, the "Camelot" aspect of the Kennedy reign was entirely the work of Jacqueline herself, and it bored Jack. But nothing resembling her Versailles-like banquet at Mount Vernon had been seen within living memory, or ever since.

THE SHIFT OF THE GLOBAL struggle from Europe—a stalemate there, backed by nuclear weapons—to the Third World had begun already during the Eisenhower administration. This new, wider conflict presented a more difficult and complicated set of problems. In the foreground for Kennedy were now not only Berlin, but the Congo, Southeast Asia, and Cuba. But in the view of Burnham's "Third World War" column, U.S. foreign policy under Kennedy was not conducted as the deliberate pursuit of a coherent national goal. It comprised, rather, most of the time, a number of different and conflicting goals pressed into a loose amalgam by such abstractions as "peace" and "democracy."

In Henry Kissinger's language, there was no "conceptual paradigm" to Kennedy's foreign policy. Thus, during the last year of his life, Kennedy sought and achieved a ban on above-ground nuclear testing. He received applause for having fostered "peace." But at the same time the Soviet Union supported revolution in Southeast Asia, Latin America, and Africa. In an editorial (August 20, 1963) Burnham asked:

> From the point of view of its American proponents [this] strategy looks both realistic and attractive, since they see it as the road to agreement between the two decisive world powers. From the point of view of the Kremlin it also looks both realistic and attractive: they see it as the best method for burying us.

National Review saw that the major foreign policy crises of the Kennedy administration possessed inner connections. The Vienna summit and the alarming deterioration of the situation in Laos occurred early and simultaneously. At Vienna, Khrushchev sized Kennedy up as weak and inexperienced, and Laos reinforced this impression, to be confirmed by Kennedy's blundering and weak handling of the Bay of Pigs affair in the spring of 1961. Before the result of that effort to topple Castro was known, *National Review* editorially defined the stakes this way:

> The decline in U.S. prestige during the Eisenhower Administration was a favorite point in Mr. Kennedy's election campaign. If President Kennedy fails now in Cuba, the Eisenhower years will come to be thought of as the Golden Age of our world reputation.
>
> We write, "If President Kennedy fails," because if the freedom fighters are smashed, it is the President who will be held responsible. But it will be the

nation, too, of course, along with the President and the slaughtered freedom fighters, that will have to suffer the catastrophic consequences. . . . Cuba is not Laos, 10,000 miles away on the enemy's border. Cuba is just ninety miles off our coast, in a sea under our domination. It is Khrushchev, not Mr. Kennedy, whose geographic and technical position is—materially—hopeless.

When the invasion was crushed, the magazine analyzed the reason:

The invasion of Cochinos Bay did not presuppose a mass uprising of the cowed Cuban population against a bristling militia backed by a highly mechanized army; but rather the maintenance of a protective air umbrella over the small landing force. *The last-minute decision to deny the patriots this basic component shattered the entire project.* [italics added]

A genuine beachhead, to have been followed by a landing of the provisional Government on freed territory, diplomatic recognition by the U.S. and other anti-Communist governments, and immediate logistical and military support to the invaders, was not inconceivable. *The negative decision, obviously, was made by President Kennedy.* [italics added]

The added emphases highlight where *National Review* believed the crucial decision had been made. The public impression has been that President Kennedy was misled by the CIA and the military to believe that there would be a general uprising when the landing occurred. If Burnham and *National Review* were correct, Kennedy crumbled into a Lord Jim moment of funk and fear. Allen Dulles and others dutifully resigned to protect him.

Beyond this fatal decision, the planning and execution of the whole operation was astonishingly incompetent. The original landing point was changed, disadvantageously. Some 14,000 men would land, only 135 of them trained soldiers. The planners were aware that they would be opposed by a heavily armed force recently equipped by $50 million invested in modern weapons by the Soviets. American air support was sketchy at best. The second strike was cancelled because Kennedy was unwilling to disclose our complicity, it was said. That was an extraordinary thought. Who else would have supplied the planes, the warships, the transportation for the landing force? Only a powerful second strike from the carrier *Essex*, obviously planned, could have destroyed Castro's Soviet tanks and perhaps saved the operation by maintaining an enclave at the landing area as "Free Cuba."

In the wake of this tragic fiasco, Kennedy called a bipartisan selection of "wise men" for advice, and as a symbol of unity—among them Eisenhower. Stephen Ambrose in *Eisenhower: Soldier and President*, drawing on Eisenhower's diaries, and well worth quoting at some length, describes Ike's reaction:

> Eisenhower asked Kennedy why on earth he had not provided air cover for the invasion. Kennedy replied that "We thought that if it was learned that we were really doing this rather than those rebels the Soviets would be very apt to cause trouble in Berlin." Eisenhower gave him another long look, then said, "Mr. President, that is exactly the opposite of what would really happen. The Soviets follow their own plans, and if they see us show any weakness then is when they press the hardest. The second they see us show strength and do something on our own, then is when they are really cagey. The failure of the Bay of Pigs will embolden the Soviets to do something they would not otherwise do."[4]

Khrushchev, the smasher of Hungary, must have chortled over the Bay of Pigs imbroglio. Kennedy had been unprepared for the Bay of Pigs, and he had not prepared well for his first encounter with Khrushchev at Vienna. As *National Review* commented about that event,

> The young man who said he never would go to the Summit without adequate preparation went to the Summit last week fully prepared after two weeks of concentrated study. The warrior who said he would not talk about Laos until a cease-fire, talked about establishing a cease-fire. The President, after he had heard Mr. Khrushchev say that "no man is neutral," agreed to work for a neutral Laos.

While the discussion went on at Vienna, the Kennedy administration was beset by a deteriorating situation in Laos, where North Vietnam was bringing the nation under pressure by proxy fighters and infiltrators. *National Review* in its lead editorial paragraph on June 3, 1961, indulged in some macabre humor:

Having looked and looked for the New Frontier, we spotted it last week when negotiators foregathered to seal the fate of Laos. It's 500 miles closer to us than the Old Frontier.

The southern part of Laos, as a glance at the map indicates, is a primary route from North Vietnam through Cambodia into South Vietnam, on the way to control of the rice bowl of the fertile Mekong Delta, a principal goal of Hanoi. It was time to step up the improvement of the Ho Chi Minh Trails through the jungles, which provided excellent camouflage for infiltrators headed south. *National Review* viewed Vietnam as a theater for the implementation of the containment strategy.

During the period of visits by the "wise men" to Kennedy after the Bay of Pigs, General MacArthur, not famous for caution, made a cameo appearance to vouchsafe the president some thoughts on Vietnam. According to Thomas Reeves, he met with Kennedy in late April 1961, and following a thirty-five-minute discussion the president recorded in a memorandum: "He thinks our line [of defense] should be Japan, Formosa, and the Philippines."[5] MacArthur had been much more militant in Korea; but there we controlled the sea approaches and a line could be drawn across the peninsula. Vietnam was a sieve. MacArthur's advice was excellent, if elementary. As Napoleon had said, "Geography is destiny." In Korea there had been no infiltration routes, no amorphous small unit action in jungle and rice paddy, no opportunity for "asymmetrical" warfare, human bodies against steel. The strategy for containment was obvious in Korea. Vietnam was another thing altogether.

What Kennedy might have done in Vietnam had he lived remains a matter of debate. At the time of his death in 1963, the number of U.S. troops there had risen to 16,732. His admirers tend to think that he would have pulled out eventually. On just how he might have proceeded, they are vague. He left the problem to Johnson, who in turn left it as a poisonous legacy to Nixon.

No doubt Khrushchev had multiple reasons for his decision to install long-range ICBMs in Cuba during the spring of 1962, along with technicians and a large contingent of heavily armed Soviet troops. This was an enormous gamble, risking no less than the existence of the Soviet Union.

The wild gamble ended by costing Khrushchev his job. He must have thought he had reason to believe the risk acceptably small.

His stated reason for the missile gambit was the defense of Cuba against the United States, which indeed had attempted to overthrow Castro in the Bay of Pigs, and afterwards sponsored assassination attempts. But defense of a small distant nation did not merit ICBMs. Those, to a degree, altered the nuclear ratio in favor of the Soviets. They would have been a huge propaganda coup. They would have raised Soviet prestige immensely in the Third World political battlefield, especially in Latin America. But such incremental benefits did not come close to outweighing the risks.

As would be expected, there has been a great deal of speculation in the serious literature about Khrushchev's motives and why he evidently misjudged the risk. Khrushchev's calculation of the risks in his Cuban venture probably were importantly shaped by that first meeting with Kennedy at Vienna, by his passivity when the Berlin Wall went up, and by the fiasco at the Bay of Pigs.

We do have some direct evidence concerning Khrushchev's probable conclusions about Kennedy at Vienna. Historian Michael Beschloss has assembled some reactions from people close to Kennedy.[5] Kennedy's friend Lem Billings found that Khrushchev's bullying "absolutely shook Kennedy," and that Kennedy "had not come face to face with such evil before." Averell Harriman found Kennedy "shattered." Senator Mike Mansfield concluded that Khrushchev had regarded Kennedy as "a youngster who had a great deal to learn and not much to offer." Vice President Lyndon Johnson chortled when he told his cronies that "Khrushchev scared the little fellow dead." Khrushchev was a rough character of peasant stock, annealed in the dangerous Kremlin power struggles, and the transcripts of the summit show that Kennedy again and again permitted Khrushchev to harangue him without reply. It is difficult to believe that Khrushchev's calculations on the Cuban missile gambit were not affected by this weak performance, in addition to what he saw at the Bay of Pigs.

As everyone knows, in response to Khrushchev's ICBMs Kennedy decided on the naval blockade, demonstrating to all, especially in Latin

America, the impotence of Soviet sea power in this hemisphere, most immediately in the Caribbean. He also accorded Khrushchev some face-saving
dignity with a pledge not to invade Cuba and, secretly, a further pledge to
dismantle U.S. ICBMs in Turkey. Kennedy's deal saved Khrushchev from
himself, and everyone from disaster. *National Review* applauded editorially.

Kennedy's pledge not to invade Cuba in the future was ambiguous; he
contented himself with assassination attempts, all of them feckless. In a
final assessment of the Kennedy foreign policy legacy, reflecting on how the
situation in Vietnam would develop following the overthrow of President
Diem and his subsequent murder, Burnham once again saw things clearly.
This editorial appeared on November 19, 1963, three days before the murder of Kennedy himself:

> The socio-political process that President Kennedy initiated can be predicted
> with near certainty. The new regime, or rather succession of regimes, will
> begin disintegrating at once. Its leftward elements will inevitably make con-
> tact with the National Liberation Front (are doubtless already in contact), the
> crisis will become even louder. "Down With the Reactionary Puppets! An
> End to American intervention in Vietnamese Affairs! Peace, Independence,
> Neutrality!"

There would be no surprise in it at all for Burnham, or his readers, when in
1975 Saigon fell to the North Vietnamese army deploying billions of dollars
worth of Soviet heavy equipment.

On November 22, 1963, Lee Harvey Oswald assassinated John F.
Kennedy in Dallas, and the Spirit of the Sixties announced itself, as it were,
with a bang.

Thomas Reeves has come up with a suggestive episode that took place
not long before John Kennedy was assassinated:

> In early September 1963 the Cuban premier [Castro] talked with an Ameri-
> can reporter at a cocktail party and warned against assassination attempts. He
> stated, "We are prepared . . . to answer in kind. United States leaders should
> think that if they assist in terrorist plans to eliminate Cuban leaders, they
> themselves will not be safe."[6]

Reeves does not conclude that Lee Harvey Oswald acted under Cuban instructions, but does point out that in June 1963, a few months before this conversation in Havana, assassination attempts against Castro had increased in frequency, and that a new Cuban exile base had been set up in Guatemala.

Immediately after the Kennedy assassination, speculation swept the country, verging on certainty, to the effect that Oswald had been a right-wing fanatic. This was unfair, but not gratuitous, since right-wing fanaticism in fact was in the air and, indeed, Adlai Stevenson had recently been insulted and assaulted by a mob in Dallas. *National Review* was able without much effort to collect a number of overheated statements from usually dignified liberals blaming the "right wing."

But it soon became evident that Oswald had been a self-indoctrinated Marxist, thoroughly alienated from American society. He had defected to the Soviet Union where he married the daughter of a KGB man, had then returned to the United States with his wife Marina, switched his Marxist attachment to Castro and Cuba, and become active in the Dallas Fair Play for Cuba Committee. He had a powerful short-wave radio in his room and regularly listened to broadcasts from Havana. A bullet fired through the living room window of retired General Edwin Walker, prominent in John Birch Society activities, missed him by inches and it seems likely that, now armed with his mail-order rifle, Oswald had fired the shot.

During his brief custody in prison before being murdered himself by Jack Ruby, Oswald requested that he be represented by the Communist lawyer John Abt.

The portrait of Lee Harvey Oswald is absolutely clear. He was not a madman. He was an alienated isolate and an autodidact Communist, whose politics now attached him passionately to Castro. To him, Kennedy was a man of the right and a Cold Warrior—and in particular, an enemy of Castro who had once tried to invade Cuba. The shots he fired were political. There is much about Oswald, indeed, that was prophetic of the alienated frenzy of the Sixties.

Soon after the death of her husband, Jacqueline Kennedy phoned Theodore White from Hyannisport and asked him to see her there. He was famous for his admiring view of the candidates and presidents in his popular making-of-the-president accounts. She broached with White the idea of Camelot as a way to characterize the Kennedy White House. White wrote it up in an article for *Life* and "Camelot" caught on, a nice way of recalling the style and the brilliance of the artistic-cultural side of those White House years. This is what is remembered—not the sordidness or the absence, as *National Review* emphasized, of a coherent foreign policy. Today, polls show that a majority of Americans consider Kennedy to have been a great president, a most doubtful judgment. But the Nightingale sings in our collective memory, and the eternal flame of the spirit burns brightly at his grave in Arlington.

11

The Goldwater Revolution

"Let's draft the son of a bitch."
"What if he won't let us draft him?" somebody objected.
"Then let's draft him anyway."
— William Rusher, *The Rise of the Right*

Few sensed at the time that the nomination by the Republican Party of Senator Barry Goldwater in 1964 was a transforming event. Most commentary regarded it as an aberration. But the Goldwater candidacy marked the shift of power in the Republican Party southward, to the Old Confederacy and the Sunbelt; it simultaneously amounted to the suicide of the Eastern Establishment, which since the Civil War had regarded the Republican Party as its home.

The emerging candidacy of Goldwater also brought about a division within *National Review*. Bill Rusher was enthusiastic about the Goldwater movement, seeing it as a populist revolt; he was one of the leaders in the Draft Goldwater movement. James Burnham was cool to the movement from the outset—inevitable, perhaps, given his hope for a reformed Eastern Establishment and his sense of possibility in Nelson Rockefeller. Buckley, closer to Burnham on this, feared that Goldwater might wreck the conservative movement. He had never been an admirer of populism but had been willing to make use of it tactically, as in his backing of McCarthy. This division, muted at the time, possessed a prophetic quality concerning the future of the Republican Party, possibly one reason for the chill from both Burnham and Buckley.

Barry Goldwater, senator from Arizona, did not win the nomination in the usual way. He won at the San Francisco Convention because of the early effort, against his will, of a small group of friends who were political professionals. The key role in all this of William Rusher, publisher and senior editor at *National Review*, gave the magazine direct knowledge of what was taking place—on this score far ahead of the disbelieving media, which complacently assumed that Rockefeller would be the nominee.

Many of the conspirators had been members of the National Young Republicans. They shared two important insights: (1) Senator Goldwater was the principal conservative political figure in America now, and had been since his 1960 address at the Nixon convention. "Grow up, conservatives," Goldwater had bellowed, urging them to unite behind Nixon. (2) The Eastern Republican Establishment might now be something of a paper tiger. Population and wealth had moved south and west, along with an assortment of new industries. The California-based Bank of America could gaze evenly across the nation at Chase Manhattan. Might not the sleepy old Establishment, too confident of nominating Nelson Rockefeller, be ripe for defeat? In fact, the old elite had lost the toughness, the élan, and the energy that had built the great post–Civil War fortunes. It now seemed soft at the core. Who could really be afraid of John Lindsay, Nelson Rockefeller, or Bill Scranton? In addition, most of the conspirators, coming from the Midwest or otherwise outside the metropolitan centers, had a populist tendency, and would be pleased to wallop the Eastern (Liberal) Establishment.

FOR A CONTEMPORARY ACCOUNT by a participant in the Goldwater coup, you have to turn to the pages of *National Review*, beginning in 1961, and to Rusher's *The Rise of the Right* (1984), key parts of which had appeared in *National Review* between 1961 and 1964. In what follows we will depend to a considerable extent on firsthand reporting by Rusher, who, along with

Rep. John Ashbrook of Ohio and F. Clifton White, a political scientist from upstate New York, were very *modern* political strategists and technicians. They were the ones who organized the nomination of Goldwater. Almost before anyone else knew what was happening, they had sewn up enough delegates to win on the first ballot. The *New York Times* awoke appalled.

In *The Making of the President 1964*, Theodore White expressed his estimate of the Goldwater phenomenon as a "rendezvous with disaster." *The Rise of the Right* begs to differ: chapter six is titled "The Watershed Year: 1964." Rusher summarizes it all with clear vision:

> It is a commonplace to say that 1964 was a year of disaster for American conservatism, and of course, in one sense it was: Lyndon Johnson defeated Barry Goldwater that November by 43,126,506 votes to 25,176,799, or 61 percent to 39 percent. Goldwater carried only six states (Alabama, Arizona, Georgia, Louisiana, Mississippi, and South Carolina) with a total of fifty-two electoral votes. It was indeed, as the media proclaimed, a "landslide."
>
> But to say that, and stop there, is to overlook almost entirely the real political significance of 1964. On any serious accounting, 1964 was the most important and truly seminal year for American conservatism since the founding of *National Review* in 1955. It laid the foundations for everything that followed. Before 1964, conservatism was at best a political theory in the process of becoming a political movement; after 1964, and directly as a result of it, conservatism increasingly became the acknowledged political alternative to the regnant liberalism—almost fated, in fact, to replace it sooner or later.

The surprisingly young band of twenty-two brothers, the Goldwater nomination conspirators, first gathered at the Avenue Hotel in Chicago on October 8, 1961. They realized that something was visible out there, available to anyone—in the demographic charts, in the tables of regional per capita income, in the district-by-district voting data and other such material—but not yet seen as a political possibility. Over the telephone and through the mails, these young men pulled it all together.

They knew that the population center of the nation had shifted markedly south and west, and with it the balance of forces in the wealth of the nation. The so-called Sunbelt, even the Old Confederacy (Mencken's "Sahara of the Bozarts"), was now far from poor, in fact was experiencing rapid growth. Republicanism's center of gravity, once in Ohio and New York, was potentially shifting. Rusher says this breezily. But to put Ohio and New York—meaning the entire upper Midwest, New England, and the states down to the Mason-Dixon line—up for grabs was an astonishing idea. It sacrificed or put in jeopardy all of the old Republican base, in exchange for the southward shift. The full implications of this, including its cultural implications, are not analyzed by Rusher.

Spin the reel in reverse for a moment. A year earlier, at the 1960 Republican Convention in Chicago, Vice President Richard Nixon had arrived with enough delegates for a solid majority and the nomination, but Goldwater also had 287 delegates and friendly editorial interest from *National Review*, while Nelson Rockefeller had been sounding mutinous. To quell trouble on his liberal flank, Nixon flew to New York the weekend before the convention, met with Rockefeller in his apartment, and agreed to what was to be called the Treaty of Fifth Avenue. This included language suggesting Eisenhower's weakness on national defense and also, provocatively, praising the southern lunch-counter protest sit-ins. The solo trip by Nixon to New York, plus Rockefeller, plus the treaty, outraged a good number of Republicans in Chicago and they flirted with the idea of nominating Goldwater from the floor. Goldwater vetoed this, but gave a preview of the future when, speaking to the convention, he told his fervent supporters to "grow up, conservatives":

> We are conservatives. This great Republican Party is our historic house. This is our home. . . . I am going to devote all my time from now until November to electing Republicans from the top of the ticket to the bottom of the ticket, and I call upon my fellow Republicans to do the same.

The drumbeat of 1964 echoed in those words, and conservatives heard it. Less clear was something less welcome and less heard. Barry Goldwater was a conservative of a distinctive kind. But he was also a *Republican*. He had a profound respect for his fellow Republicans in the Senate, and for the professional party people out around the country. He would be depicted as an extremist, even a madman, but he was very deeply a party man, not in the least a revolutionary or a wrecker.

But by 1961, conservatives were organizing in the precincts, at the Young American for Freedom meeting in Sharon, Connecticut, in the Young Republicans, at *National Review*, and at the Avenue Hotel in Chicago, where the Draft Goldwater Committee met. They were "new men" in the sense of putting together available knowledge into a revolutionary opportunity not grasped elsewhere. They were anything but "primitives." In fact, they were trailblazers in terms of political techniques and the use of advanced technology. At their initial meeting in Chicago, Cliff White was easily installed as chairman. A very modern, even prophetic figure in his expertise, a leading Young Republican through the 1950s, both a theoretician and a nuts-and-bolts man, he had degrees from Colgate and was a professor of political science at Cornell and at nearby Ithaca College. He, Rusher, and Rep. John Ashbrook of Ohio had been close friends in the Young Republicans, as had many others then on hand. One important (obvious) thing they knew was, to quote Rusher:

> Republican presidential candidates are nominated . . . by [the majority of] 1300 specific and carefully chosen delegates, chosen by varying processes, not all of them highly democratic, in every state and congressional district in the country. . . . It is the historic victory of Cliff White and his colleagues in the Draft Goldwater Committee that they brought about that surrender [of control of the GOP by the "Eastern Establishment"] on the *first ballot*—and laid thereby the foundation for the ultimate victory of the conservative movement in the United States.

The members of the committee had political friends at the precinct level all over the country and, one by one, White kept track of the Goldwater delegates as the total mounted. By the time the delegates were arriving in San Francisco, White had calculated that Goldwater would win on the first ballot, with 883 votes out of 1,308. Goldwater in fact received 884. Rusher estimates that, numerically, their national organization grew larger than the expensive Rockefeller team could put together. The difference between the Goldwater team and Rockefeller's was that Goldwater's was alert and hard at work, Rockefeller's rusty and overconfident.

YET THINGS DID NOT GO smoothly for the Draft Goldwater Committee. One problem, not small, was Goldwater himself. In the September 10, 1963, issue of *National Review*, Rusher reported:

> Early supporters of Barry Goldwater will always look back on the winter of 1962–63 as their own private Valley Forge. Their man, unconvinced that the 1964 Republican nomination was worth having, sternly and publicly repudiated all efforts to promote his cause. The press blithely ignored the grassroots sentiment for the Arizona senator and, without the slightest basis in any plausible count of the likely convention line-up, all but unanimously hailed New York Governor Nelson Rockefeller as the odds-on front-runner.

Even before White's delegate totals began to approach a condition of certainty, the Draft Goldwater men had carefully considered history, recognizing the current they were swimming in to be dynamic. Rusher outlines this in an August 11, 1964, *National Review* article. What strikes one now is the detailed professional knowledge of Republican Party history:

> Under the Eisenhower Administration, the Republican Party had been more or less jointly controlled by a coalition of its liberal and centrist elements, with the latter having perhaps the larger voice. This alliance was ratified anew when Nixon, upon being nominated in 1960 [in fact before being nominated], capitulated to Rockefeller on key platform questions in their famous "Treaty of Fifth Avenue" (which Barry Goldwater promptly denounced as a "Munich"). . . .
>
> The old Dewey machine, too, which had thrice run the New York governor for the Presidency and then twice elected Eisenhower, had lost much of its potency. (Dewey and Brownell, its two key figures, had retired irrevocably to private law practice.) And, while Nixon had inherited the shards of the Dewey-Brownell organization, including one or two top-flight political operatives (notably former Attorney General Rogers), Nixon's 1960 defeat made it impossible for him to assume control of the Party again unless he could first rehabilitate his image as a winner—e.g., by election as governor of California in 1962.

Nixon had failed at this, reaching a nadir in his post-election "Last Press Conference," where, disheveled and seeming hungover, he delivered a vulgar denunciation of the press: "You won't have Nixon to kick around anymore." Now a tectonic shift was underway. Being displaced was the old Republican elite, based for generations on the wealth generated by hard men dealing in hard substances: coal, iron, steel, railroads, shipping, oil-drilling machinery. That elite, educated and refined, had run the nation, with infrequent exceptions, since Lincoln. In its latter days it looked upon the new "conservatives" with profound aversion, as, for example, did Nelson Rockefeller.

In *The Making of the President 1964*, Theodore White evokes the social texture of the passing Eastern Establishment, a marvelous thing in its way. He uses proper nouns with a loving resonance:

> It dwells, generally, on the East Side of Manhattan in the Perfumed Stockade that runs from the East Nineties south to the East Fifties and from Fifth Avenue to the river. There is, indeed, no greater assembly of executive ability, inherited wealth and opinion leadership than is domiciled in the Perfumed Stockade. Four Rockefeller brothers live here, several Whitneys, three Kennedy families, six Harrimans, half a dozen Strausses. There are Sulzbergers, Bakers, Millikens, Clarks, Sloans, Piereponts, Roosevelts—old names without number—but also an equal number of new names. Their children go to the same half-dozen Manhattan private schools (all excellent) whence they emerge, go on to boarding school, and hope to attend proper Ivy League colleges. They meet at dances, charities, art festivals, dinners, as neighbors. . . .
>
> Washington is only a half hour-away by shuttle plane, and Paris or London seven hours. The ambience of conversation and contact here is one of great affairs. All of the United Nations embassies cluster around the Perfumed Stockade; eminent visitors from abroad or from the hinterland linger longer than in Washington; many linger and stay. Three High Commissioners of Germany live here (none native to New York); two former ambassadors to England, fourteen Cabinet members of various administrations. . . . The community intermeshes a span of American life that reaches from the brightest young playwrights from Broadway (if successful) to such patriarchs as Herbert Hoover and Douglas MacArthur (born, respectively, in West Branch, Iowa, and Little Rock, Arkansas), both of whom chose to spend the end of their days in the Waldorf Towers.

The members of this cultural community of manners, wealth, influence, and understanding included Democrats and Republicans of the right sort, moving back and forth between administrations of both parties, as had Henry Cabot Lodge Jr. and Nelson Rockefeller. This elite included such "wise men" as those who had been "present at the creation" of such institutions as NATO and the Marshall Plan, essential barriers to the westward thrust of the Soviet Union: Acheson, McCloy, Lovett, Harriman, Kennan, Marshall. This old elite, as is characteristic of elites, was beautiful in many ways, as were its social and educational institutions and its manners, an American version, derived at a distance, of those of the English gentleman—understated, deferential, restrained, and unflappable. Display was frowned upon. Notoriety was worse.

But now that elite was facing a lethal challenge, or challenges, from the direction of actuality. One challenge involved a governing coalition that was shaping up based on the South and the West against the East. The band of brothers on the Draft Goldwater Committee found the prospect of such a new elite congenial. "It was to prove less so," Rusher notes in *The Rise of the Right*, "to some of my colleagues when they first became aware of it toward the end of the decade." It is easy to infer that Rusher had Buckley in mind here, as well as Burnham. *God and Man at Yale* can be read as expressing a desire to make Yale more conservative, recall it to itself. Buckley sent his son Christopher to Yale. He may have hoped to make the Eastern Establishment itself more conservative in the long run.

Perhaps in the long run the Eastern elite did become more conservative, but Buckley's loud support for McCarthy minimized at least for a while any role for him in this development. Yale long afterward did award him an honorary degree, and he was pleased to teach some courses in writing there. Unlike Rusher, he never became a rebellious populist.

But for now, the Eastern Establishment had demonstrated suicidal incapacity, helpless before the Black Revolution that was erupting in riots, property destruction, arson, and murder in urban centers across the nation. In due course, New Yorkers would exchange Yale's John Lindsay for such very different leaders as Rudy Giuliani. Nor could the Eastern Establishment, in its Perfumed Stockades, deal with or even understand the fury and agony of the blue-collar neighborhoods, for years tribal Democrats, over the court-ordered integration of their schools in the form of "busing." On top of that, the older elite could not do what was needed to protect its own institutions, the universities for example, against the youth upheavals. It appeased. It even sympathized. Collectively, the elite had lost the courage to govern, and the odor of its weakness could be sniffed on the air.

AS THE DRAFT GOLDWATER MOVEMENT accumulated delegates, the facts caught up with the reluctant candidate. Goldwater recognized the inevitable, declaring his candidacy on January 3, 1964. But in place of the astute members of the Draft Goldwater Committee, who naturally had hoped to be his campaign team, or at least a part of it, the Arizona senator cold-shouldered the conspirators and gave control to what they called the "Arizona Mafia," friends from the senator's home state with whom Goldwater felt comfortable.

Trying to divine Goldwater's motives, Rusher says that to the senator and his friends the committee must have seemed a collection of exotic samurai and esoteric thinkers: effective theoreticians, but alien. Unconsciously, I might add, he might have resented them for running him, whether he wanted to or not; and he certainly resented leaving the Senate, which he enjoyed immensely and where he was widely liked. The Arizona cronies he gathered had no national reach, no "network," no relevant experience. In the summer of 1963 the Arizonans moved to an office in Washington, most importantly Dennison Kitchell, a Phoenix attorney, and Dean Burch, a young Tucson lawyer.

Kitchell would become campaign manager. No one knew at the time, fortunately, that this genial fellow was a member of the John Birch Society, one of the numerous members who was not a crackpot about Eisenhower being a Communist. Cliff White remained as tabulator and organizer of the delegates, and manager of the San Francisco convention, which opened in the Cow Palace on July 13. Everything was downhill from that moment, until the campaign went over the precipice on November 3.

A curious and potentially damaging disconnect occurred back at the *National Review* offices in Manhattan. There had been only three primaries in the run-up to this convention. The first, in New Hampshire, had been won in a write-in by Henry Cabot Lodge Jr., who was away as ambassador in Saigon. The second, in Oregon, had been won by Rockefeller. The third, in California, was regarded by many as absolutely necessary for Goldwater. Only insiders knew that Cliff White had already rounded up enough delegates for a Goldwater nomination, and those who were told about this at *National Review* did not quite want to believe it.

But in a sense California *was* necessary, since Goldwater did need a popular victory somewhere to legitimize his candidacy and not appear merely as the beneficiary of a coup—which in fact he was. Let Bill Rusher tell the story about what happened at *National Review*:

> Just at this point occurred one of those small hitches that can spoil, at least in the beholder's eye, even the rosiest prospect. Bill Buckley somehow became convinced 1) that Goldwater might well lose the California primary (which was true), 2) that in that case he was bound to lose the nomination (which was, at that point, flatly and mathematically impossible), and 3) that accordingly, if Goldwater did lose California, *National Review* ought to call upon him [in an editorial] to pull out of the race altogether, to avoid a humiliating defeat.
>
> I don't know what led Bill to this bizarre conclusion; like most of us, he has weaknesses as well as strengths, and a sort of coarse political horse sense has never been one of his stronger suits. (He even spent a fair amount of time during the first half of 1964 on a scheme to make Dwight Eisenhower Goldwater's vice presidential running mate.)
>
> In any case I was far too deeply committed to the Goldwater candidacy—had urged too many of my friends to support it—to call for its abandonment even if it did become futile, let alone when it was trembling on the edge of triumph. Sorrowfully, I prepared to submit my resignation as publisher of *National Review* if Goldwater lost in California and the editorial [calling upon him to pull out] appeared. Luckily Goldwater won by a whisker—1,089,133 to 1,030,180—so the problem resolved itself. When he learned that I had planned to resign, Bill urged me to tell him in advance next time: "I am medium good at finding compromises on these things."

Bill Rusher's resignation would have been a tremendous loss. He was a presence. Only a novelist could express his importance to the texture of life at 35th Street and how essential he was to the success of the equation. Even his threat to resign, and the passion behind it, was part of this. I did not, could not, appreciate his worth until I became a senior editor in 1969 and began to attend the regular editorial meetings. He added a kind of astringency that helped keep things on the tracks, a lawyer's logic, perhaps, as well as the regular arguments he had, predictable as a metronome, with Burnham and Meyer. They did have substance, but they were so predictable that it became funny. He was also a gourmet, and if he recommended a restaurant, you could count on that too. The ultimate cosmopolitan, he nevertheless was one of the architects of the disaster that overtook the Establishment, which he only seemed to embody.

THE REPUBLICAN CONVENTION was at once a technical marvel and a political monstrosity, beginning Goldwater's long slide down. Cliff White had done a perfect job of gathering delegates. Within the convention hall he deployed technology and an organized team that would henceforth be a model for both parties. Bill Rusher describes it with appropriate awe:

> Previously campaign managers had operated from the convention floor itself, with leg power supplied by aides carrying messages to delegates in distant parts of the hall. At San Francisco, however, White and his regional directors were installed in a spacious air-conditioned trailer, parked just outside the rear entrance of the Cow Palace and protected against intruders by uniformed guards. From this trailer a bewildering array of multicolored wires led to telephones at seventeen locations on the convention floor itself, where state leaders of the Goldwater delegates could pass the word to the troops. In addition, the rival candidates were authorized to have a number of roving representatives equipped with walkie-talkie radios, on the floor itself.

That was order, rationality. Everything else was irrationality. A billboard in lights across from the Cow Palace set the tone. Goldwater's slogan had been, "In your heart, you know he's right." In lights against the sky the billboard read: IN YOUR GUTS, YOU KNOW HE'S NUTS. That would be the essence of the campaign against Goldwater, begun as he had campaigned in the primaries, and it continued inside the convention hall. Goldwater had too much baggage now, having talked about nuclear weapons, defoliation in Vietnam, selling off the Tennessee Valley Authority, making Social Security voluntary—floating ideas as if in his living room among friends. His views on federal enforcement of integration allowed him to be characterized as a racist, which emphatically he was not. Rather, he was a Western individualist, hostile to government impingement on individual freedoms. As Rusher remarked, he "was, and remains, a perfectly orthodox, budget-balancing, main-line Republican, whose heart beats in near-perfect accord with Gerry Ford's." He went into the convention, however, identified for much of the public as an erratic radical.

Escaping wildly from White's control, the convention as seen by the TV viewers included the galleries booing, cat-calling, and screaming at Rockefeller when he tried to speak from the podium. Then there were Goldwater's never-to-be-forgotten words, uttered defiantly in his acceptance speech. They had been suggested by Harry Jaffa, a professor of political science at Claremont Men's College and a distinguished Straussian theorist and author of the classic work on the Lincoln-Douglas debates, *Crisis of the House Divided*. Goldwater had underlined the lines in the official text. They represented his fury at being smeared as an "extremist"—that is, as a Bircher, or worse. He roared, "I would remind you that extremism in defense of liberty is no vice! And let me remind you also that moderation in the pursuit of justice is no virtue!"

It could be argued that those propositions are true, and that if Patrick Henry had uttered them, they would be in the school books. But meaning is conditioned by circumstances, and "extremism" and "moderation" had already long been given their operative definition in 1964. People might well think that Goldwater was endorsing Birchism, and certainly the Birchers thought so. The galleries screamed their approval. Liberals and moderates who loathed Goldwater probably were delighted to have their judgments confirmed.

LET RUSHER'S *Rise of the Right* sum up the importance of what had happened in San Francisco:

Only slowly, in the deep fullness of time, would [the other implications] be revealed. Even the one visible and indisputable political change that occurred during the year—the shift in control of the GOP—looked dangerously temporary and would not be perceived clearly as the solid and permanent thing it was. . . .

Although its implications were almost totally invisible at the time, one of 1964's major developments was the appearance on the national political scene of the man who would ultimately lead the conservative movement to victory: Ronald Reagan. . . .

Now, in the autumn of 1964, Reagan was California co-chairman of Citizens for Goldwater-Miller and had taped for local use a speech on behalf of Goldwater that many people were eager to see broadcast nationally. Cliff White and others in the national campaign were enthusiastic, but—almost predictably—Kitchell, Baroody, and Dean Burch's Republican National Committee were not. The issue was not pressed, however, and ultimately Goldwater himself authorized the expenditure. It proved to be the best investment of the whole campaign, because Reagan's speech (broadcast nationally on October 27) was, by almost universal agreement, a tremendous success.

It was not, to be sure, enough to elect Goldwater. But fate has a curious way of hiding its pearls in the most unlikely places, and it outdid itself on this occasion. In the last week of Barry Goldwater's doomed campaign—out of its very ashes like a phoenix—arose his successor as leader of the conservative movement.

So, there were two consequences of 1964: a shift in control of the GOP and the debut nationally of Ronald Reagan. A third, surprising at the time and thereafter, was former senator Goldwater's very early endorsement of Richard Nixon, on January 22, 1965, for the Republican nomination in 1968. But Nixon had campaigned hard for Goldwater in 1964, all over the United States. Not one other major Republican had done so—not Rockefeller, of course, but not Scranton, Romney, Javits, Lodge, not one representative of the old Establishment. Now it was payback time, and Goldwater would hold firm for Nixon all through 1968, and very importantly at the Republican Convention in Miami. In the end it meant the presidency, finally, for the battle-scarred and perhaps psychically wounded Nixon.

Looking further into the future, the Republican shift toward the South and West gave rise to two quite different tendencies within the party, one represented by Reagan, the other by George W. Bush. Both Goldwater and Reagan were Western individualists, libertarian in their leanings. Reagan did nothing serious on "social issues" during his presidency, and Goldwater, had he won in 1964, even more emphatically would have regarded abortion, for example, as not the concern of the federal government. George W. Bush, in contrast, a southern evangelical and moral authoritarian, certainly does regard many moral issues as being within the sphere of government.

Another important result of the 1964 election occurred at *National Review*. The odor of the John Birch Society had been so strong and so intolerable, and so damaging to Goldwater, that *National Review* decided that for the future of American conservatism, decisive distance had to be laid down irrevocably between the magazine and the society. An editorial titled "The Question of Robert Welch" about the bizarre fantasies of that powerful individual had run in February 1962, but that had not been enough. The distinction would now have to be made, once and for all, between a viable conservatism and the fantastic theories that energized the leadership of the JBS. This would be a major step for *National Review* toward national credibility.

12

The John Birch Society: A Menace

Today, hardly anyone remembers much about the John Birch Society and its ever-widening and fantastic conspiratorial convictions. During the early 1950s, however, the JBS became a menace to reasonable conservatives, who became suspected of craziness themselves by association. One of *National Review*'s finest exercises in political sanity was demonstrating definitively the difference between acceptable conservative convictions and those of Robert Welch.

A successful businessman in Belmont, Massachusetts, Welch was the founder and maximum leader of the society. He had been startled into re-flection by repeated Communist advances worldwide at the expense of American interests. The United States, he reasoned, was a supremely pow-erful nation. It followed—did it not?—that American reverses could only be the result of conspiracy and treason. From this, it followed ineluctably that Dwight Eisenhower had long been under Communist Party control, and that the United States government was in fact 40–60 percent similarly obedient to the Kremlin. By 1955, for obscure reasons, Welch upped the figure to 70 percent. How else could Communist success be explained? Welch published these figures in *The Politician*, a work circulated to mem-bers of the society; that work was mandatory dogma for the higher-level elect. Within this cult-like insider group, Welch exercised complete control. Similar "information," along with other material, appeared in a regular magazine: *American Opinion.*

One problem in attacking the society as a whole was that many of its ordinary members believed none of the insider nonsense. The ordinary members were likewise alarmed by the world situation and were anticommunists—decent people who wanted to *do something*. In 1965, after much reluctance, but stung by the damage allegations of Birchism had inflicted on the Goldwater candidacy, *National Review* resolved to undertake a cleansing operation.

LEADING TO THIS DECISION were a number of considerations that had matured as early as 1958. All pointed in a direction the magazine would continue to steer. By 1965, *National Review*'s tenth anniversary, subscriptions had reached 100,000, which meant an estimated 250,000 readers. At the beginning Buckley had projected a magazine that would have influence among educated readers, and he had in mind as liberal models the *New Republic* and the *Nation*. He had estimated that to reach his goal *National Review* would have to have a circulation of about 30,000. That goal had long been surpassed, and *NR*'s prominence now entailed special responsibilities.

Possessing a strategic vision for *NR*, James Burnham likewise had a sense of what the magazine should have as its goals in tone, style, and overall approach. With Whittaker Chambers, he had advocated a "practical" or "strategic" conservatism; he pursued credibility and influence. With important support from Gerhart Niemeyer, he worked to make *National Review* more aware of its responsibility to seriousness. Niemeyer was a professor of political science at Notre Dame, an expert on Eric Voegelin, and a theoretician in the mode of Leo Strauss or Willmoore Kendall. His writing appeared in the *Review of Politics* and other professional journals. His contributions to *NR* added philosophical depth to the magazine.

Early in 1958, Niemeyer wrote a memorandum to Buckley counseling that the magazine cease sounding as if it represented an embattled outsider position. Two years later Burnham elaborated on the points Niemeyer had made, giving them added force because of the passage of time, increasing circulation, and Burnham's influence at the magazine. Niemeyer had summed up *National Review*'s message as follows:

1. Liberals are in power.
2. Conservatives are out of power.
3. Liberals form a solid block of people with fairly and basically unchangeable views.
4. Conservatives are also a group with fairly consistent and clearly identifiable views.
5. Conservatives have no prospect of coming to power or directing the course of events in our lifetime.

Those points were not exhaustive of *National Review*'s message, and one would have to qualify them for accuracy. But they were correct in saying that the magazine spoke with the voice of a saving remnant, expressing a marginalized attitude. Such a stance fostered, not incidentally, institutional high spirits. But Niemeyer argued that this attitude would become self-fulfilling, to some degree ensuring that conservatives would never gain real power in America, and it tended to make liberals even more united against *National Review*.

Burnham included Niemeyer's memorandum in his own 1960 communication to Buckley, the same year he unsuccessfully urged the magazine to support Nixon against Kennedy. Burnham now argued that during its first five years of existence *National Review* had achieved most of its initial goals, had become the recognized voice of American conservatism, and had represented a variety of the assorted themes within that position. He put the choices in colorful terms, but these were deliberately opaque and needed analysis—a fine example of Burnham's diplomatic indirectness:

> Now I suspect that you are inwardly divided on the choice between a sectarian stand—or the bayou—and the main stream. To be the honored, responsible, and enlightening leader of a . . . sect (I use this word in default of a better) is a sympathetic role in many ways; and a career of heroic size if the

seeming side channel is in truth the main stream, and if the deviating bulk of the flood will some day—as if of its own accord—burst back into the home bed. And maybe it is so. Maybe it is enough to lecture history from the bank. But it may also be necessary to wade further into the mud.

Burnham's language was purposeful, but—as suited a philosopher once specializing in aesthetics, or, indeed, as an old Trotskyite faction fighter—suggestive without being directly offensive to colleagues, such as Frank Meyer, whom he considered sectarians. Burnham's "bayou," for example, has fun with the southern or Agrarian aspect of *National Review*. That position was, he implied, not only a "side channel," but—perhaps?—silly. The term "sect," as he twice uses it here, has negative connotations, despite its accompanying honorific adjectives: "sympathetic," "heroic."

The "flood" metaphor is also suggestive, but difficult. What is the nature of the "side channel" if it "bursts back" into "the home bed"? Does it displace liberalism? Does it absorb it? Is liberalism even the "home bed"? What does "wade further out into the mud" mean? And for that matter, what about "further?" Had the magazine already waded into the mud? Whatever advice all this represents, such a venture into the "mud" seems necessary to follow it.

The upshot of the memorandum was, agreeing with Niemeyer, that the manners of *National Review* should be more mainstream, thus indicating that the magazine itself was ready to play a mainstream role. Characterizing the course he was advocating as practically "mud" might appease his adversaries, the dogmatists. There *are* choices available for the magazine—available if it tilts strongly against the "purists," that is, against Meyer, Rusher, Bozell, Rickenbacker, the "paradigm" men. In effect, the memo endorsed the direction which Burnham had already chosen. Still, it contained nothing insulting to the others. In the context of the John Birch Society war, Burnham was a hawk. He wanted to bomb it.

BEFORE THE FULL-BLOWN assault of October 19, 1965, there had also been, in 1962, one cautious but, one might have thought, adequate attempt to distance *National Review* from the JBS. The names of people friendly to or even associated with the magazine had begun to turn up connected in various ways with the society. They included, on its national council, Spruille Braden, Adolphe Menjou, Clarence Manion, and Revilo Oliver. Except for Oliver, it was highly unlikely that any of these people credited the baroque reasonings of Robert Welch, or had even heard of them. It turned out that Oliver, sound in his field, was indeed among the true believers; a fine portrait of him, indeed a *rara avis*, appears in Buckley's novel *Getting It Right* (2003). William Schlamm, a founder but long since gone from the magazine, and Medford Evans, an occasional contributor, were on the board of Welch's *American Opinion.*[1] It was coming to light that rank-and-file members of the society at state and local levels included two congressmen and a state senator. In Young Americans for Freedom, the Birch Society was playing rule-or-ruin factional politics, and New York Republicans were using Birch Society allegations to smear the nascent New York Conservative Party— like YAF, an organization Buckley had helped to found.

Nevertheless, Buckley's 1962 editorial ran into opposition at the office. Burnham and Priscilla Buckley favored it, while Rusher, Meyer, Bozell, and the new senior editor Bill Rickenbacker opposed. They argued that attacking the JBS would cause a distracting faction fight on the right, that there would be cancellations of subscriptions and loss of advertising and contributions to the annual fund drive, and that many JBS members did not endorse Welch's fantasies. Nevertheless, the decision was made to run the editorial. Buckley's "The Question of Robert Welch" ran on February 13, 1962, at extraordinary length, covering pages 64 through 88. As its title indicates, it focused on Welch and otherwise employed as gentle a tone as possible, concluding that "Mr. Welch has revived in men the spirit of patriotism, and that spirit now calls for rejecting, out of love of country, his false counsels."

The magazine did lose some financial support and some subscriptions, but not to the extent that had been feared. After the editorial appeared, the magazine's most generous supporter expressed deep regret but promised to continue his support. Between 1962 and 1965, however, there intervened the Goldwater phenomenon, accompanied by charges of "extremism" and "Birchism," persuading the editors that more was needed.

NATIONAL REVIEW CAME FORWARD with a root-and-branch attack in the October 19, 1965, issue, titled "The John Birch Society and the Conservative Movement," a special section bringing together columns by those antipodal figures, Burnham and Meyer, representing different strands of the conservative movement, and containing endorsement letters from retired admiral Arthur Radford, Senator John Tower, then-prominent California conservative Joseph Schell, Russell Kirk, and, of special importance, former senator Barry Goldwater. Here, to give an impression of the whole, are the contents of the special section: "1) The Background; 2) Three Columns; 3) The John Birch Society; 4) Get Us out!; 5) Questions and Answers; 6) Commentary." Such was the material in the section, covering pages 914 through 929 of the issue. The section was attributed to "The Editors of *National Review*," embracing all factions.

We will look first at the opening salvo, the first long paragraph in "The Background." Unlike the 1962 editorial, which is polite, this one is an act of war, and it takes no prisoners:

> In the opinion of the editors, the time has come to look once more at the John Birch Society and evaluate its role in the current American political scene. There are several reasons why the moment is now. 1) The Society is very plainly the beneficiary of the distress that has ensued on the defeat of Senator Goldwater in his race for the Presidency last year. Enormous sums of money are pouring into the Society, which money is being spent—or a great deal of it—in cultivating points of view whose bearing on the anti-Communist struggle is harmful. 2) The Society has launched a great campaign to conscript new membership. The materials being used in that campaign are disingenuous. One Sunday supplement, for instance, published in many major cities of the United States, carried a picture of Dwight Eisenhower, with a text that seemed to say that Dwight Eisenhower approves of the John Birch Society. (It continues to be the belief of Mr. Robert Welch, the Society's founder and plenipotentiary executive head, that Dwight Eisenhower is a Communist.) 3) The Society, as witness Mr. Welch's single most important publication in any given year, the annual "Scoreboard" issue of *American Opinion* published every summer, seems to have reached, this summer, a new virulence, a new level of panic. That issue of the Scoreboard (see below) concludes that at this point the United States is "60–80 per cent" Communist domi-

nated. 4) Political contests of major significance are coming up involving important anti-Communist conservatives—for instance, Senator John Tower's campaign in Texas, and Ronald Reagan's campaign for the governorship of California—in which the John Birch Society will figure. It is important to win victories in Texas and California—and elsewhere; and important, therefore, to raise the question of whether the activities of Mr. Robert Welch and some of the members of the John Birch Society are at the margin helpful to such men as Tower or Reagan, or hurtful to them. And 5) the President of the United States is engaged in anti-Communist action in Southeast Asia, and for that reason is under great pressure from the American Left. But he is also, astoundingly, under pressure from a segment of the American Right—which has been taught by Mr. Robert Welch that apparent anti-Communist action undertaken by the government of the United States cannot really be anti-Communist for the reason that our government is controlled by Communists. Such reasoning, depriving us as it does of the benefits of public support by conservatives for anti-Communist action when it does occur, needs to be analyzed and resisted.

What followed in the special section were three nationally syndicated "On The Right" columns by Buckley, one closely following the other in August 1965: August 5, August 17, August 21. As a unit, these were a powerful analytical statement reaching a nationwide audience of newspaper readers. After that came an expanded "Principles and Heresies" column by Frank Meyer, then a "Third World War" column by James Burnham titled "Get Us Out!" exploring the weird alchemy according to which the Birch movement had transformed an international struggle against communism on the march into a domestic struggle in favor of isolationism against a U.S. government dominated by Communists.

There followed a section of "Questions and Answers" that might reasonably be put forth, such as: "How do you account for the fact that *The Politician* was never reviewed, not by a single newspaper or magazine in the country?" The answer: "Because not a single newspaper or magazine in this country believed the thesis that Eisenhower—*The Politician*—was a Communist worth even considering." Finally came letters of agreement and endorsement.

A magazine could do no more. *National Review* had nailed to the mast the distinction between American conservatives and Welchites. It was done.

No mistakes were possible. Self-serving obfuscations would be obvious. A year later, in 1966, when Ronald Reagan ran successfully for governor of California, he would be asked about his support from the John Birch Society. He could relaxedly reply, "I don't care. They can support me. I don't support them."

National Review had come together and begun to consolidate a prudential, effective conservatism, supporting, in Buckley's formulation, "the most rightward electable candidate." That was a definition of mainstream. *National Review* would try to follow intellect. James Burnham was where he wanted to be—advancing a politics of reality. Richard Nixon much later remarked in conversation that only Buckley could have handled the Birch problem so effectively.

13

Farewell, Willmoore

Willmoore Kendall died in June 1967 while leading the innovative Ph.D. program he had devised at the University of Dallas, a combined study of political theory, philosophy, and literature. At the time of his death, his published work did not reflect his great gifts. He had disbursed his efforts through a mammoth correspondence, marginal quarrels, strange escapades, and other distractions. Posthumous publication awaited two important books, his *Basic Symbols of the American Political Tradition* and his translation of, and introduction to, Rousseau's *Government of Poland*. The latter substantially revises our opinion of Rousseau, no small achievement. Most of his extensive correspondence awaits editing and publication, perhaps the equivalent of several more books. His lasting fascination as a personality and as a teacher is testified to by his appearance in Saul Bellow's *Mosby's Memoirs* and in Buckley's *Redhunter*.

He left *National Review* in 1963 under—typically—exacerbated circumstances. By that time James Burnham had gradually assumed more authority among the senior editors, and in effect had become Buckley's deputy, he and Priscilla Buckley responsible for most of the regular editorial tasks. Meyer had taken his place as Books editor, apparently without objection. After the buy-out of his tenure at Yale, Kendall had joined the faculty of the young University of Dallas.

Between 1959 and 1961 friction arose between Kendall and *National Review*—or rather, more friction than usual. Kendall sent in occasional articles, sometimes from Spain, and bridled at minor revisions, even threatening resignation. To be sure, he was an original and careful stylist, yet such revisions should not have evoked the threat of resignation. At the fall 1963 regular senior editors' meeting, the idea found favor of making Kendall a contributing rather than a senior editor, which seemed justified in light of his erratic contributions and minimal personal participation. When Buckley wrote to him broaching this idea, Kendall—clearly regarding this as insubordination on Buckley's part—wrote back and resigned, calling his demotion an "honor."[1]

Even from a distance, the reasons for this acrimony seem clear. Along with Burnham, both William Schlamm, virtually a cofounder of *National Review*, and Kendall, Buckley's most influential professor at Yale, had been with the magazine since its beginning. They all had reason to consider themselves not only older and more experienced but also more learned than Buckley. First Schlamm, and then, evidently, Kendall resented their inferiority to Buckley in the running of the magazine.

Kendall, I later concluded, had wanted to be *the* theoretician of the American conservative movement, and on the road to that goal, the theoretical impresario of *National Review*. He regarded Burnham as highly intelligent, but his *realpolitik* as of limited application. He thought of Meyer, Kirk, Bozell, and others as irrelevant—and Rickenbacker as silly. Burnham, in contrast to Schlamm and Kendall, was content, indeed seemed delighted, to have Buckley as benign monarch. He stayed, and had an enormous influence on the magazine.

I mentioned that I shortly gained a good deal of personal knowledge of Kendall, whom I found to be excellent if remarkable company, and he still is influential in my own thinking. He probably was the most original and adventurous thinker on the magazine, and his posthumous books are a continuing influence. It was only at the very end, in our final friendship, that I saw directly his darker side, related to his hopeless ambition to take the lead role in the intellectual shaping of American conservatism. This is a fascinating story, appropriate here chronologically in this narrative as we approach 1967, the year of his premature death.

CIRCUMSTANCES HAD ARRANGED that both Kendall and I were in Europe during 1965–66, he in Paris working on his *Rousseau*, I on leave from Dartmouth with a research fellowship to work on a book about Burke. I had admired Kendall's work in *National Review* and had written about his ideas in *An American Dissent*, a forthcoming account of ten years of *National Review*. I had even written to him at the magazine, unaware of his resignation. Finally, I had decided to spend the summer of 1965 on the Spanish Mediterranean coast and arranged to visit him in Paris on my trip back across France in the fall.

It was a leisurely Volkswagen drive up from green and ochre Catalonia through the border town of Portbou (where the Marxist critic Walter Benjamin, escaping from the Nazis, had committed suicide or perhaps been murdered by Stalin's agents) and across France to Paris where I had a sort of appointment to meet Kendall. I knew that he was an exceptional political theorist. But he turned out to be the most drastic personality I have ever met. I had never met Nietzsche, of course, or Thorstein Veblen, or Charles Sanders Peirce, who had disgraced himself at Harvard, spoiling an experiment by Charles Eliot, a chemist, as a practical joke. As Harvard's president, Eliot made sure Peirce became unemployable in the academy.

As I drove across France I was aware of the Kendall legend: a very young Rhodes Scholar, a disciple of Leo Strauss, author of an important book on John Locke, the debacles at Yale and at *National Review*. Arriving in the City of Light and Revolutions, I managed to find his address in Meudon-Bellevue, a working-class suburb in what is known as the "Red belt," not necessarily for its brothels but for its communism. This was not exactly a slum, but close.

What answered his doorbell was a tall, gray-haired man in a sleeveless T-shirt, dirty khakis, and sneakers without socks. His hangover, obviously, was of cosmic proportions. He mumbled that we should meet later for dinner at a certain Greek restaurant on the Left bank. I doubted that he would be able to show up.

Nonetheless, he arrived transformed—shaved now, wearing a gorgeous blue-gray Harris Tweed jacket and a black turtleneck. He would have been at home at Maxim's or Wimbledon. We sat at an outside table under a blue-and-white striped awning, and first he chatted with the *maitre d'* in perfect French. We sipped cocktails. When the waiter arrived, he ordered for us from among his favorite Greek and French dishes, plus a bottle of white wine. Henry James would have loved him. His work on Rousseau was going well, he said. It was to be an edition of Rousseau's recommendations for a Polish constitution, important for a window on Rousseau's actual politics. The *Social Contract* was not the whole story. The *Poland* was important for majority-rule theory. He was sure that I did not believe all that nonsense about Rousseau from Irving Babbitt and Kirk. I was working on Burke? Burke and Rousseau were in theoretical agreement on many important matters. (Much later, I found out he was right.) Rousseau, he thought, was an incomparable political theorist.[1]

He poured himself another glass of wine. "Right over there," he said, pointing across the wide street, "once stood one of the great monasteries of Cluniac reform—a stop on the pilgrimages down this road to the shrine of Santiago de Compostela in Spain. Those pilgrimages were central events of the Middle Ages, like Chaucer's pilgrimage to the shrine of St. Thomas à Becket at Canterbury." I knew that he was a Catholic convert. He said that the historical role of the church was to keep reminding the West of what it essentially is, despite barbarians, Vikings, Moors, and heresies. He had two annulments going through the Rota simultaneously. Was this a first?

We enjoyed that late summer evening there at that Greek restaurant. There could have been no more civilized host than Willmoore Kendall. He spoke of his new Ph.D. program at Dallas. Had I realized that Camus' novel *The Plague* is a perfect illustration of Rousseau's political theory? No, I had not. I told him I had a book about *National Review* and contemporary political thought in America going through the press at Doubleday. There was a chapter on Willmoore. He eagerly asked to see the galleys when they were available. He wanted to see whether I got his "teaching," as he called it, right. We gossiped. He could be wicked. About Cleanth Brooks, he said, "Cleanth is always the next most conservative person in any room."

About Frank Meyer and Russell Kirk, he said, "Nothing they write has anything to do with America." He thought Buckley "devoured" people.

Before leaving Paris, I invited Willmoore to visit me in England, and he agreed to. He would like to visit his old college at Oxford, Pembroke. So I drove back to the coast and the channel boat to Folkstone, and on to Oxford, where I bore down on Burke there and at the University of Sheffield, where the great modern edition of Burke's correspondence was coming out, volume after volume. I had had the idea of writing a brief critical life of Burke, but the footnotes to his letters were so comprehensive that the book I had in mind would have been redundant; so I concentrated on essays about one or another aspect of Burke's thought.

Meanwhile I lived in a hamlet near Oxford named Aston-near-Bampton, where most of the cottages had thatched roofs and the butcher's son was a socially conservative Labour MP. But what was available to me was a large, draughty country house named St. Anthony's Hall, in memory of the owner's brother who had died on the Somme in the Great War.

WILLMOORE SHOWED UP that winter for the promised visit. He stayed for about ten days and we spent hours in conversation on politics and political theory. But I drove us in to Oxford every morning to work on our projects, he on Rousseau, I on Burke, moonlighting on C. S. Lewis. He drank very heavily, morning, noon, and evening, starting with a "wake up" whiskey at breakfast. I ceased trying to keep up with his daily celebrations. We met for lunch at an Oxford pub named the Turf, where he downed a pint or two. The Turf was a marvelous place, in a back yard, reached through a mere crack of an alley between the two walls of adjacent Oxford colleges. Its men's room was famous for inventive graffiti: "Rupert is in love with the manikin in Marks and Spencer's window"; and, under a drawing of two cubes, "Balls by Bracque," the Cubist painter. Later there was the cocktail hour, dinner with wine, cognac, and coffee, and of course before going to bed a couple of nightcaps. One afternoon, he had to lean against the wall of Balliol College, short of breath. He popped a nitro pill and the heart seizure passed. Our joint daily alcohol intake was such that, though he was miles ahead of me, when he finally left I jogged for the first and only time in my life to sweat it off.

But there were marvelous times that early winter at Oxford. The aged master of Pembroke, who had known Willmoore years before as a young Rhodes Scholar, put on a black-tie banquet for him in college. This involved numerous dons from all over Oxford as well as celebrity intellectuals up from London. Willmoore himself looked tall and regal in his evening clothes, and the toasts to him were obviously knowledgeable and sincere. The old master declared that the two most intelligent students he had known in his many years at Pembroke were Willmoore and then–prime minister Harold Wilson. Willmoore and I chose to interpret this as a compliment.

Oxford gossip was wonderful, including the howler that the warden of All Souls, John Sparrow, had made ridiculous all those liberal-minded bishops and other clergymen who had testified to the high morality of *Lady Chatterley's Lover*. Sparrow showed, by carefully reading the text, that Mellors, the gamekeeper, practiced anal intercourse with Lady Chatterley. All Souls was stratospheric academically, lived on a medieval endowment, and accepted no students. There was talk of taking a Marxist for a year as a visiting fellow, for the public appearance, and as an inside joke at All Souls.

Once we rolled out a pint or two of Red Barrel at a pub near Oxford where we picked up a jovial game of darts with a couple of active-duty British paratroopers. When they understood that Willmoore was living in Paris the paratroopers were flabbergasted. "Why in the world Paris, mate?" they asked. Willmoore tried to explain about Rousseau and theory. No luck. "Mate, the niggers begin at Calais." This opinion of the French was not confined to the rougher types. One of the leading English poets, who had fought in the war, once remarked to me, "It was rather a good war. But it would have been much better if we had been fighting the French." I recalled that Robert Graves had about the same opinion in *Goodbye to All That*. Those chalk cliffs of Dover are not especially welcoming to emanations from the Continent. It did not help at the time that French prostitutes were coming across on the channel steamers to get free abortions from the Health Service.

As the days and nights passed I received a thorough lecturing, Socratic fashion, on Willmoore's "teaching"—not "philosophy, or, God forbid, ideology," but "teaching." That term seemed more accurate, and more "American," or something like that.

I remember sitting with him through a long afternoon at a country inn called the Rose and Crown, about ten miles from Oxford. Nearby, the Thames, Conrad's waterway of the fleet and empire, was a small clear stream patrolled by swans. It was Matthew Arnold country, the neighborhood of the Scholar Gypsy. "Flow softly, sweet Thames," wrote Spenser, "until I end my song,/ Flow softly, for I speak not loud or long." We sat over the usual pints of Red Barrel, and I listened as he developed an informal lecture, asking questions and trying to lead me to the true "teaching." The only other person I have known to do this kind of thing so effectively is Milton Friedman. What I was hearing would be published posthumously in 1970 as *The Basic Symbols of the American Political Tradition*. As I listened to Willmoore speak, I sensed the presence of the clear, dry light that for many of us surrounds the great founders of the American constitutional system, men such as Hamilton, Jefferson, Madison, Gouverneur Morris, Franklin, Washington: "Gentlemen, we have given you a republic, if you can keep it."

There was an orthodox American political tradition, Willmoore thought, and a constant campaign to derail it, by plebiscites or by newly proclaimed "rights." The 1787 Constitution designed in Philadelphia was virtually a sacred text to him, perhaps touched by the divine, the source of being. Its foundation was established in the first irrevocable three words of the pre-amble, written by Morris: "We the People." Government by "We the People," according to Willmoore, has been the great accomplishment of the United States, and its example remains its mission to the world, symbolized by the torch the Statue of Liberty holds aloft. That torch, despite Emma Lazarus's famous but mistaken inscription, has nothing to do with welcoming immi-grants, wretched or not.

Following "We the People," the preamble sets forth the six goals of the new government of the United States. The term "rights" is never men-tioned, here or elsewhere in the unamended document.

Everything that follows the brief preamble—that is, the rest of the text of the Constitution, as ratified and amended—amounts to a mechanism for achieving the six goals of the preamble. It is striking that the six goals are syntactically equal. Which of the six takes precedence at a given juncture depends upon "discussion" within the government set forth in the rest of the Constitution. No goal is absolute, except the preservation of the United States, which transcends all. This is a "deliberate sense" theory of government, "sense" emerging through "deliberation."

This mechanism of self-government was, as I say, sacred territory to Willmoore. He had been a man of the Left until he had gone to Spain as a journalist during the Civil War and seen there the variety of ideologies that are alien to America, that is, to the Constitution. Such alien ideologies included royalism, communism, fascism, anarchism. His understanding was that the ratified Constitution represented a permanent agreement on the orthodox American theory of representative government.

I associate Willmoore's teaching with the skeptical-prudential conservative tradition in politics. This includes such names as Montaigne, Montesquieu, Hume, Samuel Johnson, Burke, the American founders, maybe Michael Oakeshott. Its ideal citizen knows too much to be a relativist but too little to be an absolutist or a utopian. Opinion filtered through accumulated experience, embodied in habits, assumptions, and institutions, subject of course to change and the people's "deliberate sense," appears to be the optimum arrangement. Human imperfection makes representative government necessary, curbing power when need be.

Toward the end—which we did not know was toward the end in those days—Willmoore became slightly edgy about that as a final formulation. In our talks, as if aware of Macaulay's judgment—though I cannot recall him mentioning it—that the American Constitution is "all sail and no anchor," Willmoore wanted a yet firmer foundation, firmer than his concept of the "virtuous"—that is, prudent—"People." He seemed to be finding it in the work of Eric Voegelin. That is the meaning of "basic symbols" in the title of his posthumous *Basic Symbols of the American Tradition*, completed seamlessly by George Carey, who knew Willmoore's work intimately.

In his magisterial *Order and History* and in *The New Science of Politics*, Voegelin holds that "symbolizations arise from a people's experience of order, first from experience of the cosmos, then from the order of the soul." Such symbols, Voegelin holds, are ways of making the essentially unknowable order of being available and intelligible, as far as is possible. A symbolization is in effect a revelation, a breakthrough in which human beings attempt to grasp the very nature of things. There were the cosmic symbol-izations with astrology, polytheism, and the god-kings, those of ancient Israel and of the Polis. The Burning Bush was such a symbol, never seen before, signaling the utterly new. The Ten Commandments another, shaping a people toward the one God. Thus, these and hundreds of others are not "mere" symbols, but stand in an intense relation to truths we can know only in this way and not directly. In *Basic Symbols*, while setting forth an independent exposition of the relation of the Mayflower Compact to the Declaration and the Constitution, Willmoore argues as well that these are also symbols in the Voegelinian sense, rooted in the order of being, or permanent actuality—and what's more, that they were "breakthroughs," revelations of the new and unfolding *American* experience. I find this a plausible epistemology; Macaulay might not agree, perhaps snorting from the heights of his Whig superiority.

FROM THESE ARCADIAN HEIGHTS, I then had my own Kendallian experience, in 1966, not long after I had returned from England. At the time, Buckley was visiting me at my home in Vermont. Willmoore had stimulated an offer to me of a post at the University of Dallas in his Ph.D. program, I assume mostly in the literature end. It was obvious that Willmoore was ambitious to make this the training ground for leadership in the theoretical direction of American conservatism, a sort of West Point of political theory. Naturally, he would be the director. Obviously also, I would be a disciple. I admired the work of two other professors there, M. E. "Mel" Bradford, a fine critic and good friend of mine, and Frederick Wilhelmsen, a philosopher and contributor to *National Review*. Still, I was not inclined to give up my post at Dartmouth, where things were going well, and so I had declined.

Willmoore's reply came while Buckley was visiting. It took the form of a note written in Willmoore's green ink on several small pages of a desk notepad. Among a few other choice things, it said that I was "more corrupt than Buckley," whom he evidently regarded as a Sultan of Corruption. I passed this missive over to Buckley himself to read. He was sadly amused. It was déja-vu all over again.

Not long after that, on June 30, 1967, Wilmoore passed an ordinary academic day. He picked up his mail and had a conference with a student about a paper. After lunch at home, he lay down for a nap and did not awaken. He was 58. R.I.P.

14

Not *All the Way with LBJ*

"**A**rrgh."

Such, in full, was the lead editorial paragraph with which *National Review* welcomed Lyndon Johnson's landslide 1964 victory over Barry Goldwater. Earlier, on December 17, 1963, the magazine had commented as follows on Johnson' first month as president: "The editors of *National Review* regretfully announce that their patience with President Lyndon B. Johnson is exhausted."

Looking back, these can be seen as a refreshingly light-hearted and endearingly innocent ways to welcome one of the most ragged and unsettling periods in American life. It is colored in memory with the smoky reds and blacks of Dante's *Inferno*, with Charlie Manson and his grisly coven of doped and demonic girls, armed with knives, peering at you through the smoke. Johnson escalated the number of troops in Vietnam to 550,000, knowing neither how to win nor how to get out. He also pushed through an ambitious legislative program, propelled by grief over Kennedy and the landslide over Goldwater, which gave the new president a large Democratic majority. The years after 1964 also brought multiple assassinations at home and abroad, years comparable to the uprisings of 1848 in Europe. Quite possibly, 1968 was the most turbulent one in American history, bringing not only battlefield defeat but also a society demoralized and sliding toward anarchy.

At the same time, by the negative power of all this, a counterreaction built up, a conservative resurgence that initiated deep-running changes in American politics, and indeed in American life. Finally, Richard Nixon, the long-distance runner, would win a close election to the White House.

When *National Review* ran that light-hearted lead paragraph in 1964, it was well aware of the power and potential of Lyndon Johnson. Ascending as if to his rightful place after the assassination of President Kennedy, he seemed, at his peak, a kind of Roman emperor. Burnham wrote of his global trip in accents that recalled Gibbon on the Age of the Antonines:

> It was a dazzling display, that pre-Christmas orbit. . . . [W]e can all of us see, unblurred by the usual fog of words, what it is to be a global power, to be *the* global power.
>
> This display dramatizes also the marriage of global power with advanced technology. . . . Air Force One, moreover, was not merely a vehicle carrying the person of the President, his aides and guards, over these fantastic distances. It was also, while the President was aboard, the seat of government of the global power and the Supreme Headquarters of its land, sea, air and space forces. . . . The red button that could annihilate the world, like the finger that may push that button, rode the global sky on Air Force One.

Johnson was a colossal figure. To quote Burnham again, a January 1965 editorial recorded:

> The House passed the Administration's aid to education bill, then the Senate passed it intact; not so much as a comma changed. The House passed the Administration's Medicare bill—intact. And the Senate will soon endorse it. The voting bill is at least being scrutinized, but constitutional objections notwithstanding, it is certain to go through. The Congress has become the President's lady-in-waiting. . . .

At that moment, Lyndon Johnson had it all. His Civil Rights Bill passed 71–29 in the Senate. Though Johnson was concerned about resistance to voting rights and desegregation of public facilities in the South, resistance was light, at least relative to the refusals and riots over the "judge-made" school integration decision of *Brown v. Board*. Johnson's War on Poverty programs sailed through, including the soon troubling Aid to Families with Dependent Children, which became enormously unpopular as rewarding "welfare mothers" without fathers in the home. Medicare, at first popular, would pose dangerous budgetary problems down the road.

In the passage quoted a moment ago about Johnson's imperial tour, Burnham's baroque prose hints at what Shelley knew in "Ozymandias"— the usual fate of excessive power:

> *I met a traveler from an antique land*
> *Who said: "Two vast and trunkless legs of stone*
> *Stand in the desert . . .*
> *Near them on the sand,*
>
> *Half sunk, a shattered visage lies . . .*
> *Round the decay*
> *Of that colossal wreck, boundless and bare*
> *The lone and level sands stretch far away.*

By the beginning of 1967, as Robert Dallek records,

> the dissent over Vietnam, urban riots, political reverses, and doubts about the administration's programs to elevate poor folks into the middle class and transform America into a Great Society made Johnson wonder why he had ever wanted to be President. In the winter of 1966–67, even before a host of new difficulties appeared, he found himself defending his administration from attacks by friend and foe alike. Governor Warren Hearnes of Missouri told Johnson that if he were running in his state now he would lose by 100,000 votes.[1]

ON MARCH 1, 1968, three years after his landslide 1964 victory, President Lyndon Johnson went on national television to address the nation and the world. He looked worn, even ill. His physician had warned him about his heart. He shocked everyone who heard him, everyone in his White House except his closest confidants and writers:

I have concluded that I should not permit the presidency to become involved in partisan divisions that are developing in this political year. . . . Accordingly, I shall not seek, and I will not accept, the nomination of my party for another term as your president.

The Vietnam troop increases and the bombing in the North had made no appreciable difference in the enemy capacity to carry on the war in the South. Long before this, two years before, in a March 23, 1965, "Third World War" column titled "What Are We Doing In Vietnam?" James Burnham had laid down the theoretical basis for the war. He concluded:

If we have an excuse for being in South Vietnam, it can only be *our own* security. Our security would be critically threatened by the advance of the Communist enterprise into Southeast Asia and the South Seas; we therefore resist that advance by what means are necessary.

Our action, if successful, will incidentally make possible a free, peaceful Laos and South Vietnam, but its fundamental aim should be to meet the challenge of the Communist enterprise. Only thus understood can our action in Southeast Asia be effectively conducted, intelligibly explained and convincingly justified.

The problem, however, was that the war had become one of attrition, the fighting in the South sustained by a supply of soldiers and materiel from the North down the Ho Chi Minh Trails. Far from being a single trail, this was an elaborate jungle network begun in 1964, when United States involvement was minimal. The war looked to the world like a guerrilla war; in fact, it was an invasion from the North backed by the power of China and the Soviet Union. The local Vietcong in the South were numerous and organized, but mainly useful as a mask for the real power.

Looking at the map, one sees a multi-road invasion extending from Laos in the north, across the border from Khesanh to Tayninh in the south, not far from Saigon: about a thousand miles of admirable engineering through supremely difficult terrain that provided excellent jungle camouflage. When Johnson offered Ho Chi Minh the big bribe of a TVA on the Mekong in exchange for a settlement—as if he were dealing with a stubborn American governor—the grim merriment in Hanoi can be imagined.

James Burnham was much to the point in a 1968 "Third World War" column when he wrote that our air strikes had failed to persuade Hanoi—and behind them, Beijing and Moscow—that we were serious about winning the war.

ON JANUARY 31, 1968, Americans in the field and those watching television at home, received a terrible shock. Some 75,000 Communist fighters suddenly sprang, as if from nowhere, to launch attacks throughout South Vietnam. This violated a truce that had been agreed upon to honor Tet, the lunar New Year. Crashing into about a hundred cities, including Saigon, the attack demonstrated a striking ability to coordinate such an enterprise without being detected. The enemy had shown spectacular capability. The Tet Offensive also punctured the optimistic statements coming from the Johnson administration and the generals.

Exclusive responsibility should not be placed upon Tet for the fall in Lyndon Johnson's support, however. Before Tet, in its January 16 issue—which means his observations had been made substantially earlier than Tet—*National Review* published an important article by Ferdinand Mount, who had sampled opinion across the country about Lyndon Johnson. It began:

> During a recent coast-to-coast odyssey, I idly ventured the proposition that Lyndon Johnson is the most unpopular President of modern times. Whether on radio and television, campus or the golf course, round the cocktail cabinet or in the coffee shop, never a voice was raised in dissent. This is extraordinary, for normally there is no public figure so fatuous or wicked that some people will not say that he's not such a fool as he looks. . . . But Mr. Johnson has effected a transition from consensus to nonsensus in a bare two years, which is remarkable even granted the traditional fickleness of the citizenry. . . .

Mount had written this, to repeat, before Tet. Even more important than the public at large, confidence in the war was evaporating not only in the highly visible media but also among bankers, corporate boards, investors, and big political contributors. Their influence began to weigh heavily on bureaucrats, politicians, and even on Johnson himself.[2]

THE BLACK RIOTS IN WATTS in 1965 inaugurated a prolonged period of traumatic domestic violence. And further up the California coast, a "free speech" movement at Berkeley began a period of campus chaos, contributing to an atmosphere in which Johnson's policies plunged in public opinion, and with them his own ability to govern. What was the relevance now of aid to education and civil rights legislation? What relevance even the surging economy? Unmanageable tides were flowing.

On April 4, 1968, the Rev. Martin Luther King was murdered by rifle bullets as he stood on the balcony of a motel in Memphis. In *National Review*, Buckley reflected somberly on the King murder:

> [Nothing] in the whole exclamatory spring—not the war, not a Presidential race—shocks the sensibilities so stunningly as Martin Luther King's death in Tennessee . . . [a] breathing ugliness, coiled like a clock spring, gathered itself and struck.

Buckley was alert to the violence now being urged by some in response to the crime:

> [It] was not King alone who had died that Thursday evening. Julian Bond was at Vanderbilt University on Friday: "Brotherhood was murdered in Memphis last night. All that is good in America was murdered in Memphis last night." In Washington, civil rights leader Julian Hobson offered blacks advice: "The next black man who comes into the black community preaching non-violence should be violently dealt with by the black people who hear him." . . . Stokely Carmichael received the press in Washington: "Black people know why they have to have guns."

That summer, I happened to be in Sacramento as a writer for Reagan—arranged by Buckley, since Reagan was an unannounced candidate for the Republican nomination—and I found the madness around California dizzying. At about the same time King was murdered, Reagan made emphatic his own attitude toward revolutionary violence, including, importantly, his willingness to act against it if necessary. Across the bay from San Francisco, on the other side of the Golden Gate Bridge, the city of Oakland was a center of Black Panther activity, including murder, drugs, prostitution, and shakedowns. At one of his weekly news conferences, the governor was asked by a reporter what he would do about the current Panther threats of a "blood-bath." Reagan answered, "Well, if they want a bloodbath, they can have a bloodbath." This was the atmosphere in which Patty Hearst later was kid-napped by some murderous crackpot "revolutionaries" calling themselves the Symbionese Liberation Army, most of whom died in fire and a hail of bullets from the California Highway Patrol.

At his regular press conferences, Reagan was invariably straightforward about how he would deal with violent groups: by force, if necessary. Even hostile reporters found themselves liking him. Behind the friendliness there was purpose, resolve, but also wit. At a press conference he was asked whether he had seen the war protesters outside the state capitol. "You mean," he said, "the ones with signs that say, 'Make love not war'?" "Yes, Governor." "Well, if you ask me, they couldn't do much of either."

DURING THE SUMMER before his assassination, Martin Luther King generally had been thought of as a disciple of Gandhi. He is remembered for his "I have a dream" speech. But this was 1968, and even King had moved in a radical direction. When he was murdered, he had arrived in Memphis to lead a strike of the Memphis sanitation workers, about half of whom were white. This hardly seemed a "civil rights" issue. According to Jules Witcover,

> On the day before [he was murdered], King had returned to the city, and learning that a federal injunction had been obtained against a planned dem-onstration two days hence, warned that "we are not going to be stopped by mace or injunctions." He told reporters, "We stand on the First Amendment. In the past, on the basis of conscience, we have had to break injunctions, and if necessary we may do it. We'll cross that bridge when we come to it."[3]

Gandhi and nonviolence had apparently become shaky by 1968. King was about to enter a Memphis vibrating in anticipation of violence. As Frank Meyer observed in one of his "Principles and Heresies" columns at the time:

Dr. King, unlike many of the other leaders of the Negro revolution, still wears the fig-leaf of non-violence, if somewhat rakishly askew. But if there were ever any doubts as to his insurrectionary intentions against constitutional government, his program for 1968 dispels them once and for all. What Dr. King has done, after three years of mounting violence culminating in Newark and Detroit, is to announce the organization this spring in Washington of a massive campaign of civil disobedience, that is, an effort to bring the functioning of the government to a stop until Dr. King's ideological program has enacted, in his words, "massive dislocation" of the capital "until America responds."

THE MURDER OF ROBERT KENNEDY in a pantry corridor of the Ambassador Hotel in Los Angeles later that summer by Sirhan Sirhan was *political*, as had been the crime of Lee Harvey Oswald, and probably of King's assassin, James Earl Ray. Jack Kennedy had been murdered by a homemade Communist admirer of Castro, while Robert Kennedy's murderer Sirhan was a Palestinian bringing the Mideast war home. According to Jules Witcover, on Monday, May 27,

Kennedy had made an appearance at the Neveh Shalom Synagogue in Portland, where he was campaigning successfully, and stated his position on Israel: "Our position is clear and compelling. We are committed to Israel's survival. We are committed to defying any attempt to destroy Israel, whatever the source. And we cannot and must not let that commitment waver."[3]

Witcover adds:

Later in the day, his words were carried on television, including in Pasadena, California, where in the house of a Jordanian family named Sirhan, a young man watched. According to his brother in a later report to an Egyptian correspondent, the young man became greatly upset at the sight and words of Kennedy in the temple. "He left the room putting his hands on his ears and almost weeping," the brother said of the scene.[4]

Sirhan was a Jordanian born in Jerusalem; he had been in the Los Angeles area since 1957; two notebooks were found in his Pasadena home containing a "direct reference to the necessity to assassinate Senator Kennedy before

June 5, 1968"—the first anniversary of the end of the six-day Arab-Israel war.[5] In 1968, politics took a turn toward guns and murder.

That summer, Senator Eugene McCarthy had been Robert Kennedy's rival for the Democratic nomination; he had lost narrowly to Kennedy in the California primary. Though usually cool compared with Kennedy's feverish rock-star-hot, women-leaping tours, with longish hair awry in the motorcades and hoarse shouts of "We can do better, we can do better," McCarthy was refreshingly aloof and ironic. Yet even he felt so drained after the Kennedy murder that he took refuge for a while in a Minnesota Benedictine monastery. Quite in tune with that year, one night a drunken monk with a revolver was subdued by other monks outside McCarthy's room.

Understandably, security was tight in and around Governor Reagan's office, but I had errands occasionally, as a sort of emissary from Reagan to beleaguered faculty at Berkeley. There, Telegraph Avenue, the main street, was heavy with marijuana fumes. The street was festooned with countless posters of Mao and Che, and many young men looked like Charles Manson. In fact, back in Sacramento, even the young men at the supermarket checkout cash registers looked like Manson.

The Countercultural Revolution of 1968, led by the younger generation, was not confined to the United States. Similar youth-centered uprisings took place in France, Germany, Italy, Greece, England, Mexico, even Japan. Everywhere it began with a parochial complaint—at Columbia, about the construction of a new gymnasium near Harlem. *National Review* ran several articles and editorials on all this, covering especially the Columbia uprising, which shattered the morale of that university for some time to come.

Meanwhile, throughout the early months of 1968, Richard Nixon had moved toward the Republican nomination with a campaign of professionally beautiful quality, as if deliberately designed to be everything the wilder and hairy elements despised. In Sacramento, Reagan undertook a tacit campaign for the nomination as the true conservative candidate, believing that Nixon was then and had always been a loser. As he put it in one of his movie metaphors, Nixon was "the fellow who doesn't get the girl." For

Reagan, the immortal figures on the screen, never aging, were like the Greek gods and heroes, fictional but real, available as models and as warnings.

THE REPUBLICAN CONVENTION in Miami stands as one icon of 1968, while the Democratic Convention in Chicago stands as another; together they symbolized what the upcoming campaign would be about: the war, and restoring to the presidency the ability to govern.

An August 20, 1968, editorial in *National Review* by James Burnham, lyrical with intellectual pleasure, celebrated the Republican Convention, including its transitory beauty, with the title "Moon Over Miami":

> Through one of the most skillfully conducted campaigns in the nation's history, the Nixon forces were occupying what looked like an unbeatable position as the final battle opened. He had early seized and managed to hold, throughout, the party's broad middle ground, thereby splitting his rivals and effectively preventing an effective consolidation of opposing forces. He did not make a single error in tactics. Against continual provocation from all quarters, he held to his bold decision not to exploit the Paris peace talks as a basis for silence on Vietnam and to stop aggressive operations in the primaries. His opponents were thereby left flailing in the air.

Only one footnote should be added to that. During this flawless campaign, with victory in every primary he entered, Nixon addressed Vietnam frequently, promising to "end the war and win the peace in Vietnam." He refused to elaborate, on grounds of the ongoing Paris negotiations, and therefore the media said, often snidely, that he claimed to have a "secret plan" for peace in Vietnam. It was not really secret, unless *Foreign Affairs* is an underground magazine. I began to realize just how lazy the major media could be. In October 1967, with the assistance of wordsmith William Safire, Nixon had published in *Foreign Affairs* an essay titled "Asia After Vietnam," advocating an opening to China as a means of setting up tension between China and Russia. Implied was pressure on North Vietnam to settle the war. But beyond that, the essay looked to a more permanent stability through a balancing of interests after the war. This plausible idea would inform his

1972 trip to Beijing, after which Moscow did "tilt" toward the United States. Both pleaded with Hanoi to be "sensible."

In endorsing Nixon editorially, with Burnham writing, *National Review* approved of the tone of his whole operation, implicitly contrasting it with the style of the late Kennedy brothers:

> In their actions at the convention, by the platform they adopted and the candidate they chose, the Republicans have committed themselves to an old-fashioned campaign in the American style. It is not to be a crusade, a Gideon's Army rushing along in the wake of a charismatic leader. Richard Nixon is a competent, intelligent, experienced, professional politician; but he does not have the "crowd magic"; he is not and cannot become a charismatic leader. . . . The Republican Party has arranged itself to function, in the old American mode, as an election machine, an apparatus built out of diverse groups and interests merged for the purpose of taking administrative control of the government.

This editorial accurately expressed the style and operative goals of the Nixon machine. But the editorial concluded, presciently, on a worried note:

> There is, yes, a lot to be said for the election-machine style of politics; we even may say that the nation where it works is therein blessed. The prevalence of this humdrum, vulgar, uninspired and uninspiring style of politics expresses the fact that within the nation there is an implicit consensus about at least the general rules of the game, and no irreconcilable divisions. . . . If so, there may be an impasse ahead for a Nixon or a Humphrey move into office as the executant of machine-style politics. President Nixon-Humphrey may find it increasingly difficult not only to put enlightened and fruitful policies into effect, but merely to govern; even impossible.

This was a fine exposition of American consensus politics, a skeptical conservatism going back to the Constitution and the *Federalist Papers*. Burnham here applies it to American politics in 1968, knowing its vulnerability, at least in the short run.

But the convention ran like a clock inside the auditorium, with the unity Burnham describes. Nixon delivered an acceptance speech, quite lyrical—unusual for him—and based upon the rhythms and emotions of Martin Luther King's "I Have a Dream" speech of distant 1963. Nixon began with "I see a boy," evoked his childhood in Yorba Linda, his devoted mother, a boy who in his bed heard trains leaving in the night, a young man who owed much to a teacher and a football coach and to others, who hoped much . . . ending, "And tonight I stand before you, nominated for the presidency of the United States." It was the American Dream. No one wondered whether Nixon, on that long train ride from Yorba Linda, might have accumulated so much emotional baggage in the form of defeats, rejections, humiliations, resentments, and manifest unfairness, as he saw it, that he might be unfit to govern during a crisis of the house divided. He had arrived with an "I'll get those bastards" anger boiling up within him, well concealed.

NATIONAL REVIEW PUBLISHED a great deal in its coverage of the 1968 Republican Convention, as was to be expected, including a long article by Garry Wills titled "The Nixon Convention." Wills followed this up with a still longer companion article about the Democrats in Chicago. As with his earlier review-essay on Baldwin's *The Fire Next Time*, several editors at *National Review*, most emphatically Frank Meyer, resisted the publication of both convention articles, understandably. To have rejected either or both would certainly have meant a permanent rejection of Wills, though in retrospect, and in several ways, these articles look like Wills's rejection of *National Review*. His sensibility had mutated; he had "grown," in the ironic sense of the term.

The thing that strikes the reader about both articles is Wills's criterion for moral judgment, political opinion taking the form of aesthetic (really social) evaluation. Republicans and conservatives are . . . vulgar. Their clothes, especially, are out of date or lower-middle class, while the Kids rioting in Chicago turn out to be strange, inviting, fuzzy, soft, attractive—and socially, aesthetically, higher.

For example, Reagan's exterior marks him as a philistine and a bad guy:

> He was wearing what would be his uniform for the next week—light sport jacket (thin stripes that blur to a solid at any distance), dark slacks, and—so

help me—brown shoes straight out of the Forties, the kind with the all-white panel out in front of the laces. His wife, very small despite her large actor-features, gazed at him, as always, with utter devotion. In a husband adoration contest with Lenore Romney, Nancy would, after hours of hard work at the awe machine, melt first. There is an impure admixture in Lenore's rapt eyes, of *command* ("If you don't make it this *time*, George. . . .")

This kind of writing involves greater risk for the writer than he may think, or want, and amounts to unearned expression of superiority based on "taste," an aesthetics of personality dangerous to political judgment: even a badly dressed leader might do the right things. Wills fails to let his reader know that Reagan had been a successful governor of a state with the sixth largest Gross Domestic Product in the world, and that he came to the convention with standing as a conservative leader who just might win the nomination. Or consider Wills's paste gems in this:

> Scranton, a raven too pleasant to croak, was on hand at least to coo his Nevermore. He came out of the hotel wearing a seersucker sport coat and his baroque *putto* smile. A woman recognized him, and cried "Governor!" He turned angelically, smiled (at the wrong lady), waved (at an empty space of driveway), and bumped into the unmothballed battleship of the convoy, Len Hall. Willie [Scranton] then rebounded on a waiting car, which he tried to enter, but as Hall insisted it was not theirs, he caromed genially round to the proper car door, dove in and drove off. It approximated Rocky's gyrations at, from, and into candidacy.

No doubt about it, many people reading this kind of thing feel that they are experiencing good writing. But it does not bear much examination. Possibly Scranton might be compared to Poe's raven, thereby suggesting the defeat and possible death of liberal Republicanism. But that is probably attributing too much content to the allusion. The seersucker coat adds some visual quality here, of a so-what kind (there must have been thousands of them at Miami Beach), but "baroque *putto* smile"? Seems a stretch. And just how do angels *turn*? Len Hall was a large man, so maybe "battleship" works, sort of—though battleships usually are not employed in convoy duty, and never by themselves, as Hall is here. But "unmothballed"?

Perhaps this extravagance means to suggest Hall's age and many battles, but it all remains more metaphorical than the energy of the idea can bear, if there is an idea. Comparing Scranton's supposedly comic caroming behavior at the car with Rockefeller's in-and-out campaign seems a rhetorical effort to no purpose, except to suggest Marx Brothers comedy. Yo-yo or revolving door would be just as good, or bad. Wills's comparisons fail to give even a spark of light in the dark cellar of such prose.

There is more:

> Out at the airport, Gov. Claude Kirk [of Florida] joined this gaudy troop of losers, and a quick Florida rainstorm made them all run for cover. Kirk's face is plastered all over Miami, on billboards, on each elevator permit; one expects, any day, to find it on the state's liquor stamps. Today he wears a bright orange sport coat, seersucker pants, black socks, white shoes.

Obviously, we are invited to understand, Gov. Kirk is a man of *bad taste*, and therefore contemptible, risible: *omigod!*—black socks and white shoes! Maybe the orange sport coat can pass as his state's color, but not really. Still, his face on *liquor* stamps? Meant to be insulting, one understands, especially in its verbal proximity to "plastered." Does Wills intend the suggestion that Kirk is a drunk? And anyway, who (except Wills) expected "any day" to find it on the state's liquor stamps? What are all these sneers trying to communicate? Anything about the actuality of a political convention? No, they are false pearls cast before real swine—that is, for an audience like *Esquire*'s.

WILLS'S COVERAGE OF THE Democratic Convention in Chicago, a nine-page, twenty-nine column essay carried in the September 24, 1968, issue, may be the longest article ever published in *National Review*. It begins with a good distance-altitude view of Chicago's Lake Shore panorama. A hotel window

> looked over the green-fretted apron of Grant Park and Lake Michigan's garish blue. The scene had the too-real brilliance of a big Kodak ad, lit from behind, in Grand Central Station. The lakefront museums showed massive

through their clumps of trees. Sailboats leaned tactically in and out of the narrow gap in the long thin breakwater. And on the grassy apron, a game seemed in progress, bowling on the lawn but with no click as the balls hit—all muffled, lazy movement. It seemed crazy, but these were human beings being bowled, rolled, lifted, dragged in a general mingle of people, as at a country fair.

This works fairly well visually, and there are good things: the sailboats "leaned tactically," for example, a nice verbal Raoul Dufy. One does wonder, however, how the observer detected that those distant lawn-bowling balls were not *clicking*. Did he suddenly open the window, possibly hearing from that height? Then, with some sort of zoom lens, we find that the "balls" are really "human beings." It must have been from a very considerable distance that they were perceived as balls. Then, suddenly, we hear about their doings as people. Oh well. Flaubert this is not.

It turns out that they are the very *Kids* themselves down there on the sward, getting ready to fight with the cops in, we gather, the most important convention, the anti-convention that is far more important than the one in Miami, and more important than the one to be held inside the hall here among the Democrats. The big one, the important one, is—*in the streets*.

The reason for this, not especially discernible throughout most of the article, comes at the end in a brief section headed "Up Against the Wall," a Kids *faux*-revolutionary slogan. The only people who went up against any walls were university administrators, who went willingly. When the Kids kicked a rotten barrel, they won. But Wills's Kids, having destroyed the Democratic Convention, are going to do the same to the major institutions of the United States:

> They made a major impact on the convention; on this year's politics; perhaps on the election itself. They drew the eyes of the world to them, and discredited their country in those eyes. . . . [T]he kids might hold the crucial cards.

Wills's coverage of the Kids in the streets is a sort of pastoral prose poem. Here, the contempt earlier exhibited for figures like Nixon, Reagan,

Romney, Scranton, Kirk, and the rest, entirely evaporates. For the Kids what we find is aesthetic fascination and, yes, love. Here, as in Miami, Wills makes much of clothes, though the Kids do not wear anything so repulsive, to Wills, as old-fashioned brown shoes with white panels in front or, God forbid, orange jackets. Things like that would be all right for Hubert Humphrey, the "drugstore liberal," as people of true sensibility called him, but not for the angelic Kids. And the following amounts to a collectors' item:

> The keynote of the kids' clothing is softness. No edges. Even last year's military jackets have the padding torn out—droopy epaulettes, wilted fronts, frayed buttons, every sag and hang saying, "I ain't marchin' any more." All things tend to the shaggy—soft fringes of adolescent beard, girls' eyes in a shadowy thicket of mascara. The clothes are all of the muffled, involving sort—blankets, capes, shepherd's coats, hoods, wooly sweaters. Velvet, velour, fur—the favorite hats are Russian astrakhan, soft Indian head bead-band, Arab turbans, Foreign Legion veils, swaths, colorful (prophetic) bandages. The shoes are moccasins, soft boots, sandals worn to pliancy—Paul Krassner takes the thing to its logical term, wearing shoes made of some carpet-stuff that looks like grass. But better even than moccasins are bare feet. . . . The soft yielding quality extends to the hair, worn in two styles—first, the long divided wavering waterfall; second, the Ella Lancaster (or electrocuted) style—fizzing out in all directions. Beards are as full as they can be grown—never trimmed. The students' "underground" newspapers, when they show nudes, always feature pubic hair.

Honesty! No airbrushed *Playboy* stuff. Very good, very sympathetic indeed, this "soft-edged" evocation. For Wills, funky aesthetics and social status overwhelm ethics. He knows that many of these Kids are credit-card revolutionaries on summer vacation from fancy schools. Some of them even come from Paris, think of that, Paris itself, on leave from the Sorbonne, with plenty of francs from home.

These scholars on vacation could not be the ones who threw paper bags of feces and golf-balls with nails hammered through them at the "Pigs," could they? Or tormented the "Pigs" with filthy language? None of that appears in "Convention in the Streets." What Wills presented was a melodrama, plus a fashion show.

MUCH TO MY SURPRISE, after leaving Sacramento after Nixon won in Miami, I joined the Nixon presidential campaign. From his New York head-quarters I wrote a great deal of material, including, on the side, a *National Review* article attacking Wallace that Barry Goldwater signed, and also Nixon's critical law-and-order speech, which he delivered in Philadelphia, I think—I am uncertain about that because in a campaign plane all cities and motorcades look alike. Even more surprising than my going to Sacramento, my new position happened this way.

When Reagan lost at Miami, I bought a battered Volvo in Sacramento and headed back east on Route 66—for no other reason than the song. But the only kicks I got on Route 66 were those I administered to myself for choosing this ghastly route. The famous Route 66, at least back then, was a ribbon of black asphalt boiling under the desert sun. At maybe 120 degrees, many cars had water bags tied to their radiators as the "highway" ran through infinities of antihuman desert, every twenty-five miles or so maybe a bat-tered filling station with one or two Indians under large hats, asleep or dead, sitting outside. In Albuquerque or somewhere I considered selling the damned Volvo, which, with a few more dollars, might have bought airfare. Pushing on, I stayed one night at a 1940s vintage motel, Alfred Hitchcock style, Tony Perkins no longer there. Sitting in front of an electric fan, I tuned in a black-and-white TV, watched the *Götterdämmerung* at the Democratic Convention, and decided to check with Sacramento for phone calls. Chief of Staff Bill Clark's office told me to call a number, which turned out to be Nixon headquarters in Manhattan. It was James Keogh, the *Time* magazine editor, who was director of the Nixon writers. We made an ap-pointment, and I headed the Volvo in that direction instead of New En-gland, the green farmland of Ohio looking like the Garden of Eden. In the future, whenever I went to California it would be at 30,000 feet. Give the rest of the place back to the Indians and the Gila monsters.

15

Nixon: The Perfect Campaign

"Without the Vietnam War there would have been no Watergate."
—H. R. Haldeman, in conversation with Jeffrey Hart

Zhou En-lai: "Who was the greatest president of the 20th century?"
Harrison Salisbury: "I don't know. Roosevelt?"
Zhou: "No. Nixon."
—related to Jeffrey Hart in conversation
with Harrison Salisbury

*N*ational Review's endorsement of Nixon in 1968, hoping for the best, reflected varying estimates of the former vice president among the senior editors. William Rusher had never trusted him. Others spread out over the spectrum of opinion.

Bob Haldeman had been only half right when he said that without the Vietnam War there would have been no Watergate: for it is also true that without Nixon there would have been no Watergate. Nixon was able, intelligent, tenacious. But he was also more than that. The qualities that created the Watergate White House came from a strange corner of his mind. His failures—including his failed opportunity to consolidate a center-right political-cultural establishment—were failures of character. In every political race he had run there was something ethically questionable, with the sleazy figure of Murray Chotiner always in the background, treating every contest as a war without rules. During his second term, Eisenhower had said again and again, "Dick is maturing," for "New Nixons" had repeatedly appeared. Still, Nixon would remain Nixon. Almost always, those who talked with him one-on-one were impressed by his knowledge and intelligence. Though he told different people contradictory things, it is quite possible that he believed everything he said at the time he said it, or none of it.

The 1968 Nixon campaign proved to be a model of organization and technology, and would be a preview in some respects of the administration that emerged from the victory, its organization epitomized in Haldeman's "zero-defect" administrative procedure. The campaign represented in every detail a triumph of analysis and organization, perfectly conceived and perfectly executed, Nixon threading the needle between Humphrey on the left and Wallace on the right. Nixon, the student of detail, had learned a great deal, especially from his failed (and Kennedy's successful) 1960 campaign—learned also from his blow-up "last press conference" after his 1962 defeat by Pat Brown for governor of California. On that occasion, Nixon had been exhausted, frazzled, and apparently hungover: he would have to be more careful and self-disciplined. Tightly wound, he knew that even one drink could be dangerous. He had studied himself intently, as in *Six Crises*, with its theme of personal fragility and the dangerous temptation to "let down" after tightening every nerve during a "crisis." He knew from 1964 about the changing equation of the Republican Party, its tilt toward the South and West. In 1968, however, everything was planned to avoid all possible mistakes.

For 1968, Nixon had decided that he would both campaign for the nomination and run in the general election as an experienced, competent "unity" candidate, attracting the center of the Republican Party and reaching outward from there. Operationally, in the primaries and in the national campaign, this meant *neither very conservative nor very liberal*. This also meant *no excitement*. His goal was to reach the Silent Majority, with the emphasis on both words. He would beat back Wallace and the segregationists, letting the Deep South go, but trying hard for everything outside that Wallaceite core, especially the Border States. In that sense, he had a "Border State" rather than a "southern" strategy. He knew that Humphrey could not move too far toward the center, which meant that Nixon had a chance at moderate Democrats, especially blue-collar and ethnic voters exasperated by riots and neighborhood-busting judges.

On Vietnam, he took no clear public position, on the grounds of the ongoing "peace talks" in Paris, with which he could not interfere. On the Constitution he was a "strict constructionist," explicate that as you wish. To willing ears it seemed to mean that he opposed judicial pioneering. And he vigorously opposed street violence, agitators, and campus disrupters. He refused to debate Humphrey, explaining that Wallace would have to be included, thus giving him a dangerous platform. Wallace's rhetoric was imaginative, sometimes almost Faulknerian, comic, and entertaining.

Nixon might have remembered the joke from 1960: "Old Joe said to his son, 'Jack, I will buy you a win, but I'm not going to buy you a landslide.'" In Nixon's 1968 campaign money sloshed around abundantly, raised by the Midas touch of finance chairman Maurice Stans, later secretary of commerce. In the 1966 off-year elections, Nixon had campaigned all over the country, in congressional and other races, creating a network of permanent gratitude; and he was given considerable credit for the gain of 44 Republican seats. Everything was in place for 1968. On October 8, Burnham wrote a *National Review* editorial analyzing the success, so far, of the campaign:

> Richard Nixon is using the strategic pattern of his fight for the nomination to guide his campaign for the presidency, a precedent that must with good reason be comforting. Again, as in the nomination race, he finds himself placed by fate in a center position: between Wallace on his right and Humphrey on his left, now, as before between Reagan and Rockefeller. This gives him an ideal opportunity to offer himself to the voters as the mainstream candidate— a chance denied him in 1960—and he is systematically, sometimes it seems too systematically, exploiting his opportunity. . . .
>
> [But] Fortune is so mischievous. This has been a year of spectaculars, and there may yet be one more before November 5. It does not seem likely that Nixon, set on his course, will make a major error, and it does not seem pos-

sible that Humphrey could manage an impressive enough coup to pull him out of his bog. But there's still a President, and Lyndon Johnson might, just might, want to do something startling before he leaves the big stage.

That was, *in medias res*, an extraordinarily prescient analysis. In the final phase, Humphrey did make a speech in Salt Lake City in which, moving crabwise, he put enough space between himself and Johnson to barely mollify the left. As between Nixon and Humphrey, the final margin was paper-thin. But that was not the whole story.

WHEN I ARRIVED FROM Sacramento at 450 Park Avenue as a speechwriter, I saw that the team of writers assembled there represented a Nixonian coalition: with William Safire, more liberal then than later as a *New York Times* columnist, but then also an old Nixon hand from vice presidential days; also Ray Price, a former editorial writer for the liberalish *New York Herald-Tribune*, writing the lofty family-of-man prose; and George Gilder, later a self-made genius in microchip communications, then still a liberal from the failed Rockefeller operation; and Pat Buchanan, an undoubted conservative who had been with Nixon early on, and the main writer from the right; and I, who had come from Reagan. That team more or less represented the Republican Party as it was in 1968.

As I had found in Sacramento, friendliness increased spectacularly as soon as I made it clear that I had no desire to go to the White House if Nixon won. Our director of research was Alan Greenspan, an economist and former Ayn Randian. He had Jeffrey Bell, a former student of mine at Columbia, as an assistant. Buchanan and I had the principal task of fending off the Wallace threat. Not writing but supervising the writers was Jim Keogh, who had come over from *Time*. Working in a cubicle at 450 Park Avenue, I learned in a practical way from Keogh how Nixon was presenting himself when he handed my first efforts back with the comment that they were suitable for Reagan but not Nixon. Too "heroic." Nixon was running as *reliably professional*. Experienced. Measured. Mature. He would look foolish trying to sound like Reagan—or like Henry V at Agincourt. I quickly rescored my lyric in the direction of prose. As always, the purpose of a political speech was to establish communion with the target audience: you conveyed that this candidate understood your needs and your situation. Even facts are subordinate to that goal. In 1968 the song went, "You can trust Nixon"—a steady man, in turbulent, even revolutionary times. Steadiness, however, turned out not to be his strong suit.

Probably my most interesting effort was Nixon's "law and order" address, to be delivered in Philadelphia, an effort to attract Wallace voters while also putting space between Nixon and Wallace. In a nice example of Nixon's strategic goal of creating and exploiting a hospitable center-opportunity between Humphrey and Wallace, Nixon himself suggested that the official title be "Order and Justice under Law." This combined Humphrey-like "justice" with Wallace-like "order" and made "law" the Nixon bridge. Nixon himself loved my abuse of Johnson's unpopular attorney general, who was against the Vietnam War and saw criminals as victims of society. I called Ramsey Clark a "conscientious objector in the war against crime."

Kevin Phillips, whom I did not know then, was working for campaign manager John Mitchell across the street from 450 Park Avenue, squirreled away in an obscure office complex over a bank. Phillips knew the voting history, ethnic composition, and other relevant facts of every county in the United States. His charts were helping to shape the campaign strategy. A predecessor to George W. Bush's Karl Rove, Phillips would soon set it all down in the highly original and prophetic *The Emerging Republican Majority* (1969). He was right that the South was trending Republican; he did not then notice the probable costs of making the South a Republican bastion. He saw it only as a pool of votes.

The Nixon speechwriters proved sometimes to be humorous at Nixon's expense, something unthinkable in Reagan's Sacramento. Sometimes, after working late, we would gather for beers at P. J. Clarke's saloon a few blocks away from 450 Park, and here the jokes flourished. One I remember caricatured Nixon's deft style for smearing an opponent:

> "Now, fellow Americans, I know some of you are calling Professor Schlesinger a nuclear spy. But I must remind you that freedom of opinion is the American way, and, fellow Americans, we are all Americans together."

Another went:

> Q: "How can a man who looks like that have two such pretty daughters?"
> A: "Never ask that question."

BY THE THIRD WEEK of September, the Gallup Poll showed Humphrey trailing Nixon by fifteen points. Worse, if possible, Humphrey was only seven points ahead of George Wallace. It was not impossible that the Democratic candidate could come in third. At his campaign stops, Humphrey was being heckled brutally and obscenely by war protesters, disappointed Gene McCarthy and Bobby Kennedy people, anarchists, and more. The catcalls flew: "Baby Killer," "Nazi," "Dump the Hump," and worse.

Even Lyndon Johnson had not suffered these ignominies. After intense cerebration among his advisors, Humphrey, on the night of September 30 in Salt Lake City, made a tiny declaration of independence from LBJ. He came forward with a three-point program, which included the offer to risk a complete bombing halt for the sake of peace, waiting to see what the response might be, while reserving the right to resume the bombing if no adequate response were forthcoming. In substance, this was next to nothing. It was hardly more than a pause—perhaps even a practical necessity, for resting the crews and maintaining the bombers. But seldom had so little produced so great a political effect. The word *peace* did the trick. Perhaps the Kennedy and McCarthy people needed something to save face. They began to flock back to Humphrey, who suddenly focused his attack with traditional working-man themes. His poll numbers began to climb.

Around the middle of October polls showed Massachusetts swinging to Humphrey and Michigan a tie. The Democrat was picking up Wallace voters. Pat Buchanan said he could hear Hubert coming up, his footsteps pounding close behind the Nixon campaign. Big Labor started savaging Nixon. After an emergency meeting in Key Biscayne with his top advisors, Nixon began to pour it on with once-a-day radio speeches, partly with long-distance truckers in mind. We had to turn out those little bombs almost by mass production.

As Humphrey was closing to single digits, *National Review* took account of the continuing Humphrey torment over Vietnam, as in an editorial (October 15) titled "Vietnam Tightrope":

> Mr. Humphrey has not, at this writing, clarified his statement that he will Stop the Bombing—more or less, sort of, *if*. And, as we all know, he has a lemming-like urge to clarify anything he says until the original statement is barnacled beyond recognition. But today, just the bare bones: He would stop bombing the North "as an acceptable risk for peace," and weighing that risk he would "place key importance on evidence . . . of Communist willingness to restore the DMZ. . . ."
>
> The new position seems to be but a teentsy de-escalation, not nearly enough to satisfy either Hanoi or the peace Democrats, both of whom demand an unconditional halt to the bombing.
>
> To be sure, Eugene McCarthy and the other men at the top have already decided to back Humphrey—as little and as late as possible; just enough to ensure that their bid to take over the party in 1972 will not be met with charges of disloyalty. But the rank and file McCarthyites, who have never understood the realities of party politics, will want a lot more.

This is a shrewd editorial, especially in its prescient look at the coming 1972 convulsion in the Democratic Party, symmetrical with the Goldwater 1964 intraparty victory that shifted the Republican base southward.

THOUGH IT WAS THE BEST campaign that could have been designed under the circumstances, the perfect Nixon campaign had irremediable flaws. One was strategic: Nixon's calculated centrist position. As a consequence, he had no sizeable fully committed base, one that would hold firm in any weather. Even if what the nation needed was cool professionalism and a politics of the center, such did not breed conviction. Pat Buchanan later told me that over the last weekend of the campaign, hour-by-hour Nixon polling had shown Humphrey actually nudging *ahead* nationally.

In a November 5 editorial titled "Nixon for Prez," important for conservatives and for the overall evolution of the magazine and appearing in its last issue before the voting, *National Review* supported Nixon, swallowing hard:

It goes without saying that the editors of *National Review* endorse the bid of Richard M. Nixon for the Presidency. We have given, extensively, the reasons why we believe that George Wallace is unqualified, and we join with Senator Barry Goldwater and Congressman John Ashcroft (*NR*, Oct. 27) in fervently hoping that those who are disposed to vote for Mr. Wallace *in protest against the march of events* [italics added] will take thought before Election Day, and help the country at this moment of travail by rendering efficacious aid (Nixon's election) instead of exemplary warning (a Vote for Wallace). . . .

In its endorsement of Nixon, *National Review* reaffirmed the practice— albeit here, somewhat unhappily—of prudential and "strategic" politics. Wallace, a mindless populist, was entirely unacceptable, his opportunistic bigotry perhaps only slightly in abeyance. The editorial goes on, aware that Nixon is a virtuoso of disappointment:

If Mr. Nixon is elected, there undoubtedly will be plenty to criticize in his administration of the nation's affairs. But there will be cause for gratitude that the nation's affairs are in his hands, rather than in those of his amiable opponent, whose loquacious romance with orthodox liberalism will not be sundered in this world.

Concerning Mr. Nixon's human qualities, we confess to a great respect for the way he has conducted himself and his campaign. His rise from 1962, at which point he reached a low as low as Harold Stassen's, is nothing less than heroic, and it is good to see heroism rewarded; and good, also, to know that non-telegenic heroism still happens to stand a chance in the modern age.

THE NIXON PARTY ARRIVED from the airport at the Waldorf Astoria on Park Avenue around 7:00 p.m. on election night. I happened to be in the lobby looking for friends when Nixon arrived. The candidate looked gray, exhausted. John Mitchell had him by the arm and was steadying him as they disappeared into a Waldorf Towers elevator. I heard from someone who had been in the Nixon suite that he had been put in a tub of warm water to relax.

I had been given a necklace with a plastic identification card for Maurice Stans's suite. The place was packed, drinks flowed, and TV coverage remained inconclusive. Around midnight, Pat Buchanan, who was roaming through the suites, told us that things looked good. Certain counties in Virginia had gone for Nixon, and this meant the whole crescent of the Sunbelt, around to southern California, looked good too.

As the night dragged on into the small hours, nothing seemed likely to happen any time soon, so I went back to the New York Yacht Club where I had been staying, had a double bourbon, and slept well. As the results finally came in the next day, the foreground consisted of the extreme closeness of the race between Nixon and Humphrey. The final tabulation was Nixon with 43.4 percent of the popular vote, Hubert Humphrey with 42.7 percent. Very close. But when Wallace's 13.53 percent is figured in, the result, 56.93 percent, represents a landslide against the Democratic Party, a seismic shift against what had been almost a permanent majority since 1932.

AT *NATIONAL REVIEW*, A GRADUAL change had been effected, from paradigm conservative politics to consensus, strategic politics. This can be seen in the framing of the 1968 situation by Frank Meyer, until now the magazine's chief ideologue. Meyer now sounded like Burke, even like Willmoore Kendall:

> [I] voted for Nixon as the choice of a preponderantly conservative convention, and as far and away the best of the three candidates. I, like most of his supporters, hope from him a presidency that will restore order at home and American order and prestige abroad. Wallace spoke of these things, too, in some ways more forcibly than Nixon. But he spoke and speaks of other things as well. He translates the frustrations, the legitimate fears, of the solid Americans to whom he appeals, into hatred. Not content with castigating the errors of our recent leadership, he appeals to the lowest instincts of the demos. By tone, by innuendo, by his whole style, he tries to convert those frustrations into hatred of established institutions and procedures, of the rule of law, of differentiations among men. . . .
>
> The instincts of the people are in general sound. There is no question but that the leading sectors of our society have lost touch with these instincts. But the task of conservatives is, while remaining in consonance with those instincts, to channelize them, to find ways whereby those sound instincts may be expressed without destroying the fabric of society and disrupting the com-

plex arrangements within it that have made civilization possible. The conservative mind does not, as does Wallace, play to the emotions of the people and stir them up, but, recognizing the legitimate sources of those emotions, guides them to reach the civilized solution. . . .

The reader here notices some familiar phrases, though not earlier familiar in Meyer: "established institutions and procedures," "the instincts of the people are generally sound," "complex arrangements," "conservative mind." Meyer has come in from the cold of his Woodstock aerie to the lived life of men in the world.

Meyer goes on:

This is the challenge that faces Richard Nixon as President. He will represent an overwhelming American conservative consensus: not merely his own voters, but most of those who voted for Wallace, and a great many even who voted for Humphrey. No President in the history of the republic has faced a more difficult task, but no President will ever have had more solid support, if he recognizes the character of his mandate and finds the means to carry it out.

National Review looked forward on that optimistic note, suitably qualified. In 1968 Nixon had united the antiliberal vote. He had the historic opportunity to create a new conservative governing establishment. But with Nixon nothing ever was as it seemed.

16

Nixon: In the Arena

"Far better it is to dare mighty things, to win great triumphs even though checkered by failure, than to take rank with those poor spirits who neither enjoy much nor suffer much because they live in the gray twilight that knows neither victory nor defeat."

—Theodore Roosevelt, often cited by Richard
Nixon, as in his resignation remarks to his staff

Uh oh: It is reported that the Senate Caucus Room, in which the Watergate hearings are being held, was first used when Congress investigated the sinking of the Ti-tanic.

—*National Review*, July 6, 1973

The current administration has given a new meaning to the phrase unimpeachable sources.

—*National Review*, November 23, 1973

"Commentators on Richard Nixon's inaugural address have found in it what they wished to find." That opening sentence to *National Review*'s February 4, 1969, editorial resonates in memory. Still, no doubt like everyone else, *National Review* found things to praise in the speech:

> [The] important thing about Nixon's speech was its non-utopian character. No hubristic Great Society was adumbrated; Nixon pointed to no glittering New Frontier. Indeed, he identified the rhetoric of facile aspiration as a principal source of our troubles. "America has suffered from a fever of words; from inflated rhetoric that promises more than it can deliver."

Good for Nixon. He was no blowhard, no utopian.

In retrospect, though *National Review* found much to discuss and to argue about in Nixon's first-term domestic program, when all is said, such discussion and such argument did not have much point. To adapt Gertrude Stein's comment on Oakland, there was simply not much there there. *NR*'s tepid opening editorial thus has a prophetic quality, for Nixon's proposals had no center. A Family Assistance Plan for liberals, a good Supreme Court nominee, Clement Haynesworth, for the conservatives. But both failed, the FAP in Congress, Haynesworth, unjustly, in the Senate.

One day during Nixon's third year I was floating around in the White House looking in on friends from the campaign and I stopped to say hello to John Ehrlichman, the domestic policy advisor. I asked him what Nixon had done for Middle America. He seemed nonplussed, finally answering: *postal service reform*. That about sums it up. A centrist politics needs a vibrant center. Nixon often asked his speechwriters for "the lift of a driving dream." That absurd expression shows why he never had one.

On foreign affairs, Nixon at least came forward with things worth discussing, whether good or bad:

First, opening to China, and downgrading Taiwan. As he had written in *Foreign Affairs*, Nixon hoped for "triangulation" between China and the USSR. While a field of force was established, this did nothing to end the war in Vietnam. Possibly Nixon did not expect it to, but had in mind the postwar power equation. *National Review*, sensing abandonment of Taiwan, urged continuing loyalty.

Second, détente, arms negotiations, SALT (Strategic Arms Limitation Talks). Complex and generally appealing to liberal negotiationists. *National Review* was skeptical and considered détente a Kissinger illusion, since one side continued to wage global war. Kissinger wanted merely to "manage" the Soviet Union; *National Review* saw that stance as static and weak.

Third, Chile and Allende, etc. The near-satellization of Portugal by Communists was avoided. In Chile, Allende took office as a minority president and proceeded to move the country rapidly toward Castro and communism. Nixon made the Chilean economy "scream," but Allende was overthrown by his own armed forces when he tried to move leftists and Castroites into command positions.

OF COURSE, THE VIETNAM WAR, passed on from Johnson to Nixon, had to be the main problem for Nixon's foreign policy. In retrospect, Vietnam and Watergate, closely related, became the defining features of his presidency. Abundant evidence indicates that Nixon and Kissinger regarded the war as impossible to win. They wanted to liquidate America's position there on the best possible terms, while attempting not to sacrifice American "credibility" by perpetuating too visible a disaster. The earliest exponent of that interpretation, so far as I know, was Richard Whalen, a *National Review* contributor who had worked for Nixon early in his run for the nomination. In 1972 he published a thoughtful book, titled *Catch the Falling Flag*, about his growing disenchantment with Nixon.

According to Whalen, as early as March 1968 Nixon had firmly stated his conclusion to Whalen, then a speechwriter, who was taking notes on what he said:

> [As] he announced the conclusion he had reached and the course he intended to follow, my pen stopped. "*I've come to the conclusion that there's no way to win the war. But we can't say that of course. In fact, we have to say the opposite, just to keep some degree of leverage.*"[1] [italics in the original]

A great deal of later evidence exists that supports Whalen's account, as does *National Review*'s coverage of the Vietnam situation as it developed.

But there exits another level, so to speak, to the Nixon-Kissinger strategy. They not only regarded the war as lost, but also as a nuisance to their much larger strategic goal of "managing" relations with the Soviet Union, a far more dangerous nation than China to U.S. foreign policy aims. Nixon and Kissinger wanted stability, which was more important than Vietnam, and this dictated "triangulation," the opening to Beijing putting pressure on Moscow. Of course, the actual strategy had to be maintained out of the public eye, in deep secrecy.

Such statecraft was profoundly Bismarckian, the Iron Chancellor being its greatest practitioner and a major hero to Kissinger. It was, of course, coldly cynical, despite the summits and talk of "peace." More cold-blooded was "Vietnamization," training the ARVN (Army of the Republic of Vietnam) to fight largely on its own after American withdrawal. Neither Nixon nor Kissinger believed this could work: the ARVN was only a mask for incremental withdrawal, and consequent "Vietnamization" under Hanoi. This would make it look as if the ARVN had lost the war, not the United States. Nixon and Kissinger were more interested in post-Vietnam great-power politics than in South Vietnam.

Not long after Nixon's resignation, early in Ford's term, North Vietnamese troops and Soviet tanks invaded the South and quickly reached Saigon. The Nixon and Kissinger plan entailed the death of 20,552 American soldiers between 1969 and 1972. How much American "prestige" had been preserved by this maneuver remains hard to prove. A nation with a large nuclear arsenal probably has enough prestige. The need of Nixon for the utmost secrecy in protecting this devious plan constituted a motive for frequent wiretapping and bugging to detect leakers. This made necessary the secret "Plumbers" operation in the Old Executive Office Building, the Plumbers being the ones who would carry out the Watergate break-ins, though they were not responsible for the myriad dirty tricks that John Mitchell would call "the White House horrors." Beyond that, however, something even less rational was involved, what Bill Safire in *Before the Fall* (1975) called the "dark side of the moon" aspect of Nixon's mind.

EARLY IN NIXON'S FIRST term I was in San Clemente to visit Nixon and others at the summer White House to research an article I was writing. As it happened, Chief-of-Staff Bob Haldeman gave me a lift in his limousine up the Pacific Coast Highway to the Newporter Inn where I was staying. On the way, Haldeman, tanned, crew-cut, tight as a violin string, said something memorable: "You know, this could be a great presidency." I remember that because of its *could*. Haldeman, with his "zero defect" system now in place in the White House, had known Nixon for a long time. He certainly never suspected that he might go to jail. His system worked well—below the "Boss," that is. But there was nothing much he could have done about that.

Nixon liked to boast of "firsts," as in his pride at being the first American president to stand on the Great Wall of China. In 1974, with the resignations of first the vice president, then the president, amidst charges of corruption and other offenses, and with imminent impeachment looming, Nixon became the unchallenged champion of American presidential firsts. As Watergate unfolded, an astonished *National Review* finally turned against both Agnew and Nixon with admixtures of disgust and fury.

From the beginning, *National Review* had expressed a tough skepticism about Nixon, as in these early editorial comments on March 18, 1969:

> President Johnson stopped the bombing of North Vietnam last November 1 because time was running out on Hubert Humphrey's campaign for the Presidency. Mr. Johnson tried to disguise his political motive and protect his party from charges of surrender. . . . That Mr. Johnson's negotiators actually won no concessions from the Communists has not affected tactics on the battlefield. . . .

Ahead, for the Nixon administration, lay mounting resistance, uproar, and violence on the university campuses, mass demonstrations, Kent State, intense media hostility, a sense of social disintegration, all despite Nixon's massive victory in 1972 over the protest candidacy of George McGovern. Already by the fall of 1969, *National Review* recognized what actually was taking place:

> Richard Nixon is playing for time. Time is the top stake in this fierce, delicate, Southeast Asia game. Mr. Nixon knows there cannot be an *honorable settlement* in Vietnam unless the anti-Communist side holds on; and the anti-Communist side cannot *hold on* if the Americans do not. How long? Long enough. Long enough to convince Hanoi and its backers that America will not permit the Communists to take over South Vietnam. [italics added]

This sounds stern enough, except that the amount of time they must hold on is not specified. In an October 14, 1969, editorial, the scope of the problem was coming into view:

> The outlines of President Nixon's Vietnam policy have now become clear. During the next eighteen months a substantial number of American troops will be withdrawn—around half the number now there. Vietnamese troops and regional forces will 1) greatly reduce American casualties, and 2) *eliminate the possibility of a Communist takeover*. Those American troops remaining in Vietnam will be volunteers, largely professionals, rather than draftees. [italics added]

The italicized goal was, of course, an impossibility. Indeed, why would the North offer better terms, let alone give up its goals, while American forces were *leaving*?

On November 6, 1969, *National Review* ran an important editorial probably written by Burnham. *There did exist a way, or ways, of winning*:

> It is true, to be sure, that abstracted from its concrete political circumstance this war presents no great military problem. North Vietnam could be knocked out of the war quickly by: 1) Bombing the Red River dams, bombing the power grid, and, if necessary, obliterating its cities and towns. If it be argued that only military targets are legitimate objects for bombing, the obvious answer is that as far as countries on the Asian mainland are concerned, the main— and sometimes the sole—military resource is population. 2) Closing Haiphong by any of several methods. 3) Biting off a chunk of North Vietnam by an invasion across the DMZ, or, more elegantly, by a large and menacing assault.

The magazine did not return to any of these options. Any sort of land invasion would have brought the United States itself to the edge of nervous breakdown and revolution. Any of the options, by themselves, would have defeated the North. The best might have been destroying the population to the point where not enough manpower would be available to enter the invasion trails. That would have been a legitimate military option. We had been willing to use population destruction in Japan to avoid an invasion after the carnage on Okinawa. But Vietnam was backed up by *China*. It seems likely that destroying North Vietnam by devastation from the air, and thus annihilating its military capacity, would merely have resulted in what was left becoming a vassal state of China. Losing this war, on the other hand, could issue in a "Titoist" Vietnam, a nation that had been resisting China for centuries. It was the strategic location of China that made winning the war impossible.

Nixon visited China, Buckley in the traveling party and covering the visit extensively in *National Review*. Buckley thought Nixon's deference to Mao excessive and undignified, but Nixon expected much from the diplomacy. His triangulation of Beijing, Moscow, and the United States *did* in fact tend to isolate Hanoi, but it had no discernible effect on the war. Prime Minister Pham Van Dong of North Vietnam did travel to Beijing and appealed to Mao to rescind the decision to receive Nixon for his 1972 visit. Mao not only rejected this plea, but urged the emissary to seek a compromise settlement of the war. This was exactly as Nixon had intended.[2] A parallel result was achieved in Moscow, where Brezhnev refused to cancel the planned summit, urged Hanoi to be reasonable, and then reached agreements with Nixon on Berlin and other outstanding matters that might otherwise have been more difficult or impossible.[3]

Diplomatic "signals" thus were sent to Hanoi, though for the time being material aid to the North did not cease. The most to be expected from Nixonian diplomacy was achieved, but the only difference it made to Hanoi was to produce anger at the three nations' failure to achieve full Communist cooperation. Hanoi would fight on as before, indicating a degree of independence from both Beijing and Moscow.

THE ASSUMPTIONS BEHIND Nixon's Vietnam strategy faced a brutal test in April 1972, when General Giap suddenly launched an all-out conventional attack on the South with Soviet-supplied heavy equipment and high-quality regular North Vietnamese forces. *National Review* responded in an April 21, 1972, editorial:

> [We] confront the first critical and perhaps decisive test of the President's
> Vietnamization policy. Whatever the ambiguities in which it has been for-

mulated, the American public has been led to believe that Vietnamization promises withdrawal of American military forces from Indochina in a fairly short period of time *and* the survival of an independent South Vietnamese government. Many strategic analysts have held all along that the attainment of *both* these goals, however desirable, is not possible. We shall soon have new and compelling evidence by which to judge their doubt.

As, indeed, we did. Almost at once, B-52s flying from Guam smashed the April Fool's day invasion. Beijing did nothing, and in Moscow the summit went forward. But American airpower won that battle, not the ARVN.

The response in Beijing and Moscow corresponded exactly with what Brezhnev, in a good phrase, sometimes called the "correlation of forces." The Saigon army could not match the fighting power of the North Vietnamese. With the total withdrawal of the Americans, South Vietnam would remain a rump state, with the proven fighting power of the North arrayed against it, backed by China and the Soviet Union with diplomatic and logistical support. Brezhnev and Mao knew very well that American opinion was divided on the war. Time could only work against Nixon.

In his April 24, 1972, column, Burnham began to draw this conclusion:

> Conceivably South Vietnamese troops plus U.S. air power and naval guns will stop and push back this North Vietnamese advance. But the underlying issue will not be affected. For Richard Nixon, South Vietnam's survival as an independent non-Communist state has a lower priority than American withdrawal and his own re-election. It is therefore probable that South Vietnam will not so survive, just as, in an analogous structure of priorities, Free China did not survive as a U.N. member.

As Burnham hinted at that point, about four months before the 1972 Republican Convention in Miami, Nixon was in good shape for reelection. As it turned out, the nomination of George McGovern by the Democrats would hand Nixon a landslide. But Burnham's accurate assessment of the actualities regarding Vietnam made him one of the first to see through the rosy atmosphere surrounding the January 27, 1973, "peace" accords signed in Paris. Was peace really "at hand," as Kissinger claimed?

As Burnham was one of the first to notice, the "peace" accord accepted, and by so doing legitimized, the continuing presence of substantial numbers of regular North Vietnamese troops in South Vietnam. This, as U.S. forces approached the vanishing point. Was such a thing not a compromise of South Vietnamese sovereignty, as well as a strategic asymmetrical defeat for U.S. policy? Burnham expressed his doubts in a February 16, 1973, "Protracted Conflict" column titled "Peace, Peace, But Is It Peace?"

> It is not a treaty of peace and does not end the war. So far as Southeast Asia is concerned, it is not even an armistice. . . . Essentially the agreement would be accurately entitled: A Protocol of American Military Disengagement from Vietnam. We may confidently predict that many provisions of the agreement will not work out. Some of them are obviously impossible from a technical standpoint. The international commission could not and did not assemble in Vietnam within the prescribed 24 hours after signing, much less start effective functioning. Nor, for that matter, will it ever function effectively. Its assigned tasks cannot be carried out by the specified 1,116 men, even if they had the wings of angels. . . . The suggested precedents of Germany and Korea do not hold. In Germany in 1945 and Korea in 1951, the armistice line coincided with the military line. But in Vietnam and Indochina, the DMZ does not mark an established power division. The maps of Indochina showing areas controlled by the Communists, and confirmed to their control by the agreement, look like the x-ray of a chest with metastasized cancer.

The disgraceful tragi-farcical end came in 1975 under President Ford. It consisted of an ignominious Dunkirk, with frantic helicopter evacuations from the roof of the American Embassy in Saigon and some million Vietnamese "boat people" embarked upon the South China Sea while hundreds of thousands of their countrymen went to "reeducation camps."

In 1979, four years after the fall of Saigon, Kissinger published the first volume of his memoirs, *White House Years*, concluding with the year 1972 (before the collapse) in a chapter titled, surely with some macabre humor, "Peace at Last." It ends as follows, describing Kissinger's supposed feelings as he initialed the Paris "peace" accords:

> Enveloped in an intractable solitude, [Nixon] nevertheless saw before him a vista of promise to which few statesmen have been blessed to aspire. He could envision a new international order that would reduce lingering enmities, strengthen friendships, and give new hope to emerging nations. It was a worthy goal for America and mankind. He was alone in his moment of triumph on a pinnacle that was soon to turn into a precipice. And yet with all his insecurities and flaws he had brought us by a tremendous act of will to an extraordinary moment when dreams and possibilities conjoined.

This is astonishing. Anyone might be excused for mistaking it for a translation of Virgil's *Fourth Eclogue* welcoming a golden age, or perhaps of Isaiah on the lion and the lamb.

In his less lyrical moments, Kissinger had a much more realistic sense of international affairs, as did, certainly, Nixon himself. Nixon was darkly Hobbesian. Once, in conversation at San Clemente, he remarked to me concerning international relations, as if about the ocean outside his office, "That's not Charlie the Tuna out there. It's Jaws." I will add here one anecdote evocative of Nixon's Hobbesian side, and his confidence as regards Europe. On another occasion at San Clemente, he took obvious pleasure in telling me this, and I quote from memory:

> Brezhnev was in here a week or so ago. He had a big blonde with him. His *masseuse*, as he called her. The first night, at the Casa, Brezhnev got drunk as a skunk, and in the middle of the night Mrs. Nixon got up to get something in the kitchen and she ran into Brezhnev in the hall, stark naked, chasing the big blonde, also naked, around the halls. Well, next morning at nine o'clock sharp, Brezhnev was here in this office with his interpreter and he seemed cold sober. He took a cup of coffee. I said to him, "Mr. Chairman, before we get to our agenda I want to tell you this. If there is a Russian tank attack across the German plain, the war will go nuclear immediately." Well, Brezhnev paused for a minute. Then he said, "Mr. President, I'm glad you told me that."

Nixon's mind worked more surely in Europe than in Asia; the boundaries of possibility were established in Europe. From the beginning, Nixon was aiming for a good agreement on Vietnam, if he could get it—but a bad one, if he could not. He took the second. On Whalen's evidence, cited earlier, he probably knew all along that he would.

IN HIS 1982 MEMOIR *Witness to Power*, John Ehrlichman includes this anecdote:

> On January 23, [1973,] the President announced the peace agreement in a short, televised address. The next day I talked to Henry Kissinger briefly in the doorway of the Roosevelt Room. After congratulating him, I asked about the future: "How long do you figure the South Vietnamese can survive under this agreement?" I expected Henry to give me some assurances. Instead, he told me the truth, and it shook me badly.
>
> "I think," Henry said, "that if they're lucky they can hold out for a year and a half."[4]

What Ehrlichman reports here was consistent with the facts, though not consistent with the prose poem in Kissinger's autobiography. We must agree, on the evidence, with the strategist Anthony Hartley, reviewing (December 14, 1992) in *National Review* Walter Isaacson's biography of Kissinger:

> In 1969 the United States was fighting its way out of the impasse into which the efforts of previous Administrations—not least the soaring ambitions of the Kennedy years—had led. When Richard Nixon took office, with Henry Kissinger as his National Security Advisor, the United States was losing the war in Vietnam. It was Kissinger's task to find a way out of Vietnam that was not too humiliating and not too destructive of America's credibility. He did it, but there was no elegant way to retreat. The path out of Vietnam was unpleasant and devious. Kissinger was clear that the war must end, but in a way that would not leave America's allies or enemies with the impression that the country had been crippled by the experience.

Whether the result achieved did salvage American prestige and credibility, and whether it was worth all those American lives, historians will continue to ponder.

Fifth anniversary dinner: (L to R) Natalie and Garry Wills; Frank and Elsie Meyer; Joan and Neil McCaffrey. A lighter moment for the *NR* editors (1956): (L to R) Priscilla L. Buckely, Suzanne La Follette, James Burnham, Willmoore Kendall, and WFB.

TO ARTHUR M. SCHLESINGER, JR.
HARVARD UNIVERSITY

NATIONAL REVIEW'S Special Award For
Promise In Political Prognostication

NR editor as public intellectual: (clockwise) WFB keeps *National Review* in the limelight through public speaking; hosting *Firing Line*; and running for public office (1965). The first issue: November 19, 1955. *National Review* celebrates its tenth anniversary (November 30, 1965).

IN THIS ISSUE: A NEW BOOK By JEFFREY HART

$1.00

NOVEMBER 30, 1965

NATIONAL REVIEW

A Journal of Fact and Opinion

10

TENTH ANNIVERSARY ISSUE

EXTRA: THE COMPLETE PHOTO-STORY OF THE DINNER, WITH STEVE ALLEN • **WM. F. BUCKLEY** • JOHN DOS PASSOS • **SEN. BARRY GOLDWATER** • CLARE BOOTHE LUCE • ADM. LEWIS STRAUSS • PLUS THE INSIDE STORY OF NR BY PRISCILLA BUCKLEY

NATIONAL REVIEW

20 Cents
November 19, 1955

A WEEKLY JOURNAL OF OPINION

Peace — with Honor
WILLIAM F. KNOWLAND

They'll Never Get Me on That Couch
MORRIE RYSKIND

I Raised Money for the Ivy League
ALOISE HEATH

Articles and Reviews by • • • • • JOHN CHAMBERLAIN
JAMES BURNHAM • RUSSELL KIRK • FRANK S. MEYER
WILLMOORE KENDALL • FREDA UTLEY • C. D. WILLIAMS

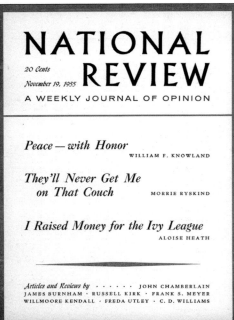

Keeping the ship afloat. The 1970 National Review Board of Directors: (L to R, back row) Dan McGrath, Neal Freeman, Joe Donner, Jim Buckley, Jim McFadden, Roger Allan Moore (chairman); (front row) Tom Bolan, Bill Rusher, Van Galbraith, WFB, Arthur Andersen. A 1972 editorial meeting: (L to R) Priscilla L. Buckley, WFB, and James Burnham.

(Clockwise) Goldwater, Reagan, and WFB; Joe Sobran, Kevin Lynch, and author; 1980 staff; *NR* sponsors Michael Oakeshott lecture at Hunter College, 1975; Clare Boothe Luce.

NR contributing editors: (counter-clockwise) Jeffrey Hart, ONI, circa 1955; L. Brent Bozell; William Rickenbacker; John Chamberlain; and Russell Kirk with WFB. Frank Shakespeare and WFB visit the Oval Office. WFB interviews Richard Nixon on *Firing Line* (1968).

30th anniversary gala attendees: (clockwise) CBS mafia join James Buckley, Roy Cohen, Henry Kissinger, and Erik von Kuehnelt-Leddihn; along with George Will, Mrs. Reagan and WFB; thanks from cartoonist Jeff MacNelly. *NR* evaluates the Reagan Revolution. *New York Times* reports news fit to print.

National Review Losing Buckley As Chief Editor

By ERIC PACE

William F. Buckley Jr., the founder and ranking editor of National Review for 35 years, said last night that he would soon step down from his position and become the editor at large of the conservative biweekly magazine.

Mr. Buckley, who is 64 years old, disclosed his plans at the end of a banquet held at the Waldorf-Astoria celebrating the 35th anniversary of the magazine's founding.

He said the anniversary issue, which is to be published in two weeks, would be his last as the top editor.

Mr. Buckley told the nearly 800 guests in the hotel's grand ballroom that he had stayed so long at the magazine, which has a circulation of 152,000, because "there never was anything else around seriously to tempt me" to leave.

Smiling broadly, he said, "We did as much as anybody, with the exception of

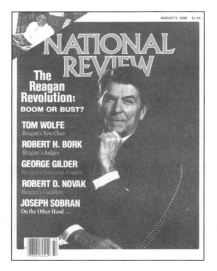

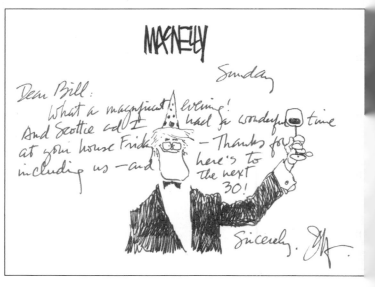

AUGUST 5, 1988 $1.95

NATIONAL REVIEW

The Reagan Revolution:
BOOM OR BUST?

TOM WOLFE
Reagan's New Class

ROBERT H. BORK
Reagan's Judges

GEORGE GILDER
Reagan's American Empire

ROBERT D. NOVAK
Reagan's Coalition

JOSEPH SOBRAN
On the Other Hand ...

(Clockwise) Bill Rusher and Linda Bridges, 1985. Ed Capano, 1990. Dinner at Nicola Paone's, 1988: Bill Rusher, Tom Bolan, and Wick Allison are joined by Jim McFadden, John O'Sullivan, and WFB. Contributors Ernest van den Haag and Richard John Neuhaus with WFB at the 1991 *NR* Christmas party. A special guest celebrates the openning of the *NR* Washington office, 1983.

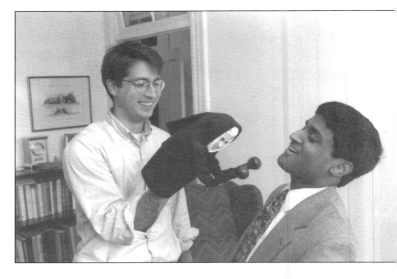

Buckley Retires As Editor

National Review Founder Steps Down After 35 Years

By E.J. Dionne Jr.
Washington Post Staff Writer

Thirty-five years ago, William F. Buckley Jr. founded National Review, a conservative magazine that set itself a preposterously ambitious goal. "It stands athwart history yelling Stop," the magazine said of itself in its first editorial.

Yesterday, 2,750 issues later, Buckley quietly said Stop himself and announced that he was stepping down as National Review's editor in chief.

In financial terms, the announcement was without significance. Buckley will continue to hold all of the National Review stock, which, he noted, "commercially is about as valuable as Confederate bonds." And he pledged to look over the shoulders of his editors to keep the magazine on

(Clockwise) John Derbyshire; Rich Lowry boxing Ramesh Ponnuru, 1995; Tracy Lee Simons and Richard Brookhiser at editorial meeting, 1995; WFB at the office. *Washington Post* on retirement.

17

Watergate: Nixon X-Rayed

"The lengthened shadow of a man
Is history, said Emerson. . . ."
—T. S. Eliot, "Sweeney Erect"

Watergate has become part of our national legend, unfolding, as it did, day by day on television. Its cast of characters outdid anything Hollywood could have imagined. Obscure Nixon staffers such as the resonantly named Jeb Stuart Magruder and the young, blond presidential counsel John Dean were suddenly pushed out into the daylight from the corridors of the Executive Office Building. The now famous figures Haldeman, Ehrlichman, and Mitchell turned in their performances, as did comical Damon Runyon gumshoes, plus creatures from even darker depths. And always the question echoed through the Ervin Committee's Senate hearing chamber, the insistent question about the spider at the center of the web: "What did *he* know and when did *he* know it?"

National Review responded to the developing scandal with condemnation for the violation of constitutional norms mixed with a great deal of disgust; it came close to lacking even residual loyalty to Nixon. *NR* viewed the "President's men," the aides closest to him, as technicians of no discernible principle, all products of their relationship to Nixon and otherwise ciphers with no personal identity. It regarded Nixon himself as the shifty politician the magazine had always known. James Buckley was the first senator to call for Nixon's resignation as an "act of courage" on Nixon's part. Of course, Nixon did no such thing until forced to.

What strikes anyone going back over that period, and what certainly struck *National Review* at the time, is the conspicuous presence of an absence—or the deafening noise of a silence. Why did those closest to the president in the administrative structure—namely Haldeman, Ehrlichman, and Mitchell—not once, ever, say to themselves or to each other, "President Nixon would never approve of this"? What did Nixon say to himself when thinking of those portraits of past presidents in the halls of the White House? When he took office, Nixon had Woodrow Wilson's desk taken out of storage and used it in the Oval Office. What would the Presbyterian straight-arrow Wilson, a minister's son, think just now? The echoing silence of Nixon's aides can only be understood through a grasp of the political atmosphere of the time, itself amply reported in *National Review*: a rancid division into mutually loathing parts, all but in name engaged in civil war, pullulating with hatred—and some of it, but by no means all of it, Nixon's fault.

On the day following his August 9, 1974, resignation speech, Nixon met in the East Room with his family, his Cabinet, and what remained of his staff, to bid farewell to those who had served him and the nation, the whole thing televised and macabre. When the sliding doors opened and Nixon entered, his Marine Corps aide Colonel Jack Brennan boomed, "Ladies and gentlemen, the President of the United States of America and Mrs. Nixon, Mr. and Mrs. Edward Cox, Mr. and Mrs. David Eisenhower." The words and their entry evoked thunderous applause. Nixon had difficulty quieting the crowd; some were weeping. His words were moving. He included the quotation from Theodore Roosevelt about the man in the arena, which he had often used, and this thought:

> Always give your best, never get discouraged, never be petty; always remember, others may hate you, but those who hate you don't win unless you hate them, and then you destroy yourself.

That comes pretty close to a confession. But characteristically, Nixon makes of this self-disclosure a generalization, even a warning to *others* in the room. Those with a good memory might have recalled the Nixon of *Six Crises*, the Nixon of the self-destructive, badly hungover 1962 "Last Press Conference," the Nixon always in danger of cracking under pressure—and the Nixon who, during the March on Washington, had visited the enraged but astonished demonstrators in the middle of the night and talked about football, his nerves almost out of control. Whether to pity him or loathe him at that moment has to be a close call.

Nixon, as even a casual reading of his biographies reveals, suffered from a sense of resentment about factors beyond his control that had so often frustrated him. He had been admitted to Harvard, but his pinched family could not afford it. He made the best of Whittier College. There, he played mediocre football, and in some especially awful episodes, while courting Pat Ryan, drove her to dates with other men. Instead of one of the elite law schools, he went to Duke, where his hours in the law library earned him the nickname "Iron Butt." Despite high grades, he could not get an offer from a prestigious Eastern law firm. He was hurt by that as much as by his earlier failure to attend Harvard.

Biographers say that perhaps the happiest period of his life occurred much later, when he was a partner in John Mitchell's Wall Street firm and living in the same apartment building as Nelson Rockefeller. Nixon was then at last a member of the Eastern Establishment, sort of. But as a young law school graduate, failing to secure a post at a prestigious firm, he took a minor federal job. After the World War II Navy and the Pacific, he ran for Congress, then for the Senate, clawing his way to victory with dubious tactics, coached by Murray Chotiner, who came to the White House with him in 1969.

Both he and Chotiner saw electoral politics as war. He believed the Eastern elite never forgave him for his successful work in exposing Alger Hiss, whose Harvard law degree and elite manners antagonized him. He took more seriously than he should have those cartoons by Herblock which pushed him, always unshaven, down into the gutter. As vice president, he knew that Eisenhower—and the right word is difficult to find here—but perhaps, "faintly loathed him" will have to do. During the 1960 campaign, Ike, asked on TV to name an important Nixon contribution, replied, "If you give me a week, I could think of one." Nixon exposed his feelings of injured merit when, in his 1962 "Last Press Conference," he angrily told reporters, "You won't have Nixon to kick around any more." But, oh yes, they would.

Finally, and this is subjective on my part, Nixon must have known that his appearance was far from pleasing. All too conspicuous was his *nose*: not its ski-jump shape, but, looked at from the front, its awful *width*. And his jowls. Someone said he looked like a malevolent chipmunk. Add to that his five o'clock shadow, his fair skin so transparent that his black stubble showed through, especially under television glare. Everyone is aware of appearance, and how it affects people. Reagan from an early age must have known that people usually were immediately pleased to see him. Nixon must have sensed the opposite.

In sum, we have here a difficult personality, one who had succeeded by effort, endurance, intelligence, one who had made his way to the top against tremendous difficulties. Injured merit may have been his driving emotion. *They were not going to take it all away from him.* The identity of "they" might change, but he was a suspicious man and so saw plots all around him, enemies—which of course he had. He could be cold and ruthless. He cut corners, always wanted an "edge," as he called it. In retrospect, with his fragile nerves he seems unfit for the presidency, especially during a quasi-revolutionary period.

SECRECY SEEMS TO HAVE BEEN almost an obsession for both Nixon and Kissinger, heightened by the requirements of the complex project of withdrawal from Vietnam. Bill Safire was angry for a long time when he discovered that Kissinger had caused *his* phones to be tapped, as seems to have been endemic to the Nixon White House. The infamous Plumbers Unit, designed to stop "leaks," G. Gordon Liddy and E. Howard Hunt its guiding spirits, can be seen as a natural product of comprehensive suspicion. Both Nixon and Kissinger could be devious, as circumstances sometimes demanded: but circumstances did not *always* demand it. Kissinger's excellent *A World Restored* (1957) praised the skills of Metternich, diplomatic genius of the Congress of Vienna, about whom the following no doubt apocryphal story has been told: When a diplomat at the congress suddenly died of a heart attack, Prince Metternich mused aloud, "I wonder what he meant by that." Both Nixon and Kissinger sometimes suspected hidden motives and agendas where none could reasonably be discerned.

Desiring secrecy, ostensibly for diplomacy and security, Nixon wiretapped the White House and even taped himself in the Oval Office. Nothing resembling this voice-activated system had ever been used before. It seems almost inevitable, even poetic justice, that finally his own tapes of himself are what caught him, convicted him, and could have sent him to prison.[1]

Nixon also gave hints in his farewell remarks to his staff that *he would be back*. Which, indeed, he would—remarkably, as a sort of ruined Elder Statesman. An accurate count of his "comebacks" is probably impossible.

Many anecdotes reveal a side of Nixon that few people saw. In his book about the Reagan presidency, *The Role of a Lifetime* (1991), Lou Cannon tells this anecdote, shocking in its way. On March 14, 1970, at a banquet at the Capitol Hill Hotel in Washington, Cannon was placed in the receiving line next to Governor Reagan. Then President Nixon came in,

> waved his aides aside, and walked down the receiving line. Reagan warmly greeted him and introduced me by saying, "Hello, Mr. President, this is Lou Cannon. He's just written a book about me." Nixon stopped in his tracks, looking as if he'd just been slapped. He glared at me, as if he could not understand why anyone would conceivably write a book about Reagan. Then he glared at Reagan. "Well, I'll *scan* it." Reagan saw that I was shaken by the unexpected ferocity of Nixon's response. He waited until Nixon was out of earshot and said quietly to me, "Well, Lou, he just took care of you—and me."

Cannon interprets that as an example of Reagan's view that Nixon had "bad manners." That is certainly true, though sometimes Nixon could be prissily correct.

The incident, however, in an overall view of Nixon, is suggestive of much more than bad manners. Nixon had a wolfish contempt for anyone he considered his intellectual inferior, and he considered Reagan an ignoramus. Perhaps worse, two years earlier, in 1968, Reagan had tried to thwart him at the Miami Convention. Reagan must have been on some Enemies List in his mind. Of course he envied, feared, and hated the Kennedys: first Jack, handsome, wealthy, whom he also considered an ignoramus, and who had thwarted him in 1960, and later Ted—until that Kennedy was ruined by Chappaquiddick.

To Nixon's mind, not only were the war protesters an obstacle to his plans for a slow extrication from Vietnam, they were also traitorous, and their numbers legion. Daniel Ellsberg had copied the Pentagon Papers at Rand, but after all, they had nothing to do with Nixon. Nonetheless, Ellsberg, a hero to the liberals and to the *New York Times*, had to be ruined. Not in the least original in this surmise, my own conclusion must be that Nixon's personality created an atmosphere of suspicion, enmity, and deep hostility within his inner circle that spread through the entire White House and ultimately explains the "White House horrors," as John Mitchell called the fantastic plots and schemes revealed during the Watergate investigations: the break-ins, the proposed murders and fire-bombings, kidnappings, smears, and more. Meet G. Gordon Liddy, dark spiritual son of Nixon. The spreading Nixon atmosphere enveloped even straight arrows like Haldeman and Ehrlichman, and many others who, in the absence of Nixon, would never have seen the inside of a jail cell.

NIXON GLIDED TO HIS 60–40 landslide over McGovern in 1972, but the various investigations of the Watergate break-in had only been postponed into the new year. Nixon knew that his greatest protection was his physical possession of the tapes. He knew that they contained much that was dangerous, especially the June 23, 1972, and March 21, 1973, tapes, from which it could be inferred that Nixon had indicated to his counsel John Dean "we could get" the hush money and pay it, and had ordered Haldeman and Ehrlichman to have the CIA tell the FBI to pull back from its investigation on national security grounds. Smoke was pouring out of those "smoking guns," but there was much to fear from other guns as well.

As early as August 6, 1973, *National Review* expressed exasperation with White House obstruction tactics in an editorial titled "A President and His Privileges":

> Skepticism escalates to cynicism as the battle over "executive privilege" rages between the Senate and the White House. The captains of both sides, hands on hearts and eyes to high heaven, invoke the loftiest of constitutional principles, while they meanwhile try to hide the muck they are wading in. . . . And what is this Caesarist wall defending? The shoddy little trail of this pipsqueak Watergate business. As Vermont Royster wrote in the *Wall Street Journal*: "The real mystery of Watergate . . . is why the Nixon administration at this late date is letting a caper turn into a political calamity."

Before long, editorial comment became angry:

> It seems most probable that President Nixon could have reduced the Watergate affair to a ten-day wonder. . . . All he needed was clear and unequivocal disapproval and, if necessary, letting a few heads roll.

If only it were so. What Nixon had to guard against was exposure of the whole truth on the tapes, the truth about *him*.

National Review tried to take some comfort in the fact that Judge Sirica, in the process of breaking the case open, was a conservative Republican. The magazine was looking for some small conservative gain amidst the debacle, as in such a characterization of the president's men as this (May 18, 1973):

> A final, and interesting, sidelight: The outgoing bad boys [mainly Haldeman and Ehrlichman] were all technicians, men with little experience in politics other than as faithful aides and supporters of Richard M. Nixon. None had come up through grass-roots political activity. They understood the meaning of power only too well—power is to have the ear and the confidence of Numero Uno.

This is only partly true. Haldeman and Ehrlichman, and their immediate subordinates, such as Haldeman's assistant Magruder, were technicians, and like their boss they were take-no-prisoners political operatives, but they were also fierce patriots and despised their enemies on the Left, whom they regarded as weak in the American cause. They also loathed the counterculture and the sexual revolution; they were religious, teetotalers, and did not smoke.

With the resignation of Haldeman and Ehrlichman, public testimony before the Ervin Committee, a steady stream of indictments, and the advancing struggle over the tapes—finally settled by the Supreme Court in favor of disclosure—the walls of the Nixon White House began to crumble. Elements of comedy began to enter the picture, notably in *National Review,* when Hugh Kenner shaped excerpts from the tapes into pseudo-poems, inventing a fictitious book titled *The Poetry of Richard Milhouse Nixon*, compiled by Jack Margolis (Cliff House Books), unpaged, $1. Kenner "reviewed" this concoction as if it were a real book, praising the Nixon poems as "A New Voice" in the July 19, 1974, *National Review.* Here are just a few excerpts, of Kenner's spoofing, pretentious commentary:

Here are no sonnets for an idle hour. Stark, terse, hard-bitten, cunningly disequilibriated—tip-toe, in fact, on the needlepoint of a century's anguish—these poems speak to and for the thwarted Tamburlaine that lurks in the heart of urban America. Make no mistake, ours are not easy times. Old certainties dissolve. On every front—ecology, government, Raquel Welch—we face both ways while poet Nixon speaks for all of us:

> *Mixed Emotions*
>
> *I still have mixed emotions on it.*
> *I don't know.*
> *I don't know.*
>
> *I have been one way at one time*
> *One way another.*

By contrast, how quintessentially *English* was Tennyson's "This way and that dividing the swift mind," a genteel stab at comparable authenticity. Mr. Nixon has nothing for the ear of Queen Victoria: no periphrasis, no effete pentameter. The American idiom beats in his *Threepenny Opera*, which in frank concession to our decade's theme, inflation, is entitled "One Million Dollars":

> *We can get that.*
> *On the money,*
> *If you need the money,*
> *You could get that.*
>
> *You could raise a million dollars.*
> *You could get it in cash.*
> *I know where it could be gotten.*
> *It is not easy,*
> *But it could*
> *Be done.*

One of the funniest passages comes near the end of this spoof:

But more often, as in the "Who Are They After?" (a profound reversal of Wyatt's "They Flee from me," effected by a student of "The Hound of Heaven") Nixon will pare away the merely formal core to leave free-standing:

> *Who*
> *the hell*
> *are they after?*
>
> *They*
> *are*
> *after*
> *us. . . .*

Kenner as *faux* critic comments:

Face to face with such quiet mastery, one is startled to learn from the dust jacket that this is Mr. Nixon's first book of poetry. Surely we may expect more from his Sony? We have no right to expect better. So consummate is such an achievement, one is quietly satisfied to remark, that it certifies to the viability of the middle American lifestyle. Yorba Linda has given tongue to Pittsburgh, to Winnetka. Here is no footloose vagrant, no sandaled unshaven bum. Un-like Homer or Allen Ginsberg, Mr. Nixon is a civil servant, is content to reside in Washington, D.C., with his wife "Pat."

BUT THE MILLS were grinding steadily and exceedingly fine, as indicated in a *National Review* editorial on January 1, 1973, "Can the President Continue to Rule?":

> It is generally accepted that if, *per impossible*, the President were found to have been responsible for Watergate, or for covering up after Watergate, he should be impeached. That is the view, for instance, of Senator Barry Goldwater, and the view of columnist Stewart Alsop. Congressional leaders who have a keen eye for the demands of social stability are not pressing for impeachment, nor even arguing lasciviously, that impeachment must result from any adverse findings by grand jury or congressional investigating committees. They are saying—some of them sadly, some of them exultantly —that the president will not exercise power after the stains of Watergate.

That was an institutional overview. But soon a major *National Review* opinion in the form of a Buckley "On the Right" column took a more personal view in a consideration of Nixon's character:

> Nixon is not other-worldly in his habit of operations. His character is well-known to the American people, who cannot easily be convinced that his preoccupation with cosmic concerns so absorbed him as to leave him transfixed, like Socrates in one of his philosophical trances, while such petty matters as Watergate flurried about him. Mr. Nixon is a man of compulsive curiosity concerning matters of potential political moment. Mr. Gallup has not released the figures, but it is likely that a considerable majority of the American people believe that Richard Nixon knew way before April 17 that people surrounding him were not merely standing aside from the Watergate investigation, but were in fact conspiring—a word used here with precision—to obstruct justice. That belief will in due course crystallize into a legal formulation: namely, that President Nixon was guilty of misprision of felony. Misprision of felony is itself a felony. It is predictable that a motion would then be introduced to impeach President Nixon, and it is imperative that that motion be defeated.

In that formulation, the tapes are confirmatory evidence of what we already surmise through past knowledge; and that such evidence is necessary to impeach Nixon, and that we should insist, upon the evidence: Guilty, but not proven.

Then this column continues, in a second part, to make an important moral point:

> The trial of Daniel Ellsberg in Los Angeles is grinding at last to its end, and, indeed, just in time: For the big name indictments and trials arising out of Watergate are about to commence. But no one has pointed out how intimately connected the two are.
>
> In a recent column James Reston viewed Watergate as connected to an atmosphere of "suspicion" pervading the Nixon White House, but "suspicion" is hardly the right word. It is too psychological to do justice to the reality, and it does not raise the question of the extent to which that "atmosphere" was justified. Reston assumes that it was not.
>
> As a matter of fact, Watergate, like Ellsberg's copying and disclosure of the Pentagon Papers, is an episode in a kind of civil war that has been going on in this country for the past seven or eight years, and which doubtless has roots which go much further back than that. Both Ellsberg and the Watergate operatives behaved as if they were dealing not merely with political opponents but with enemies.

But whatever Nixon's fate, *National Review* assured its readers that all was relatively well, since the sturdy Vice President Spiro Agnew stood ready to take over, observing editorially on June 8, 1973, "Richard Nixon may be forced to resign":

> That possibility is no longer in the realm of abstract theory. . . . In cold political terms an incoming Agnew Administration could be in a strong position.
>
> "After all," writes syndicated columnist Kevin Phillips, "Agnew is not remotely implicated in the Watergate Syndrome; he should no more be affected by its fallout than Calvin Coolidge was by the scandalous odor attached to the Administration of Warren G. Harding. . . . Similar success can await Agnew. If Richard Nixon were to leave office within the next year, then Vice President turned President Agnew would have nearly three years to gain the nation's trust, affection, and respect.

That was in the spring of 1973. By the fall, Agnew was desperately dealing with prosecutors and trying to stay out of jail.

By July 20, 1973, *National Review* had just about reached the end of the line with the Nixon White House, about the break-ins, the cover-up, and a myriad of other things, as in this major editorial titled "The Line Must Be Drawn Somewhere":

> The testimony and documents that have been made public in or through the one forum or another since the break-in at the Democratic Party headquarters in June 1972 have shown beyond reasonable doubt that President Nixon's immediate staff have attempted to use and in fact have used official agencies of the United States government for partisan, factional, and personal ends unrelated to the public and national purposes for which such agencies have been created and funded by law.
>
> The evidence and indications are that this sort of thing is not the . . . occasional deviation of a few individuals but, in intent at least, part of the operational style of the White House staff as a whole, inclusive of its topmost echelons.

At about the same time, *National Review*'s new Washington columnist George Will began to perfect the style of political comment that combined relentless logic with understated scorn for felons and fools and would make him famous. His handling of the upcoming Spiro Agnew scandal would alienate some at *National Review* as too severe a way to treat a friend, but it was also just, and it impressed a national audience with his integrity. Will soon moved to the *Washington Post* and *Newsweek*. James Burnham considered him potentially as influential as Walter Lippmann had been in his prime.

Spiro Agnew went out rotting. As *National Review* said editorially:

> On September 29 then-Vice President Spiro Agnew told fifteen hundred Republican women in California assembled, and through them the nation, that he was totally innocent of all the crimes and misdemeanors, high and low, with which public rumor had charged him, and that in the face of these charges he would not resign ("I will not resign. I will not resign") but would meet them head-on and fight them all the way. His words brought those ladies cheering to their feet. . . .

Spiro Agnew knew then that 17 days earlier his attorneys had opened up negotiations with the Justice Department and the White House seeking a deal whereby he would a) resign, b) on a plea of *nolo contendere* be sentenced to one of the lesser crimes on the list, and c) stay out of jail. Agnew admitted receiving crooked payments both as governor of Maryland and as vice president, was fined, became a self-defined felon, and avoided prison. He quickly found his level as part of the crowd around Sinatra's Rat Pack in Hollywood and Warm Springs, fitting right in with that glitzy riff-raff.

Now, with the rest of the nation, *National Review* welcomed Gerald Ford as vice president, sharing in a collective sigh of relief. Vice President Ford appeared to be, and established himself utterly as being, a *normal person*. By this point, normality seemed remarkable. *National Review*'s words about him upon his becoming vice president reflect the spirit of this transition:

> Few of the initial comments on the President's nomination of Representative Ford were flatly adverse, but many of them considerably underestimated, we believe, Gerald Ford's talents, personality, and experience. . . . [H]e has shown himself responsible, generally conservative without being doctrinaire, and prepared to make an honorable compromise without which a democratic republic cannot successfully function. He is literate—he actually reads and studies books. And his years at the center of the infinitely complex congressional maze has given him an incomparable chance to study men, the beginning of all wisdom, and particularly of political wisdom.

There we can savor the style and politics of James Burnham, seeing in Gerald Ford his own ideal of a nondoctrinaire conservative, no utopian, a man of experience, judgment, and integrity. For Burnham, "nondoctrinaire" was especially important. Ideology edited experience and corrupted judgment.

After Nixon's resignation in August 1974, the nomination by Ford of Nelson Rockefeller as his vice president could not have been expected to be as welcome at *National Review*. After all, Rockefeller loathed *National Review* conservatism, which had fought him vigorously over the direction of the Republican Party. William Rusher in particular was vociferous in disapproval of Ford's choice, but Burnham had long viewed Rockefeller with modified favor, and he wrote the editorial—a particularly important one from a historical point of view—about Ford's decision (December 6, 1974):

> Many conservatives are unhappy with the President's choice. It is hard for conservatives to see why a man who has been decisively rejected for its national ticket by the Republican Party, and who in vivid memory refused support to the Party's Presidential candidate, should be preferred to all others by a Republican President presiding over a Republican Administration elected by a massive majority of the citizens. . . .
>
> With his Midwestern roots and conservative ethos, Gerald Ford knew himself to represent the principal geographic and social sectors that made up the electoral majority in 1972. As we see it, the choice of a Vice President from the same political location as his own would have risked accentuating the deep divisions in this country instead of healing them. By naming Rockefeller he was symbolically bringing together, in the nation's service, the Northeast with the rest of the country; the moderate liberals with conservatives. . . .

This represents a superb exposition of a Burkean conservative politics applied to the situation of the nation as it actually was. It also expressed the direction in which Burnham wanted *National Review* and the nation itself to move: a center-right politics. Would that be the road taken—or the road not taken? That question would reverberate and gain in importance decades down the line. Would the Republican Party be center-right or doctrinaire?

18

Meyer Sets the Bar High

When Frank Meyer took over the "back of the book," *National Review* was far from an attractive place for young and ambitious writers to contribute. Against all plausibility, given his Communist background and fugitive existence up a mountain road near Woodstock, New York, using his books and culture section as a recruiting tool, he made the magazine a very good place to publish for a variety of writers. Widely read in the classics, in fact almost homemade after his break with the party, Meyer quickly transformed *National Review* into a place for young writers to appear, and even for difficult highbrows to find a wider audience. He accomplished this through astonishing energy, putting in hours every day on the phone, and unexpectedly welcoming a great variety of talents—unexpectedly, because he remained a rather schematic thinker, but nonetheless gave wide freedom to writers with whom he might disagree.

I remember him getting on the phone in 1963 and not getting off the line until, though busy teaching at Columbia, I finally agreed to contribute my first review. Between 1957 and his death from lung cancer in early 1972, he turned the Books, Arts and Manners section into one of the great strengths of the magazine. He fulfilled Buckley's founding hope of appealing to educated people and shapers of opinion. Meyer was a proud, intelligent, and intellectually aristocratic embodiment of *National Review*'s original purpose. In his performance, he set the bar high for his successors in running the section devoted to the arts, to books, and to civilization: first, briefly, his wife Elsie, then George Will, Chilton Williamson, Brad Miner, David Klinghoffer, Adam Bellow, and Mike Potemra would be his worthy successors, but none would surpass him.

A LARGE PART OF the April 28, 1972, issue of *National Review* consisted of an assessment of Meyer's achievement and tributes to him, as well as recollections of the man himself. The issue was introduced by Buckley in an account of Meyer near his death:

> I called him from Peking (which I knew would give him a kick) and he told me that the cause of the pains that had begun to hamper him seriously had not yet been diagnosed, that the culture sent out a few weeks earlier to discern whether he was suffering from tuberculosis had not yet matured, that meanwhile he had no appetite, but that he was beginning to get on with his work as usual. "I never guessed that I would sit here hoping that I had tuberculosis," he said, and quickly got on to Nixon's mission in Peking. . . . By Frank Meyer's standards, it wasn't a long conversation, though I assured him that the telephone rates in Peking were modest. . . . But I caught a quiver in his voice when I spoke to him next . . . and then the day after returning to New York, the news came in. Cancer. Inoperable. . . . On Thursday he spoke for the first time in ten days—there was not such a stillness since quiet came to the Western Front.

There followed recollections from what sounds like a Who's Who of *National Review* contributors. One from Garry Wills seems remarkable, in that Meyer had reviewed his *Nixon Agonistes* scornfully, identifying its sentimentalities, but Wills was both generous and accurate:

> One encounters real teachers in one's lifetime—and most of those do not do their teaching in a classroom. To meet one of my own favorite teachers, I had to go, fifteen years ago, to a lonely mountain top—which fit almost ridiculously the picture of a youth questing for a guru. . . .
>
> [But] he sat on that mountain like its very active volcano opening, spouting opinion, debate, reminiscences, and unfinished projects. . . . His Books

[section] contained the literate judgments of Guy Davenport, Hugh Kenner, Theodore Sturgeon, Arlene Croce, or Francis Russell. And Frank knew the review-page advantages of an Anglophile long before *The New York Review of Books* was born.

Though we all live inevitably toward death, Frank also moved very consciously toward a faith that would account for man's weird vitality of spirit to challenge that death. In one brief day last week, those two journeys converged for him. Lucid in the afternoon, as he prayed aloud through cancer-ravaged lungs, he was baptized—and then the tensest of vibrant men relaxed. Six hours later he was dead; three hours after, it was Easter.

This was an extraordinary tribute, generous in spirit, to a man often seriously at odds with Wills, and who had said so with asperity.

Wills mentioned Hugh Kenner, the Poundian-Joycean intellectual aristocrat who helped to build the Books section's distinction, and so, among many other tributes in this memorial section, we will quote from his, in his carefully wrought prose:

One way to tease Frank Meyer was to put his zip code on the envelope and hope he'd notice. He disapproved of zip codes, though telephone numbers were passable, perhaps because they weren't assigned in Washington. Late at night, in Woodstock, amid that midden of magazines that were always to be put in order, he would moralize with genial passion, sorting out the phenomena of living, those symptomatic of our social damnation, those not yet contaminated. Oscar Wilde said that his brother could compromise a locomotive, and I think Frank could have ideologized the Big Dipper.

So his book review section was in constant tension between his generosity and his vigilance. Generosity had the best of it, usually. That was why it was comfortable to review for NR. He trusted his reviewers, and passed for publication all manner of statements his principles urged him to worry like a pup. Being the most deductive of libertarians, he deduced the need to give writers liberty, though what they did with it was in frequent collision with all his other deductions. His was a nineteenth-century virtue, called Liberalism before the liberals made off with that word, and he'd probably like it if I called him a Victorian sage. Many doughty debaters have awaited his coming in heaven. The next time you see sheet lightning, you can fancy it's Frank Meyer taking on Carlyle.

A footnote should be attached to that notice of Frank's love of principled argument. His conversion, finally, was held up by an argument he had with the priest about the church's condemnation of suicide. It is my understanding that the matter was deferred to the presumptive wisdom of the ancient church.

AN ACUTE SENSIBILITY can illuminate the reasons for literary failure and its paradoxical popularity. In 1961, Joan Didion, one of Meyer's discoveries, reviewed J. D. Salinger's *Franny and Zooey*. She begins with a snippet of recent autobiography, which should be remembered in view of her future development:

> When I first came to know New York in the fall of 1956, I went to a party on Bank Street, which I remember with particular clarity for a number of reasons, not the least of them my surprise that no one present wished William Knowland were running for President. (I had only been in New York a few days, and the notion that Democrats might be people one met at parties had not yet violated what must have been, in retrospect, my almost impenetrable innocence.)

She goes on to marvel at the popularity of Salinger:

> Among the reasonably young people in heart, he is surely one of the most read and re-read writers in America today, exerting a power over his readers which is in some way extra-literary. Those readers expect him to teach them something that has nothing to do with fiction. Not only have his vague metaphysical hints been committed to rote by *New Yorker* readers from here to Dubuque, but his imaginary playmates, the Glass family, have achieved a kind of independent existence; I imagine that Salinger readers wish secretly that they could write letters to Franny and Zooey, and their brother Buddy, and maybe even the Jesuit Walker (apparently less disturbed than his kin).

With "metaphysical hints" she has identified one of the weaknesses of Salinger's writing, unearned and sentimental glimpses of Something. She knows, in her ironies, that this badness is what makes him popular, offering a free ride to the Eschaton. She would not have been surprised, on her evidence here, that he would abandon the finiteness of words altogether, to listen to the sound of one hand clapping in a New Hampshire country town.

Here we can bring two of these *National Review* contributors together, with Guy Davenport's review of Hugh Kenner's magnum opus, *The Pound Era*. This book itself is a work of art, taking Kenner a decade of scholarship and careful prose to sculpt into a most unusual artifact. Davenport's historical-critical prose proves equal to the challenge:

> A little past one o'clock on the fifth of June 1915, Corporal Henri Gaudier of Seventh Company, 129th Infantry, Captain Menager commanding, ordered his squad to fix bayonets and deploy themselves in diamond formation around him as they went over the top. The artillery began to crack its flat thunder behind them. . . . In the charge Corporal Gaudier was cut to pieces by machine-gun fire. He was 23 years old. He was descended from sculptors who had worked on Chartres. . . . This Corporal Gaudier, cited for bravery, remembered by his fellow soldiers for his intelligence, was one of the greatest sculptors of our century. He signed his work Henri Gaudier-Brzeska, adding the name of his Polish mistress to his own.

The point of this narrative is that the modernist movement did not begin with the First World War, as Paul Fussell maintains in his *Great War and Modern Memory*, but much earlier, and to a considerable extent lost major talent in that conflagration. Picasso's cubist landmark "Young Ladies of Avignon," for example, was painted in 1908; Eliot's "Prufrock" was published in 1915. An extraordinary number of young modernists, like Gaudier-Brezska, died on the Western front. Davenport comments:

> Mr. Kenner's study (a history book full of explications, "an X-Ray of a moving picture," as he calls it) . . . is not so much a book as a library, or better, a new kind of book in which biography, history, and the analysis of literature are so harmoniously articulated that every page has a narrative sense. Mr. Kenner's prose, always a miracle of compression and robust grace, is here brought to perfection. Has anyone since DeQuincy written such English with such verve and color? Has any scholar ever been so thorough?

Marvelous as Kenner indeed can be, it should be added that occasionally he does assume that expectations amount to fulfillment, as when he fails to see that in Pound's *Cantos* the "Adams" sections consist in substantial part of Adams's own prose, worked in to prove Adams's nobility of spirit, when they in fact are merely flat and boring; or, worse, fails to see that Pound's "Hell" Cantos consist of nonsensical economic theory and mere anti-Jewish name-calling, dying as language long before they flunk moral judgment. Unfelt ideological poetry is a pig attempting to fly.

What has been on display here amounts to one aspect of Buckley's aspiration for *National Review*. He wanted the magazine, from the beginning, to appeal to an audience with an educated taste. But he also wanted to ally the magazine with potential power, and to challenge the liberal Establishment. He would value the populist appeal of the populist demagogue, Joe McCarthy. Yet there was beauty in the Eastern Establishment, even at Yale.

MEYER'S OBVIOUS TEACHING intention at *National Review* was to school the conservative movement by exposing it to master intellects viewed as on the conservative side. Examples of this are Hiram Caton's review of Leo Strauss's *Liberalism Ancient and Modern* and Robert Nisbet's review of Steven Lukes's *Emile Durkheim: His Life and Work*. Walter Berns contributed a long piece, "The 'Essential Soul' of Dan Berrigan." Berns, then at Cornell, had witnessed the pied-piper priest's leadership role in the effort of fools to destroy that great university, with queasy or threatened professors frequently decamping elsewhere. The foundations of the modern conservative mind continued to be explored in a December 1973 section on "The Achievement of Leo Strauss," marking the death of that major figure.

In May 1973, Robert Moses, a villain to liberals like his biographer Robert Caro, contributed an essay about the aesthetically aristocratic landscape planner of Central Park, Frederick Law Olmstead. The park is in its way a conservative entity, a patch of nature in a city unimaginable without it. *National Review*, in a major omission, too seldom celebrated beauty in its widest sense, Burke's "unbought grace of life," and this essay was a welcome departure.

Comedy, as in Shakespeare, can often come mixed with tragedy, laughter the signature of man's fallen state. So during the 1970s, comedy raised its grinning head with the regular appearance of the columns of the young D. Keith Mano, much admired by Hugh Kenner, and whom I would describe in the *Sewanee Review* as the best novelist of his generation. His column "The Gimlet Eye" delighted in an antiwar rally, for example, featuring "Atrocity Jane" Fonda, "dressed *à la chinoise*":

> It's homecoming. The old grads assemble. Class of '69, '70, '71. Jane brings them out. Reminiscence and cheap embraces on the Washington Square Church stoop. "Terry. She cut her hair. Tom's teaching in Colorado. Sexual politics." The girls jerk stringy hair back from their eyes; men sport beard pieces, a sort of pacifier. Beautiful, oblique glances. They're so sincere, they stutter. . . . You can understand radicalism socially. It's cheaper than a Grossinger's weekend. . . . Finally the show is on. A young man dedicates his nice folk song "To the 300,000 prisoners in South Vietnam." Up 100,000 already; a go-go stock. Holly Near sings, "No more genocide." Must make Thieu glad.

Mano's profound Christianity had an unusual dimension which was creative artistically, a very strong sense of sin fused with comic laughter. He covered the *National Review* pre-Christmas trip to the Soviet Union, and there, confronting the pickled corpse of Lenin in Red Square, shivered as the thought occurred that he was looking at the Antichrist.

This has been an excursion into Frank Meyer's mental country, antipopulist, courageous and energetic, brilliant, homemade and aristocratic. Kendall had gone, now Meyer. The mower was at work among the *National Review* originals, who had educated themselves and then each other, on the way educating an American conservatism. The great originals had set the course, and the only task would be to keep the ship on course as conservatism became institutionalized as a movement. As Lionel Trilling suggested in *The Liberal Imagination*, liberalism transformed into a movement had brought with it the defeat of intelligence. That is the fate of movements, as less independent spirits try to belong, hewing to the party line rather than thinking freshly as circumstances change.

19

Ford Transition: Populism Growls at NR

O n December 3, 1973, as he succeeded to the vice presidency, Gerald Ford described himself agreeably as "a Ford, not a Lincoln." The refreshing candor of that remark would characterize his subsequent presidency, marked by a lack of pretension that contrasted amiably with much that had marked the style of the Nixon White House, including the comical uniforms temporarily sported by White House guards. That odd Nixon whimsy looked more musical-comedy Ruritanian than DeGaulle-stylish, as Nixon had hoped.

William Buckley once remarked, only partly in jest, that "Switzerland has the perfect politics. Nobody knows the name of the President." The natural desire of most people is for political tranquility. Burke thought that was one goal of politics; but it stands as a goal because it is seldom achieved, especially in the revolutionary twentieth century.

With the Ford-Carter interregnum the nation enjoyed a brief calm. The Republicans had been through Nixon. The Democrats had joy-ridden to the left disastrously with McGovern. For a long moment both looked for a return to "normalcy," a now famous neologism used by Warren Harding in offering a relief from the crusading Wilson. Ford served as *I am not Nixon*, and though challenged by Reagan, won the nomination in 1976.

That year, the Democrats turned south, where great repair work was needed, and nominated the *I am not McGovern and I am not Nixon* Jimmy Carter, a scarcely known recent governor of Georgia, the most conservative Democrat who could be nominated: religious, Annapolis graduate, nuclear submarine commander. He ran for the nomination as a "nuclear scientist" (which he was not), as a man who "would not lie to you," and as being "as good and truthful as the American people." He summed up his candidacy with, "Why not the best?"—the assumption unstated that Nixon had been the worst. It did not hurt at all that he promised the big teachers' unions a bribe in the form of a new Cabinet-level Department of Education.

He easily defeated the strongest Democratic candidate from the Left, Senator Edward Kennedy, who was still damp from his swim in Poucha Pond and had made an inarticulate appearance with Roger Mudd on CBS. Evidently Kennedy was helpless without his staff's cue cards. If Kennedy had claimed to be "the best," the nation would have laughed. Carter won on evident moderation, his moral stance, southern appeal, and the unfamiliar possibility for the Democrats of winning—which he did, edging Ford very narrowly. Ford and Carter were all about political repair work, but what Ford had embarked upon in 1974 was a roller-coaster ride to his defeat in 1976.

NATIONAL REVIEW ENTHUSIASTICALLY welcomed the Ford presidency after the *Sturm und Drang* of Nixon. The man from Grand Rapids was steady, intelligent, athletic, decent. He had ranked in the top third of his class at the University of Michigan and played center on its 1932, 1933, and 1934 football teams, during the first two of those years ranked first in the nation; in his sixties and even into his seventies he could ski parallel turns in the Colorado powder. He graduated from Yale Law School, paying his way by coaching Yale football and also working as a model. Lyndon Johnson famously mocked the better-educated Ford's intelligence, but Ford never admired the feral modes of the LBJ mind.

In 1949, Ford ran for the House from Michigan's Fifth District, won, and declared that being a congressman would be his life's work. It proved to be secure employment. In 1963 he ran for chairman of the House Republican Caucus and won, and the following year he ran for party leader in the House and upset Charlie Halleck. Ford's record, like Halleck's, had been somewhat to the right of the center of the Republican Party, but he was liked, he listened, and he was trusted.

His ambition had been to be Speaker of the House, not president. Thoroughly a man of the House, he raised the perennial question of whether experience in the legislature, without executive experience, was good preparation for the White House. His tenure in the presidency proved to be a mere transition, a complicated one, buffeted by political changes in the Republican Party beyond his understanding or control.

Two weeks into his presidency, a *New York Times* poll showed for his performance so far 73 percent approval, 3 percent disapproval, based on his wholesome demeanor. Hugh Sidey remarked in *Time* that "Everywhere there was the feeling that the American Presidency was back in the possession of the people."

On Sunday, September 8, at 11:00 a.m., President Ford went on national television from the Oval Office and announced:

> Ladies and gentlemen, I have come to a decision which I felt I should tell you and all my fellow American citizens as soon as I was certain in my own mind and in my conscience that it is the right thing to do. . . . Now, therefore, I, Gerald R. Ford, President of the United States, pursuant to the pardon power conferred upon me by Article II, Section 2, of the Constitution, have granted and by these presents do grant a full, free, and absolute pardon unto Richard Nixon for all offenses against the United States. . . .

His press secretary Jerry ter Horst (George Will wrote that his name looked like a typographical error) resigned.

Inevitably, theories shot up about a secret deal with Nixon for the vice presidency, on condition that Ford would pardon him. But biographer Richard Reeves—anything but an admirer of Ford—remains persuasive when he observes that Ford, a prayer breakfast regular, told an August 28 news conference when asked about clemency that: "In the last ten days or two weeks I've asked for guidance on this point," and goes on to say that when Ford told the American people "I must do this,"

I tend to believe those words were literally true. The decision was between Gerald Ford and his God, and his painfully personal rhetoric reflected his personality and the psychological pressures that made pardon inevitable. The Lord may have had a bit of help from Al Haig and the political judgment that it was better to get the political controversy over before the 1976 election, but Ford almost certainly, consciously or unconsciously, had decided to pardon Nixon before he became President on August 9, no matter what the consequences. Gerald Ford Jr. did it because he is what he is—and he probably would have done it even if he knew for certain that it would destroy his Presidency.[1]

It almost did, and some think it cost Ford the close 1976 election against Carter, though of course there were many other factors there.

In a syndicated column republished in the September 13, 1974, issue, but published first on August 22, before the pardon announcement, Buckley gave the rationale for clemency:

Why is it right to decline to prosecute Nixon, having proceeded to prosecute his subordinates? To answer that question clinically, you just have to tear yourself away from the absolutization of republican principles. It is okay to go about saying: no one is above the law. But that is only mostly true. Our Presidents are expected to take certain risks, and generations of them have done so. *Quod licet Jovi, non licet bovi.* [What is permitted Jove is not permitted a cow.] The risks Richard Nixon took were for tawdry motives, and he has been punished as surely as Napoleon was punished when his empire was taken away from him. But they didn't take Napoleon out and shoot him, even though he had led, in his disastrous campaigns, hundreds of thousands of men to their deaths. We were shocked, not satisfied, at the execution of Nicholas II.

A long editorial in the September 27, 1974, *National Review* made many points in favor of the pardon, including the one articulated by Buckley, adding also the likely distortion of the political process by a trial that Special Prosecutor Leon Jaworsky estimated might drag on for a year of more, the sensationalist quality of this trial, and the fact that the unconditional pardon clause had been put into the Constitution for undefined extraordinary situations, of which this was perhaps one.

MEANWHILE, FORD HAD HIS problems in the White House. His own staff as a congressman, even as minority leader, was not first-rate. Ter Horst had been engaged in a brutal influence contest with another newspaperman, the bibulous Bob Hartman, long Ford's friend and speechwriter. Ford retained many of Nixon's staff, including former congressman Donald Rumsfeld. As ambassador to NATO, Rumsfeld had immediately flown back from Paris to undercut Al Haig and seize the post of chief-of-staff, which he won.

On a comical level, Nixon had brought into the White House in his time of troubles Rabbi Baruch Korf and former Jesuit John McLaughlin, to provide religious cover during the scandals. Korf had departed, but McLaughlin tried to hang on with Ford. Pat Buchanan quipped, "I know the blonde who laicized him." Eventually he was shoehorned out and became an effective Washington correspondent for *National Review*, later a TV talk-show host of the stentorian school. Ford had trouble in reconsidering, let alone modifying, the Nixon policies already moving through the pipeline, and more or less consigned foreign policy to Henry Kissinger. Things were slightly out of control.

THE MARCH 28, 1975, *National Review* published a positional essay by John Chamberlain titled "Ford's Hundred Days." It did not offer a definitive assessment, but defined the ongoing and emerging problems. It focused on the economy, the deficit, the apparent slide toward recession, but also went on to strategic nuclear matters and to Vietnam. There was the questionable balance of nuclear strike capability, and here *National Review* was none too favorable to Nixon-Ford-Kissinger. The magazine continued to worry about the sufficiency of Kissinger's doctrine of sufficiency. Chamberlain kept his fingers crossed as regards Vietnam, but leaned, justifiably, toward pessimism:

> Communists, of course, have their troubles too. Their invading armies do not operate well during the Cambodian and South Vietnamese rainy season. The Hanoi Politburo is split between those who want to go for broke quickly in South Vietnam and those who think the Thieu government can be counted

on to eviscerate itself. . . . The Soviets still show an interest in acquiring Western technology.

Translation: Storm warning. In fact, the heavily equipped and battle-ready divisions of the North Vietnamese army soon Blitzkrieged their way through the crumbling ARVN resistance. No B-52s would fly from Guam this time, and what was left of a U.S. presence in Saigon grabbed the last helicopters from the roof of the American Embassy in soon-to-be Ho Chi Minh City.

Far from being blamed, Ford saw his popularity take a surprising jump over the handling of the *Mayaguez* affair. Seized and held by Communist Cambodians, the situation of the ship was an embarrassment on top of the collapse in Vietnam. Ford ordered a heavy bombing of surrounding areas and a shock helicopter assault on the ship itself by Special Forces. This was immensely popular, the public appreciating it when a president commissions successful military action. George Will wrote one of his regular "Capital Issues" columns, titling it "Early Peak":

> Regarding 1976, perhaps Gerald Ford has peaked a little early. . . . But life must look sweet from his current peak. He got there a boost from the Cambodian Communists, who stole a country and a boat. No one blamed Ford for the former, and Mr. Ford looked convincingly Presidential in response to the latter.

It would be up and down from that "peak," mostly down. *National Review* commented editorially:

> The specific mission was achieved 100 percent. The *Mayaguez*, its entire crew of forty, and all its cargo were recovered undamaged. . . . Suddenly this country had a government—something that had been missing for the past two years. Until May 15, Gerald Ford had been an interim, caretaker President. This *Mayaguez* affair legitimized his Presidency, as was immediately evident in the attitude of Congress as well as the citizens in general. . . . The odds lengthen against attempts to deny him the Republican nomination, if he wants it, or, for this next period at least, to swing Republican conservatives—who were unanimous in approval of Ford's *Mayaguez* conduct—into an anti-Ford new party alignment.

That last, about a new party, must have been puzzling to casual readers or to those outside *National Review* altogether. It signaled a development within American conservatism, and within *National Review*, of a prophetic and sometimes acrimonious kind. Publisher and senior editor Bill Rusher, a principal architect of the 1963–64 Draft Goldwater Movement, was getting extremely restless. He had seen the Goldwater Movement crippled by the assassination of Kennedy in 1963, and though Goldwater did get the nomination, the geography and other factors in his contest with Lyndon Johnson made his electoral task impossible. In 1968, the combined votes of Nixon and Wallace would have meant a landslide against Humphrey rather than a photo finish; but the Nixon administration had not been able to bring those two (Nixon-Wallace) slices together, until the Democratic nomination of McGovern and the assassination-attempt crippling of Wallace did so. The 60-40 1972 landslide went to Nixon alone against McGovern.

The accession of Ford, plus his choice of Rockefeller as vice president, seemed to Rusher to portend further paralysis. The division of tendencies at *National Review* was indicated by Burnham's praise for the choice of Rockefeller by Ford. In the May 23, 1975, issue, Rusher published a lengthy piece titled "A New Party: Eventually, Why Not Now?"—an excerpt from a new book he was publishing with Sheed and Ward. President Ford was of course being criticized by the Left; here came disaffection from the populist Right. One problem was that, seen historically, populism is never conservative, except by accident. The Constitution, it is hardly necessary to say, is designed to cool off waves of populist emotion.

At the time, Rusher's efforts were tolerated and not considered of much importance. Ronald Reagan, who would be elected in 1980, held the uneasy national conservative coalition together. It is not too much to say that Reagan on a national political level was analogous to the unifying figure Buckley was at *National Review*. But a southern-based populism would eventually triumph in the Republican Party with the narrow election of Texan George W. Bush in 2000 and his reelection in 2004.

FROM SPECULATION ABOUT Ford "peaking" too soon, *National Review* began to be increasingly critical of his performance. In an editorial with the title "Summer Book," the magazine provided a summary of the situation:

> After the *Mayaguez* affair President Ford's stock rose sharply. Conservatives were pleased by his vetoes of big spending bills. His approval rating rose in the national approval polls by a dozen points. In political Washington it became a commonplace of conversation that Ford was a shoo-in for the nomination and was probably unbeatable in the election. Interviewers discussed his "confidence," and *Time*, reviewing his first year, pronounced him "Secure in the White House."

But all that did not reflect the deeper political realities. With the advent of August a subtle change in the political atmosphere is already perceptible. *National Review* commented:

> Henry Kissinger has been doing the President very little political good. The Solzhenitsyn affair was one political stink bomb, the fumes blotting out the effects of Mayaguez.

Ford's refusal to meet one of the master spirits of the age was a tremendous mistake. *The Gulag Archipelago*, an account of prisoners, often by name, in the vast network of Soviet concentration camps, was a literary masterpiece, Joycean in its verbal artistry, fully appreciated only in the original Russian. It also proved to be an irreparable blow to intellectual communism in Western Europe. Not since the Hitler-Stalin Pact had so many French intellectuals left the Communist Party. By indicating that he disapproved of Solzhenitsyn in a transparent move to please Brezhnev, Ford demeaned himself and his office.

As 1975 wore on, a vague but now widespread discontent with Ford began to be sensed. He was becoming an object of mild scorn, on the way to Romneyization. A November 14 editorial asked, "What's wrong with Ford?":

> Poor Gerald Ford must be feeling, these days, like Alice when she reached the other side of the looking glass and found that, no matter how fast she ran, she couldn't make any progress. . . .

And, somehow, symbols of rather bumbling ordinariness multiply around these provincial junkets: stumbling of aircraft exits, fender-bending drives, head-colds at awkward moments, a wife who won't keep her mouth shut, slips of the tongue. Even two assassination attempts somehow don't attain Presidential level, and rapidly fade into sordid counter-culture vagary.

The author of this, James Burnham, interpreter of Machiavelli, knows that the "Prince" should maintain a distance to preserve his aura of authority. Burnham sees the symbolic quality of the tiny slips: in themselves they are nothing—Ford had been a great athlete—but they became clues to something else.

It is hardly surprising that by August *National Review* had begun to editorialize along the lines of "Reagan Must Run" (August 28). Thus, the magazine—which earlier had praised Ford enthusiastically—was swinging against his nomination.

RUSHER CONSIDERED that the Goldwater transformation of the Republican Party was now being frittered away. The magazine itself saw Reagan as the truer direction for the Republican Party. Rusher's vision was akin to that of Kevin Phillips in *The Emerging Republican Majority*, virtually scripture to Rusher. His inspiration, however, found few or even no disciples at *National Review*, certainly not in Buckley or Burnham. It amounted to a frontal attack on their strategic, prudential, and therefore gradualist conservatism.

National Review, after all, had been founded as a magazine of ideas, an attempt to change the mind of the American intellectual elite in a conservative direction. Burnham had looked with favor on Nelson Rockefeller and might have been comfortable on the conservative edge of the Establishment, now occupied by Harvard's Kissinger. Buckley had gone to Yale, was erudite, liked yachting, classical music, painting, and skiing. Meyer had gone to Princeton and Balliol, Priscilla Buckley to Smith. Burnham had gone to Princeton and Balliol and had taught philosophy. His tastes were exquisite. *National Review* was an educational endeavor, based on the conviction that ideas have consequences. This dictated the mission of such a magazine as *National Review*, that it would be directed at opinion makers, the educated, at the governing class in the broader sense of the word; or, to put it as a synecdoche, Buckley wanted to change the direction of "Yale."

And the magazine had made considerable progress in this enterprise. It had brought forward a host of new writers and was fashioning a conservative intellectual establishment. Its writers and readers were active in the universities, journalism, the arts. In essence, it articulated an aristocratic conservatism, however the result might or might not appeal to Joe Six-Pack and NASCAR fans. *National Review* did not speak to them, and its newly fashioned elite cohort would be uncomfortable in a regime dominated by people like them, which Rusher's projected New Majority regime apparently promised, or threatened.

What was going on here? Rusher provides the answer in his *The Rise of the Right*, in the context of the Goldwater movement's goal of routing Rockefeller and the Eastern Establishment. Rusher shrewdly notices that this was to prove "less attractive to some of my colleagues at *National Review* when they finally became aware of it toward the end of the decade," but,

> To me personally—given my Midwestern cultural background, my boyhood hostility to things Eastern, and my political record (in the Young Republicans) of alliances with upstate New York against the city, and national coalitions against Rockefeller—the concept of a southern-and-western-based coalition against the East was both familiar and thoroughly congenial.

One might suggest, also, that Rusher, an expert on the Communist movement, loathed the likes of Alger Hiss, who was free from scorn around Cambridge, Massachusetts. But if Rusher's neopopulism made a kind of psychological sense, it tended to isolate him at *National Review*. One could discern a form of it, however, in the blue states/red states configuration of the 2000 Bush-Gore result, both coasts against the South and Heartland.

Another theoretician of such populist politics, Kevin Phillips, initiated an argument with Buckley that he couched in unduly personal terms. Phillips had been important to the 1968 Nixon campaign as a strategist, but Nixon had deliberately excluded Wallace himself while trying to attract some Wallace voters. For 1976, Phillips in his syndicated column advocated a Reagan-Wallace ticket, which Reagan would never have accepted.

More annoying, because closer to home, was an attack from the once-conservative Left, in particular from Garry Wills, who had veered off in 1968 with the "Kids" in Chicago and his sympathy for the Panthers and his admiration for the renegade Jesuit Berrigan Brothers. It looked as if he were being "Leonard Bernsteinized," moving toward what Tom Wolfe had called "radical chic."

Something was going wrong at *National Review* and in the mind, perhaps, of the conservative movement. The magazine, in large part because of Buckley's magnanimity, had been able to hold together an intellectual coalition stretching from the individualism of the libertarians to the Willmoore Kendall/Edmund Burke kind of conservatism. Meyer had tried "fusionism," individual freedom combined with a freely chosen traditional morality. Willmoore Kendall combined a Heartland Americanism (Oklahoma) with an aristocratic constitutionalism. Buckley held it all together. The political answer would be provided for eight years by Ronald Reagan. *But, what then?*

THE APPEARANCE OF Michael Oakeshott as guest of honor at *National Review*'s twentieth anniversary celebration in 1975 might certainly be seen as a highbrow rejection of Yahoo populism. This elegant sequence of events began with an address at the Hunter College auditorium by the British philosopher. His succession to the chair previously held by Harold Laski at the London School of Economics had seemed to herald a conservative renaissance in the realm of high theory. Oakeshott was a major figure, looked at in one way as a direct descendent of Burke in his regard for nonrational cognition. Thus, in the *Reflections*, Burke's hero-statesman was Lord Somers, who knew from long experience that the time had come, necessity dictated, that King James II had to go, or England would be ungovernable. Somers did not reach this conclusion by consulting some book of "rights" or "principles." Oakeshott could put this in a homely way: a good chef knows things a cookbook cannot teach, and this truth extended to all areas of human activity. Oakeshott explored this insight with impressive intellectual energy into areas of great complexity, expressing a permanently valuable theory of human behavior, including politics.

Oakeshott was a dandy in dress, and in prose style an aesthete, achieving a beautiful lucidity. He also had a slightly scandalous reputation concerning women and favored canary-colored waistcoats. He did not admire the philosopher Isaiah Berlin, whom he considered shallow: Oakeshott once disconcerted Berlin by introducing him to an LSE audience as a "Paganini of thought," a fancy insult for cognoscenti. The idea of having Oakeshott address a *National Review* twenty-fifth anniversary audience seemed perfect. A principal stipulation was that the public address had to be previously unpublished and would be published first in *National Review*. Oakeshott could be expected to deliver something important. The first hint of trouble appeared when the manuscript of his projected talk arrived at the *National Review* 35th Street offices. I was trapped into an unwelcome role.

Sitting with nothing much in mind in the office shared by James Burnham and Priscilla Buckley, I suspected nothing when Burnham turned to me with an innocent smile and said, "I have just read the Oakeshott manuscript. Now, Jeffrey, you know that in journals of philosophy, the editor sometimes inserts brief interruptions to guide the reader, stating in a couple of sentences where the essay has been and where it is going. Some of our readers might appreciate it if you did this for the Oakeshott piece. Okay?" Sure, no problem. Nothing I had read by Oakeshott, including his recent collection *Rationalism in Politics*, posed any difficulties at all.

This essay, however, was impenetrable until about the third reading, a dense argument from definition about the nature of the modern state. Its upshot, a useful term Sidney Hook favored, was an attack on the "teleocratic" or purposive state, the state with a plan, which by its nature involves coercion. Oakeshott favored the state as "association," or the state as "rules keeper," composed of individuals who decide on their own purposes and work toward them within the rules. Oakeshott's argument was a powerful attack not only on totalitarianism, but also on socialism and modern liberalism, which drive teleocratically toward *equality*. But Oakeshott took a long time to get there, beautifully of course. My guideposts sentences appear in the essay as it was excerpted in the twentieth-fifth anniversary *National Review*.

The Hunter College auditorium was packed. We had a panel on stage to ask the first questions of Oakeshott after he finished speaking: Burnham,

Priscilla, Rusher, and me. Burnham "honored" me with the assignment of asking the first question.

As Oakeshott spoke for more than an hour, the audience listened in bewildered and stunned silence. There were few questions from the floor, these at best tangential. Then, long silence, and "Thank you very much." Afterwards, in the crowd crunching toward the exits, I overheard a woman say, "That wasn't Michael Oakeshott. This was Buckley's greatest hoax. That was an actor playing a philosopher." It *had* been a hoax of sorts by Oakeshott, unknowing I suppose; though, maybe, from his elevation, Oakeshott was amused. The essay, as I have indicated, was a great one, absolutely convincing, conservative, important, if perhaps not susceptible to on-the-spot appreciation. And it was an honor for *National Review* to have had it on this occasion.

Much later that night, after the festivities at the Plaza, while the cleaning people were already at work in the ballroom, some friends and I, full of champagne, ran into Michael Oakeshott and a beautiful young woman near the exit. Oblivious of us, Oakeshott was saying to her, "Just call me Mickey." This chef needed no cookbook.

20

Reagan to Ford to Carter: Bouncing Ball

As analyzed by *National Review*, the story of the years 1974 to 1980—from the inauguration of Gerald Ford to the election of Ronald Reagan—constitutes an extended political interim. Yet a great deal happened in those years—in a way that leaves little trace in history. Reagan's challenge to Ford for the Republican nomination in 1976 failed, unexpectedly slowed, maybe crippled, by his loss in the New Hampshire primary, where the polls had showed a solid Reagan lead. Then Ford was edged out by Carter in the general election, for many reasons, among them a mysterious, even absurd remark by Ford in the second debate. Not since Nixon's first debate with Kennedy has a televised debate mattered so much. Carter had emerged meteorically from the peanut fields of Georgia. He possessed a peculiar charisma. He failed as a president, becoming even a joke toward the end. But at least in the eyes of the Nobel Peace Prize judges, he would become a great ex-president.

In its first editorial on the 1976 primaries (January 30), *National Review* emphasized the importance to both Ford and Reagan of New Hampshire and Florida. In an accompanying article with the strikingly unoriginal title "The Snows of New Hampshire," David A. Pietruza reported from the scene that

[i]n late January Ronald Reagan returned to New Hampshire for the second of four planned trips.

. . . On his previous trip, Reagan's opponents had drummed up a great foofaraw over his plan to transfer $90 billion worth of federal functions to the states. This was the time to set the record straight, if it could be set straight.

It was no "foofaraw," and it could not be set straight. What Reagan thought his proposal meant was that New Hampshire voters could get rid of federal programs they did not need or want. What it meant in practice to those voters was the installation of a state income tax to pay for programs they wanted, but preferred the federal government to pay for. The state slogan, emblazoned on the New Hampshire license plates, was "Live Free or Die." This was a 1776 battle cry, but it would do in 1976 too, and in practical terms it meant federal money.

Inevitably Reagan's early lead in New Hampshire quickly evaporated, and a March 19 article reported from the scene, "During the last ten days of the campaign, it appears, the large undecided vote broke in Ford's direction." Not usually a detail man, Reagan had depended on his staff for political advice, and it had not told him about the New Hampshire Republican hatred of the idea of a state income tax. Reagan would need advisors more alert to local conditions.

Ford's New Hampshire victory translated into strength in Florida, also previously thought to be leaning toward Reagan. The Reagan slide stopped in North Carolina, however. *National Review* in the next issue observed editorially,

> In North Carolina, particularly toward the end of his campaign there, Reagan stressed foreign policy issues. . . . President Ford remains the front-runner for the Republican nomination, but the North Carolina result reminds him— and Mr. Kissinger—that discontent with their performance is deep and spreading.

By August the Reagan campaign had become desperate and sought some way to break the Ford momentum. Campaign manager John Sears came up with the Richard Schweiker play: Reagan announced his choice of Senator

Richard Schweicker of Pennsylvania, a liberal, for vice president. *National Review* was as shocked as everyone outside the campaign inner circle:

> If it works—if Reagan gets the nomination—it should go into the *Guinness Book of Records* as a political masterstroke. If it fails, and Ford is nominated, it will provide only a footnote in the history of a bizarre political year. A week after Reagan chose Schweiker, the shock waves were still reverberating across the Republican landscape: but enraged conservative Reagan enthusiasts appeared to be cooling off—the line was, We will support Reagan in Kansas City, not Schweiker—and there was some small movement toward Reagan among uncommitted or Ford delegates in the Northeast, but too small a movement to be decisive or even significant.

At Kansas City, Reagan did fall short. In the end, he delivered a fine speech supporting Ford (which probably would have been his acceptance speech had he been nominated), and Ford, energized by his victory, the band playing the Michigan football fight song, delivered what must have been the best speech of his career. But the polls showed him far behind Carter. Bob Dole, selected as Ford's running mate, had made a weird mistake in his own acceptance speech, calling World War II a "Democrat War." The polls showed Ford/Dole behind Carter by double digits.

THE CARTER CAMPAIGN through the primaries had been a remarkable performance, taking advantage of the McGovern rules changes that shifted importance to the primaries and away from the machine pols. Carter proved to be charismatic in retail politics, well adapted to the New Hampshire primary. Ted Kennedy later quipped that Carter had spent so much time in that state he could have voted there. Carter's lined face had a sort of Eleanor Roosevelt homely reassurance; his broad grin was toothy; and his apparent honesty came across strongly in small groups. As a centrist candidate, and as a fresh face, he was a relief from the McGovern frenzies of four years earlier. As a southerner, he promised to offset the Republican strength in that region. His victory in New Hampshire propelled him on to Florida. One by one, Kennedy and the other well-known aspirants fell away.

But Ford surged after his convention victory and his Michigan fight song speech, and doubts about Carter began to surface. Perhaps that syrupy niceness was unsuited to a dangerous world. *National Review* noticed the remarkable evidence of the late polls: "Gerald Ford's cutting of Jimmy Carter's lead from 18 points to 2 points in five weeks was, said George Gallup, 'the greatest comeback in the history of public opinion polling.'"

That was just before the second TV debate. In that debate, Ford appeared to say that the East European Soviet satellites were free and independent nations. Stunned, the panelist even gave Ford an opportunity to clarify. Ford just let the wild claim sit there. What was going on? It was widely referred to as "Ford's Polish joke." Burnham wondered whether it were a profound and important error, and concluded that Ford's statement was no gaffe, but rather a somewhat clumsy rendition of the Sonnenfeldt Doctrine, as transmitted to him by his secretary of state, Henry Kissinger.

This new doctrine was highly controversial at the time. It had been set forth by Kissinger State Department official Helmut Sonnenfeldt and had been explicated in columns by Burnham. It has now been largely forgotten. On May 28, 1976, Burnham summed up the doctrine and stressed its importance:

> The doctrine recognizes and accepts: 1) the legitimacy of the Soviet government as ruler both of Russia and of the non-Russian nationalities now inside the Soviet Union; 2) the legitimacy of the Communist regimes in the East European nations; and 3) the legitimacy of Soviet hegemony over the East European nations. The aim of the policy is to get along with the Soviet Union.

That was a remarkable doctrine to come from Kissinger's foreign policy team. What had the Soviets done to "get along" with us? Burnham concluded that Ford's remarks in the second debate were his attempt to paraphrase the Kissinger-Sonnenfeldt Doctrine, which was unacceptable. That is, Ford was being nice, using a tiny fib with the aim of *managing* the Soviet problem. This was truly Kissingerian: like refusing to see Solzhenitsyn. And it might, as with appeasement, be destabilizing.

SOON AFTER THE ELECTION, which Carter won narrowly, *National Review* (December 3, 1976) asked the question: "Jimmy Carter Who?" That question recognized an uncomfortable truth: no one knew. This early editorial seemed to sense danger.

Carter might be a good man, and he seemed virtuous. But if he had read Reinhold Niebuhr, as he claimed, he failed to understand his teaching about human imperfection, as Niebuhr much too gently called it. Further, Carter failed to grasp Niebuhr's central distinction between private and public virtue: that private goodness is not translatable to the collective behavior of a state. Even the general will of a deliberative assembly is not likely to promote perfection of the soul. Carter evidently did not include in his political education *Federalist* 10, about the usefulness of self-interested group goals in setting limits to the desires and goals of other groups. Nor was Carter capable of learning from experience. When Henry Kissinger met him for the first time, he came away telling friends that President Carter was like "an unpeelable Brussels Sprout." When his policies eventually failed, Carter went up on his famous mountain and came down with his infamous "malaise speech," which blamed not his policies but the American people, who were far from charmed by such self-righteousness. He should have remembered that even saints traditionally combine the eagle with the dove.

From the beginning of his term, Carter had little administrative sense of government. His experience as governor of Georgia had not prepared him for Washington, with its constellations of power and its responses to interests and opinion. For example, there was no apparent rationale for the nomination of Theodore Sorensen as CIA director, Sorensen being a pacifist by personal conviction. Carter had not even discussed the matter with Senate Majority Leader Harry Byrd. He moved to close a number of old domestic military bases, a move defensible on paper but without appreciation of the fact that the interests of 289 congressmen might be more than simply military-strategic. When he sent his 1978 tax bill to Congress, he refused to negotiate or discuss concessions.

His self-cultivated image as a moralist immediately ran into contradictions when he named Bert Lance—an able Georgian small-town banker—

as director of the Office of Management and Budget. Lance immediately came under investigation for shady banking practices.

Carter's White House staff, shapeless in structure, made Ford's early in-house confusion look like sound management. The leading personnel did not appear to be of high quality, and it did not help that Hamilton Jordan pronounced his name "Jerden," *National Review* joking that this Georgian "did not even know how to spell his own name." Thereafter, at Joe Sobran's instigation, the magazine spelled Jordan's name with an umlaut: Jörden.

The result was a slide in public opinion, from a Gallup poll showing 42 percent strong approval in March 1977 to 24 percent in October.

Not surprisingly, attacks began to come from the Left, which, intellectually at least, was organized. George McGovern, rising from political death, and Ted Kennedy, whom Carter had crushed in 1976, both demanded a move leftward.

THE CARTER ADMINISTRATION also showed disarray in foreign policy, an uncertain compass beginning at the top with Cyrus Vance as secretary of state—Yale, Eastern Establishment, genteel, and moralistic—and Zbigniew Brzezinski as national security advisor, a Columbia professor representing the "realist" school of politics that focused on power. In a remarkable editorial on June 17, 1977, *National Review* took account of this contradiction, expressed in a baffling speech Carter delivered at Notre Dame, which consisted of contrasting drafts from Vance and Brzezinski, stitched together. An editorial by Burnham shrewdly defined the Carter problem:

> At Notre Dame, on Sunday, May 22, Carter delivered what may be the worst speech on foreign policy ever uttered by an American President. The effect was eerie, since Carter's rhetoric was so out of sync not only with the external actuality but with his own evident policy. "We are now free of that inordinate fear of Communism which once led us to embrace any dictator who joined in our fear," intoned the President. Tumultuous cheers came from the Notre Dame innocents. Carter would have had to have a heart of stone not to laugh.
>
> Three days later a State Department spokesman warned that the fifty Cuban "advisors" who had arrived in Ethiopia might be the vanguard of a

Cuban expeditionary force, and that, if so, it would be a "serious setback." The State Department evidently had not read the Notre Dame speech; it retained an inordinate fear of Communism, plus a lively sense of the strategic importance of the Golden Horn of Africa.

In conversation, Burnham described Carter as president in form but not in substance—though still a welcome relief from the leftward lurch of McGovernism.

National Review did not miss the concerted effort by the Soviets to turn the 1980 Moscow Olympics into a showcase for communism, while at the same time depending upon foreign contracts to install the long-distance telephones necessary for press coverage of the games. This led Burnham to form a "Committee to Save the Olympics"—that is, to marginalize the Moscow games by bringing about a U.S. withdrawal. The Soviets achieved this themselves by invading Afghanistan, the P.R. groundwork perhaps being done by Burnham's committee, which included Rep. Ralph Metcalf, who was black and had come in second to Jesse Owens in the 1938 Berlin Olympics, and Rep. Jack Kemp, who had been a star quarterback for the Buffalo Bills.

ALSO ON THE CARTER agenda was a treaty turning over sovereignty in the Panama Canal Zone, about which (September 2, 1977) *National Review* took a prudential position, out of step with much conservative opinion, which regarded relinquishing the canal as yet another U.S. retreat.

It was in the midst of the discussion of the Panama Canal issue that *National Review* suffered the tremendous loss of James Burnham, putting a severe strain on the maxim that no one is indispensable. *National Review*'s canal position had been shaped by Burnham and Buckley. Burnham held that the projected transfer of canal sovereignty to Panama was essentially a no-lose proposition. The canal was out of date, too small for the big supertankers and certainly too small for modern naval vessels—besides which we now had a two-ocean navy. Moreover, retaining the canal would inflame Latin American nationalism, highly undesirable for our anticommunist foreign policy. Buckley was also sensitive to Latin American issues, having served in Mexico City with the CIA and having long-standing family connections in the area. He thought that rather than a retreat, the transfer would look like *noblesse oblige.*

In January 1978, Buckley and Burnham had flown south to the University of North Carolina for a televised debate on the canal with Ronald Reagan, George Will, Pat Buchanan, and others. Reagan opposed the transfer—"We paid for it, we own it"—but Buckley guessed that he nevertheless favored the transfer in order to get the issue out of the way before his 1980 run for the presidency. On the return trip to New York, Burnham suddenly began losing sight in his left eye, soon after that in his right as well, signs of serious circulatory trouble.

At the office, where I had been present regularly for biweekly editorial work since 1969, it seemed to me that Burnham had aged with surprising rapidity in the last few years, becoming a bit frail, with thinning white hair, vision trouble, and uncertainty in manner (quite a change), often asking me to check his typewritten editorial copy. In 1975 he ceased coming to New York from Kent, Connecticut, to edit the biweekly "Bulletin," though he continued to contribute to the "Abroad" feature. He also turned over to me the lead cover editorial, despite the fact that I was manifestly without Burnham's strategic grasp of global affairs. Soon, during Buckley's absences, including his regular month in Switzerland, I was performing the principal editorial duties for the magazine itself. Since I remained a full-time professor of English at Dartmouth, commuting to New York by plane, this put some strain on those duties and other activities, though I continued to write scholarly articles and went on to publish books in 1982, 1987, and 1989. My chief interests remained literary, philosophical, and cultural rather than political.

The absence of Burnham, however, was a major loss in several respects: his political sophistication, of course, but also his overall balance, and, pervasively, his excellence as a stylist. His absence was also a loss to institutional memory. Except for Buckley, the founder, and Priscilla Buckley (there almost since the beginning), Burnham was the sole remaining senior figure who had been with the magazine from the beginning. His absence would be felt increasingly as years went by. He indeed had been indispensable with his prudential and strategic conservatism.

In addition to his near-blindness, between 1978 and his death in 1987 Burnham was afflicted, almost Lear-like, with a barrage of physical calamities. For example, in early November 1978, not long before his seventy-third birthday, he suffered a serious stroke, recovering enough to perform simple routine tasks but largely losing his short-term memory.

In 1980, at *National Review*'s twenty-fifth anniversary dinner, with Burnham present, Buckley hailed him as having been "beyond any question . . . the dominant intellectual influence" at the magazine. Burnham was evidently pleased. In August 1982, another blow: Marcia, Jim's wife of many years, suddenly died of a variation of pneumonia, commonly called Legionnaire's Disease. For some time, she too had seemed, though beautiful, also frail. But I and I suppose others had assumed that she would outlive her husband. Early in his first term, President Reagan awarded Burnham the Presidential Medal of Freedom at the White House—the president accurately describing him as having "profoundly affected the way America views itself and the world," and asserting that "[f]reedom, reason, and decency had fewer greater champions in this century" than James Burnham. Reagan was an assiduous reader—a still little-recognized aspect of his character, who had long been a fan of *National Review* and a good friend of Buckley's. To the extent—considerable—to which *National Review* had shaped the American conservative movement, an organized base of Reagan support, Burnham had exercised a great deal of national influence, much more than he would have enjoyed at, for example, *Partisan Review*, now long in his past.

During the spring of 1987, Burnham developed a cough and other symptoms. A medical examination diagnosed kidney and liver cancer, beyond treatment. He died on July 28. Shortly before he died he did not object to being formally received into the Catholic Church. He accepted the visits of a priest, made neither objection nor sign of acceptance, and received the last rites. His authoritative biographer, Daniel Kelly, does not decide whether this meant an actual decision to return to the church.[1]

Burnham left a sense of great absence at *National Review*. In the *Aeneid*, Palinurus the helmsman falls overboard before the Trojan voyagers reach Italy to found the city of Rome. *National Review*, in Burnham, had lost its

Palinurus, but Buckley continued to lead as Aeneas, while also replacing the helmsman.

BEFORE WE RETURN to the downward path of Carter's defeat by Reagan in 1980 and the end of the post-Watergate interregnum, a touch of humor, at Carter's expense, will provide a moment of comic relief. The lead piece in the October 14, 1977, editorial section, written as I remember by Joe Sobran, read as follows:

> Proclaiming October 19 "Lief Erikson Day," Jimmy Carter referred to him as "that courageous Norseperson." Bet he wouldn't have said that to his face. There goes the Norwegian vote.

With the gasoline shortage, the domestic political news became increasingly bad for Carter. The Gallup polls showed him sinking, while in late 1979 Reagan, if the New Hampshire primary had been held then, would be favored by 44 percent over a scattered field of Republican aspirants that included John Connally, Howard Baker, George H. W. Bush, and Philip Crane. In July 1979, a *National Review* editorial noted,

> Gasoline is President Carter's Vietnam—important enough itself, but more so in the way it strips bare his political vulnerability. Carter no doubt has his personal shortcomings—his ineloquence, his rationalist apolitical mentality, his self-   righteousness, his tropism for third-rate personnel, his provincial naiveté in foreign policy. At that level, Woodrow Wilson is with us again. But Carter's problems have always been political, and have to do with the deep and unbridgeable splits within the Democratic Party. Each of Carter's energy options can only exacerbate those splits.
>
> The Left Democrats want gas rationing, wage and price controls, severe and imposed conservation measures, heavy taxation, and the extension of government controls. Moderate Democrats want deregulation and market pricing, which they see as increasing supplies and undercutting OPEC. There's no way to reconcile that division. . . .
>
> Carter has withdrawn, like Moses to the Mountain, gathering about him various tribal representatives. He hopes to descend, delivering the Word of the Lord. But he does not possess that Word, because of his divided constitu-

ency. From a political perspective, that is the meaning of the Kennedy furor. For a Democrat to be for Kennedy in 1980 is a convenient way of not making any hard choices in 1979.

It was not until 1992 that those divisions in the Democratic Party would be papered over, by Bill Clinton—helped by the third-party candidacy of Ross Perot. Carter invited just about everybody he could think of up to the mountaintop (Camp David), but what he came down with was his "malaise speech," which in essence told the once-virtuous people just to buck up.

In November 1979, Iranian "students" seized American hostages and held them in the American embassy in Tehran. They would remain prisoners, mistreated and tormented, for a year, a feckless Carter effort to free them ending with our helicopters crashing in the Iranian desert. The hostages remained prisoners until after Reagan's election.

Under such circumstances, Reagan needed only to persuade voters that he was unthreatening and capable in order to be elected. He succeeded, a memorable occasion coming in a televised debate when, in answer to Carter's overheated allegations, Reagan seemed calm rather than dangerous, commenting, "There you go again."

Like Ford, Carter was a failed president. In the end, Carter-Mondale lost with 35.5 million votes to a Reagan-Bush landslide of nearly 44 million votes. The electoral vote spread was 489 to 49.

Making no impact at *National Review* during the Carter years—but important for the fact that it made no impact—was the defense of the Endangered Species Act by James L. Buckley (Sept. 14, 1979). The Republican Party once had led the nation in conservation, as symbolized by T.R.'s establishment of the national park system, a source of recreation and education for the public—*conservative* education, need it be said. Buckley observed that a species is much more easily destroyed than replaced. He might have urged stewardship and the collective pleasure involved in even the distant existence of the great wild creatures of plain and forest, the loss of which would be an unimaginable catastrophe: the world as strip mall, plus a zoo or two. William Buckley was sympathetic, but warned against the extremism that would protect every snail darter.

Surely that was correct. But free-market dogma ignored what Burke had called the "unbought" grace of life, surely a key dimension of the conservative mind.

21

What We All Worked For

"Ronald Reagan won the Cold War without firing a single shot."
—Margaret Thatcher

One day in 1977, Ronald Reagan asked Richard Allen, who would later serve as his first national security advisor, if he would like to hear his view of the Cold War. "Some people think I'm simplistic," Reagan said, "but there's a difference between being simplistic and being simple. My theory of the Cold War is that we win and they lose. What do you think about that?"

"I was flabbergasted," Allen later recalled. "I'd worked for Nixon and Goldwater and I'd heard a lot about . . . détente and the need to 'manage' the Cold War, but never did I hear a leading politician put the matter so starkly." He asked the governor if he really meant that. Reagan told him, "Of course I mean it. I just said it."[1]

Reagan's highly focused anticommunism had its roots in his experience as president of the Screen Actors' Guild. He was a New Deal Democrat, but as he fought off a Communist takeover of the union—an attempt at dominating the movie industry as a whole—he soon realized that the American Communists were not simply a band of idealists with a mimeograph machine. They were often thugs who would throw acid in the faces of movie stars or beat them bloody to get their way. Reagan knew that this was *not* the American way, but something sinister.

Reagan then followed up on this experience with a great deal of reading. The extent of his reading was not widely recognized until the publication of his radio transcripts, *Reagan in His Own Hand* (2001), composed between January 1979 and October 1979 when he was broadcasting regularly, and a thick volume of his correspondence, *Reagan: A Life in Letters*, in 2003. Discovered in the Reagan Library archive, these radio scripts, handwritten by Reagan on yellow pads, give evidence of the surprising scope of his reading and intellectual facility on a great variety of matters. Historians, whatever their politics, can never again consider him uninterested in matters of intellectual weight, nor as merely a pleasant fellow manipulated by handlers. Reagan read and thought his way to a principled anticommunism. And then he set out to act on his principles.

It is worth noticing that Reagan was one of the three most successful presidents of the twentieth century. All three were coalition builders, all three won second-term landslides: FDR in 1936, Eisenhower in 1956, Reagan in 1984. Reagan carried forty-nine states and—had he not declined to put more campaign money into Minnesota, giving Mondale a pass in his home state—might have made it fifty. All three presidents could be considered prudential conservatives: FDR center-left, securing the center at a time of fanaticism on both the left and right, Eisenhower and Reagan center-right. Like these three great presidents, when a leader puts together a national coalition, he guarantees that he can govern a large and various nation.

Reagan was an assiduous reader of *National Review*, had a particularly high regard for Burnham's prudential and realistic foreign policy, was a friend of Buckley, and awarded the Presidential Medal of Freedom to both Chambers (posthumously) and Burnham. He attended the magazine's thirtieth anniversary dinner at the Plaza Hotel, as well as the opening of *National Review*'s Washington office at the Madison Hotel.

From the perspective of *National Review*, and of the American conservative movement that the magazine played such an important part in shaping, the Reagan presidency was a culmination. A Western individualist like Goldwater, Reagan trusted the judgment of Americans on moral issues, and in that he leaned libertarian. If he opposed abortion, it was not prominent on his political agenda. At the same time, his own instincts were traditional, and he appealed often to the American past. He was quietly religious, in the American grain. Abroad, he was prudential, never a risk-taker, and in the end a winner, bringing down the Soviet empire. American conservatism had arrived.

Like Jack Kennedy, Reagan's oratory could eloquently remind Americans of their own best dreams, as in his optimism, his use of Governor Winthrop's "city on a hill" metaphor, and his "Morning in America" 1984 theme. His four great anticommunist speeches were moving, and sometimes alarming to Liberals, but they were correct in substance: they were *true*. History will remember his "Tear down this wall, Mr. Gorbachev. Tear down this wall." The State Department tried to block that as impolitic, but Reagan said, "I am the President, am I not?" He gave the speech as written. As his aide Martin Anderson once aptly observed, "His mind was an open book that he read to the nation." Even Gorbachev concluded that Reagan's word was good: what you saw was what you got.

Though he was Soviet communism's most dangerous enemy, he avoided major violence, as Margaret Thatcher attested; and when she told him that Gorbachev was different, that "You can do business with him," Reagan was willing to negotiate, genial though firm. He knew, and said, that the Soviet Union was a rotten barrel economically, but he gave that rotten barrel a few strong kicks.

Reagan's Strategic Defense Initiative, his proposal for a space defense against ICBMs, was a proposal the Soviets could not begin to afford, even in experimental form. SDI occupied the center of all the Politburo meetings, was Gorbachev's highest priority, but Reagan never gave in on it. He never launched an attack without the odds being wholly in his favor, as in Grenada and Libya. He put together a united European coalition to install our Pershing II and Cruise missiles, in answer to the Soviet medium-range missiles already installed—this despite a furious "nuclear freeze" movement throughout the West, backed by the Democrats, the American Catholic bishops, the Vatican, and massive demonstrations. Margaret Thatcher, François Mitterand, and Helmut Kohl did not want a Soviet tactical nuclear edge on their own borders with no matching American commitment. Forty thousand Soviet tanks on your border, considered able to reach the English Channel within a week, concentrates the mind.

Reagan was perhaps the most focused mind I have ever met. When I had been in Sacramento for a little while in 1968, I thought that every morning when he got up he probably mused to himself, "What can I do to hurt the Soviet Union today?" I was not surprised that when I met Margaret Thatcher for the first time—much more beautiful than her photographs indicate, blue suit, Liberty silk scarf, blonde hair, and that special pure English complexion—the first thing she asked me was, "How is Ronnie?" In the summer of 2004, she managed to come to his funeral in Washington, then also the funeral at the Reagan Library in California—against her doctors' advice, and though she now was old and frail. If ever two national leaders had a special relationship, those two did. Even Gorbachev concluded that Reagan's word was good: what you saw was what you got.

REAGAN'S COALITION INCLUDED all regions, East and West, North and South, blue-collar "Reagan Democrats" and former Wallaceites. Nothing had been seen like it since Roosevelt's New Deal coalition, which included everything from Ku-Kluxers to Popular Front Communists. There seemed to be a quickening intellectual mood that first Reagan year, with the publication of free-market books like George Gilder's *Wealth and Poverty*, the displacement of Keynesian orthodoxy by supply-side economics, and the growing prominence of conservative idea centers such as the Hoover Institution, the Heritage Foundation, and the American Enterprise Institute.

At times Reagan even seemed to have a quality touched by myth. Within recent memory Jack Kennedy, Martin Luther King, and Robert Kennedy had been assassinated and George Wallace had been crippled by a would-be assassin's bullets. Was the United States a banana republic? Early in Reagan's first year, an assassin's .22 caliber, exploding-tip bullet stopped an inch from his heart. Here we go again. But he lived. He even joked at death.

"I forgot to duck, honey," a line from an old movie. An April 17, 1981, editorial in *National Review* had it exactly right:

> Ronald Reagan has exorcised the national nightmare. He looked it in the eye and cracked some jokes. His own sanity was overwhelming, and the baggy neurotic devils of self-hatred slunk back into the shadows. We are not, repeat not, a sick society, Reagan told us with his jokes. His own behavior provided us with an exemplary metaphor. We cannot be defeated, at home or abroad, if we refuse to be defeated.

National Review also had greeted Reagan's inauguration with a sense of its unusual—even, to use the word again, mythic—importance:

> It often happens in history that the need to conserve essential things requires in fact drastic change. We appear to be living through just such a moment, when the will is prepared to meet the necessity. On January 20 there occurred an extraordinary convergence. Even as President-elect Reagan raised his hand to take the oath of office, the nervous choreographers—barbarians—in Teheran were releasing their kidnapped hostages. History, ineluctably, had brought the two events together. The Teheran kidnappers had little choice in the matter. . . .
>
> Hope is always renewed, both in the individual life and in the national experience. . . . Carter will go down in history as a complete cipher. The question of the hour is whether or not we are at a moment in history like 1933 when fundamental changes are set in motion.

Even nature seemed to conspire in the mythic pattern. For two weeks before, Washington shivered under an unaccustomed cold spell. Mounds of dirty snow piled up in the gutters. But as the wooden stands went up along Pennsylvania Avenue, an emotional force was felt throughout that still-provincial city, an atmosphere of waiting, or expectation. The inauguration brought spring-like temperatures—and even, among Reagan's Republican rivals, a sense of relief. They, as much as we, needed a new beginning.

THROUGHOUT HIS EIGHT YEARS as president, Ronald Reagan had four goals which informed his administration. These were not merely the most important goals among many, they were the *only* goals; and they were interrelated:

1. Restore the American spirit of confidence and optimism.
2. Get the American economy humming through cuts both in tax rates and in domestic spending.
3. Build up and renovate American military power.
4. Stop the spread of Soviet power and destroy the Soviet system in its home base through the application of moral-intellectual and economic-strategic power, that is, cancellation of the "Brezhnev Doctrine," or "What's mine ('socialist') is mine, and what's yours is up for grabs."

These four points constituted the irreducible heart of Reaganism, that "metal core," as Edmund Morris said, which lay just beneath the gentleness and geniality. Unless this is grasped, nothing is grasped.

In Isaiah Berlin's famous metaphor, the hedgehog knows one great thing, while the fox knows many and moves among them. Reagan was a hedgehog, Franklin Roosevelt a fox, experimenting with a number of ideas—at least until December 7, 1941. Except for that major difference, however, there were important similarities between Reagan and FDR, as *National Review* pointed out in an editorial (Feb. 19, 1982) on the occasion of his State of the Union address:

> In his first year, Ronald Reagan approached the new issues of the Eighties with the optimistic grace of the man whose centenary we are observing. Reagan has been the Happy Warrior. FDR suffered, and some say that it deepened him: a failed marriage, polio, an unfulfilled love. Reagan has had his own family problems; he also met his attempted assassination with the same personal grace FDR managed against polio. The nation correctly appreciated the symbolic character of both ordeals. If Roosevelt prevailed, the nation too might walk. If Reagan, seriously wounded, joked, then we might as well stop wringing our hands.

Reagan's focus on the essential things that lay before him may go far toward explaining his occasional inattentiveness at Cabinet and other meetings, often bound to involve clouds of words irrelevant to a highly focused president.

Reagan's goal of restoring the American spirit was integral to the achievement of his other three goals. In that sense, he was an idealist, and as such he had roots in the American tradition and can be associated with Emerson, his idealism wholly practical and a paradigm for behavior. Reagan also had his personal myths. Hollywood movies played a large part in his imagination, a fact he shared with most Americans, especially those who lived through the Depression and war years. So too did historical and even sports figures. His role as George Gipp, the Notre Dame football star, was as real to him as Homer's Achilles was to the ancient Greeks; Alexander the Great even imagined himself another Achilles, and with such imaginings conquered most of the known world. Churchill, Franklin Roosevelt, and Lincoln loomed large in Reagan's responsible dreams, to use Yeats's sense of that word when he wrote, "In dreams begin responsibilities."

On February 18, 1981, Reagan spoke to a joint session of Congress and asked them to join him in "restoring the promise that is offered to each of us in this, the last best hope of man on earth." This echoed Lincoln, as Reagan combined an inspiring model with a concrete request asking Congress to cut $4.1 billion from the current Carter budget and enact a 30 percent income tax reduction over three years, while also increasing defense spending.

Reagan made clear how central his economic commitments were at the beginning of his administration, as *National Review* recognized editorially on January 23, 1981:

> So far President-elect Reagan has stopped Establishment politicos and naysayers in his entourage from selling out the supply-side economic issue on which he campaigned. Mr. Reagan has let it be known that Kemp-Roth and a supply-side tax cut are presidential decisions *that have been made*. He has designated David Stockman, a Kemp ally, as director of the Office of Management and Budget to be sure that the tax cuts do not fall victim to spending increases. Other members of the President's team, with varying degrees of

enthusiasm and reluctance, are lining up behind the President's supply-side policy. . . . For the first time in a long while, the chances are good that the economy can be refurbished on a free-market basis.

By September 30, 1983, *National Review* could print a triumphant editorial titled "Reaganomics: A Short History":

> By the summer of 1981, Reaganomics was already "hurting the poor." By late 1981, with recession setting in five minutes after the first phase of the Reagan tax-cuts was installed, Reaganomics had "caused the recession."
>
> Throughout 1982, Reaganomics "prolonged" the recession. In mid-1982, signs of recovery began to appear. It was feared that Reaganomics would "delay" or even "kill" a full recovery. As the recovery continued, the question was whether it could continue to survive Reaganomics. Today the recovery appears strong. It has, of course, nothing to do with Reaganomics. The misery index is under 12 percent.

By then, Reagan was grinning and quipping in his speeches, "They used to call it Reaganomics." He was too considerate to recall that during the primaries, George Bush, now his vice president, had called it "voodoo economics."

Two books stand out as articulating the rationale for what was taking place: Jude Wanniski's *How the World Works* (1978) and George Gilder's *Wealth and Poverty* (1981). Rep. Jack Kemp, the Republican cosponsor along with Democratic Rep. William Roth of the Kemp-Roth tax cuts, was a favorite of *National Review* and a charismatic advocate of tax cuts. Kemp's easy-to-grasp formulation persuaded many: "When you tax something you get less of it, and when you reward something you get more of it." This held for investment as well as for welfare dependency. Celebrating the "Ship of State to Starboard" (August 21, 1981), the magazine distributed congratulations:

> The passage of Ronald Reagan's package of tax and spending cuts sharply reverses the leftward course of economic policy in the United States. It demonstrates that fundamental change is possible, and shatters that stultifying concept of "politically impossible"—long the knee-jerk answer of political moderates to conservatives pressing for a restoration of the formulas of American success. . . .

The termination of this process two hundred days into the Reagan Administration seems so sudden as to be magical. Few expected it, and that in itself contributes to the image of Ronald Reagan waving a magic wand. In a morning-after editorial, the *Washington Post* expressed its own great surprise at the decisive change in economic policy. . . . The *Post* owes its surprise to its unwillingness to recognize the rising influence of the editorial page of the *Wall Street Journal* and the efforts of people like William Simon, who established a style of refusing to defer to the "politically impossible."

There was abundant credit to go around. In fact supply-side economics was a reformulation of Says Law, named after the classical economist who held that supply creates demand. Thus, there was little demand for petroleum until the invention of the internal combustion engine, and no aviation industry until the invention of the airplane. But the counterintuitive "magic" of the "new" economics did run into all-too-solid flesh in the form of House Speaker Thomas P. "Tip," or "All-Politics-is-Local" O'Neill, who regularly pronounced Reagan budgets "dead on arrival." Thus, domestic budget cuts proved insufficient to prevent deficits.

After all, irrational as many budget items may seem on paper, in fact they are in the budget because they have constituencies, and these have clout in Congress. This is just a fact of representative government, probably correctable only piecemeal. In addition, the sharply increased defense spending added to the deficits. Nevertheless, supply-side economics opened an entire vista of fresh thought.

TIGHTLY CONNECTED with the first two Reagan goals were the third and fourth: the build-up and renovation of American military power and stopping the spread of Soviet power and destroying the Soviet system in its home base. Reagan considered the time ripe for what had been called a "forward" or "liberation" policy toward the Soviet empire. What had begun as "containment" after the Second Word War had been formulated by George Kennan and implemented by Wise Men such as Acheson, Marshall, McCloy, and Harriman, representatives of the Eastern Establishment. They had held the line, supported by Truman and all subsequent presidents. Now, a new phase was at hand.

22

Reagan: The World Transformed

Now, the climax of World War Three, as the scales of power tip fatally against the Soviet Union. Never had a huge empire fallen apart with so little peril to those around it. The moment was fortunately almost unique, given the relationship between Ronald Reagan and Mikhail Gorbachev, and their success in playing a peaceful endgame was a tribute to both men—and unthinkable with a more typical Soviet figure such as Brezhnev. This peaceful conclusion also took special qualities in Reagan as well—to see the possibilities and to rest real confidence in his Soviet counterpart, a man from what amounted to a different planet.

What we will be dealing with is a great whirlpool of history sucking down ever more rapidly and irreversibly to its extinction the great Soviet empire, with one of the most remarkable presidents in American history riding in the whirlwind—to use Addison—and directing the storm. The man and the moment had arrived together. *National Review*, with moments of doubt, enjoyed the implementation of policies it had urged in outline from the beginning. It was possible to imagine that the policies it was now commenting on had been designed by James Burnham himself. Reagan meant to win the Cold War. And that meant building up and restoring American military power at home, halting the spread of Soviet power abroad, and destroying the Soviet system on its home turf.

First of all, Reagan's Protracted Conflict or World War Three strategy focused directly on the Soviet Union. Germany, and derivatively Berlin, was the prize, and had been so since 1945. Khrushchev's repeated threats to blockade or dominate Berlin reflected this. His erection of the Berlin Wall in 1962 was an attempt to staunch the hemorrhage of the best and brightest westward through Berlin. Both Moscow and Washington knew that an assault westward across the 1945 line of settlement would mean an exchange of ICBMs.

The strategy of the Kremlin therefore was to "decouple" Western Europe from the United States by neutralizing it or, in the argot of the period, by "Finlandization"—or else by biting off pieces through local seizures of power, as had almost come to pass in Portugal. Meanwhile, advances might be made in Latin America and elsewhere in the Third World. "Decoupling" Western Europe would resolve the Third World War in the Soviets' favor with a united and dominated Europe. So, as then-president Eisenhower had remarked in 1956, you had to "kill the head of the snake" first. Eisenhower meant Moscow.

President Reagan made his intentions clear in four great positional speeches. In themselves, they put pressure on Moscow by indicating that a fresh policy was in place. Each drew the lines not only between the USSR and the United States, but within the United States, between Reagan's forward engagement and Nixon-Kissinger's détente, and further, between both and the spreading "nuclear freeze" movement and assorted quasi-pacifist groups, including the American Catholic bishops and other clergy.

Speaking before the British Parliament on June 8, 1982, the president, ignoring diplomatic catchphrases, laid out the historical assumptions underlying the policies he would pursue:

> In some sense Karl Marx was right. We are witnessing today a great revolutionary crisis, a crisis where the demands of the economic order are conflicting directly with those of the political order. But the crisis is happening not in the free, non-Marxist West, but in the home of Marxist-Leninism, the Soviet Union.

As Reagan uttered those words, shipyard workers in Gdansk and workers elsewhere in Poland were seething with national and religious passions, as well as with economic discontent, that would shake the Soviet empire, "the prison house of nations." Reagan continued:

> The dimensions of this failure are astounding: A country which employs one-fifth of its population in agriculture is unable to feed its own people. Were it not for the private sector, the tiny private sector tolerated in Soviet agriculture, the country might be on the brink of famine. . . . Over-centralized, with little or no incentives, year after year the Soviet system pours its best resources into the making of instruments of destruction. The constant shrinking of economic growth, combined with the growth of military production, is putting a heavy strain on the Soviet people. What we see here is a political structure that no longer corresponds to its economic base, a society where productive forces are hampered by political ones. . . . [The] march of freedom and democracy . . . will leave Marxism-Leninism on the ash heap of history.

Words as direct, truthful, and searing as these are seldom heard in global politics. Marx's term "ash heap" must have grated on some of the MPs, especially those of the Labour Party, but Reagan was here playing the anthem of the future.

In this first address, Reagan had turned Marx's economic forecasts against the Marxist homeland. In the second, on March 8, 1983, before the National Association of Evangelicals in Orlando, Florida, he set forth the moral and religious case:

> Yes, let us pray for the salvation of all those who live in their totalitarian darkness—pray they will discover the joy of knowing God. But until they do, let us be aware that while they preach the supremacy of the state, declare its omnipotence over the individual man, and predict its eventual domination of all peoples on the earth, they are the focus of evil in the modern world. . . .
>
> You know, I've always believed that old Screwtape [the devil in *The Screwtape Letters* by C. S. Lewis] reserved his best efforts to those of you in the church. So, in your discussions of the nuclear freeze proposals, I urge you to beware the temptation of pride—the temptation of blithely declaring yourselves above it all and labeling both sides equally at fault, to ignore the facts of

history and the aggressive impulses of an evil empire, to simply call the arms race a giant misunderstanding and thereby remove yourself from the struggle between right and wrong and good and evil.

Peter Robinson—then a Reagan speechwriter, a young Dartmouth and Oxford graduate, a former student and now friend of mine—recalls in his White House memoir *How Ronald Reagan Changed My Life* (2003) that for months he "could count on seeing that phrase 'evil empire' referred to in a newspaper or magazine at least once a week. *National Review* and the *Wall Street Journal* applauded it. Nearly every other publication denounced it. But the phrase continued to echo."[1]

The phrase "evil empire" did violate international protocol, but how many of the greatest spirits of twentieth-century history would have cheered and applauded, a long roll-call of honor including Orwell, Chambers, Koestler, Malraux, Borges, Milosz, Mindszenty, Solzhenitsyn, Pasternak, Akhmatova—and fading away into the mists of the past the millions of *zeks* who had died in the frozen gulags?

Perhaps the best remembered of Reagan's four great addresses was delivered in Berlin on June 12, 1987—best remembered because he employed so effectively the concrete imagery of his setting, the Brandenburg Gate and the Berlin Wall. The speech referred to Mikhail Gorbachev's recently declared policies of *perestroika*, or restructuring, and *glasnost*, or openness. Its central passage:

> We hear much from Moscow about a new policy of reform and openness. Some political prisoners have been released. Certain foreign news broadcasts are no longer being jammed. Some economic enterprises have been permitted to operate with greater freedom from state control. Are these the beginnings of profound changes in the Soviet Union? Or are they token gestures, intended to raise false hopes in the West or to strengthen the Soviet system without changing it. . . ? There is one sign the Soviets can make that would be unmistakable. . . .
>
> General Secretary Gorbachev, if you seek peace, if you seek prosperity for the Soviet Union and Eastern Europe, if you seek liberalization, come here to this gate.

> Mr. Gorbachev, open this gate! Mr. Gorbachev, tear down this wall!

Peter Robinson, who had written the draft submitted to Reagan, comments that, "Like the phrase 'evil empire,' the phrase 'tear down this wall' echoed for months." And well it might have. It was comparable to asking Louis XVI to "Tear down this Bastille." Even more so. In 1989, when the wall did come down, an enormous exodus flowed through and the evil empire was finished. In his memoir, Robinson recounts how the "tear down this wall" phrase came to him. At a social gathering in Berlin, the guests began talking about the wall, and the Berlin hostess angrily exclaimed, "If this man Gorbachev is serious with his talk of *glasnost* and *perestroika*, he can prove it. He can get rid of this wall."

Robinson records that both the State Department and the National Security Council tried to block the speech, submitting alternative drafts. This continued until the morning of the speech, when Reagan said he "was determined to deliver the controversial line. Reagan smiled. 'The boys at State are going to kill me,' he said, 'but it's the right thing to do.'"

The last of the four major addresses was delivered by Reagan on May 31, 1988, during his visit to Moscow. At the State University, with a large marble bust of Lenin looking on behind him, he spoke to several hundred students:

> Freedom is the right to question and change the established way of doing things. It is the continuing revolution of the marketplace. It is the understanding that allows us to recognize shortcomings and seek solutions. It is the right to put forth an idea, scoffed at by the experts, and watch it catch fire among the people. It is the right to follow your dream, or stick to your conscience, even if you're the only one in a sea of doubters.
>
> Freedom is the recognition that no single person, no single authority or government, has a monopoly on the truth, but that every individual life is infinitely precious, that every one of us put on this world has been put there for a reason and has something to offer.

Robinson concludes: "The fortieth President, describing freedom to the children of the apparat. The Cold War was over." There remained another year before the wall came down, and for the forty-first president to negotiate our response to the astonishing change and try to keep it peaceful.

REAGAN HAD SET FORTH the ideas in his public addresses. The material foundations that had to be laid in order to realize them were plain enough and had to be addressed right from the beginning. Two of *National Review*'s earliest editorials during the Reagan administration took up this problem, the first addressing strategic realism in relationship to the confirmation hearings of Alexander Haig (March 21, 1981):

> Amid the cant characteristic of such proceedings, there were impressive glints of candor and wisdom at the Alexander Haig confirmation hearings—for example, Haig's explicit avoidance of sentimental generalizing about the so-called Third World, unbudging endorsement of the strategic good sense of the Christmas bombings in the Vietnam War, and assertion of the existence of "more important things than peace." That last utterance departed from a ritual mode persistent through six Administrations beginning with Eisenhower's.
>
> Such thoughts—there were many others—bother tender minds. The *Washington Post*'s Philip Geylin envisioned Haig carrying a metaphoric swagger stick. The *New York Times*'s James Reston depicted "a Secretary of State who, right or wrong, regards diplomacy in military terms with a Simple answer to all problems: more arms." Such simplism is not borne out by the hearing record. What is revealed, rather, is an outlook properly attuned to George Washington's counsel "always to keep ourselves by suitable establishments in a respectable defensive posture." . . . Military strength, on Haig's reckoning, is indispensable in managing external affairs but not the all-encompassing end.

To be sure, military strength had to be funded. Reagan's program was also intended to put pressure on Soviet research and development, as with advanced jet fighter and bomber aircraft, and his proposal of a defense against ballistic missiles, which he announced on March 23, 1983, after being persuaded of its eventual technical feasibility. This lay in the then-distant future, but its significance was far from lost on Mikhail Gorbachev and his advisors. *NR*'s March 20, 1981, editorial made the general point:

> President Reagan's intentions concerning improvement of U.S. defense capa-
> bilities were made clear in his budget address, which specified defense as the
> single exception to plans to slow down rates of increase in federal expenses in
> general. The question here is how much, not whether. Comparison with what
> the previous Administration had in mind may help in understanding the mag-
> nitudes. . . . The Reagan proposal is for outlays of $175 billion above the more
> recent Carter projection for the quinquennium.
>
> . . . What can be said at the moment is that the figures very closely corre-
> spond to estimates of the defense requirements put forth by the Committee
> on the Present Danger. Big figures, indeed—but the necessity is obvious to
> us.

In early August, the president also struck an exemplary blow abroad, on the
north coast of Africa. President Muammar al-Quaddafi of Libya had
advanced the territorial waters of that country by drawing a "line" in
international waters across the Gulf of Sidra. After first informing President
Sadat of Egypt about his intention to send American warships across the
line—Sadat answering, "Magnificent"—Reagan did so. On August 19,
1981, when two advanced F-14s crossed the line, two Soviet-built SU-22s
intercepted them—and were obliterated by a barrage of heat-seeking
Sidewinder missiles. Carter wasn't president anymore.

UNKNOWN TO *NATIONAL REVIEW*, and everyone else, during the early
years of the Reagan administration a spectacular covert initiative was also
being carried out against the Soviet Union. The revelation of some details
of this effort in early 2004 should silence the claim that the Soviet Union
collapsed entirely from within and that its demise owed nothing to Reagan.
In his book *At the Abyss: An Insider's History of the Cold War* (2004), former
Reagan Secretary of the Air Force Thomas C. Reed recounts that the CIA
had uncovered a massive Soviet effort to steal Western industrial technolo-
gies. Reagan's CIA responded with a program to plant defective technolo-
gies so that they could be stolen. "One result," writes Reed, "was the most
monumental non-nuclear explosion and fire ever seen from space." This
occurred during the summer of 1982 in a vital Soviet natural gas pipeline.
This CIA effort was known as Operation Farewell.

But the bigger game took place in Europe, where the Soviets had deployed medium-range SS-20s in East Germany. This was fundamentally a political move. The SS-20 could not reach the United States, but the Europeans knew that the United States would not respond to a threat to use the SS-20 against Europe by threatening to retaliate with ICBMs from America. Risking Boston, New York, and Washington on behalf of the Ruhr, Paris, or London would not be a credible threat. The Soviet political goal was to decouple Western Europe from the United States by leaving it naked before Soviet nuclear intimidation: and so to win World War III.

Obviously, it had become a matter of the first importance for the United States to install its own medium-range nuclear weapons in Europe: that is, the Pershing II and Cruise missiles. Yet this strategic necessity ran up against fierce opposition from the "nuclear freeze" and "peace" movements, sweeping the United States and Europe as they had not since 1968–72, often with the same leadership and enlisting the same groups of "clergy concerned," "academics against," and so forth. The "nuclear freeze," now supported by the Catholic bishops, was endorsed by Walter Mondale in 1984 and made its way into the Democratic platform that year. Obviously, freezing the prospective deployment of the Pershing II and the Cruise, while leaving the SS-20 in place, would be close to suicidal.

The freeze movement lasted through most of the Reagan administration. Naturally, *National Review* devoted a great deal of space to it, because it had ramifying implications, assorted groups losing while others gained authority and political power. In one form or another, and with different substance, the struggle has persisted. Here, our purposes require only a representative sample, as the movement got rolling.

Very early, an editorial (April 2, 1982) attempted an overview:

> It will be very important for the Reagan Administration to handle correctly the nuclear freeze movement now shaping up as this spring's mass effort, and for it to be handled correctly its *politics* must be thoroughly understood.
>
> The nuclear freeze movement represents a *political* initiative. It arises out of the political *success* Reagan has so far achieved. . . . It has attracted the support of most of the defeated political figures of the past generation; but, on that very account, it should be handled with a political response.

Let us pause there. There plainly is something to that. Liberal Democrats had come up with no fresh proposals, ideas, or compelling personalities. But the freeze was becoming popular internationally, quite apart from Reagan. Protesters were parading with skulls drawn in white on their faces, clergymen were making speeches—all good footage for the media. The editorial enumerated the popular and beneficial things that Reagan had already accomplished, including the ascent of economic indicators, and continued:

> In this political Alamo what does liberalism *do*? It comes out against . . . death. No doubt there's still a majority to be had there.
>
> Make no mistake about it, the nuclear-freeze movement is gaining momentum. As soon as good weather arrives, we can expect to see large-scale demonstrations in Washington, backed up by the national media. . . . Already, this movement has attracted the fading political stars of yesterday. Senator Kennedy speaks in apocalyptic tones: "Today the arms race rushes away toward nuclear confrontation that could well mean the annihilation of the human race. And the nuclear-freeze movement has enlisted the support of people who have not had any recent purchase upon the direction of American politics." Walter Mondale, Father Theodore Hesburgh [then president of Notre Dame], Senator Mark Hatfield, the reverend Billy Graham. They hope to lead an emotional, apocalyptic movement around which liberalism and the Democratic Party can rise again.
>
> But they have a problem.
>
> The only politically acceptable American formulation calls for a "mutual" freeze on nuclear weapons delivery systems. Worse still, it calls for a "verifiable" freeze. If the anti-nuclear movement called for a unilateral freeze, it would soon cease to be a movement; it would be reduced to its core of the usual people.
>
> President Reagan has already shown how to de-fang movements of this sort politically with his call for an elimination of all medium-range nuclear weapons from Europe. The Soviets disappeared into a squid-like ink of technicalities.

Very fine and very rational, but the movement flowed on. *NR*'s editorial ignored some of the nonrational factors at work. The reasonable trade-off *NR* (and Reagan) envisioned was boring compared with orating and parading around dressed like a skeleton; a stance that can advertise as *moral* can appeal to individuals as long as the consequences will be postponed for others to deal with; a lot of liberals simply hated Reagan.

ABOUT A MONTH LATER (May 14, 1982) came another editorial, "Anti-Nuclear Politics":

> We have just come to Ground Zero Week, an anti-nuclear mobilization centered on the campuses and churches, which by all accounts met with mixed results. There are those who think, however, that with the advent of warm weather, the demonstrations and protests will gather greater numbers. . . .
>
> Some signs support such an estimate. Jonathan Schell's *The Fate of the Earth*, a nuclear nightmare forecasting human extinction—an update of Nevil Shute's 1957 *On the Beach*—has become both a canonical work for the movement and a runaway best-seller.

This editorial went on to note assorted examples of gathering strength in the American freeze movement, but correctly pointed out where the more serious political problem would lie: Europe, the primary area of political tension, threatened by the Soviet missiles, and without a deterrent.

> It would be a mistake, in our opinion, to assume that the European and American anti-nuclear movements are identical. There is overlap, to be sure, but the two are differently rooted.
>
> This consideration suggests that the European movement is likely to be more enduring, because it rises out of certain undeniable military realities. That is, a limited nuclear war (i.e., one employing tactical nuclear weapons) against the Warsaw Pact forces would initially be fought in West Germany. A datum of that kind concentrates the mind, and, not surprisingly, the European anti-nuclear movement is strongest in West Germany.

There is where the political battle would be fiercest, and would be carried on by European leadership, with West German Chancellor Helmut Kohl playing the vital role, and deserving Reagan's lasting gratitude.

Editorial after editorial in *National Review* followed the course of the movement, with its focus of its energies in the churches, the media, and on the campuses, and the circus-like atmosphere of the rallies, with rock stars performing and old protesters always prominent—career protesters, as it were: Jane Fonda, Bella Abzug, Benjamin Spock, Episcopal Bishop Paul Moore. Even Reagan's then-rebellious daughter Patti joined the throng.

As things grew more and more frenzied, there was even an independent creative aspect, with gruesome puppet shows and artists *manqueés* wearing inventive costume, dressed as cylindrical bombs. A Republican convention was never like this. *National Review*:

> The anti-nuclear rallies scheduled to coincide with the United Nations Second Special Session drew large though not unprecedented crowds (Simon and Garfunkel pulled 400,000 last year). Singers sang, poets read poems, politicians tried to hitch free rides. A number of innocents appeared, while Mayor Koch, who is not innocent, but who must shore up a crumbling left flank, announced his sympathy with the spirit of the occasion.

In Rome, the prizewinning young poet Daniel Mark Epstein, who in 2002 would begin to contribute to *National Review*'s new poetry feature, took all this in as the subject of his ironic "Ode to Virgil," the great poet of Rome and European civilization:

> *The children of Europe are striking, Virgil*
> *and Rome is paralyzed. Nothing works.*
> *The docks are striking, and airplanes and freight-trains,*
> *gears are locked, the dynamos freeze, the piston*
> *sticks.. . .*
> *I myself am striking in self-defense.*
> *Vergilius Maro, this is your young American correspondent in Rome.*

But, probably inevitably, there was management concealed behind the spontaneity and the anarchy. A November 12, 1982, *National Review* editorial communicated some basic facts about military hardware and then about Soviet involvement. This should be read with the close attention it deserves. The Soviet Union had an evident stake in the antinuclear movement, and drawing on a new book by John Barron, *National Review* turned to this aspect of the question:

> The Soviets' interest in a freeze grew out of strategic realities. At the time of Ronald Reagan's election, the Soviets had 42,500 tanks in Eastern Europe and 315 multiple-warhead SS-20s aimed at Western European cities. The neutron anti-tank warhead (a.k.a., "neutron bomb") had been cancelled by Carter. None of the Pershing II missiles—requested by Western Europe to counter the SS-20—had been installed. The MX and the B-1 were in abeyance.

That is to say, as Reagan became president, the whole idea of deterrence hung in the balance, which had tipped strategically toward Moscow. An all-out Soviet tank thrust across the West German plain was a possibility. A united Germany under Soviet domination would shift Europe toward the Soviet bloc, but for that reason, such a thrust would probably be answered by American long-range missiles.

However, its monopoly of medium-range missiles on the continent also gave the Soviets the opportunity for irresistible political pressure and so for "peaceful" domination—victory in World War III, without firing a shot. And so, as *National Review* went on to observe in this editorial, Soviet intelligence was at work within the freeze movement:

> On February 23, 1981, Brezhnev called for a freeze on the development of all new nuclear weapons systems. The Soviet PR machine swung into action.
>
> KGB agents fanned demonstrations in Western Europe. Occasionally they were careless. In April 1981, the Dutch expelled a KGB officer, masquerading as a TASS correspondent, who had boasted in his cups: "If Moscow decides that fifty-thousand demonstrators must take to the streets, then they take to the streets." In October, the Danes arrested one Arne Petersen, sponsor of the Oslo-to-Paris peace march, as a Soviet agent (Petersen had met with the KGB's agent in Copenhagen 23 times). Norway and Portugal expelled other KGB "peace" organizers.
>
> Soviet agents attended all the important early strategy sessions in this country. Yuri Kapralov, nominally counsel to the Soviet Embassy in Washington, in fact a KGB officer, sat on the discussion panel of the first meeting of the American Nuclear Freeze Campaign at Georgetown in Mach 1981.

That month, the International Physicians for the Prevention of Nuclear War held a meeting in Virginia. The main Soviet representative was Georgi Arbatov, ostensibly a sort of sociologist (he heads something called the Institute for the U.S.A. and Canada), whose speech was greeted by thunderous applause.

In May, freeze supporters in the House invited Romesh Chandra, president of the World Peace Council, to meet with them. Chandra is an Indian Communist, and the WPC is a Soviet Front. The U.S. Peace Council, the WPC's local affiliate, sent representatives to a disarmament strategy session in Nyack, N.Y., in October, and held a meeting of its own in New York City in November, also attended by congressmen.

Yuri Kapralov (*supra*) was on hand to help kick-off the Riverside Church Disarmament Program. The Reverend William Sloane Coffin, senior minister at Riverside, had picked Cora Weiss, once a cheerleader for Hanoi, as the program's director. Other KGB agents, stationed at the UN as diplomats, have participated in the Riverside program. And so on, and so on.

From Brezhnev to the Reverend William Sloane Coffin, et. al., and the Riverside Church originally financed by the Rockefellers. At *National Review* around this time, the imaginative Joe Sobran applied the perfect metaphor: the Hive. When the Queen Bee in Moscow buzzes, the buzz goes down all through the Hive, buzz buzz buzz. . . .

THE FREEZE MOVEMENT collapsed amidst a remarkable constellation of forces and events leading up to the November 1984 forty-nine-state victory of President Reagan over Walter Mondale and Geraldine Ferraro. In retrospect, the period between 1982 and 1984 has a revolutionary feel to it when considered as an independent whole. To do so, let us list some of its major events approximately in chronological order, and without attempting to assess their relative importance. To use Brezhnev's felicitous phrase, probably found in some Marxist manual, a momentous change was taking place in the "correlation of forces":

1. In 1982, Poland was in turmoil. The Solidarity labor union, led by Lech Walesa and by the first Polish pope, was crystallizing problems of religion and nationalism for which a Communist answer was difficult to discern.

2. On March 23, 1983, in a televised address to the nation, Reagan announced his Strategic Defense Initiative. Though ridiculed as "Star Wars," this put enormous pressure on the USSR and remained in the foreground of negotiations with Gorbachev.

3. On September 1, 1983, Soviet interceptors shot down Korean Airlines Flight 007, a passenger plane. Reagan's response was far from conciliatory, and the event dramatized the nature of the Soviet regime and raised questions about its control of its own defense and retaliatory forces.

4. On October 25, 1983, alarmed by a Cuban presence in Grenada and the danger to resident U.S. medical students, Reagan ordered an invasion that seized the island. This was an example of a new decisiveness.

5. On November 22, 1983, in a tremendous political victory for Chancellor Helmut Kohl, the Bundestag approved deployment of medium-range U.S. missiles on German soil.

6. Dramatic changes were also taking place within the Soviet leadership. Leonid Brezhnev, First Secretary since 1964, died in November 1982, two weeks after delivering a fiery attack on Reagan as threatening a nuclear war. He was succeeded by Yuri Andropov, former KGB chief, who died of kidney disease in February 1984, to be succeeded by the aged and ill Konstantin Chernenko, a veteran apparatchik who dropped Brezhnev's demand that the American medium-range missiles be removed before any further talks could begin. But Chernenko also died after little more than a year, to be succeeded by Mikhail Gorbachev, 54, an engineering graduate who had risen through the party ranks. This did not seem promising at the time. Indeed, the glacial Andrei Gromyko, 76, assured the Politburo in an emotional speech that, "Comrades, this man has a nice smile but he's got iron teeth."[3]

National Review, in a light-hearted moment, began an editorial section with: "There is room for optimism over the accession to power of Mikhail Gorbachev. He has never been directly linked to the shooting of the Pope." And compared with the potato-sack wives of previous Soviet leaders, Raissa Gorbachev was virtually a Hollywood beauty. Her husband, trying to reform communism in order to save it, instead helped to liquidate it. Soon after the inauguration of George Bush, on February 1, 1989, Reagan reminisced a bit:

The only reason I'd never met with General Secretary Gorbachev's predecessors was because they kept dying on me. He was different in style [and] in substance . . . from previous Soviet leaders. He is a man who takes chances and that's what you need for progress. He is a remarkable force for change in that country.

The Great Man theory of history will be endlessly debated, and the issue is probably irresolvable. An approach might be to discuss what might have happened differently had Walter Mondale been elected in 1984. Also debated has been what the demise of the Soviet Union meant in terms of Jeane Kirkpatrick's famous view that "authoritarian" governments can be overthrown from within, but "totalitarian" ones cannot. Certain is the fact that the Soviet Union had come under the pressure of tremendous forces, economic, political, and religious—or "contradictions," as Marx had called them. The CIA had consistently overestimated Soviet economic capability.

In the foreground by 1983–84 was President Reagan's remarkable European political victory in the deployment of the Pershing II missiles, a triumph also for Helmut Kohl, Margaret Thatcher, and François Mitterand. Here, let us look at one unexpected evaluation in a *National Review* editorial citing the *New Republic*:

In the years since Martin Peretz assumed overall direction of *The New Republic*, the magazine has been rejuvenated. . . . [The] magazine today is not knee-jerk in its analysis. For example, the lead editorial in its February 20 [1984] issue was entitled "The Upside Abroad," and it took direct aim at the charge that the Reagan Administration has accomplished nothing in foreign affairs. It enumerates: "First there is the Euromissile victory. There are some for whom hitching the word 'missile' to 'victory' makes an oxymoron, but that is a sentimental view. . . . The Soviets' huge arsenal of SS-20 missiles was designed exclusively for the intimidation of Western Europe. Had the Soviets been able to exercise a veto over a Western deployment whose aim was never more than parity, NATO would have sustained the most serious setback in its history, and perhaps the last. . . . Yet it is hard to think of a single Democratic candidate for President who would have toughed it out the way Mr. Reagan did."

We will return to that last sentence in a moment; meanwhile, the editorial goes on to Grenada: "The success was not that the U.S. Army was able to overcome a platoon of Cuban teamsters, but that an American President could gain the support of the country for intervention against a particularly obnoxious regime aligned with the Soviet Union." And finally: "The third success has been the rebuilding of American defenses." The editorial quotes a critic of Reagan who "acknowledges that what the Soviets call the 'international correlation of forces' has shifted in favor of the United States. In short, the Soviets are in a hole."

National Review praised this "clear-headed assessment" but went on to observe that, even while the *New Republic* could not name a single Democratic candidate for president who would have achieved these things, it nevertheless, in 1984, would support Mondale or Gary Hart against Reagan, and in 1980 had supported Representative John Anderson against Reagan.

That certainly was a contradiction within Martin Peretz's new *New Republic*. It can be explained this way. The magazine essentially was (the late) Scoop Jackson–Democratic, and Mr. Peretz wanted to reconstruct the Democratic Party from within—that is, roll back 1972 and McGovernism, recoup Jackson's defeat that year, and make the party a responsible governing institution. This would be the goal of the Democratic Leadership Council, which, in turn, would later be the springboard for Bill Clinton's 1992 victory and, perhaps, his "triangulation" policy while in office.

NATIONAL REVIEW OF COURSE gave extensive coverage to Poland, Lech Walesa, and Solidarity, and it was far from alone in this. The combination of religion and nationalism was explosive within the Soviet's Eastern European empire, nor was it obvious that it could be controlled, as it had been in 1956 in Hungary by Soviet tanks. In three columns recently established in the magazine, John Roche provided a valuable labor perspective, Erik Kuehnelt-Leddihn a traditional Catholic one, and Brian Crozier, successor to James Burnham, a strategic one.

The distinguished historian John Lukacs, brought to *National Review* by his friend, then–Books editor Chilton Williamson, urged the magazine not to overrate the influence of communism in the Eastern European nations. His opinions could not be ignored or dismissed. From a very long-range perspective, perhaps religion and nationalism *were* more fundamental than communism. Still, unless one thought in terms of epochs or centuries, Lukacs seemed to be sleepwalking through modern history. Lukacs, who lived in Pennsylvania and was wonderful company, seemed spiritually located in nineteenth-century Budapest.

National Review, during this hinge of history, provided a perspective and quality of journalism unique to it and not matched in quality by other publications of the same kind. For example, in its January 23, 1981, issue, *National Review*, extensively covering his growing power, named Lech Walesa "Man of the Year," and the great Solzhenitsyn contributed his European perspective in "Communism at the End of the Brezhnev Era" (January 21, 1983).

Adding to the mounting pressure put on the Soviet position in Poland by Solidarity and Lech Walesa was the Polish Pope John Paul II, whose 1983 visit to Poland *National Review* celebrated (July 8):

> Poles were said to be joking that General Jaruzelski had permitted the Pope to visit only so that, by riding in a motorcade with John Paul, the general could find himself, for once, amid an enthusiastic crowd. If so, he paid dearly for the experience. The Pope boomed out his censure of Polish repressions while a fidgety Jaruzelski stood beside him. The scene occurred on national television. *Nothing* like this has ever happened in a Communist-ruled country. . . .
>
> John Paul showed the world a model of correct diplomacy vis-à-vis Communism: he was polite, but uncompromising. He called not only for justice but for specific reforms, including an independent Poland. He spoke with rich sentiment of Polish culture and history. He formally beatified a nineteenth-century nun who had secretly worked to keep the Catholic faith alive under Russian occupation.

In retrospect it seems inevitable that Moscow would try to do something about this pope. When a Turk named Mehmet Ali Agca attempted to assassinate John Paul II in St. Peter's Square and proved to be in league with the Bulgarian intelligence services, the shock, but not the surprise, was widespread.

Bulgarian intelligence did not freelance independently from the KGB. Complicity was soon all but proved by 25,000 pages of documentation collected by Italian authorities. *Cui bono* spoke for itself. The Reagan administration let the assassination attempt merely sit there in the daylight, stinking. *NR* worried editorially that, with the KGB trying to pull off a murder in St. Peter's Square, the president himself might be in danger. Even the metaphor "rode in the whirlwind" might be weak for these counterrevolutionary—or revolutionary—times.

ON THE TECHNOLOGICAL FRONTIER, *National Review* commented editorially with vigor, establishing a regular "SDI Watch" written by former NASA scientist Robert Jastrow. There is no doubt that in negotiations with Gorbachev SDI exerted intense pressure on the Soviets. The president's vision was a powerful one, rooted in his oft-expressed horror of nuclear war, of Mutual Assured Destruction as the basis of deterrence. He was urged to seek a defense in space against incoming missiles by Edward Teller, by Navy chief-of-staff Admiral James Watkins, and by advocates of the earlier "High Frontier" project. On March 23, 1983, Reagan began the peroration of his televised address to the nation with these words:

> Wouldn't it be better to save lives than to avenge them? Are we not capable of demonstrating our peaceful intentions by applying all our abilities and ingenuity to achieving a truly lasting stability? I think we are. Indeed, we must.
>
> After careful consideration with my advisors, including the Joint Chiefs of Staff, I believe there is a way. Let me share with you a vision of the future which offers hope. It is that we embark on a program to counter the awesome Soviet missile strength with measures that are defensive. Let us turn to the very strengths in technology that spawned our great industrial base and that have given us the quality of life we enjoy today.

Such a proposal was inseparable from Reaganism and was part of its power. Reagan knew enough about the history of science and technology to believe that he should not bet against them. Galileo and Columbus were canonical for schoolboys. Men had recently walked on the moon. We had satellites in orbit, and they were integral to our modern military.

But more than that, Reaganism was part of the American spirit, at one with Whitman's open poem, William James's open philosophy, and Roosevelt's "The only thing we have to fear is fear itself." If the usual suspects immediately ridiculed SDI as "Star Wars," the joke might well be on them. In the immediate future, moreover, they seemed to be betting against technology. Soon after the speech, I had a chance to ask Richard Nixon what he thought of it. He replied that it would be useful as "a bargaining chip," certainly safe enough to say, and as it certainly proved to be in Reagan's summits with Gorbachev.

But there were deeper forces at work now, and here Edmund Morris is riveting:

> Few Americans—let alone that archive of obsolete information, the Central in-telligence Agency—realized just how decrepit the Soviet Union really was. Gorbachev's own privately researched information showed that its gross national product was half that of the U.S., while its economic development was lagging "ten to fifteen years behind the capitalist countries." This "exceptionally grave situation" was worsened by a new sense of inferiority, brought about by the Reagan Administration's arms buildup. All signs pointed to "further weakening of the USSR's international position, and its decline into a second-rate power.[2]

Such, in part, was the unequal position with which Gorbachev finally undertook face-to-face negotiations with Reagan at Geneva on Tuesday, November, 19, 1985, when he struggled to play a weak hand.

Parenthetically, here I will add a personal footnote to Morris's characterization of the CIA as an "archive of obsolete information." During the 1980 primaries, in which George Bush was campaigning against Reagan in New Hampshire, I had a pleasant conversation with Bush. I asked him whether we might not spend the Soviet Union into strategic defeat. I knew that among his many posts he had been CIA director. Genially, he answered that no, the Soviets would match anything we might spend. This was conventional wisdom at the time, evidently also at the CIA.

Edmund Morris's footnote to this passage, remarkable and revealing, contains information I have not seen elsewhere, and provides the source and validation for his generalization about the Soviet economy:

> "Manifesto for Socialist Renewal," a secret document made available by Acting Secretary Gorbachev to Dwayne Andreas, the American business tycoon, in December 1984. Copy in Author's Collection. Since Gorbachev was then clearly the next leader of the CPSU (Chernenko, dying, had just made his last public appearance), and since Andreas was known to be an old friend of RR, delivery of such a self-condemnatory document can only be interpreted as a private *cri de coeur,* a plea to the White House for technological aid and relief from crippling military expenditures.

Without reliable knowledge of the economic condition of this closed society, *National Review* was of two minds about the Soviet situation. It published a signed editorial by the eloquent Peggy Noonan to the effect that Gorbachev was playing possum as a modernizer, and therefore was doubly dangerous: "iron teeth." But it also ran another editorial, "Thinking the Unthinkable" (June 24, 1988):

> Strange things appear to be happening within the Communist world. . . . The Communist idea, or system of ideas, grew up amidst many other protests against capitalism. . . . Practically all of Marx's philosophical, historical and other ideas had been exploded by experts by about 1910. . . . Dialectic was "mysticism." When Sidney Hook . . . tried to synthesize Marx and John Dewey, every time he got near an acceptable philosophical formulation Dewey was in and Marx was out.
>
> Now those readers who can remember or even imagine the period immediately following World War II will recall how powerful the Communist idea seemed at the time. . . . In Malraux's *Man's Hope,* the Revolution is man's hope. In Chambers's *Witness,* the ex-Communist believes that in leaving the party he is on the *losing* side, the West. . . .
>
> Well, the great Communist parties of the post-war period, in France, in Italy, and (underground) in Spain, are virtually out of business.
>
> Recent material indicates that the USSR is in terrible economic shape, far worse than CIA estimates had indicated—that, in fact, it is in the process of becoming a Third World nation in terms of productivity, per-capita in-

come, life expectancy, individual weight and height, and other indices. The bureaucratized "command" economic structure has been a disaster.

We remain skeptical about the ultimate outcome of what Gorbachev is doing, but he is certainly attempting something.

This editorial represented *National Review* opinion, but only partially. It was signed: J. Hart. A more pessimistic view continued to be expressed, prudently enough.

To be sure, Soviet economic debility could be inferred from Soviet behavior. The most spectacular evidence, perhaps, was the explosion and meltdown of the nuclear power plant at Chernobyl just before May Day in 1986. According to Morris, thirty-two people died immediately, and 133,000 were moved out of the "dead zone." The tonnage of lethal particles released and drifting across Europe was equal to ten Hiroshimas. Gorbachev waited almost two weeks before explaining to the world what had happened.

Meanwhile, *National Review*, beginning with Reagan's March 23, 1983, TV address on the promise of SDI, enthusiastically supported the vision. It made some political points (April 15, 1983):

Set aside for the moment the question of feasibility. If the President were to go on TV tomorrow evening and announce that we had developed and deployed an effective defense against missile attack, would that not, self-evidently, be cause for rejoicing? We have of course been inundated with accounts of the horrors of nuclear war. . . . If nuclear warfare could be apocalyptic, would not a defense against nuclear attack be good news?

It is difficult not to believe that if such a defensive effort had been proposed by, say, Kennedy or Mondale, it would have been received very respectfully—would indeed, quite probably, have been hailed as courageous, progressive, humane, pioneering.

President Reagan's proposal that we pursue a serious nuclear defense effort met, instead, with a chorus of instant rejection and ridicule. . . .

If Reagan's proposals were so self-evidently absurd as his critics claim, why then did Mr. Andropov react so violently to them? . . . It would take a bold prophet to guarantee that *no* such defense is feasible.

Politically, the President scored psychologically against the freeze advocates and their apocalyptic backers, and placed himself visibly on the side of saving lives and cities. It was no doubt this political aspect that infuriated his critics, that and their instinctive suspicion of any proposal that would enhance American power and security.

An interesting sidelight from a perspective twenty years later, of lasting relevance about the character of the 1980s opposition, was the issue of the "Neutron Bomb." In 1985, the Soviets still had more than forty thousand tanks on the West European frontier. The kind of mega World War II Battle of Kursk for which these were designed probably will never happen again because of military evolution, but in their day they were a major military and political force. The radiation from a neutron howitzer shell would knock out tank personnel, but its lack of major blast effect would leave buildings intact: the perfect antitank weapon. *National Review* supported the development and deployment of this weapon in Germany from the beginning of the Reagan years (September 4, 1981):

> In the first place, the thing is not a "bomb." It is an eight-inch artillery shell, which can be either fired from a gun or mounted on a Lance missile. The semantic edge gained by calling it a "bomb"—and thus associating it with weapons of mass destruction is simply a part of the political power struggle over the weapon.
>
> Second, the neutron shell is almost entirely a defensive weapon, an anti-tank weapon. Its principle use today is to offset the 4-1 tank advantage enjoyed by the Warsaw Pact over NATO. It should be noted that NATO is not planning a tank attack upon East Germany or Poland. Therefore Soviet, threats to develop their own neutron warhead are hollow. . . .
>
> In one of the more bizarre, but successful operations in the history of psychological warfare the Soviets succeeded is establishing the formula that the neutron warhead is a typical capitalist weapon because it kills people while leaving property intact. This had had surprising resonance. But, of course, the *tank* is not an enemy. It's only a piece of metal. The personnel inside the tank are what determine its mission and political use.

Right there we have what may be the permanent interest of the debate.

Sam Cohen, the Pentagon scientist who invented the weapon, published *The Truth About the Neutron Bomb* (1983), a history of its engineering and the rationale for its strategic importance; *National Review* articles editor Kevin Lynch reviewed the book very favorably (April 29, 1983). This gave rise to a lunch Buckley and several editors had with Cohen, an engaging man who had been startled by the fact that the official Vatican newspaper *L'Osservatore Romano* was attacking the neutron weapon in terms identical to those of Soviet propaganda: it kills people, but leaves property intact.

Cohen was shocked that the Vatican was thus echoing Moscow, and, he recounted, he had arranged a meeting with Pope John Paul II and flown to Rome. In the Vatican, the ancient cardinals and other prelates had treated him as if he were Dracula dripping from a feast, horrified, virtually fleeing his presence. The pope himself had been the only person who seemed to know what a tank was. And Cohen had expected the Vatican to be anti-communist.

The *National Review* editors were also "shocked," but in the *Casablanca* sense. Someone remarked that Cohen should be glad that the taking of interest on loans was no longer a violation of canon law, and that the pope himself is usually more critical of capitalism than of socialism. In the event, the neutron weapon was overtaken by Reagan's deployment of the intermediate nuclear weapons in Europe, reinforcing the earlier deployment of nuclear howitzer shells. But the success of the "peace" camp on the neutron bomb issue has lasting historical interest, as well as serving as an example of the intellectual shortcomings of the modern Christian clergy, when otherwise the modern intellect in their area of religious concern has opened greater opportunities than it has had for more than a century.

ALL OF THESE FORCES—economic, nationalist, political, religious—and the leadership of the free world were concentrated cruelly upon Mikhail Gorbachev when he and President Reagan met at the first of their summit meetings on November 19, 1985, in Geneva. No doubt the "correlation of forces" is the dominant element at any such antagonistic encounter; and there Reagan held every high card. But the personal element does matter, as no doubt Hitler's estimate of Neville Chamberlain and Edouard Daladier mattered to him—not just on his immediate demands regarding Czechoslovakia, but on his much riskier decision to invade Poland in 1939.

Gorbachev had to decide whether Reagan could be intimidated or bamboozled. Thus, this first meeting of Gorbachev and Reagan takes on enormous importance. Unlike the experimental earlier part of his book in which fact mixes with fiction, the account by Edmund Morris of the Reagan years 1981 to 1989 possesses great narrative power and credibility, and it is meticulously footnoted. In the palatial chateau *Fleur d'Eau* on the shore of Lake Geneva, where Reagan and Gorbachev were to meet, Morris, present then in person at the outset, describes the tension as Reagan waits on the steps and Gorbachev's Zil limousine pulls up at the end of a gravel path. The account is worth quoting at some (excerpted) length for its artistry as well as its historical importance:

> Despite three degrees of frost, [Reagan] wore no overcoat. There was not a hint of tremble at the cuffs of his suit. Silence fell. Then a long, black, prismatically polished Zil flatnosed its way around the corner of the villa. . . . A KGB man got out and opened the rear right door.
>
> The forty-eight seconds that followed replay in my mind in extreme slow motion, as if each frame were too fraught with drama to roll any faster. Similarly the sounds I remember are dry and distinct, although they must have been part of a larger web: the first crunch of Gorbachev's shoes on the gravel, the answering swish of Reagan's on lichened stone, the surgical sound of a hundred camera shutters slicing the light, and a mysterious roar that gathered overhead as the two leaders drew near. It was, of course, the pass of some military jet, but so intent was I on the business at hand that I subconsciously equated it with blood thundering through Gorbachev's birthmark.
>
> Not that anyone could see that famous stigma at first. He emerged from the Zil wearing the traditional homberg of the *nomenklatura*. Its low rim and the mass of his unbuttoned overcoat (widening as he raised both hands to adjust a loose scarf) made him look shorter than his five feet nine. The President, descending tall and tailored in the near foreground, took advantage of the laws of perspective to dominate their encounter. . . .
>
> I see them now closing with the static momentum of spacecraft. Reagan's elegant silhouette, still airborne, begins to blot out the tangle of clothes. Gorbachev's left hand rises a third time, reaching for his hat, then disappears along with the rest of him, as the blue bulk reaches center foreground. . . . Contrary to expectations, Gorbachev looks scared.
>
> His right hand moves forward in greeting, and for a moment Reagan's

left seems to be aimed at parrying it. But their trajectories are different, and do not intersect. Instead, Reagan's right sweeps around in a beautiful arc, neither cramped nor exaggerated. Just as flesh touches flesh, that higher left hand reaches the thick folds above Gorbachev's elbow, so he is both welcomed and caressed simultaneously. He breaks into another smile, broad and relieved this time.

He looks into Reagan's eyes and sees—what? All *we* can see is the back of the president's pompadour, glossy and impenetrable. The roar in the sky drowns out their initial exchange—perhaps mercifully, since neither man can understand the other. Reagan points twice, with easy authority at the steps, and inch by inch those two figures, ill-matched in shape and size yet already companionable, move across the screen of memory and ascend out of frame.

This extraordinary description, so visual, so evocative, not only captures those few minutes but sees that the attire and the body language here speaks loudly: Reagan graceful, cordial, dominant, and knowing all the strengths he brings. He has nothing to fear, certainly not fear itself. At a lecture he gave before the publication of this memoir, Morris returned to that moment when Gorbachev's brown eyes gazed into Reagan's blue ones, and recalled that, years later, he had asked Gorbachev what he had seen in Reagan's eyes. He said that Gorbachev had replied—and here Morris imitated Gorbachev with gobbledygook syllables—and reported that he had asked the translator what Gorbachev had said. The reply had been that the word was difficult, but that it meant something like, "strength, because all of America was behind him." The academic audience listening to Morris did not seem to relish that.

Morris presents many fascinating details regarding the summit, but one item stands out above all the rest. In Russian, SOI. In English, SDI. Gorbachev repeatedly insists that with agreement on that, anything is possible. Without agreement, nothing is. SOI must be confined to the drawing board and the laboratory, no testing. Reagan is immovable. But they will talk again. It remains a literary tragedy that Morris introduced fictional characters into the first half of *Dutch*. Once we get to the Reagan inauguration in 1981, *Dutch* becomes a great work of biography because so much of it was witnessed directly by the author.

National Review's attitude toward the Geneva summit was, to put it very mildly, restrained. Writing before the conclusion of the meeting, it editorialized:

> We go to press with the Geneva Summit still in progress, our skeptical and anxious hearts sustained by the thought that it is Ronald Reagan, not Jimmy Carter, who represents the nation there, and that the proceedings, when you read this, will not have ended with a smooch.
>
> The trouble is that Summits by their nature require shrewd men to utter Carteresque words, and so we find the President quoted as saying, "I believe we both do share the same goals. . . ."

On September 31, the summit concluded, and *National Review* relaxed with "Realism in Geneva":

> Whatever else may be said about the Geneva Summit, it was plainly the most realistic of the 13 U.S.-Soviet Summits held since World War II. President Reagan went to Geneva with no illusions about what summitry could accomplish. He gave away nothing vital, and he shrugged off Gorbachev's threat to torpedo the whole affair if concessions on SDI were not made. The Russians are not used to having their temper tantrums ignored. They seemed to have left the Summit a bit shaken. Reagan had succeeded in demonstrating to the whole world his willingness to seek peace, without giving up real security to make the point.

True, but minimal. During an exchange in Geneva, Morris chanced to view a private exchange between Reagan and Gorbachev over SDI in which the meeting ended with Gorbachev throwing his pencil on the table in disgust and walking out. But he would come back the next day. Similarly, there would be repeated summits, in gray, icy Reykjavik, and in Washington, where both Mikhail and Raissa were great popular successes.

It was in Washington, on December 8, 1988, that Reagan and Gorbachev signed an intermediate nuclear forces treaty, designed to reduce Soviet intermediate-range missiles to 1,836, and U.S. equivalents to 849, over a three-year period. Reducing nuclear arsenals by 4 percent, this was largely atmospheric, a detail in the tilt of the correlation of forces against the Soviets;

but it tended to revive public approval of Reagan amid the poisonous clouds of Iran-Contra.

To Reykjavik on October 11, 1986, Gorbachev came armed with a briefcase full of complex arms control and reduction proposals, but in the end, everything came down to SDI. Reagan held firm, and *National Review* heaved a large sigh of relief (November 7, 1986), applauding,

> Ronald Reagan's refusal to yield the Strategic Defense Initiative to Mikhail Gorbachev's blandishments in Reykjavik required some Spartan-like determination of his own and he came through. Add it to the list of occasions for which America can be grateful that Reagan sits in the White House.

The comment was apposite for that moment. But even then the question must have lingered in the minds of thoughtful people, at *National Review* and elsewhere: Just why had Gorbachev been so desperately anxious to derail SDI, to make it the center of his negotiating agenda? The *sine qua non*? Especially since it was unlikely to be realized for some time, if ever. The answer has to be that the Soviet Union could not afford the program, the testing and development of components, even to keep pace. Even though Reagan had offered to share the research. This was remarkable. If its ICBM arsenal were to be neutralized by a successful SDI, it would be clear that this constituted the Soviet Union's sole claim to superpower status.

It might have been guessed then, and it appears clear now, that Gorbachev's Soviet Union was close to the bottom of its economic barrel, and that Reagan had been correct in his Westminster address about the bankruptcy of Marxism and the waiting "ash heap of history." In retrospect, Reykjavik can be seen to mark the end of the Cold War. Economically desperate, its empire crumbling, Gorbachev ran into the rocks. The United States and NATO had won the Third World War.

ALTHOUGH THIS COULD NOT have been not grasped at the time, the year 1986 marked the apex of Ronald Reagan's popularity and power while in office. On Election Day 1986, the evening news broadcasts announced not only that the Democrats had regained control of the Senate but that something strange had happened in the Middle East. The Lebanese weekly *Al-Shiraa* had carried a story to the effect that National Security Advisor Robert McFarlane had recently appeared in Iran wearing an Air force uniform, and in disguise, bringing with him two planeloads of weaponry. It later developed that accompanying McFarlane had been Lieutenant Colonel Oliver North and Howard J. Teicher, employees of McFarlane's National Security Council, and two CIA operatives, one of whom spoke Farsi.

Thus began what soon became known as the Iran-Contra scandal, a plot reaching high in the Reagan administration. It linked hostile Iran to the continuing Nicaragua–El Salvador problem in Central America, where the administration had been seeking to empower the Contra guerillas despite an increasingly skeptical Congress. Beyond the communism of the ruling Sandinista junta, the problem reflected the continuing inability of former Spanish (and Portuguese) colonies, as distinguished from former British colonies, to achieve decently stable government.

As the Iran-Contra scandal unfurled in public, Congress investigated, high officials proved to have been involved, some eventually resigning or being convicted of felonies. Reagan's approval ratings plunged from 86 percent to abysmal figures, and the word "impeachment" did not seem outlandish.

At *National Review*, opinion tended to be divided among the senior editors as to the seriousness of the affair. Buckley was furious, but chose to say publicly that though covert action had its uses, this example had been grievously mismanaged. Of course *National Review* followed the unfolding events avidly, commenting in a January 30, 1987, interim update on the affair, edited by senior editor Richard Brookhiser. His introduction provides an outline of the then-known Iran-Contra facts:

In August and November of 1985, Israel, with American encouragement, sold two batches of anti-tank missiles to Iran. In January of 1986, President Reagan signed an intelligence finding authorizing direct American sales, which began in February and continued at intervals continuing through September. Meanwhile, sometime in the spring, the Iran deal spread out beyond Iran, as profits from the sale—some $10 million—were routed to the "covert" war against the Sandinistas. The story of the arms sale was first leaked by Iranians to a Lebanese magazine which broke it in early November. Three weeks later,

Attorney General Meese revealed the Nicaraguan angle.

The potential improprieties are many. As far as the Iranian half of the deal goes, there are laws regulating arms traffic with terrorist nations. The National Security Act also requires that Congress be notified of any covert intelligence operation "in a timely fashion"; Congress had to wait ten months. Beyond the law, there is also the inconsistency of condemning the thuggery of terror while at the same time dealing with thugs, or their close friends.

As far as Nicaragua goes, there is no inconsistency. The Reagan Administration has never been a fan of the Sandinistas. But the legal situation is still more tangled. From October 1984 until three months ago, Congress, though it voted small amounts of "humanitarian" aid for the Contras, specifically forbade any American military assistance.

The impresario of both the Iranian and Nicaraguan halves of the deal was Lieutenant Colonel Oliver North, until November a staffer with the National Security Council. . . . Iran's downpayment on the American arms was paid by Adnan Kashoggi, a multi-millionaire Saudi businessman. According to the *New York Times*, Kashoggi got $35 million last summer from a Saudi "closely linked to the royal family. . . ."

[Reagan] says he did not know about it until the week before Thanksgiving. His "only criticism" of Oliver North, he told *Time*, "is that I wasn't told everything." But it seems implausible that a lieutenant colonel, even a hotshot, would buck $10 million to a different war and hemisphere on his own authority. Whose authority *did* he have?

The contributors to the special *National Review* section on the affair would offer a variety of theories about the workings of the plot, pending congressional testimony; but the overall public impression was highly negative. The deal apparently had been rewarded by the release of some American hostages held by Shiites in Lebanon. But arms-for-hostages was contrary to Reagan's own announced policy: it rewarded kidnapping. And the combination of the theocrat fanatics' Iran and hostages had been pure poison since the fiascoes of the Carter administration. Arms for a regime that had called the United States the "Great Satan"? Laws appeared to have been broken.

Worst of all, Reagan's statement that he "had not been informed" about the arms sale or the diversion to the Contras indicated that the president himself had not been part of important policy decisions in his own administration. This was reminiscent of his administrative style as far back as the mismanaged 1976 primary campaign in New Hampshire.

While the Senate inquiry was going on in the committee room and on television, little was revealed about the central question: Who was in charge? On June 15, 1987, *National Review* began its close coverage and evaluation of the Senate hearings. For example, the magazine examined the testimony of Robert McFarlane, who had resigned as national security advisor because of "family matters"—and visible exhaustion—as the Iran-Contra matter was coming to light:

> Bud McFarlane was supposed to cook the President. Senator Inouye said as much before McFarlane testified. It has not happened. McFarlane has so far come across as a dignified, intelligent, and frank patriot. In his lengthy exchanges with Senator Paul Sarbanes, for example, McFarlane did not come off second best, though operating in a complex policy area. . . . The great failure of the Reagan Administration as regards Nicaragua has been that the President has failed to persuade the American public that a Soviet base in Central America would matter. . . . In the larger political sense, therefore, it does not much matter what the Secords and McFarlanes testify to.

Much awaited was the testimony of Admiral John Poindexter, McFarlane's successor as national security advisor, and Lieutenant Colonel Oliver North. *National Review* commented:

> In two and a half weeks, it seemed, the world turned around. Admiral Poindexter, emotional as a Frigidaire, explained that, no, President Reagan did not know about the now-famous diversion. Lieutenant Colonel North, who was anything but cool, explained what he was doing and why. The Left's best hope of pinning a wrong on Reagan vanished.

This was true but inadequate. If the best that could be said for Reagan was that he was in the dark, this was still a political mess. Reagan went on national television to explain that yes, the evidence did show that arms had been traded for hostages, that this was against his established policy, but that at the time he did not think that this was what was happening. Then, it was widely speculated, there was always the possibility that the deal was made to enhance the stature of supposed Iranian "moderates," but this idea had next to no traction. The only figure to emerge with a plus from the whole thing was Oliver North, handsome and purposeful on TV in his Marine uniform, a hero to many, a future star on the speakers' circuit, and an unsuccessful senatorial candidate in Virginia.

But what had happened there in the murk? The testimony of McFarlane, Poindexter, North, and others did not clear this up. A large amount of paper had been destroyed. The testimony of principals had been confusingly contradictory. At the end of the day, it looked as if McFarlane had been in charge of the Iran end, while North had taken over the Nicaragua diversion. CIA Director William Casey, a longtime covert operations practitioner, had by this time been hospitalized incommunicado and was dying of brain cancer. His testimony was not available.

Based on subsequent research, including extensive interviews, Reagan's biographer Lou Cannon stresses Reagan's emotional concern for the hostages in Lebanon, the pleas of their relatives, and reports he knew about concerning their mistreatment to account for his approval of the Iran arms transfer. Cannon adds the strategic interest of McFarlane in countering Soviet influence in Iran. He further believes it was Casey and North who put an emphasis on the diversion of funds to the Contras. The picture then becomes one of Reagan sitting atop a plot of astonishing complexity by subordinates operating largely independently.

In examining Reagan's diary, Edmund Morris reaches a different conclusion. He concludes that Reagan approved of the deal when he was recovering from intestinal cancer surgery in Bethesda Hospital and was only half aware of what he was doing. Morris describes the situation on July 18, 1985:

> Let us in fairness consider this diary entry of a half-deaf man who has, only five days before, been hacked open from pubis to breastbone, and, seventy-two hours before, received about the most terrifying news that doctors can deliver: a positive biopsy. He has been awake since 5:15 a.m., and is trying without much success to get his shocked and shortened intestinal system back into action. At 10:22 a.m. (the diary's paragraph arrangement is misleading), an expressionless little man comes in and drones something about wanting to meet with some reform-minded Iranians. Even Don Regan, who monitors

the briefing, hears nothing but a "general" mention of hostages still in captivity. If there is any implication that McFarlane's foreign contacts might be "helpful" one day in springing them, it is vague enough not to alarm the famously reactive Chief of Staff. Reagan, like Regan, hears nothing about hostages worth recording. He hears only the encouraging words *want* and *talks* and *neutral* applied to two Iranian "government" officials, together with what sounds like a request for travel. He says yes, and the little man is gone by 10:45.

Here is the diary entry for July 18, 1985. The reference to the Iran matter is meager and out of sequence with surrounding events:

> Nancy and I had lunch, I find that I can eat only a few mouthfuls. A lot of cards and messages to look at. Then around 4:30 p.m. a wave out of the window to press and down to X-Ray.
>
> Bud [McFarlane] came by—it seems two members of the Iranian govt. want to establish talks with us. I'm sending Bud to meet them in a neutral country.
>
> Gorbachev has passed the word that he'd like to establish a private channel of communications.

And that is all there is about Iran-Contra. The mass of evidence, such as it is, remains to be interpreted.

Definitiveness seems out of the question. If this diary entry is accurate and complete about Reagan's authorization—and Regan's hovering presence might suggest that it is—then the president was in no condition to approve of any Iran initiative as extensive as McFarlane undertook. If that is so, McFarlane seriously underestimated the seriousness of what he was about to do. Iran was no "neutral country," just to begin with. In effect, McFarlane was taking a huge step, without proper authorization.

If that is so, discipline on Reagan's staff was extraordinarily lacking. And even when disaster became evident, McFarlane was allowed to resign without penalty, to be replaced by his deputy, Admiral John M. Poindexter. Could it be true that Reagan entertained no suspicions? In addition to McFarlane's role, and with the $10 million available, it looks as if the play then went to North and the diversion to the Contras. Perhaps North thought he *knew* Reagan's feelings in this matter. If so, the leash on the staff was extraordinarily loose, and staff members believed it was safe to operate at a great distance from control by the center. This would have been astonishing insubordination. The investigation by what became known as the Tower Committee implicated McFarlane, North, and Poindexter, but cleared Chief of Staff Donald Regan and the president.[3] Further speculation here would lead us into a Great Dismal Swamp of hypotheses.

If we locate the Iran decision in Bethesda Hospital on July 18, 1985, as Morris and Cannon and Regan agree, then things get even more difficult. Over a year later, on October 24, 1986, President Reagan was in Reykjavik handling Gorbachev masterfully, winning the Cold War. That means that all this time the Iran-Contra matter had gone forward, Reagan oblivious, only to be revealed in the Lebanese journal on Election Day in November 1986. It just doesn't figure. It may be legitimate to say that Reagan had chronic trouble with staff discipline and supervision. Whatever may be the truth, the Iran-Contra scandal certainly haunted Reagan's last year in office, the sense of an administration somewhat out of control making him seem, perhaps, *old* for the first time.

THE WORD "BORKED" has now entered common usage, meaning a public figure wrecked by a savage media-political campaign directed against him. In an earlier era such efforts had been condemned by the *bien pensant* as "McCarthyism." Reagan nominated Judge Robert Bork, a former professor at Yale Law School and one of the most distinguished legal minds in the nation, for a Supreme Court vacancy on July 1, 1987. Up to that point, Reagan's nominees had been broadly acceptable and were confirmed without undue fuss in the Senate. Though Bork had long seemed the preeminent conservative choice for the Court, Reagan had made a campaign pledge in 1980 to place the first woman on the High Court, and so in 1981 he had nominated Sandra Day O'Connor to replace Potter Stewart. She was highly qualified and was easily confirmed. When Chief Justice Warren Burger retired in January 1986, Reagan nominated the sitting justice William Rehnquist for chief justice, and with only slight resistance to his conservatism, the Senate confirmed him. Then came Antonin Scalia to fill the Rehnquist seat. This surprised conservatives, notably Buckley, because after the nomination of O'Connor Buckley had received a personal note from the president saying that he would certainly name Bork next. Yet Scalia had the intellectual brilliance; on legal philosophy he resembled Bork; and at 50, he was eight years younger. That Scalia was ethnically Italian might have counted with Reagan's political advisors. The Senate confirmed him unanimously.

So far, conservatives had cause for enthusiastic approval. Finally, in 1987, with the retirement of the moderate conservative Lewis Powell, came the Bork nomination. Some important things had changed in the political landscape since 1981. Importantly, Democrats had regained control of the Senate in the 1986 elections. But also of critical importance was the effect of the changes Reagan had made in the Court.

From a long-range historical point of view, the great domestic issue in American politics had become the role of the judiciary, and most importantly of the Supreme Court, in the balance of powers within the federal government. To an ever greater degree, to put it one way, the Supreme Court had been performing as a legislative body, "interpreting" the Constitution in order to, in effect, pass new laws. In the polemical phrase, the Supreme Court had become an out-of-control legislative branch, not simply "supreme" over other courts, but supreme over the other branches of government. This, despite the fact that the first three words of the Constitution are "We the People," implying the relative supremacy of the popularly elected branches of government, and despite the fact that Congress constitutionally has weapons superior to those of the Court. Reagan's new justices appeared to be slowly shifting the balance against the Court's assumption of legislative powers, and so were threatening the liberal agenda.

Bork's nomination thus became critical, and this probably would be Reagan's last opportunity to fill a vacancy. No one should have been surprised that the fight to block Bork would be savage. But surprisingly, only the opposition to Bork was ready to fight. Bork's backers were lulled and complacent because of his obvious qualifications, and also surprised (!) that, here and now, qualifications hardly mattered. They should not have been: if the Court had become a legislature, congressional seats were usually hotly and not always nicely contested.

National Review's editorial commentary on the Bork struggle is of the first quality and of historical importance. Just before the Judiciary Committee hearings began, Joe Sobran contributed an editorial (July 31, 1987). Part one is well worth quoting:

> Nominating Robert Bork to the Supreme Court, Ronald Reagan has kept his promise to foster the principles of "judicial restraint" and "original intent." Bork has made powerful arguments for both.
>
> This is important. Bork is anything but the "ideologue" the Democrats and their media allies portray. That is, he doesn't yearn to impose an agenda by wielding judicial power. On the contrary. The paradox is that so many legislators are enraged at a nominee who believes in legislative prerogatives.
>
> Time and again he has made his view clear. "Courts must accept any value choice the legislature makes, unless it clearly runs contrary to a choice made in the framing of the Constitution." In ruling against a claim of homosexual rights in 1984, he wrote: "If the revolution in sexual mores . . . is in fact ever to arrive, we think it must arrive through the moral choices of the people and their elected representatives, not through the ukase of this court." He speaks of his philosophy of "deference to democratic choice" and attacks "judicial imperialism."
>
> This attitude makes him critical of many Supreme Court decisions and willing to rethink them. "Since the legislature can do nothing about the interpretation of the Constitution given by a court," he has said, "the court ought to be always open to rethinking constitutional problems." That, of course, is what alarms partisans of the Court's leftist activism: Bork wouldn't treat prior rulings as sacrosanct. He has taken his analytical scalpel to a number of "historic rulings" including ones on abortion, busing, school prayer, the exclusionary rule, legislative reapportionment, capital punishment, and pornography. Bork takes the general position that the "right to privacy," as limned by the Court since 1965, is unprincipled and incoherent and has no constitutional basis. There is no clear way, he complains, for lower courts to apply such an amorphous concept; it invites judges to impose their own policy preferences, for "the truth is that a judge who looks outside the Constitution always looks inside himself and nowhere else." He likes to cite Jefferson's remark that "whatever power in any government is independent is absolute also."
>
> But Bork is hardly the radical his opponents depict. He was after all, unanimously approved by the Senate (yes, including Edward Kennedy) for his present seat on the federal court of appeals for the District of Columbia.

All of his majority opinions have been sustained by the Supreme Court, which has also agreed with several of his dissents and has overturned the rulings they disputed. Bork wouldn't be a misfit on the Court; he'd probably vote with Antonin Scalia as often as anyone.

Despite the current hysterics, Bork has no ties to the anti-abortion movement. He'd probably vote to return the issue to the states, and he has questioned the constitutionality of a federal human rights bill. Although he thinks the first amendment doesn't protect pornography, he has taken the side of the press in matters of libel. He has his own principles, but they don't follow any party line.

Conservatives shouldn't get their hopes up just because liberals are caricaturing Bork as a right-wing caveman; he would probably disappoint, now and then, the people who most ardently support his nomination. What is safe to predict is that Robert Bork would raise the general level of legal debate on the Supreme Court. His major contribution would be to deflate judicial arrogance.

This editorial amounts to an anthologizable summary statement of what is probably the core position of American conservatism. The basis of the American constitutional system is specified in the first words of the Constitution, "We the People." Their decisions, made "deliberately," and based upon their individual and collective experience and with whatever reading, philosophizing, and tradition they bring to the voting booth or assembly, should result in the right laws about how they are to be governed and how they are to live. The laws reflect the deliberate sense of a free people and not the absolutist dictates of some minority.

This position generally informed *National Review* conservatism, pulled in the direction of an emphasis on power by James Burnham, toward an aesthetic-Tory reverence for tradition by Russell Kirk, toward individualism by Frank Meyer. Others might find absolutes as they chose, but they were not part of conservative governing. The absolutists' position on whatever issue was before us had first to command a consensus. In general, this theory of the American mode of government was that of the editorial majority at *National Review*, though here and there a monarchist or an anarchist might float around; the view had been most forcefully and thoroughly articulated by Willmoore Kendall.

It will be seen immediately that this theory of American government distinguished American conservatism from that of Europe. Since the French Revolution, European conservatives had distrusted the people, whom they visualized as the Paris mob. This distrust and fear was amply reinforced by the populist nature of national socialism in Germany and fascism in Italy, the "revolt of the masses." American experience trusted the delaying mechanism of the Constitution to ensure that the "sense" of the people was "deliberate." The Court was supposed to be part of the delaying mechanism, not a vanguard quasi-revolutionary body. At bottom, what rose to the surface in the Bork fight was the fact that modern liberalism simply does not trust the "deliberate sense" of "We the People."

Sobran went on to explore thoughts such as these in part two, titled "Why All the Shouting?":

> Bork's nomination, in eliciting an orgy of vituperation, has already had one good result: It has brought the Democrats out of the closet as an ideological party, America's Party of the Left.
>
> Senator Joseph Biden made it official on *Face the Nation* that Democrats feel entitled to demand "ideological purity" of a Supreme Court appointee— even a Reagan appointee. Gone is last year's pious talk of "highest judicial standards" and an "independent judiciary," pretexts on which Biden & Company tried to block other Reagan appointments but which won't do this time around. Abortion has emerged as the sort of "litmus test" the Democrats hotly accused the Administration of applying in lieu of pertinent professional qualifications.
>
> Qualifications? Bork's are tops. But the Democrats have come up with a new criterion: "balance." For the first time, a nominee's fate depends not on his merits, but on who else is already on the Court. The Democrats want to assert restrictive quotas on conservatives.

A brief comment is appropriate here. Sobran's singling out of "balance" indicates the emerging identity of the Court as a nonelected legislative body. "Balance" would usually apply to an individual's judgment—that is, the individual "balances" one consideration against another. But, here, "balance" refers to the more or less predictable voting behavior of individuals in a deliberative body. Sobran continues:

"Balance," in this context, means freezing the Court's recent imbalance. Suddenly the retiring Justice Lewis Powell is being hailed as a "moderate," an encomium that needs unpacking: A "moderate" is a Republican who seldom impedes the Court's leftward momentum, sometimes gives it crucial support, and—above all—never, never tries to reverse it. The *New York Times* bade Powell farewell as a "model conservative," i.e., one who "took firm progressive positions" when it counted, as on abortion, affirmative action, and aid to private schools.

With Bork on the Court, the Left's long judicial winning streak could, for the first time, be reversed, not just slowed. It's not any agenda of Bork's that drives Biden, Kennedy, Hooks, and Smeal to hysteria; it's his willingness to look hard at their "gains," and to reassess the opinions of their predecessors. The Left's power depends on a fragile mystique of irreversibility, a domestic counterpart of the Brezhnev Doctrine ("What we have, we keep").

Given Bork's respect for the legislative branch, why are there so many legislators so frenzied about him? Simple. They're ideologues first, and legislators second. In the ecology of the Left, the dirty work of the progressive agenda, acting as the cutting edge on social issues where even the most left-wing elected officials usually fear to tread, belongs to the Court. (Who wants to vote for legal porn?) But once the Court has taken the lead, its congressional allies cover for it, blocking any move to clip or curb judicial powers on the specious grounds that the Court is only performing its constitutionally appointed role of "interpreting" the fundamental law, however bizarrely. Until now, the system has served the left well. As Lino Graglia has noted (*NR*, July 17, 1987), the Court has, on major social issues, consistently "adopted and furthered the policy preferences of those of the far left of the political spectrum, and has done so in many cases over the strong opposition of a majority of the American people." . . .

By appointing a spectacularly qualified legal scholar, Reagan has given the Democrats everything they said they wanted. Now they're starting to tell us what they really want.

By appointing Bork, Reagan had certainly opened these issues, and done so invaluably from the standpoint of political thought. But for a moment, and from that standpoint, it is important to raise a question about Sobran's generally excellent editorial by focusing on his explanation of why many legislators are "so frenzied" about reexamining contentious positions on which feelings are strongly held—such as abortion, now one "litmus test," as Sobran says, regarding Bork, but also school prayer, affirmative action, and others. They are "frenzied," Sobran says, because "They're ideologues first, legislators second." Maybe, but doubtful.

What may instead be operative, at least often, is "the intensity factor in majority rule," as political theorists call it. To a legislator—even, in fact, to the members of a group of merely social friends—an intense minority can often overrule a majority. The intense, committed minority on any position might be more threatening, or maybe just an especially unpleasant nuisance, to a legislator. In responding, the legislator (perhaps rising above principle or personal belief) may precisely be behaving as a legislator: negotiating, keeping the peace, getting reelected. John Adams said famously that in 1776 only about a third of the people supported independence: look what one-third got.

Most Senate races are decided by five points or less, and candidates do try to calm if not enlist passionate advocacy groups. Where abortion is concerned, at the time of *Roe v. Wade*, state legislatures were moving, variously, toward relaxing their abortion laws. This probably would have spread much further as the various states were energized by the women's revolution, but Bork probably paid the price for apparently being willing to trust the deliberate sense of the people arguing the issue in the state legislatures. He antagonized the intense affirmative action group, the "cutting edge" secularizers on school prayer, and so on. Small wonder the constellation of opposition proved to be intense. Those who differ from the energetic groups learned in the Bork fight that they in turn have to argue intensely.

Conservatives at *National Review* have taken many views on abortion, Ernest van den Haag permissive, Buckley holding that Catholics should not try to impose their views on others, Senator James Buckley supporting a constitutional right-to-life amendment. Where Reagan himself stood on abortion is not clear. He opposed it in his public statements but signed a liberal law in California and never did anything about it with his executive authority or his early huge popular majorities. His main focus was limited: the American spirit, the economy, Moscow. With his nomination of Bork—indeed, with his other previous Court nominations—

he went for majority rule, as, from personal preference, he probably did naturally.

The Senate hearings on Bork were a circus, of course. As *National Review*, in a later editorial (November 6, 1987) groaned (but certainly enjoyed), Teddy Kennedy found yet another way to disgrace himself, saying thunderously (as always) concerning the distinguished Yale professor and outstanding federal judge, who had been rated "exceptionally qualified" by the ABA, and whom he, Teddy, had recently voted to confirm to the federal bench:

> Robert Bork's America is a land in which women would be forced into back alley abortions, blacks would sit at segregated lunch counters, rogue police would break down citizens' doors in midnight raids, school children could not be taught about evolution, writers and artists could be censored at the whim of government, and the doors of federal courts would be shut on the fingers of millions of citizens for whom the judiciary is—and often is the only—protector of the individual rights that are at the heart of democracy.

Of course no one believed that sort of thing. Kennedy's language was disgraceful; but this was not a seminar in New Haven, it was hardball in Washington.

The White House had been complacent because of Bork's credentials. In the failure of the Bork nomination, it followed up with Douglas Ginsberg, a good nominee, but one who, it turned out, had smoked marijuana as a professor at Harvard Law School. Democrats and liberals generally were *shocked*, in the *Casablanca* sense, by the very idea of marijuana. Ginsberg dropped out as advised by William Bennett, then secretary of education, and was succeeded by Anthony Kennedy, an unthreatening conservative who was unanimously confirmed by the Senate on February 11, 1988.

As the Anthony Kennedy confirmation came through, the 1988 primaries were already in full swing, leading by November—through many a close call—to the election of George H. W. Bush, the country voting in effect for a third Reagan term. Yet in his only term as president, George Bush quite mysteriously tried to move as far as possible from Reagan, in both personnel and policy.

As Reagan prepared to depart from the White House, Edmund Morris interviewed the new president-elect in his home, the former Naval Observatory. His account is brief, hilarious, and rich as metaphor, epitomizing the complex attitudes of Barbara and George Bush toward the Reagans. Depending for his national office almost entirely on Reagan, beaten badly by him in the 1980 presidential primaries, overshadowed between 1980 and 1988, ignored, disappointed, yet admiring, George Bush—and Barbara also—is uncomfortable, and yet not willing to seem ungrateful. Morris makes the complexity dramatic, the passage is very funny, and for the pleasure of the reader, this anecdote is worth quoting in full:

> Christmas Eve 1988. I go around to the President-elect's house to interview him. Barbara sits knitting, dangerously *à la* Madame Defarge. They clearly have something to get off their collective chest about their eight years as "the help," but Bush's preppy politeness keeps moderating their fury.
>
> "Gotta tellya, I really love that guy, he's such a terrific fellow. Only one thing kinda bothered me, whichistersay, just never been able to understand — guy never seemed to *need* anybody." "Except Nancy," says BB, needles *accelarando*.
>
> "Off to Camp David every weekend, never took their *kids* with 'em! Bar and me," the VP allows, "we'd go *crazy* if we found ourselves up there without a whole bunch of family runnin' around."
>
> "Anything else about the President bother you?"
>
> "Listen, he was a prince of a feller, I'd never say anything against him. Nancy neither. . . ." There is a pause as the Bushes exchange glances. "Well, sometimes," he says reluctantly, "I kinda wish they'd shown—y'know, a little appreciation. Didn't seem to want us upstairs in the White House."
>
> "We would always thank them for their gifts," BB says pointedly.
>
> "Guess they didn't always thank us," he goes on. "Gave him, oh such a neat present for his seventy-fifth birthday, took a whole lot of trouble customizing it to the right measurements, borrowed his boots so it would stand up real pretty. . . ."
>
> He notices my perplexity and stands up, a huge, hurt, loveable, distressingly ordinary man. "Lemme show you. We had a duplicate made."
>
> He escorts me to a bathroom upstairs, outside of which stands the single most terrifying piece of kitch I have ever seen. It would not be out of place at Auschwitz. There, standing booted and spurred, are *Dutch's feet and lower legs,*

supporting, like some flattened dwarfish torso, an embroidered seat, with the presidential seal *au centre*.

While I marvel, as so often before, at the aesthetic perversity of well-born WASPs, Bush shakes his head and says in the same hurt voice, "Not a word of thanks."

As George Bush the First took office, perhaps those legs came to life as a declaration of Bush independence—by kicking Reagan.

23

Bush One: Train Wreck

"Read my lips: no new taxes."
1988

"A kinder, gentler nation."
1988

"Message: I care."
1992

George Herbert Walker Bush always seemed a better man than he was a president. Thus, *National Review*'s examination of his unfolding public performance involves sadness and personal tragedy. He did not come from major wealth, as did Jack Kennedy, but from affluence and hereditary social position. He attended the best schools, filled in the boxes across the page, and was successful in an established sort of way, energetic, and full of promise. His father, Prescott Bush, managing partner of Brown Brothers Harriman when George was at Andover, later became a United States senator from Connecticut. A good student at Andover, George Bush was president of his senior class, captain of the baseball and soccer teams, playing manager of the basketball team, treasurer of the student council, deputy house master, and member of assorted other teams and clubs.

Immediately after Pearl Harbor, he enlisted in the Navy Air Corps at eighteen and became the youngest combat pilot in the Pacific. In 1945, flying an "Avenger" bomber off the carrier *San Jacinto*, Bush was shot down by antiaircraft fire while attacking the heavily defended Japanese communications station at Chichi Jima, about one hundred miles from the more famous fortress Iwo Jima. He was rescued from the ocean by an American submarine and received the Distinguished Flying Cross for this mission: his plane crippled, he nevertheless had completed his bombing run. Other navy fliers shot down and captured by the Japanese were beheaded. Some were cannibalized. This story has been well told by James Bradley in *Flyboys* (2003).

At Yale, Bush was captain and first baseman on the baseball team, a member of Skull and Bones, and with James Buckley one of the most popular members of the senior class. After a successful career in Texas as an oil entrepreneur, he entered politics.

There again he prospered. A congressman from Texas, he was urged by Richard Nixon to run against Lloyd Bentsen for the Senate. He had little chance and was roundly defeated, but he won Nixon's gratitude for serving the party. This put him on the path to appointed offices under Nixon and Ford—as ambassador to the United Nations, chairman of the Republican National Committee, de facto ambassador to China, and director of the CIA. These appointments gave him the springboard from which to try elective politics once more.

He lost again, badly, to Reagan in the 1980 presidential primaries, perhaps indicating genuine electoral weaknesses. Winning the Iowa caucuses, he had approached the New Hampshire primary proclaiming that "the Big Mo"—momentum—was with him. This was slightly goofy, an aspect of his personality that hurt him on the national stage. Reagan beat him in New Hampshire and pulled his campaign together for the ultimate victory. At the Detroit convention, Reagan put Bush on the national ticket to reassure eastern Republicans, and also to stop a delegate surge on the floor to nominate Jack Kemp. As Reagan's vice presidential candidate, Bush stopped talking about "voodoo economics," an unfortunate term as it turned out, and together with Reagan coasted to victory over Carter-Mondale. Bush had not yet shown that he could appeal to voters on his own.

Early in 1982, *National Review*'s Washington correspondent John McLaughlin evaluated Bush's performance as Reagan's vice president in terms that would soon seem astonishing:

> One of the remarkable phenomena of the Reagan Administration is the change in conservative perception of George Bush. When Reagan chose his leading opponent in the primaries, many conservatives winced. They looked on Bush as light and Left. Instead, he is turning out heavy and Right. Lampooned by some hard-liners as an arch-preppie Eastern Seaboard centrist, Bush is bringing to the Vice Presidency a record of quiet substantive achievement.

McLaughlin's success as Washington columnist led to an important change in *National Review*. This success, and the presence of Reagan in the White House, led to the establishment of an *NR* Washington office and the designation of McLaughlin as Washington executive editor, the occasion celebrated by a gala cocktail party at the Madison Hotel. This development gave the magazine a new Washington orientation and, in turn, a greater emphasis on Washington politics, along with growth in the Washington staff. When John O'Sullivan became Buckley's successor as editor in 1991, the Washington coverage intensified.

With Reagan's landslide over Mondale-Ferraro in 1984, however, the evaluation by the magazine of George Bush as a prospective presidential nominee altered drastically from that of McLaughlin's column of 1982. For example, a March 28, 1986, editorial asked, "Can George Do It?" The answer seemed, almost, to be No:

> He is even now the front-runner for the 1988 Republican nomination. . . . So what's his problem? He certainly has one. In the last few weeks he hasn't just been attacked, but treated with contempt, the contempt reserved for the weak. Even his defenders, by seeming over-protective, reinforce the impression that he can't defend himself.
>
> Most notably, he was the target of a scalding column by George Will. . . . As Bush goes about trying to ingratiate himself with conservatives, wrote Will, he omits "a thin, tinny 'arf'—the sound of a lap dog." Supporters of

Bush's main opponent for the nomination, Jack Kemp, quickly distributed thousands of lapel buttons reading simply "Arf." The Johnny Carson jokes can't be far off.

All this was cruel, but substantive. Bush won the nomination as Kemp split the conservative vote in New Hampshire with Pete Dupont and Pat Robertson.

Bush-Quayle would go on to defeat Dukakis-Bentsen in 1988 with the help of Bush's Reaganesque pledge of "Read my lips: no new taxes." Dukakis's unjustified posthumous pardon of Sacco and Vanzetti proved symptomatic. And Lee Atwater's ads attacking Dukakis's furloughs for murderers serving life sentences were fully justified by the case of Willie Horton, a murderer who committed further violent crimes on his furlough. During the election campaign Horton, now serving a life sentence in Maryland, endorsed Dukakis, embarrassingly enough remarking, "What do you expect?" In a TV ad, Dukakis looked like a foolish child as he rode in a tank to show his supposed strength on national defense; and he was unable to answer with any emotion a televised presidential debate question as to what he would do if a man broke into his home and raped and murdered his wife. The dry technocrat could muster only a lecture against capital punishment. The joke about Dukakis at the time was that on vacation he would read a book on beach erosion.

In this comical contest, poor Dan Quayle's reputation never recovered from his befuddlement in his TV debate with Lloyd Bentsen. Addressing Quayle's assertion that, like Jack Kennedy in 1956, he would not be too young for the vice presidency, Bentsen answered, "I knew Jack Kennedy, senator. Jack Kennedy was a friend of mine. And you're no Jack Kennedy." This was a solid, indeed personal punch. Quayle looked, it was said, like a deer caught in an automobile's headlights. Instead, he might have said— his wife being named Marilyn—"You're absolutely right, senator. I married Marilyn," alluding to Kennedy's well-known affair with the late Monroe. Laughter, knockout counterpunch. Quayle's aide, Bill Kristol, should have coached him on the likelihood that the icon Kennedy might come up apropos of the age question.

But despite Quayle, the Bush-Quayle ticket prevailed, the first electoral office Bush had won on his own since winning a House seat in Texas at the beginning of his political career. His political record so far had given little clue about how he would perform as president. The Bush train was on the tracks for the 1992 wreck.

In his only term as president, and supposedly serving in Reagan's "third term," Bush worked a negative miracle, turning gold into lead. He managed to transform a 91 percent favorable rating in March 1991, after his Desert Storm victory, into a humiliating 38 percent of the vote in November 1992. In 1991, a happy moment to remember, President Bush awarded the Presidential Medal of Freedom to William F. Buckley.

HERE IT WILL SERVE our purposes to look at the jolting events unfolding on the tracks toward 1992 through the eyes of *National Review*, with some on-the-scene help from John Podhoretz, who was a Bush speechwriter, using his book *Hell of a Ride: Backstage at the White House Follies, 1989–1993* (1993). The results of the previous three years all came together in 1992, achieving dramatic clarity. But first an anecdote from Podhoretz about Reagan's own reaction to the impending disaster:

> In the weeks before the 1992 election, when it became clear that Bush was going to be brought low, Reaganites tended to react to Bush's misfortune with a kind of cold glee. And in the weeks before Election Day, a story began circulating in Reaganite circles from Los Angeles to New York. The details were a little sketchy, but it seemed that the old man himself had been having dinner with members of his "kitchen cabinet," the California brain trust and financial backers who had turned him from actor into governor and financed his three races for the presidency. As they discussed the coming electoral disaster, Reagan said, "I guess I really effed it up in 1980." Meaning, if he had chosen a better vice-president, none of this would have happened.[1]

In 1988, *National Review* had strongly endorsed Jack Kemp for the nomination, and it could be argued that the 1992 results confirmed that judgment:

Bill Clinton: 44,908,254 (370 electoral votes)
George Bush: 39,102,343 (168 electoral votes)
Ross Perot: 19,741,065 (0 electoral votes)

Given those figures, Bush might have slid in without Perot in the race, since Perot—eccentric and possibly beyond the pale, but no liberal—very likely drew much more heavily from Bush than from Clinton. *National Review* even briefly considered Perot a plausible protest candidate.

But no, the magazine concluded, Perot was not plausible enough. Still, Bush's 1992 defeat had been coming on ever since his election in 1988, and in retrospect it seems inevitable. In almost every detail of his performance as president, and with an almost oedipal urgency, he had distanced himself from Reagan. He seemed to be trying to govern with a platform Reagan had defeated in the 1980 primaries. Despite his "Read my lips," he signed OMB Director Richard Darman's 1990 budget deal, persuaded that increased tax revenues would be matched by major cuts in congressional spending. Of course Congress balked at the latter half of the deal, spending being a congressman's road to reelection. A recovery did begin during Bush's final term, picking up momentum during Clinton's first term, but this was too late to save the Bush presidency. Bush also won Desert Storm. But Saddam Hussein remained in power, gassing and crushing the Kurds in the North, whom Bush had encouraged to rebel but did nothing to help when they did so. Saddam also slaughtered the rebellious Shiites in the South.

With the help of John Sununu, who had been governor of New Hampshire in 1988, Bush managed to survive the primary there although Pat Buchanan had taken 40 percent of the vote, another Bush display of electoral weakness. Sununu and Richard Darman were bright, and they annoyingly let everyone on the mediocre White House staff know it at the staff meeting every morning. Bush in 1992 could claim the Americans with Disabilities Act, the Clean Air Act, and child-care legislation—perhaps "kinder and gentler" measures, but hardly galvanizing issues.

NATIONAL REVIEW VIEWED this performance with apprehension and even disbelief. For the January 20, 1992, issue, William McGurn, a tough-minded political analyst and *National Review*'s new Washington Bureau chief, wrote a laughing-through-tears editorial, "Memo to the President," as if from "Jimmy Carter":

> Well, the big day—the State of the Union—is fast approaching now, and though I can't say we've been particularly close, I feel a certain kinship with you watching the talk shows these days. You probably heard Carson the other night. You're finally honest enough to admit we might now be in a recession, technically speaking, and he says he has another news flash for you: "Lindbergh made it." Or you try to show your concern for the common man by going to J.C. Penny and picking up $28 worth of socks, and Jay Leno tries to twist it around to suggest you don't care ("You think that Bush is unpopular now, wait until his grandchildren get their Christmas presents."). Or you try not to alarm people on the economy, and David Letterman puts out a list of ten ways of telling us we're in a recession (No. 4: "Hey, we're still better than any South American country you want to name.") I know how it feels, I've been there. . . .

But nothing at all changed as November 1992 approached.

On foreign affairs, especially where United States–Soviet relations were concerned, Bush was also clueless, confident that Gorbachev was the man to back in the interest of stability. In the January 20, 1992, issue, senior editor and foreign affairs specialist Peter Rodman contributed two important editorials on the emerging situation in the disintegrating Soviet Union. The first, titled "The Last General Secretary," implied by that title that Gorbachev was far behind the curve, the Communist Party doomed:

> Mikhail Gorbachev will go down in history as the man who destroyed the Soviet system, by mistake. This explains the great debt that the world owes him, and the inevitability of his downfall.
>
> His reform program consciously and deliberately discredited the old Soviet system—its stultified ideology, its empire ruled by brute force, its foreign adventures. But events went far beyond his intention. Until the bitter end, his vision was not of a constitutional democracy but of a more benign, reformed Communist structure that would thrive because he had put it on a new basis. . . .

The second editorial, "The Ash Heap of History," regretted that Bush was clueless:

> Mercifully, the destruction of the Soviet state came with a whimper instead of a bang. It is now a safer and better world than it was a month ago. We wish the Bush Administration would get into the spirit of things instead of moping about it. The Administration seems to view the old regime nostalgically as an efficient system of command and control over nuclear weapons; it forgets that it was also a system of command and control over people. The people who suffered under it have no such nostalgia. Neither should we.

Instead, Bush and his national security advisor Brent Scowcroft wanted to go slow when the disintegration of the Soviet empire was moving swiftly. So in his address in Kiev, Bush warned the Ukraine against a "suicidal nationalism," when, of all the nationalities, the Ukrainians probably hated Moscow the most. This became known derisively as the "Chicken Kiev" speech.

After the Berlin Wall went down in 1989, fear disappeared and refugees from the former East bloc poured through the Brandenburg Gate and across borders. Nothing could save the empire or Gorbachev's kinder, gentler communism. Gorbachev and Bush both belonged to the past. The Bush presidency involved a post-Reagan loss of energy from the Republican Party and a transition to eight years of Clinton dominance, an attempt, in historical perspective, to move the post-McGovern Democrats back toward the center. The 1992 election and the demise of Bush loomed, but *National Review*, too, was entering a period of transition.

A PERIOD BEGINNING in Reagan's second term and embracing the first Bush administration brought important changes at *National Review*, and these accumulated to modify the character of the magazine. Priscilla Buckley now retired as senior editor, having stepped down as managing editor at *National Review*'s 1985 thirtieth anniversary celebration. She was now editing a *National Review Reader* and remained on the board of directors.

With the exception of Buckley, Priscilla was the one remaining link with the founding of the magazine in 1955. Her retirement-cum-seventieth birthday party took place at the Union League Club in New York. She and Burnham had been the steadying anchors at the magazine, recognized as such by all connected with it. And so the *ave atque vale* that evening was both festive and touched by sadness. The sense of farewell resonated with changes and transitions that were on everyone's mind that night, amid the humor and eloquent tributes.

The magazine was undergoing an inevitable generational transition. Burnham was gone, following Kendall and Meyer. The passing of Burnham in 1987, dying of cancer after years of incapacity, left a void that nothing— still—can fill. During the magazine's formative years, he gave to it a philosophical depth and a series of prudential lessons that had been indispensable to its success. He possessed an experienced detestation of ideology as pre-fabricated and often contradicted by reality, and therefore doomed to failure politically. In a memorial issue of September 11, 1987, Buckley wrote in his introductory words that,

> [b]eyond any question, he has been the dominant intellectual influence in the development of this journal. He brought widely advertised qualities as a scholar, strategist, and veteran of the Cold War. He had been a practicing philosopher, and editor and author of seminal works on the nature of the current crisis.
>
> Other qualities he brought to the magazine are almost certainly the primary reasons for its survival. He had, to begin with, a (totally self-effacing) sense of corporate identification with it. He devoted, over a period of 23 years, more time and thought to more problems, major and minor, than would seem possible for an editor resident in Kent, Connecticut, who came to New York only two days a week.
>
> Every aspect of the magazine interested him. Its typography, just for instance. He cared always for what he would only call "tone." He believed in sentiment but not in "sentimentality." At the regular editorial meetings, which by tradition we began by listening to his recommended list of issues about which we should write that week, his comments were always made calmly, with the kind of analytical poise one associates with the professional philosopher. Notwithstanding the gentleness of his manner, he brought great passion to his work: not ungovernable passion, because Jim doesn't believe that passion should be ungovernable. But his commentary, during such crises as are

suggested by mentioning Budapest, Suez, Berlin, the Bay of Pigs, Vietnam, was sustained by the workings of a great mind and the palpitation of a great heart.

Although he told me that twenty years of teaching was enough . . . his natural instincts were always pedagogical. Probably fifty writers have in the past 25 years had editorial experience in the offices of *National Review*. I don't think any of my colleagues would question the figure for whom they had the greatest respect, and the greatest feeling of gratitude, was Jim Burnham, who was never too busy to give the reasons for thinking as he did, or too harassed to interrupt his own work to help others with theirs. His generosity was egregiously exploited by one person, whose only excuse is that at least he has documented his gratitude by penning these words.

Not a word of that is inaccurate or overstated for the occasion. I would add that, as I hope has been shown earlier, he helped shape *National Review* in the direction of becoming a maker of the American conservative mind, and that in doing so he rescued it from dogmatism and utopianism. Without this it would not have succeeded as it did, nor would it have come to exert so much influence, not least in the case of Ronald Reagan. Burnham had been Buckley's indispensable guide, philosopher, and friend.

At *National Review*, Burnham achieved an influence he never would have approached at *Partisan Review* had he remained there—a magazine, for all its fame, too Manhattan-provincial to accommodate his strengths. At *National Review* he did his best writing, forced by unfolding events to modify his Hobbesian sense of political power as force and to take account of contingency, personality, and the indeterminacy of luck—politics as an art, not a Machiavellian "science."

NATIONAL REVIEW DURING THIS period was in the process of renewing itself, as all institutions must; this process included major shifts as well as small nuances that affected the nature of the magazine. In 1985, with the departure of Priscilla Buckley, Linda Bridges, her assistant and a meticulous copy editor, replaced her as managing editor. Linda, though a Californian who had gone to USC, was unexpectedly attuned to odd old things and such Englishnesses as P. G. Wodehouse and the Anglican Church. She worked at a rolltop desk in a littered office that rivaled Joe Sobran's squirrel-like office clutter. She should have, but did not, write with a quill, and might be called an antiquarian traditionalist in the mode of Russell Kirk. Chilton Williamson, a short-story writer with longings for the American West, became Books editor.

Joe Sobran contributed to the thirtieth anniversary issue a long and important profile of the contemporary ideal conservative mind, a kind of paradigm of conservatism, titled "Pensées: Notes for the Reactionary of Tomorrow." This splendid piece of prose gave no hint of the personal hurricane to come. President Reagan himself attended the 1985 anniversary gala at the Plaza Hotel. *National Review* had come a very long way in its first thirty years.

Around the time of the anniversary, though I cannot pinpoint the year, senior editor Richard Brookhiser—we had become good friends—indicated that he wished to talk with me about his career. He had come to Buckley's attention with a letter written when he was in high school, of all things, and he began contributing to *National Review* while at Yale. In 1977 Buckley talked him out of going to law school—this, a major service all around—and he began coming to the magazine on a regular basis as a senior editor. Naturally, the usually unspoken thought at *National Review* was that he would eventually succeed Buckley as editor-in-chief, which, given his talent, was an entirely plausible thought. I invited him to dinner at the Century Club.

The discussion had to do with the overall direction of Brookhiser's career as a writer. He had demonstrated his gifts as an editorial writer, and also of articles and reviews. He was working on a book to be called *The Outside Story*, about the 1984 presidential election. He was good at on-the-scene reporting. I finally asked him what he saw himself doing in ten year's time, maybe contributing to the *New Yorker*? He said Yes, and then he said something defining, and very well put. He wanted to be, he said, "a writer who is a conservative, not a conservative writer." This seemed to me to rule out editor-in-chief of *National Review*.

I myself had intermittently served as editorials editor after Burnham had stepped down and Buckley was away from the magazine. I would fly to

New York from Hanover, preside over the biweekly meeting, and put the editorial section to bed. I told Rick that by no means did I envision leaving my faculty post at Dartmouth to take a full-time permanent position at *National Review*. My commitments were to literature and, derivatively, to history and philosophy. I was not consumed professionally by current events, as a chief editor must be, and I was anything but an administrator.

This genial discussion left the editor-in-chief post out of both our plans, whatever Buckley might have had in mind. Brookhiser would go on to write his notable series of Plutarchian biographies of America's founders, beginning with *The Founding Father: Rediscovering George Washington* (1996). These were relatively brief, stylish works (more useful for many purposes than the familiar three volumes), and they deserved their wide readership. They possessed an eighteenth-century lucidity and wit appropriate to their subjects, books on Hamilton, the Adams family, and Gouverneur Morris following the one on Washington. In the Plutarchian tradition, invented by the Greeks as a branch of moral philosophy, such preeminent statesmen, faults and all, were meant by Brookhiser as examples to be contemplated of what makes a leader in a republic. These books made Brookhiser famous, and along with his continuing work as a senior editor, were also an asset to the reputation of the magazine. He had become "a writer who is a conservative."

John O'Sullivan became an editor as Buckley's "deputy" in 1988, then editor in 1990, with Buckley as editor-at-large. Shortly thereafter Wick Allison, a successful young magazine publisher in Dallas, replaced the now retired Bill Rusher as publisher. His views for the direction of the magazine foreshadowed long-term—and perhaps not always desirable—developments, though his direct influence is not traceable. Allison maintained that the magazine had heretofore been written as if a monthly, when it should be written as if a weekly. This would mean, if pushed too far, topicality to the exclusion of serious reflection, and indeed, the exclusion of probing controversy. Yet these features—serious reflection and probing controversy—had been a major strength of the magazine, making for sustained interest beyond the week's news, and tending to ensure some philosophical rationale for such policy positions as the magazine might take. These features also served an educational purpose, especially for young conservatives, or would-be conservatives.

Buckley now never appeared in the office, but he emphatically remained a presence as editor-at-large, able to oversee editorial operations from afar. John O'Sullivan brought formidable professional and personal qualities to the magazine. Splendidly educated at the University of London, he was widely literate and had abundant experience in journalism as part of the Rupert Murdoch organization, as at the *New York Post*, where some of the *National Review* editors knew him. He was closely associated with Margaret Thatcher and assisted her with her autobiographical volumes. He brought some new emphases to *National Review*, especially a desire for a strengthened "Atlantic" relationship with Britain and both a theoretical and a practical focus on the negative aspects of immigration, most pungently articulated by Peter Brimelow, a senior editor at *Forbes*. Given the "national" adjective in the title *National Review*, O'Sullivan's position as editor-in-chief involved a certain peculiarity, as would an American editor in charge of, say, the British *Economist*, but his obvious talents made the question of his citizenship marginal.

DURING THE 1992 PRESIDENTIAL primary, some events eventually unsettling for *National Review* took place. From New Hampshire, Brookhiser reported on the New Hampshire primary, where Pat Buchanan carried 40 percent of the vote in that solidly Republican state, demonstrating dangerous Bush weaknesses. Brookhiser noticed that,

> [c]ompared to Buchanan the columnist, Buchanan the candidate is a cautious fellow. . . . [He] wore a white shirt and navy blue suit, the sharp part and tightly combed hair of the Fifties, his decade, and his characteristic look, which he owes to the lines of his forehead, of perpetual worry. . . .

That mention of Buchanan's syndicated columns leads Brookhiser to the following:

> Then there is the Jewish Question. All the times Buchanan has been right (as in his defense of John Demjanjuk) and all the times he has been wronged (as when A. M. Rosenthal equated him with David Duke) do not drain away the residues of animus. Buchanan's columns have picked away at Jews the way a

kid picks at a scab. Buchanan's speeches will have to find some way to make amends.

Coincidentally, at about the same time, Joe Sobran began to show symptoms of being deeply bitten by the anti-Semitic bug.

It was in this context, in 1992, that Buckley published *In Search of Anti-Semitism*, one of his best books, making fine distinctions and performing some surgery necessary to the process of shaping the American conservative mind. Based upon the analysis in Buckley's book, excerpts of which were published in *National Review*, the story, highly condensed, goes something like this. According to Buckley, both Joe Sobran and Pat Buchanan stood in an unacceptable relation to anti-Semitism, if not shown actually to be anti-Semitic. In the accumulation and frequency of their questionable statements, they had given rise to a justified view that they were in fact anti-Semitic. The very subtlety of that statement demonstrates what a minefield this area in fact is.

Nothing published in *National Review* by Sobran ever gave rise to a suspicion of animus regarding Jews. On the basis of his syndicated column, however, Buckley became worried and, at a friendly dinner in Paone's, warned him about the direction his column was taking. Six months went by, alarm increasing enough to have Buckley meet three times with the senior editors, two of the meetings with Sobran present. One of the columns, for example, had praised a magazine of microscopic circulation named *Instauration* as having an aptitude for "wit and trenchancy." *Instauration* was a walk on the wild side, with its flagrant hatred of Jews among other groups. Its editor used a pseudonym, not at all imprudently.

The Sobran columns were discussed by the senior editors, with the result that in the July 4, 1986, issue Buckley published an editorial, "In Re Joe Sobran and Anti-Semitism." This long discourse discussed the frequency with which Sobran had reflected on Judaism going back to the philosopher Maimonides, and also on the internal behavior of Israel toward Christians. This editorial concluded, "I here dissociate myself and my colleagues from what we view as the obstinate tendentiousness of Joe's recent columns," ending with a hope for better judgment on Sobran's part.

This did not suffice. Sobran wrote a long, unrepentant reply in *National Review*, pulled back to a degree in his columns, but at length offended again sufficiently to be asked by Buckley to read to him on the phone any column he might write about Jews or the Middle East. At first he complied, but soon relapsed. Then he opposed Desert Storm, unrelentingly, despite the invasion of Kuwait, attributing the war to Israeli influence, whatever the wide support for the war among a great many who by no stretch could be accused of being influenced by Israel. In September 1990, Sobran sent Buckley two pieces for *National Review* that Buckley deemed unpublishable, indeed, "indefensible." Buckley composed a letter to Sobran urging him to resign as senior editor while continuing to contribute reviews and so on if he wished.

But Buckley did not send this letter, because "I was persuaded by my colleagues that it would be a mistake to proceed against Joe, and distracting attention from *NR*'s thirty-fifth anniversary and its special edition, the subject of a thousand hours of labor." Then, three months later, becoming, as Buckley writes, "effectively a part of the American pacifist movement," Sobran agreeably resigned as senior editor, agreeing to have no connection with the magazine's editorial content, and agreeing to contribute to the cultural side of the magazine, which he did.

But there is another side to this story, less documented, on which I am hazy as to chronology. Writing in a tiny Catholic newspaper called the *Wanderer*, Sobran said personal things about Buckley. One of these columns, for example, reported imaginatively on a dinner he and Buckley had at Paone's, Buckley purportedly saying that the opinions of "ordinary" Catholics did not matter, and advising Sobran to attend to people who counted, a notion entirely uncharacteristic of Buckley, who denies saying any such thing.

At some point, Sobran vanished from *National Review*. Again, at some point later, I asked Buckley whether there was anything Sobran could do that would allow him to return to the magazine, such was my regard for his talent as a writer, not to mention the pleasure of his wit. Buckley said that no, he could never again trust him.

Sobran's departure proved to be a tremendous loss to the magazine, not only because of his beautifully natural prose style, which rendered closely the rhythms of his thought processes, but also because of his wit in conversation. Around the office he was a joy, rushing around to show everyone the latest editorial witticism he had dreamed up; he was one of the best conversationalists I have known.

In Search of Anti-Semitism concludes:

> It does not occur to Joe to meditate on the exchanges with his colleagues during the period in question: three protracted sessions, two of them lasting over two hours, at which other Senior Editors, plus the Managing Editor, plus the Publisher, endorsed the analysis that went into the editorial he classifies as "strange." [The editorial here is the one dissociating *National Review* from the many statements he had made on the relevant questions.] All five of us joined in warning him that what he then was writing inevitably gave rise to conclusions that what burns up Joe Sobran is the Jewish operation in Israel.

Though Pat Buchanan was not connected with *National Review*, he had been a staunch conservative for years and a good friend of mine since the 1968 Nixon campaign. Buckley detected repeated innuendo, an imputation that Jews avoided military service, while only such men as "McAllister, Murphy, Gonzales, and Lee Roy Brown" were likely to turn up for the country. Then there were Buchanan's mistaken calculations about the impossibility of gassing Jews in carbon monoxide vans, and a reference to an "amen corner" favoring Israeli above American interests: referring to the first Gulf War, he wrote, "The only two groups that are beating the drum for war in the Middle East [are] the Israeli Defense Ministry and its amen corner in the United States."

That supposedly treasonous amen corner was very large indeed: a large majority of Congress and the general public. I felt great regret about the magazine's position here, Pat always my friend, and the best company imaginable. I did not consider Pat an anti-Semite, merely a tough fighter, and I was certain that he would not ever join an anti-Semitic organization. I understood that Pat, when in the White House, had been outraged over the pressure put on Reagan over Bitburg, a visit Reagan felt he owed to Helmut

Kohl for supporting the installation of medium-range missiles, Kohl helping Reagan achieve a major victory in the Cold War. Pat's anger over this probably fueled his incautious rhetoric.

THOUGH *NATIONAL REVIEW* endorsed George Herbert Walker Bush in 1992, it did so reluctantly, while regretting his weaknesses. An important editorial on February 12, 1992 ("Four More Years?"), pointed out:

> The state of George Bush at the time of the State of the Union address was parlous. Polls never tell the whole story, but they told enough: from a post–Desert Storm high of over 90 percent approval, the President had sunk into the 40s. More alarming still, some polls showed Americans believing that the Democrats, rather than Republicans, were better able to manage the economy and that a Democrat should be given a crack at the White House.

Rumors during the campaign about Clinton's sexual escapades in Arkansas pointed to dangerous weaknesses on his part. Still, as the election approached, *National Review* told jokes touched by *Schadenfreude*: "The good news is that Imelda Marcos is running for president. The bad news is that she's running in the Philippines." After the election, the *National Review* cover showed Bush as a battered prizefighter on a stretcher, while his campaign manager James Baker walks beside him saying, "What do you mean 'we'?" Bush's legacy to the nation was William Jefferson Clinton.

24

Bill Clinton:
Was It Better Than It Looked?

No one who ever passed through an American public high school could have watched William Jefferson Clinton running for office in 1992 and failed to recognize the familiar predatory sexuality of the provincial adolescent. The man was, Jesse Jackson said that year to another point, "nothing but appetite."

So wrote Joan Didion, a former *National Review* contributor, in her 1998 *New York Review of Books* essay "Clinton Agonistes," written during the Monica Lewinsky fiasco when thong underwear and a stained blue dress were widely thought to clinch the case against the Clinton presidency. Not for nothing, however, did John T. Harris call his 2005 book about Clinton *The Survivor*. Right from the beginning, when he first came to national attention as a presidential candidate in the 1992 New Hampshire primary, Clinton had seemed to be finished by scandal.

True enough, on paper the young governor of Arkansas appeared to be the ideal candidate. He had been groomed by the Democratic Leadership Council, formed after the 1972 McGovern disaster to move the party toward the center and rescue it from the attitudes of Vietnam and the 1960s—since then, the party that always "blamed America first." Clinton was supposed to return the Democrats to the patriotic, firm on national defense, broad-based party of Franklin Roosevelt, Harry Truman, and John F. Kennedy. That would be a singular accomplishment, if he could do it. From a long-term perspective, all American citizens should have hoped that he would succeed: a two-party system requires two strong and plausible parties. A Rhodes Scholar, a Yale Law School graduate, apparently a natural leader, charismatic, Bill Clinton, the youthful face of the New South, might be just the man to accomplish this historic transformation.

But. In every defining sentence about Bill Clinton there seems to be a "but." Much in his 1992 primary campaign led many to loathe him, and also his wife Hillary, as creatures of the 1960s, the very memory of which he was supposed to expunge from the Democratic Party. It came to notice that he had been a Vietnam draft dodger, and slippery in the way he managed it. He had also smoked pot—or sort of: he claimed he "didn't inhale." Though he came with the name "Slick Willie," that claim was not very slick. Hillary Clinton, Wellesley and Yale Law School graduate, had worked for the House committee preparing the impeachment of Nixon. Obviously an ambitious woman, she said she had never intended to "bake cookies," and many considered her the epitome of the women's revolution, which they viewed with distaste as demeaning motherhood and driving abortion. Clinton said with a salesman's smile that "You get two for the price of one." That was just what many did not want: the sixties times two.

In 1992, rumors of sexual extravagance in Arkansas grew, one reporter saying in private, "If you think Jack Kennedy and Gary Hart were bad, just wait until you see this guy."[1] And sure enough, a cabaret singer named Gennifer Flowers almost derailed the Clinton campaign, taped phone calls confirming rumors of their relationship. Governor Clinton even got her a state job, offering the *Bartlett's*-worthy compliment that "She could suck a golf ball through a garden hose." Flowers herself said that she was "sexually liberated." The Democratic orchestra could as well have played, "Happy *Sixties* Days Are Here Again."

But Hillary helped save Slick Willie from the Flowers scandal. In a *60 Minutes* TV broadcast following the Super Bowl—and so guaranteeing a huge audience—Clinton admitted causing "pain in my marriage," and Hillary stood by her man, after having mocked Tammy Wynette for that very thought. In 2005, now a senator from New York, Hillary allowed rather winningly that Bill "was a hard dog to keep on the porch." There is little doubt that Hillary saved Clinton's campaign, and for that he owed her, owed her plenty. He could not refuse her claim to take charge of health care reform. His Gennifer Flowers escapade thus led directly to that disaster, and to a Republican majority in the House in 1994.

IN NOVEMBER 1992, Clinton slid into the presidency with 43 percent of the vote, then-president George H. W. Bush being handicapped by the eccentric candidacy of Ross Perot. The Clintons entered the White House with a minority vote, loathed and even seen as illegitimate by the right wing. This loathing never subsided; far from it, the loathing increased exponentially on the political Right. And in the most visible ways the young Clinton administration floundered, beginning with the nomination of Zoe Baird for Attorney General. It turned out that she had two illegal aliens as domestic servants. There followed the controversy over gays in the military; the scandal of the Travel Office firings, in which career employees were sacked on trumped-up grounds to benefit Clinton's Little Rock cronies; Clinton's uncertain approach to ethnic cleansing in Bosnia, and also to the usual impossible situation in Haiti; the imprisonment of Clinton's Little Rock golfing pal, Assistant Attorney General Webster Hubble, for crooked billing practices at the Rose Law Firm in Little Rock; allegations about implausible profits on cattle futures by Hillary while at the Rose Law Firm; allegations about the Clintons' role in "Whitewater," a suspicious Arkansas land scheme; and the extraordinary flare-up of what became known as "Troopergate."

On this last matter, the *American Spectator* published a series of articles by one David Brock, alleging, with plenty of testimony to support it, that Governor Clinton had used Arkansas state troopers to facilitate and cover up his numerous assignations with the Daisy Mays of Little Rock. His chief-of-staff there, Betsy Wright, became famous as his "bimbo suppressor," using threats and rewards to shut the bimbos up. The account in the *American Spectator*, vulnerable in some details, was nevertheless largely confirmed by a parallel investigation conducted by the *Los Angeles Times*, which was more professional in checking allegations. *American Spectator* editor R. Emmett Tyrrell had hoped that he would bring Clinton down, and for a season he was the toast of the Washington right wing. Instead, the financial extravagance that resulted from a temporarily ballooning circulation wrecked the *American Spectator*.

Possibly the worst blow to the Clintons was the suicide of Vince Foster, deputy White House counsel and a close Rose Law Firm friend of Hillary, which for a time was exploited by right-wing groups that promoted the idea that Foster had been murdered. In fact, he was a victim of depression. The bright young Clintons were off to a wonderful start.

In light of all this, who would have believed that a New Year's 1998 poll would find that for 83 percent of respondents Bill Clinton was the "most admired" man in America? And in fact, his accomplishments had been considerable. *But*—and there is that Clinton "but" again—in 1998 the "most admired" man in America had two years to go before crossing the finish line. During those two years, William Jefferson Clinton would become the costar of a pornographic nonfiction book known as the "Starr Report," published not in Paris by the Black Obelisk Press, but in Washington, D.C., by the federal government. And that "most admired" man in America would become only the second president in American history to be impeached by the House. Where was H. L. Mencken in this season of need?

IN 1998 AT *NATIONAL REVIEW*, halfway through Clinton's second term, Rich Lowry replaced John O'Sullivan as editor, *National Review* also moving from its ancient and familiar offices on 35th Street to bright new ones on Lexington Avenue near 32nd Street. O'Sullivan had left to pursue other diverse interests; Lowry, a young graduate of the University of Virginia, had been Washington correspondent, filing excellent copy from the new office in the capital.

In general, *National Review* policy vectors showed no visible change with the advent of Lowry, though he did indicate to senior people his intention of bringing fresh talent to the pool of writers, financial advisor Dusty Rhodes assuring him that funding would be available. Jay Nordlinger soon arrived from the *Weekly Standard* to become managing editor, and Linda

Bridges moved over to become special assistant to Buckley, who had many projects in hand. Ramesh Ponnuru, a young Princeton graduate, also arrived from the Washington office, while Kate O'Beirne, an O'Sullivan addition, continued to file copy from Washington.

Perhaps surprisingly, none of these now prominent figures at the magazine had been known for books or even important articles on politics or political thought. Where they stood on the spectrum of conservative thought—traditionalist, individualist, libertarian, skeptical, Straussian, Burkean, Voegelinian—was completely unknown. Ideas and arguments among exponents of various conservative strands of thought had been integral to the magazine for its first thirty-five years, but this dimension of *National Review* now disappeared completely. In effect, the Washington office, almost entirely reportorial and topical in its focus, had moved to Manhattan.

The post–John O'Sullivan and post-Clinton *National Review* was beginning to take shape, and it included the start-up of National Review Online, which proved to be breathtakingly successful. It will suffice to consider *National Review*'s handling of the Clinton administration as a continuous whole, nothing much changing in the magazine's coverage of Clinton from his 1992 narrow election, through 1996, when he triumphed over another weak Republican ticket, Dole-Kemp, until the end in 2000. Clinton was showing the Democrats one way to win a national election: nominate a center-left candidate with wide appeal, preferably from the Sunbelt, also religious, who sent signals to voters that he understood their cultural concerns, such as supporting welfare reform, school uniforms, v-chips for televisions, a national registry of sex offenders, and a national crack-down on delinquent fathers. Under 1996 electoral pressure, Clinton raised "triangulation" to a principle of governance, tacking right in order to cruise toward a not very ideological center-left. Clinton was willing to disappoint the enthusiasts in order to please the majority at the center—and to win.

IN 2003, RICH LOWRY, proving himself an admirably hard worker, published *Legacy*, a highly professional account of Clinton's two terms, focusing on policy. This was the only serious extended study of the Clinton presidency until John D. Harris's *The Survivor* two years later. Lowry takes up, for example, Hillary's IOU from the Gennifer Flowers affair, one result of which was the Hillary-care disaster. This plan was so unpopular that its ripple effect helped to elect the 1994 Gingrich Congress. Hillary teamed up for the doomed plan with Ira Magaziner, whom Clinton had met at Oxford, and whom Lowry describes this way:

> Magaziner got to know Clinton at Oxford, where he organized protests against the Vietnam War. He had a history from his student days to his career as a multimillionaire business consultant of leading large-scale totalist reforms that failed. His rationality was prodigious. It was only a feel for reality that Magaziner lacked. . . . After the 1992 election, Magaziner presided over a health-care task force of more than five hundred people in a secret, byzantine policy process involving, by Magaziner's count, some 840 policy decisions. Meetings were of a punishing, Maoist length. One lasted twenty-two hours. Magaziner himself pulled "double all-nighters," and when Clinton gave his health address to Congress in September 1993, Magaziner had gone without sleep for sixty-five hours. Out of this frantic, enormously complex process was born a plan of . . . enormous complexity.

A droll wit characterizes this profile of the flaky Magaziner making major policy. Hillary-care was the ultimate graduate-student effort, a scheme that would have reorganized, starting from scratch, 15 percent of the total U.S. economy. In Congress, it fell like a stone; and with it went Clinton's congressional majority.

There is room here for a what-if, however. Clinton had campaigned to "end welfare as we know it." Had he advanced welfare reform at the outset, he would have needed some votes from the Democratic majority, many of whom would have been reluctant; the "Hillary wing" of the administration would have been opposed; but he might well have gained from congressional Republicans more votes than he lost from his own party. The time had come for such reform. And its success would have built up momentum for his presidency. *But*. But women. There had been Gennifer Flowers, and Hillary had saved him: Hillary got health care. She never would have stood aside for welfare reform.

IN LATE 1994 THE NEW Speaker New Gingrich found a place in history by trying actually to *reduce* federal spending. In the fall of 2004, *Washington Post* columnist Anne Applebaum would write that compared with the big-time riverboat spenders of the then-adjourning George W. Bush Congress, Newt Gingrich and his followers

> tried to limit the terms of all-powerful committee chairmen, who had so skewed the appropriations process to the advantage of their constituents. He assailed what he called the "East German farm subsidy programs" that had gone unchallenged for a half-century. He even managed to pass a line-item veto, which—had it not been declared unconstitutional—would have allowed then-President Clinton to cut pork from the then-Republican Congress' legislation.... [Now] the Education Department, once slated for abolition, has experienced a huge spending boost. So has the Energy Department, once greeted with skepticism. In fact, many of the programs that Republicans promised to end in the mid-1990s . . . now have larger budgets than ever.

Whatever one might call George W. Bush politically, he could not be called a fiscal conservative. With the ascendancy of Gingrich and the Republican Congress, Hillary disappeared from political prominence—until, that is, the Monica Lewinsky affair, another chapter in the epic of Clinton's woman problem that in book form should bear the title *From Here to Infinity*. Once again Hillary stood by her man. *National Review* would joke: "The Clintons' legal defense fund mailed a pitch to Dr. Bernard Lewinsky, who replied that his daughter gave at the office."

Curiously, the Lewinsky affair began during the November 1995 modified government shutdown that resulted from a budgetary impasse between Clinton and Gingrich. On the night of the fifteenth, the White House operating with a skeleton staff, Clinton was alone in the chief-of-staff's office when the lusty intern showed up. She had been flirting with him when their paths crossed, and had caught his eye, but now she suddenly "pulled up her dress to show Clinton the straps on the thong underwear she was wearing."[2] Clinton took it from there, all the way to the Starr Report and to the televised grand jury session at which, appearing like the proverbial deer in the headlights, he said that there "is" no sexual relationship, and finally to impeachment.

Rich Lowry analyzes the Lewinsky case at length in *Legacy* and concludes:

> There were two overriding factors that would ultimately save Clinton in the Lewinsky affair, his wife and a broad cultural shift in the American public that predisposed it to go easy on him. . . . As always, she was Clinton's fiercest fighter. . . . When in her famous *Today* show appearance, she said twice that the charges against her husband would not be "proven true," she was speaking the language of the affidavit strategy. Upon returning from the appearance, she told [Harry] Thomason, "I guess that will teach them to f—k" with us."

Hillary was steel complementing Bill's flab. Lowry concludes, plausibly, that when Hillary said she had defended Clinton "as president," she should be interpreted as meaning that she did so out of self-interest. Arguably, therefore, one of the achievements of Clinton's presidency was Hillary's election as senator from New York in 2000, and possibly election to the presidency in 2008.

Lowry, we see, attributed Clinton's survival to a change in the climate of opinion regarding sex, and this is undoubtedly true. He does not seem interested in exploring reasons why this change in sexual attitudes has occurred. It must have had complex social causes of great importance. John F. Harris adds other reasons. While Republicans judged that the lurid details in the Starr Report would destroy Clinton, they were regarded by public opinion as pornography and instead ruined Starr for airing such things in public. Above all, writes Harris,

> With the stock market soaring and unemployment near modern lows, the President's private morals were of little relevance to most citizens. Yet Clinton never would have lasted were it not for the competence the voters credited to the administration for the handling of the economy. The public face of that competence, the hero of the day even to many who deplored Clinton, was [Treasury Secretary] Robert Rubin.[3]

But credit should also accrue to Rubin's first-term predecessor, Lloyd Bentsen. At his urging, Clinton exercised self-restraint, going against his own aspiration for heroic Rooseveltian spending projects and against the urging of many liberals on his staff, and taking instead the fiscally conservative Bentsen's advice. He held down spending and raised taxes moderately. As Harris writes in *The Survivor*:

> The gamble Clinton took . . . that deficit reduction would spur the economy [paid off] extravagantly. Annual growth in 1987 was 8.2 percent. The tax revenue this growth produced was erasing the deficit far faster than anyone projected—it was $22 billion in 1997, compared to $290 billion when Clinton took office. The deficit would be gone entirely by the first week of 1998—a milestone the *New York Times* called the fiscal equivalent of the fall of the Berlin Wall.[4]

Bentsen had argued that cutting the deficit would lower interest rates and buoy the economy. *National Review* took the position that the tax increases would be, if anything, negative to prosperity, and further, that the economic surge had begun during the last seventeen months of Bush One. That contention was seriously at odds with the magazine's excoriation at the time of Budget Director Richard Darman for the budget deal that raised taxes and energized the improvement of the economy. The magazine appeared to be dogmatically against raising taxes whatever the circumstances and whatever the deficit. That is, *National Review*, on the grounds that lower taxes meant less government, always supported tax cuts. But in the real world, Americans wanted such programs as Medicare and Social Security, and these had to be paid for. Ballooning deficits are not sound economics. Under Bush Two, Vice President Cheney would proclaim that "deficits don't matter." He should have checked with the money markets. Under George W. Bush, deficits would soar into the stratosphere, as he declined to veto a single spending bill. In the partisan pitch of the 1990s and beyond, was *NR* losing its independent critical edge?

As Clinton's term in office drew to an end, he made a heroic effort to end the Israeli-Palestinian conflict. Clinton and Israeli Prime Minister Ehud Barak made Yasser Arafat the most generous offer the Palestinians are ever likely to receive. It included 90 percent of the West Bank, sovereignty over the Temple Mount and East Jerusalem, and the symbolic return of some Palestinian claimants to Israel. Many believed it too generous. *National Review* speculated that, when Arafat rejected it, demanding the "return" to Israel of four million claimants (who had never lived there), as well as many other concessions, he did so because he was more comfortable as a guerrilla leader than as a negotiator and peacetime administrator.

Thus Arafat began the Intifada and rampant terrorism. As *National Review* also saw it, the Oslo path had been doomed from the start. A November 6, 2000, editorial summed up this train of thought:

> The Oslo peace process was doomed by its structural flaws. Israelis and Palestinians were to do the easy thing first and leave to the end the hard issues. Two of these revolved around the sovereignty of Jerusalem and the right of Palestinian refugees from 1948 to return. A two-stage process is like asking the parties to jump across a wide abyss by taking each stride in midair. It was an open invitation to extremists to raise their demands in the final stage of settlement, in the certainty that they could kill the idea of peace. This is exactly what happened, and the parties now lie bleeding at the bottom of the abyss. . . . Arafat concluded that Israel was on the run and that violence would bring him yet greater rewards. Violence has in fact produced the opposite of what Yasser Arafat expected. . . . Among possible nightmares are Islamic suicide bombers, kidnappings and hijackings. . . . Appeasement and retreat have brought Israel to this.

That is persuasive, though it is to some extent at odds with the notion that Arafat balked because he was more comfortable as a guerrilla leader. At the same time, the magazine never recognized that an accord—and an accord is emphatically in the U.S. national interest—required a viable Palestinian state on the West Bank, which meant a state with geographical integrity like other states, and not host to numerous permanent Israeli settlements.

SINISTER CLINTON FOREIGN policy problems now involved terrorism, and here there can be little doubt that Clinton was insufficiently engaged. In 1993, the first World Trade Center bombing killed six people. The bomb went off in the underground parking garage; perhaps the terrorists even hoped to topple the giant structure. In 1998, the bombing of two U.S. embassies in Africa killed 224. That same year, Osama bin Laden declared holy war against the United States, putting his head, one would think, in the bull's eye of our targeting. Indeed, President Clinton announced that, "We will use all the means at our disposal *to bring those responsible to justice*, no matter what or how long it takes [italics added]." Bring them to justice? This was *war*, not a matter of criminal justice.

Clinton's chance to kill Osama bin Laden apparently arrived during the fall of 2000. Unarmed Predator spy planes flying over Afghanistan took aerial photographs of known al-Qaeda camps that showed military training activities taking place. At CIA headquarters in Langley, analysts identified a tall man (bin Laden is 6'5") in flowing white robes surrounded by a group of guards or attendants. The location in these pictures was the Tarnak farm, the walled compound where bin Laden was known to live. Just why we did not vaporize this place with as many cruise missiles as necessary has never been explained satisfactorily. Was Clinton in a "bring him to justice" mode?

Shortly before the 2000 election, on October 12, an unidentified small boat cruised up to the destroyer USS *Cole* in the Aden, Yemen, harbor. A man smiled from the boat's deck. Seventeen American sailors died in the subsequent explosion. Just why the unidentified boat was allowed to get so close has never been explained. It seems that neither the Navy nor Clinton thought we were really at war. *National Review* rightly criticized Clinton's lack of action in response to the *Cole* attack. 9/11 was a little more than a year away.

On Iraq, *National Review* noticed that Saddam Hussein was evading sanctions, discouraging inspections, and consolidating his power by assaults on Kurds and Shiites. The Afghanistan training camps of al-Qaeda drew only pinprick cruise missile attacks. *National Review* recognized that Clinton did intervene to good effect to stop genocide in Kosovo—but criticized him for doing so on humanitarian grounds, not in an effort to further the national interest of the United States. That may be a false dichotomy: the national interest did not lie in ethnic war in the Balkans. In addition, public opinion was strongly opposed to intervention, and Clinton succeeded with a solid NATO coalition plus airpower. When we turned out the lights in Belgrade, Milosevic caved. Overall, *National Review* judged Clinton's foreign policy to be weak—and dangerous, in that it encouraged enemies to think the United States passive and unwilling to strike.

NOW WE COME to the big, or at least one of the biggest, questions about the performance of Bill Clinton: *de-McGovernization*. This, for the future of American politics, was Clinton's historic political mission, dating from his early role in the Democratic Leadership Council. Such a project faced serious obstacles. The original McGovern reforms had democratized the primaries. Popular votes now chose state delegates. In practice, this proved *less* democratic in the kind of delegates it sent to the party's national convention. Before the reforms, officeholders and party officials exercised predominant power while attending to a variety of interests, including local opinion. The McGovern reforms magnified the importance of activists, people who had time to work in the primaries and who were likely to be energized by "principle"—for the Democrats, meaning positions far to the left of the American mainstream. The focus now tended to be on "correct" politics—meaning expressive and "moral"—rather than on the job of *winning*.

Beginning in 1972 with the McGovern convention, far more delegates were academics and Ph.D.s, with time to spare and the most abstract of concerns. This was a recipe for the permanent marginalization of the Democratic Party. Nevertheless, for the September 13, 1999, issue of *National Review*, Norman Podhoretz contributed an important essay arguing for the proposition that Clinton deserved credit for some normalizing of the Democratic Party, in effect restoring the American two-party system. This large issue fell outside the scope of Lowry's reporting in *Legacy*.

Podhoretz's essay was an effort at discerning major political consequences within the flow of discrete events. It was of a sort that had become almost extinct in the pages of *National Review*, where journalistic topicality now dominated the biweekly content. At one time, regular columns had expressed and examined the implications of divergent kinds of conservatism. That had largely disappeared. With Lowry, in addition, senior editors' quarterly meetings ceased, eliminating the kind of intra-magazine discussion—

and argument—that had previously quickened *NR*'s collective mind. Just how policy questions were decided now was opaque. Podhoretz's contribution, it is worth noting, came from outside the magazine, but it did reintroduce important questions, both theoretical and practical.

The Podhoretz essay also possesses special interest because Podhoretz was a leading member of the amorphous group called the "neoconservatives," which had its origin in 1972 with the rise of McGovern, the very problem Clinton was supposed to remedy. The neocons had left the Democratic Party with the eclipse of Senator Henry "Scoop" Jackson of Washington, once a serious possibility for the presidency, and with the failure of Daniel Patrick Moynihan to emerge as a party leader. Titled "The Life of The Party," Podhoretz's essay occupies five pages and provides a history of the leftward shift of the Democratic Party over Vietnam. This resulted in its capture by a combination of the New Left and the counterculture, along with the media and the academy, and produced, according to Podhoretz, the failure of Carter and Dukakis, who felt it necessary to kowtow to the McGovernites.

Podhoretz then comes to his case for the Clinton administration. The essay is intricate and paradoxical: I had to read it more than once. Clinton came to the presidency, Podhoretz argues, ostensibly as a centrist:

By now the Cold War was over, and foreign policy for the first time in decades was taking second place to domestic affairs. But the minute the newly elected Bill Clinton turned his wonkish attention to domestic concerns, he blithely stripped off the centrist mask and revealed the face of the old Adam living on below (with an even more fervent McGovernite Eve standing beside him in the form of Hillary Rodham Clinton). The DLC understandably felt like so many of the women in Clinton's life: seduced, used, and then abandoned.

At first, this brazen deceiver, having achieved power by posing as a centrist, pushed hard to the left. But to his evident astonishment, the country pushed back even harder, forcing him to abandon efforts like his campaign promise to abolish the ban on gays in the military. To top it off, the old Adam's Eve was driven out of her own little paradise by the flaming sword of public indignation at her high-handed bid to dictate the revamping of her country's entire health-care system.

Now the old Adam was born yet again as a centrist, and this time it was the turn of the McGovern liberals to feel betrayed. In January 1996, Clinton, in his State of the Union address, made what may yet turn out to be his most enduring pronouncement as president: "The era of big government is over."

It was a breathtaking renunciation not just of McGovernism, but of contemporary liberalism as a whole.

One appreciates the wit and reach here: the Trickster tricked into political virtue. Podhoretz then turns back to foreign policy, recalling that the late Meg Greenfield had once doubted whether the Democrats would ever use force short of an invasion of San Diego, and observing that Clinton *had* used force, as in Kosovo. "De-McGovernization has by now gone so far . . . that beefing up the military will not encounter anywhere near the amount of Democratic resistance it would have provoked in the past."

While aspects of this argument need to be examined with reference to the subsequent record of the Democratic Party, still, the intellectual charm of Podhoretz's overall conclusion should be savored. Podhoretz argues that Clinton *achieved* de-McGovernization, not because of his virtues but because of his faults, in particular his lack of principle—an argument, indeed, reminiscent of Machiavelli's *Prince*:

If he had been a man of any principles at all, a man with something inside him besides the lust for power (and the other lusts that power contributes to satisfying) he would have been incapable of betraying the people and the ideas he was supposed to represent. If he had not been so great a liar, he would not have been able to get away not only with his own private sins but with the political insults he was administering to some of his core constituencies. And if he had not been such a disgrace to the presidency, he would not have been impeached, and would not thereby have forced even the intransigent McGovernites of his party, who had every reason to hate him, into mobilizing on his behalf for fear of the right-wing conspiracy they fantasized would succeed him.

And so, through a kind of political and psychological jujitsu, it came to pass that Clinton's worst qualities were what enabled him to accomplish something good. Scoop Jackson, the man the DLC dreamed of seeing in the White House, was a political saint by comparison with Bill Clinton. Which may mean that he could never have done as much to de-McGovernize the Democratic Party as Clinton had managed to do.

Now, the thought there is complex. At the very least, Podhorertz did not have his nose buried in topical events. Yet despite the appeal of its ingenuity and intellectual ambition, how far do we go in accepting this argument that Clinton had, in fact, succeeded in de-McGovernizing the Democrats? Maybe? Partly? Kerry's "flip-flopping" in 2004 probably derived from his attempt to bridge an oxymoronic Democratic Party, composed simultaneously of realists and quasi-pacifists.

A further immediate question *National Review* failed to ask would arise during the 2002 blitzkrieg in Afghanistan. Where did those fancy new hi-tech weapons come from?—the anti-personnel bombs called "daisy cutters," the "smart bombs," the drones and cruise missiles, the deep-penetrating "bunker buster" bombs? It takes a while to design these and put them into use, and at any moment they may be killed either politically or bureaucratically. These weapons systems had to have been in the pipeline during Clinton's eight years. This did not sound like McGovernism. Somewhere in *National Review* this question—and the name of Clinton's second-term secretary of defense, William J. Perry—had been lost, apparently through partisanship.

Podhoretz's argument did not settle the question of whether Clinton had moved the Democratic base toward the center. But with its intellectual reach, and its focus on a major theoretical as well as practical issue, Podhoretz's article was instructive, entertaining, and refreshing. It represented the best of the *National Review* tradition. Mere opinion in the absence of sound conservative thought leads only to unfortunate and tendentious results.

WE NOW ARE ACHIEVING perspective on the wild ride of Clinton's eight years. Lowry's *Legacy* was a pioneering effort, well reported; and we now have Harris's *The Survivor*, sometimes severely critical but also fair in its judgments. Much more work needs to be done, to be sure, with archival research and recorded interviews with participants. But the following can be said with some assurance now. On domestic policy, Clinton was practical rather than ideological. He leaned toward such colleagues as Lloyd Bentsen and Robert Rubin for his successful economic policy. He embraced free trade and NAFTA against the opposition of his liberal and labor constituencies. During his eight years, twenty-two million new jobs were created and the budget began to show a surplus. Despite strong objection from liberals, he signed a welfare reform bill that was overdue and proved successful in its results.

In foreign policy, he sought to form coalitions, with considerable skill rallying NATO in addressing the crisis in Kosovo. There his intervention was successful. Whatever his relations with the generals might have been, his administration developed the advanced weapons that made the blitzkrieg in Afghanistan so successful—and the Iraq blitzkrieg equally so, if only temporarily. But Clinton had a passive side, and was culpable in failing to respond massively against al-Qaeda training camps in Afghanistan and in not seizing a chance to kill bin Laden, who would have killed as many Americans as he could, including Clinton.

As a political leader, Clinton sought to capture the center while marginal-izing the utopians and extremists in his own party. He was a man of compromise, conciliation, and a sense of contingency, preferring results to ideological satisfactions. As time goes by, Clinton is bound to be perceived through the prism of his successor's performance—on the economy, on other domestic issues, and on foreign policy. Seen that way, Clinton is even now—dismaying to conservative partisans—rising in general estimation, and no doubt will achieve a decent place in the judgment of history. *But.* But there will always be a sense of lost possibility, given his manifest talents. His personal flaws, ludicrous to contemplate, denied him a much higher place in history than he might have achieved. Yet his overall performance was better for the country than it looked at the time.

As a magazine, even when it had a small initial circulation, *National Review* had become important—that is, interesting and educational—by maintaining that the conservative mind is a model arrived at by reflection upon the best that has been thought and said. We know who we *are* by knowing who we *were*. Serious critical thought has the power to assess the politician of the moment according to the evolving model, necessarily adapting itself toward always changing social, technological, and scientific facts.

Conservatism is irrelevant unless it keeps that in mind. There is nothing higher for the mind than truth. "Facts," as Lenin said, "are stubborn." Attention to serious conservative thought of the highest quality was central to Buckley's original conception of *National Review*. He wanted the magazine to appeal to an educated readership and also to educate young conservatives in the conservative intellectual tradition. Topicality cannot accomplish that.

As the Clinton years wore on, the Books section under the splendidly literate Mike Potemra honored the standard set by Frank Meyer. A new poetry feature, installed at my urging, provided a moment of beauty and, sometimes, verbal complexity and depth. Topicality has generally meant short-changing what Russell Kirk called "the permanent things." The problem remains that the major conservative ideas and themes, a result of reflection and refining, are not usable without considerable dexterity. Edmund Burke today would apply conservative insights differently. The Burkean sense of experience as cognitive is more difficult to apply today amid the quickening pace of change, in family structure, in modes of production, in the role of women, in scientific development, especially in biomedicine and nuclear physics, than even in the recent past—but it still can be applied, and probably with greater urgency. Conservative insights remain applicable, but this takes agility. A young conservative today who cannot explicate such things as Burke's (and Oakeshott's) formulations in terms of current actualities becomes increasingly irrelevant.

Even Burke, in *Thoughts on French Affairs* (1791), realized that the causes of the revolution had been deeper than he had understood, were in fact irresistible, and that in effect he had thrown sand into the gale. This "turn" Matthew Arnold considered one of the great moments in Western political philosophy.[5]

Modern thinkers have struggled mightily to accommodate the great insights to current actuality: Lionel Trilling, Leo Strauss, Eric Voegelin, Martin Heidegger, even the widely misunderstood Nietzsche (a powerful individualist answer to Marx), as well as *National Review*'s own James Burnham and Willmoore Kendall. *National Review* itself, over its entire fifty-year course, can be read as a single text. That is, the entire *oeuvre*, consisting of fifty years of the magazine, amounts to a single great conservative *work*. Throughout most of its history, *National Review* struggled to reshape its formulation so that it responded to truth. That very struggle was conservative, in that it recognized the peril of abstraction. Ideology is always wrong, because it edits actuality and in doing so simplifies it.

RUSSELL KIRK, AN INSPIRATION to generations of American conservatives, died in the spring of 1994. A great creative spirit thus passed from *National Review,* and an extraordinary personality, Kirk's *Conservative Mind* (1953) having served as an energizing force at the beginning of modern American conservatism. He died in his picturesque home ("Piety Hill") at Mecosta, Michigan, surrounded by his family. He was the fourth of the major figures who had been present at the creation in 1955. What all four had in common was a highly individual, *homemade* American quality. They were originals.

All four had been someone else before, creating their exemplary identities. Having been someplace elsewhere in the country of the mind sharpened their perceptions and stimulated their imaginations as they moved into new territory—the birth of modern American conservatism, a cultural and political phenomenon. Kirk gave the title *The Sword of Imagination* (1995) to his autobiography. If more conventional men sometimes thought him foolish, then he was God's fool. These four major figures had not been ground into a common mold by an ideological "movement," and so their ideas were lived and experienced, not predictable. To more conventional people this sometimes made them seem unsound—unsound, that is, from a partisan perspective. Richard Nixon, for example, never knew what to make of *National Review*, because no senior person was exactly on his team.

Kirk was a natural university don and would have been perfect at All Souls, Oxford, but he never was offered a post commensurate with his distinction: remarkable, unless you know how universities actually function. Instead, he made his living as a man of letters, pouring forth an abundance of books, articles, *National Review* columns, and syndicated newspaper columns, lecturing everywhere, organizing student seminars at Piety Hill. He was a man, it seemed, turning up everywhere for forty years.

His *Conservative Mind* awakened a widespread interest in the writing of Edmund Burke, advocating tradition, prudence, awareness of history, and modesty—because man is no angel, much less a god. When it appeared, *The Conservative Mind* enabled many bright young people to entertain the idea of being a conservative for the first time, so pervasive was liberal intellectual authority at that time. Kirk accomplished this by his generous selection of passages from conservative thinkers beginning with Burke and ending with Santayana; in a second edition, he included T. S. Eliot as well, at the end. Thus, there *had* been conservatives of majestic intellect, and so who could say that there was no serious conservative stance toward the world even today?

Kirk's array of great conservatives often disagreed with one another; like Kirk, they tended to be originals. This was especially useful for young conservatives to keep in mind, since, as American conservatism became a movement, it tended toward a conformity based on a set of litmus test "positions." All movements tend toward conformity, and coarseness of formulation, a fact that Lionel Trilling combated in liberalism in his *Liberal Imagination*, considering movements to be hostile to mind itself. Young conservatives, like young anythings, tend to the condition of sheep looking to graze safely. Like other major figures in the early *National Review*, even a traditionalist such as Kirk had to be a practical individualist, fighting back the tyranny of the democratic herd.

Kirk's Burke was not the historian's Burke, or the biographer's, or the Burke of the political theorists. Willmoore Kendall had to translate Burke into "deliberate sense" constitutionalism to render him applicable to America. Kirk's Burke was a bit of an antiquarian, a lover of "old things," and more mysterious than he actually was. Burke was not mystically in awe of the workings of society but sought to understand them, which was not Kirk's strong suit. Yet even in the modern academy Kirk did stimulate a greater interest in Burke scholarship—though such scholarship often found a somewhat different hero than Kirk had imagined. Kirk's Burke was not Burke the practicing statesman, nor the theoretician of aesthetics, nor Kendall's American Burke. Kirk's Burke was something of an agrarian, like Kirk himself; and in that he came together with T. S. Eliot's social and cultural criticism.

In January of 1993, the year before he died, Kirk was diagnosed with congestive heart disease. In the tributes published in the June 13, 1994, issue of *National Review*, including a number by his friends and colleagues, T. Kenneth Cribb, president of the Intercollegiate Studies Institute, re-called that,

> realist that he was, he took the news as no more and no less than an artifact of the human condition, and in his last year and a half neither despaired in his spirit nor flagged in his Herculean literary feats. After all, he was a man who planted trees throughout his life as a symbol of our duty to strive for good we may not live to see.

> Buckley recalled Kirk's passing in a tribute delivered at the White House on October 24, 2003, and published in the February 23, 2004, *National Review*: He lived his life as he prescribed it, working long days, traveling incessantly, reading day and night, tending to his family. On that last day on earth in a life which we are here to commemorate, he awoke at Piety Hill, exchanged a few words with his wife and two of his daughters, closed his eyes and died.

In the *National Review* tributes of 1994, Gerhart Niemeyer, also long associated with the magazine and now an emeritus professor of government at Notre Dame, grasped the core of Kirk's thought:

> He understood the reality of living human beings with body and soul and spirit. He [fought against] a consciousness deliberately separated from living reality. . . . This is the ideological mind building thought systems around utopian fantasies with which to manipulate human beings into false hopes.

This was the essential insight protected by Kirk's aesthetic attraction to the old and the antiquated, which in his mind helped protect all that is human from the demons of modernity. His great contemporary hero, T. S. Eliot, had managed to be at once traditional and also a high modernist, but Kirk's mind did not work that way.

25

George W. Bush:
Transformative President

"It is far better to accept teaching with wisdom and reason than mere faith."
—Origen, second century A.D.

"It will now be our fortunate duty to assist by example, by sober friendly counsel, and by material aid in the establishment of just democracy throughout the world."
—President Woodrow Wilson, 1919

We come now to the riskiest of tasks for the historian, assessing the stream of historical events more or less as they are happening in the present. I will try to raise some large questions about the passing scene, in a spirit of critical inquiry, the founding spirit of *National Review*. After eight years of partisan conflict with the Clinton administration, conservatives welcomed the return of a Republican to the White House—and a professed conservative, too, albeit a "compassionate" one. George W. Bush's presidency began with a focus on domestic policy, but events would quickly compel him onto the international stage. In both areas, Bush was a transformative president. But were his victories *conservative* victories?

At the beginning of the twenty-first century, President George W. Bush brought religion into the foreground of American public policy in a nearly unprecedented way. *National Review* conservatives had long been critical of the dogmatic secularism of the left, and they were certain of the central role played by Christianity in the history and formation of Western civilization. But did Bush's particular brand of Christian commitment—evangelical and optimistic, nondoctrinal but moralizing—really correspond with American conservative hopes? Bush was the first president who relied for his electoral majority on an evangelical base. His election was the political high-water mark of America's third Great Awakening. But what exactly was *conservative* about this form of religious expression, with its roots in the camp revivals?

Whatever might be said against the excesses of liberal secularism, the accepted convention in America has been that religious beliefs are a private matter. President Bush challenged this convention, but he did not seem to recognize the full implications of his approach to questions of religion and public life.

In the third televised debate during the 2000 Republican primaries, the candidates were asked, "What political philosopher has most influenced you?" Bush answered, "Jesus Christ." But of course, Jesus Christ said almost nothing about politics, his teachings being focused on the innermost direction of the soul. He characteristically dealt with Moses and the prophets with the sentence structure, "It has been said . . . but I say": "You have heard it said, Thou shalt not commit adultery. But I tell you that he who casteth his eye on a woman so as to lust after her has committed adultery with her in his heart." All such teachings in his sermons as well as in his parables enjoin us against being whitewashed tombs, clean outside but corrupt within. We are told to be white all the way through. It is the heart that matters, not merely the public (political) action. Are these hard teachings? Of course they are, and Jesus knew they were. That is why he pardons the woman caught in adultery, even as the crowd stands ready to stone her in obedience to the Law. Jesus says, rather, "Go now and sin no more."

David Frum, in his book *The Right Man* (2003), describes his first day in the Bush White House, where Bible Study groups were already forming. While himself Jewish and so not expected to attend, Frum makes an important observation about the significance of this small detail of White House life: the Bush version of evangelical Christianity, marked by the folkways of Southern Baptist Texas, differed markedly from the Western kind of religious outlook seen in the conservatives Goldwater and Reagan. The Christianity of those two previous conservative standard-bearers, Frum summarizes, was individualistic, quietly reserved, and leaned toward libertarianism on moral questions. Bush's Christianity was none of these things.

Yet if Bush's evangelicalism is a distinctive historical phenomenon, *National Review* and its editors have not attempted to analyze it as such. In his syndicated column, Rich Lowry wrote instead, and applaudingly, of "Orthodoxy's Revenge" (Feb. 23, 2004). He observed that there are about one hundred million Evangelicals in the United States—mostly Protestant, but some Catholic—and that about 75 percent of such voters supported Bush in 2000. Lowry noted, no doubt correctly, that these evangelicals are Bush's "indispensable base." And these facts have implications. Lowry cites the respected foreign-policy writer Walter Russell Mead for the proposition that the "reinvigorated Wilsonian foreign policy championed by Bush—and motivated less by Wilson's secular values (international law, etc.), and more by religious beliefs (the God-given rights of all people)—is a reflection of Bush's Christian base," for example.

The question arises: Are we now seeing a military Wilsonianism, fueled by religious ideals, put to an empirical test? And further: Why does Lowry call such evangelicalism "orthodoxy"? Evangelicalism is proudly nontraditional, even antitraditional, in rejecting historic forms of magisterial Christianity. True, American evangelicals hold fast to the literal words of scripture, and they readily assent to major elements of Christian doctrine, including the divine nature of Jesus Christ, the Virgin Birth, and Christ's atonement for sin on the cross, matters on which the mainline churches have seemingly become agnostic. But evangelicalism's focus on individual experience—the "personal relationship" with Jesus as savior—works precisely against creedal Christianity, with its structure of dogma and authority.

As the historian Wilfred McClay, himself an evangelical, observed in a major lecture at the Ethics and Public Policy Center (Feb. 23, 2005), "Although many secular observers seem not to understand this, evangelicalism, by its very nature, has an uneasy relationship with conservatism." A kind of anticonservatism is built into evangelicalism with the trope of the "word of

God"—interpreted independently by each individual Christian—pitted against "the traditions of men." McClay writes that "the religious vision that energizes [Bush] is not always compatible with conservatism as conventionally understood, and may not, in the long run, be easily contained or constrained by it." McClay concludes that President Bush may be aptly described as an "evangelical conservative"—something very different from a "conservative evangelical." But he remains cautious and, as a historian, rightly so.

The first American evangelical "Great Awakening" occurred during the middle of the eighteenth century, and was associated with John Wesley (in the South) and Jonathan Edwards (in New England). Both were exceptionally learned men, sound in traditional theology. Wesley died within the Church of England; he was on friendly terms with the Tory Samuel Johnson. Edwards has a high standing among theologians, and his essays, beginning with those he wrote as a Yale undergraduate, are immensely impressive. But such learning dropped away among these evangelists' followers, who tended to populism, emotion, and immediacy. The populist energies of the first Awakening did feed into the American Revolution; but the leaders of our successful revolution, our Founders, the men who wrote the Constitution, were conservative Whig gentry. The firebrand populists such as Tom Paine, Sam Adams, and Patrick Henry faded from the foreground of politics.

The second Awakening occurred in mid-nineteenth-century New England, and its spirit can be heard in Julia Ward Howe's "Battle Hymn of the Republic," reflecting a crusading Christianity opposed to slavery. Jesus is now far away among the lilies across the sea, while in "bleeding Kansas" the murderous John Brown spread the Word with gun and broadsword. Yet the cause of Lincoln and the other pragmatic American leaders was not abolishing the sin of slavery; it was saving the Union.

After the Civil War, revivalist Christianity followed the wagon trains westward into the Great Plains, where the cultural thinness favored it more than did postwar Boston. The ecstasies and gyrations reported back from the camp meetings out West caused one Boston Episcopalian to quip, "I think they're creating more souls out there than they're saving." This second Awakening issued in such a figure as William Jennings Bryan. Though three times nominated for the presidency (1896, 1900, 1908), largely because of his appeal to Christian populism and populist Christianity, he never came close to winning—and he brought the Democratic Party into widespread disrepute.

The second half of the twentieth century seems to mark a third Awakening in America. The cultural "losers" of the Fundamentalist controversies of the 1920s retreated for a time, but then reemerged as a potent cultural force, led for many decades by the evangelist Billy Graham. Their effect on American politics has been striking, not least in the election in 2000—and reelection in 2004—of President George W. Bush, together with many of the policies he has advanced during his presidency.

It will be noticed, however, that a principal feature of these evangelical Awakenings has been the sudden rise and then no less sudden loss of energy. Hence the perpetual need for new Awakenings, new revivals. This is due to the dependence of revivalist Christianity on emotion in the absence of doctrine and institutional continuity. If a structure of Christian ideas is valid, it is so independent of emotion. In fact, its creedal formulations took centuries of concentrated thought to perfect. Such a structure of ideas is not in need of Awakenings.

So the evangelicalism of the Bush presidency presents American conservatism with a perplexity, and perhaps with a problem. *National Review* has always considered traditional religion integral to the American conservative mind, exploring that tradition through major writers past and present. One would have expected an *NR* symposium asking, in this light, "Is Evangelicalism Conservative?" Clearly, there remain fundamental questions for American conservatism—and *National Review*—to investigate and to answer.

WILFRED MCCLAY SEES THE MARK of President Bush's evangelicalism primarily in the "softer" elements of his policies: "No Child Left Behind," vastly increased AIDS funding for Africa, and, of course, faith-based initiatives aimed at reducing poverty. But there is no less religious fervor in the stated aims of Bush's foreign and strategic policy, which have proved a source of continuing controversy among conservatives.

Now, in the year 2005, we cannot know how the Iraq war will turn out, or what its ramifying effects will be for America down the road. Much that took place among policymakers preparatory to the war is still unknown; we have journalists' reports and some early memoirs, but so far no archival material and no definitive history. So the best approach here will be simply to record what *National Review* had to say about the Iraq war, with a glance first at the magazine's commentary on domestic policy during President Bush's first term.

National Review approved of Bush's stimulative supply-side tax cuts. Beyond that, however, it gave low scores to the failed immigration reform proposal. It regarded the "No Child Left Behind" education bill as over-promising in its goals, and also disapproved of its expansion of the federal role in education. The administration passed a Medicare prescription-drugs bill, which *National Review* considered to be a nightmare of cross-purposes in negotiations between the House and Senate, as summed up by Ramesh Ponnuru in the article "Pick Your Poison" (August 11, 2003). Then there was Bush's opposition to embryonic stem-cell research, and specifically his blocking of federal support for embryonic stem-cell lines created after August 2001, which the magazine strongly approved. In 2001 *National Review* had asked what "compassionate conservatism" might mean. Now it had its answer.

IN *THE RIGHT MAN*, Frum, a frequent *National Review* contributor, described a White House job interview he had soon after the January 2001 inauguration. Chief speechwriter Michael Gerson told Frum that Bush was going to remove Saddam Hussein from power: as Frum observes, this would prove a prophetic remark. In a *Vanity Fair* interview with Sam Tanenhaus published in May 2003, Assistant Secretary of Defense Paul Wolfowitz stated that it was "for reasons that have a lot to do with the U.S. government bureaucracy" that the administration emphasized "weapons of mass destruction" as the rationale for the Iraq war.

National Review observed with joy the unfolding military campaigns after 9/11, beginning with Afghanistan, as the high-tech invasion smashed the Taliban and destroyed the al-Qaeda bases. Early on, this joy was reflected in the editorial "Eloquence and Force" (December 3, 2001), which contained two items of particular importance:

> *The president and his planners say that Afghanistan is only Phase One of this war* [italics added]. Even Osama bin Laden, whose humiliation and death was one of our prime war aims, is only a pustule on the diseased body of the Middle East. After Afghanistan comes Iraq, which has been nursing its grievances and building germ and atomic weapons for ten years. After it comes Saudi Arabia, which, with its mysterious and still unexplained bin Laden connections, is the financial reservoir for terror. The Saudi royal family must understand that their days of indolence and irresponsibility are over. Whether they can transform themselves into competent rulers and reliable friends remains to be seen.

Certainly this editorial was correct that Iraq would follow Afghanistan—and when it warned that "there is a lot of work, sorrow, and nasty surprises ahead." The editorial also said that our ultimate goal—though it took the claim of WMD at face value—was to cure through modernization and democratization the "diseased body of the Middle East." In this, *National Review* correctly described the policy of the Bush administration.

After this editorial, and for some twenty-nine months, until the editorial "An End to Illusion" (May 3, 2004), the magazine followed the war with a series of editorials, along the way expressing first troubled doubt and then grim determination as the Iraq situation deteriorated badly. According to "An End to Illusion,"

> Secretary of Defense Donald Rumsfeld denied the obvious fact of a guerilla resistance and compared it to street crime in the United States. Every piece of good news was described as a turning of the corner, even as the insurgency remained stubbornly strong. . . . It is easy to pick at what seem to have been errors in the occupation. There probably were not enough troops. The administration probably was not ready for the magnitude of the task that rebuilding and occupying of Iraq would present.

This editorial said the "illusion" constituted "an underestimation in general of the difficulty of implanting democracy in alien soil, and an overestimation in particular of the sophistication of what is fundamentally still a tribal society and one devastated by decades of tyranny. This was largely, if not entirely, a Wilsonian mistake."

We Shall Prevail (2003), a collection of speeches by President Bush edited by *National Review* managing editor Jay Nordlinger, includes an address Bush made to the American Enterprise Institute on February 26, 2003. In that lecture, Bush put forward the following theory:

> Human cultures can be vastly different. Yet the human heart desires the same good things, everywhere on earth. In our desire to be safe from brutal and bullying oppression, human beings are the same. For these fundamental reasons, freedom and democracy will always and everywhere have greater appeal than the slogans of hatred and the tactics of terror.

Lowry, in a syndicated column of February 23, 2004, described this interpretation of the world scene, and the policy directives that emerged from it, as a "reinvigorated Wilsonian foreign policy," reflecting the religious beliefs of President Bush's evangelical base. (Lowry himself is not a Wilsonian and wrote a Spring 2005 *National Interest* essay attacking Wilsonians.) Others have seen the Wilsonianism here as neoconservative in inspiration, AEI being a neoconservative think tank. In any case, Bush added concerted military force to Woodrow Wilson's optimistic universalism.

Between the editorials "Eloquence and Force" and "An End to Illusion," the basic question might have been asked: Is hard Wilsonianism itself, whether the original version or one ramped up with religious fervor, *conservative?*

WITH THE 2004 PRESIDENTIAL ELECTION two weeks away, Rich Lowry's article "What Went Wrong?" appeared in the October 25, 2004, *National Review*. This represented the defining statement of the magazine on the Iraq war as of that date, covering seven double-column pages and based on many interviews with relevant officials in the Bush administration. I counted the things that "went wrong" as reported in this article and found twenty-two of importance. Lowry provides a summary:

> The story of Iraq post-war is, in part, a tale of gross intelligence failures, debilitating intramural battles, miscommunications, unintended consequences, and counterproductive half-measures. . . . *The Bush administration didn't know*

what it was getting into in Iraq, and then found itself stumbling into exactly the sort of heavy-handed occupation many officials hoped to avoid. [italics added]

This very fine piece of reporting by Lowry represents a withering criticism of the Bush execution of the Iraq project. Nevertheless, he concludes: "For all that, the administration still hasn't lost Iraq and, if it stays the course, may well prevail." *National Review* endorsed Bush-Cheney for reelection in 2004, although not without reservations:

> Bush relied on flawed intelligence about Iraq's weapons of mass destruction. When the error became apparent, he did not admit it forthrightly and explain to the American public why regime change was nonetheless necessary. Bush allowed bickering between departments of his administration to complicate post-war operations. He backed off Fallujah in April, with grave consequences. Bush's diplomacy toward Europe has lacked vigor and far-sightedness. If Bush understands that continued European integration would deprive us of many of the allies we still have, he has shown no evidence of it. The ideological component of the war on terrorism should be stronger.

At the time of the 2004 election, it had been established that no weapons of mass destruction had existed in Iraq at the time of the invasion, and also that Saddam's regime had no serious connections with al-Qaeda. Yet about half of American voters thought that Saddam Hussein had something to do with 9/11. In much of the commentary on the war by columnists and editorial writers, the fact that there were no WMD within Iraq's borders seemed to drop from the discussion, the original rationale for the war in effect forgotten, as the Bush administration emphasized democratization and freedom as America's war aims.

The Bush administration argued repeatedly that "democracies" are inherently peaceful, and so the way to ensure America's security from terrorism was to bring democracy to the Middle East—though as political developments crept along in Baghdad, the standard of "democracy" became somewhat more flexible, more culturally conditioned, less universalistic. The war went on with varying degrees of violence, as some 10,000 insurgents with no weapons heavier than a howitzer, together with land mines and suicide bombers, tied down 150,000 United States troops armed with the most modern weaponry. The bill for the war reached some $300 billion early in 2005.

Among conservatives, George Will, former *National Review* Washington correspondent, wrote that, "in American politics, optimism is mandatory, even—no, especially—when it is dubious. Everybody has a game face on. Too bad this is not a game." He compared Prime Minister Alawi with Kerensky, who held power in Russia until the Bolsheviks shoved him aside. Will concluded that when Alawi addressed Congress he would face "an audience that is sadder, and perhaps wiser, than it was 14 months ago." John Eisenhower, son of the president and collaborator on his writing, a lifelong Republican, announced that he would vote for John Kerry.

In a September 14, 2004, column titled "Dead Ahead," Buckley concluded that "in relation to the overall threat we now face [in Iraq], an effort hugely greater in scale and more refined in conception is required to signal our determination to take on the disease wherever it is nurtured." He judged that no such huge effort would be made. In a subsequent column, "Algeria Warned Us" (October 26, 2004), nine days before the election, Buckley compared our war in Iraq with the losing French battle in Algeria under similar circumstances. He concluded that the "insurrectionists in Iraq can't be defeated by any means that we would consent to use." Both columns took a dim overall view of the war.

In his September 27, 2004, *Newsweek* column, George Will made the point that "the idea—a tenet of neoconservatism—is that all nations are more or less ready for democracy. So nation-building should be a piece of cake—never mind the winding, arduous, uphill hike the West took from Runnymede and Magna Carta in 1215 to Philadelphia in 1787." Surely Iraq had proven to be an intellectual disaster for neoconservative naïveté, hard reality making a hash of the clean contours of speculative theory.

The conservative *Economist* magazine, American circulation 450,000, delivered its endorsement for president in an editorial titled "The Incompetent versus the Incoherent." Very reluctantly, the *Economist* endorsed Kerry, arguing that the United States needed a "change."

After President Bush's reelection, in its November 15, 2004, issue, the *New Yorker* carried an interview with Buckley, much of it dealing with the state of American conservatism. Buckley declared that the Bush victory had prevented a serious rethinking of conservatism. As shown here, thoughtful conservatives were all over the map about President Bush. *National Review*, for its part, had given low grades to Bush's domestic policy, and had wondered "what went wrong?" in Iraq. (After the election, Lowry wrote a follow-up titled, "What Went Right.")

On Election Day, 2004, Bush won a convincing but narrow victory, 279-252 in electoral votes, 51-48 percent (a 2.5 percent spread) in the popular vote. Analysis of state-by-state results and exit polling showed that as a war-time "leader," Bush outscored Kerry. Perhaps what this meant was that Bush had shown he could pull the trigger, whereas Kerry and his party were still not convincing about that. Now the House, the Senate, and the White House were in Republican hands. The margin of Bush's victories in 2000 and in 2004 had been small, and, as history shows, second-term overreach is a distinct possibility, even as the Wilsonian war in Iraq grinds on.

26

The American Conservative Mind: Where We Are Now

In *The Conservative Mind* (1953), one of the founding documents of the American conservative movement, Russell Kirk assembled an array of major conservative thinkers beginning with Burke and, by virtually anthologizing long passages, made a major statement. He proved that conservative thought in America *existed*, and even that such thought was highly *intelligent*, a demonstration very much needed at the time.

Today we are in a very different and more complicated situation. Nevertheless, it is possible to attempt a synthesis based on what *National Review* has achieved, and left unachieved, and on how the magazine has interacted with history since 1955. The political philosopher presiding over this synthesis will be Edmund Burke, the founder of modern conservatism, but a Burke interpreted for a new constitutional republic and, today, for modern life. This synthesis, needless to say, is my own and itself can be assessed as it attempts to cover the facts.

Over its fifty-year history, *National Review* has taken many a political position but also, and more lastingly, has taught conservatives *how to think*. Here, debate within the magazine has been the necessary condition; argument meeting with counterargument has been a refining fire. Any political position is only as important as the thought by which it is derived. Throughout its history, *National Review* has been tempted from time to time by a politics of wishing, or utopianism. Its mistakes have been instructive. That is, even the magazine's mistakes have assisted in the achievement of a normative conservatism, described by Buckley as the "politics of reality." It has been the process of trying to achieve a "politics of reality" that made *National Review* over the years the most interesting magazine of its kind in the United States. And so we proceed to my attempt at a synthesis.

1. *Hard Utopianism*. During the twentieth century, national socialism and communism tried to effect versions of their Perfect Man in the Perfect Society. One of *National Review*'s most noble enterprises from its beginning was its informed anticommunism. As Pascal had written, "Man is neither angel nor brute, and the misfortune is that he who would act the angel acts the brute." In abstract theory was born the gulag.

2. *Soft Utopianism*. Both hard and soft utopianism ignore flawed human nature. Soft utopianism believes in benevolent illusions, most abstractly stated in the proposition that all goals are reconcilable, as in such dreams as The Family of Man, World Peace, multiculturalism, pacifism, and Wilsonian global democracy. To all of these the conservative mind objects. Men do not all desire the same things: domination is a powerful desire. The phrase about the lion lying down with the lamb, adapted from Isaiah, is commonly quoted; but Isaiah knew that his vision of peace would take divine intervention, not at all to be counted on. Without such intervention, the lion dines well.

3. *The Nation*. Soft utopianism speaks of the "nation-state" as if it were a passing nuisance. But the conservative mind knows that there must be much that is valid in the idea of the nation, because nations are rooted in history. Arising out of tribes, ancient cosmological empires, theocracies, city-states, imperial systems, feudal organization, we now have the nation. Imperfect as the nation may be, it alone—as far as we know—can protect many of the basic elements of civilized existence. Hegel rather thunderously argued that the nation and its freedoms are the goal of history. He might have been wrong, but that he was wrong has yet to be shown.

4. *National Defense*. It follows that national defense remains a necessity, threatened almost always by "lie-down-with-the-lambism," as well as by recurrent, and more obviously hostile, hard utopianisms. In the earliest nar-

ratives of the West, both the Greek *Iliad* and the Hebrew Pentateuch, wars are central. Soft utopianism often has encouraged more frequent wars, since it tempts irresistibly the lion's claws and teeth. *National Review*, most of the time, has shown a healthy resistance to utopianism and its various informing ideologies. Ideology is always wrong because it edits reality and paralyzes thought.

5. *Constitutional Government.* Depending on English tradition and classical theory, the American founders designed a government that would express the "deliberate sense" of the people. The "sense" originated with the people, but it was made "deliberate" by the delaying institutions built into the constitutional structure. This system aims at government not by majorities alone but by stable consensus, because under the Constitution major changes almost always require a consensus that lasts over a considerable period of time. Though the Supreme Court stands as constitutional arbiter, it is not a legislature. The correct workings of the system depend upon mutual restraint among the branches. And the Court, which is the weakest of the three (see esp. Article III, Sec. 2, Para. 2 of the Constitution), should behave with due modesty toward the legislature. The legislature is the closest of the three to "We the people," who are the basis of legitimacy in a free society. Legislation is more easily revised or repealed than a Court ruling, and therefore judicial restraint is necessary.

6. *Free-Market Economics.* Carrying this banner high, *National Review* emerged during a period when socialism in various forms had become a tacit orthodoxy. The thought of Hayek, Mises, and Friedman, among others, informed the magazine's understanding of economic questions. At length, the free market triumphed through much of the world, and today there are no, or very few, socialists in major university economics departments, an almost total transformation since 1955. But the utopian temptation can turn such free-market thought into a utopianism of its own—that is, free markets to be effected even while excluding every other value and purpose, such as . . .

7. *Beauty*, broadly defined. The desire for beauty may be natural to human beings as such, like other natural desires. It appeared early, as in the prehistoric cave murals. In literature (for example, in Dante) and in other

forms of representation—painting, sculpture, music, architecture—Heaven is always beautiful, Hell ugly. Beauty may thus even have a theological dimension, as Hans Urs von Balthasar has argued. Plato taught that the love of beauty led to the good, *Eros* to *Agape*. Among the nonquantifiable needs of civilization are forms of what Burke called the "*unbought* grace of life," a memorable phrase from a man whom Adam Smith said was the only one in England who understood his free-market economics. In Burke's formulation, the word "unbought" should be pondered.

In *National Review* this conservative principle, beauty, has been clamorously *present* through its almost total *absence*, except for the Books, Arts and Manners section. This has been a major omission, though briefly remedied by Senator James Buckley, who continued the tradition of regard for woodland and wildlife, present from the beginning of the nation in such eighteenth-century figures as explorer, naturalist, and artist William Bartram of Philadelphia, and continuing through famous exemplars like John James Audubon, contemporary of Tocqueville, the Republican president Theodore Roosevelt, who established the national parks, and in a small but laudable way Russell Kirk, who planted hundreds of trees near his home in Mecosta for future generations to enjoy after his passing.

In its great buildings, which are history in stone, New York City would now lack most of the works of McKim, Mead and White, for example, were it not for the efforts of the Landmarks Preservation movement. Embarrassingly for conservatives (one hopes it is embarrassing), this was founded by liberal Democrats, such as Daniel Patrick Moynihan, Brendan Gill, and Jacqueline Kennedy, and continues to consist mostly of liberal Democrats. Not all ideas and initiatives put forward by liberals are bad ones. Burke's "unbought" beauties are part of civilized life, and therefore ought to occupy much of the conservative mind. The absence of this consideration remains a mark of yahooism and is prominent in Republicanism today.

Momentarily noticed by *National Review*, Governor Reagan had a good record on conservation in California, appointing leading conservationists to key positions, preserving wilderness areas in the Sierra Nevada and elsewhere, blocking unnecessary and destructive highway development and much else of that kind. Yet as if by an intrinsic law, when the free market becomes a kind of utopianism it maximizes ordinary human imperfection, unleashing greed, short views, and the resulting barbarism.

8. *Religion.* From its beginning, *National Review* has known that religion is an integral part of the distinctive identity of Western civilization, this recognition manifesting itself in the magazine as support for traditional forms of religion—repeat, *traditional*, or intellectually and institutionally developed, not dependent upon spasms of emotion. This meant religion in its magisterial Protestant, Catholic, and Jewish forms.

The magazine, to its credit, editorially criticized Catholic political pronouncements on virtually all World War III questions, including *Pacem in Terris* and *Mater et Magistra* (recall "Mater, Sí! Magistra, No!") as well as stands taken by the American Catholic bishops that were strategically suicidal. The magazine criticized *Humanae Vitae*, which reaffirmed the ban on artificial birth control, a ban widely ignored. Such teachings tend to discredit the valid core doctrines of traditional Christianity. What the time calls for is a recovery of the great structure of metaphysics, with the Resurrection as its fulcrum, established as history, and interpreted through Greek philosophy. The representation of this metaphysics through language and ritual took ten centuries to perfect. The dome of the sacred, however, has been shattered. The act of reconstruction will require a large effort of *intellect*, which is never populist and certainly not grounded on emotion, an unreliable guide. Religion not based on a structure of thought always exhibits wild inspired swings and fades in a generation or two.

9. *Abortion.* This has been a focus of conservative, and national, attention since *Roe v. Wade* (1973). Yet abortion as an issue, its availability indeed as a widespread demand, did not arrive from nowhere. One of *National Review*'s conservative guideposts had been Burke's thought, including his sense of the complexity of society, and at the same time his sense of the great power and complexity of forces driving important social processes and changes. Nevertheless, *National Review* recently has defended the "right to life" of a single-cell embryo, and it has criticized those conservative political figures who disagree with that view.

But a total ban on abortion, to put it flatly, is not going to happen. Too many powerful social forces are aligned against it, and it is therefore a utopian notion. The abortion question deserves a Burkean analysis. *Roe* relocated decision-making about abortion from state governments to the individual woman, and was thus a *libertarian* ruling. *Planned Parenthood v. Casey* (1992) supported *Roe*, but gave it a social dimension, making the woman's choice a derivative of the women's revolution: the "advancement of women," as *Casey* put it.

According to statistics available from the Centers for Disease Control, 83 percent of optional abortions take place during the first trimester. That abortion must be criminalized even during the first trimester is surely a utopian notion. The women's revolution has been the result of many accumulating social facts, as Burke would see, and such social facts would not be difficult to enumerate. The women's revolution already has been largely assimilated. Since the beginning of the twentieth century, the United States has steadily urbanized, and suburbanized; living conditions now are radically different from those that persisted in a largely rural country. Women's suffrage was an issue in the election of 1912 but today is taken for granted. Women today work in all the professions, also serving in the military. Their career preparation often lasts years. They will not surrender control of their reproductive capacity.

By 1973 and *Roe*, the women's revolution reflected a relentlessly changing social actuality. Simply to pull an abstract "right to life" out of the Declaration of Independence, as some conservatives do, is not conservative but Jacobinical. To be sure, the *Roe* decision was certainly an example of judicial overreach. Combined with *Casey*, however, it did address the reality of the women's revolution, a social process with deep roots in actuality. The question now is whether *Roe*, more than thirty years old and reaffirmed by many lower court decisions, will stand; and, if *Roe* is overturned, then what rules might issue from fifty state legislatures. No doubt in 1973 the Court should have deferred to the jurisdiction of the states. But a checkerboard of state legislation might merely increase the value of Greyhound Bus stock.

10. *Wilsonianism.* The Republican Party now presents itself as the party of *Hard Wilsonianism*, which is no more plausible than the original Soft Wilsonianism that Balkanized Central Europe with dire consequences. No one has ever thought Wilsonianism to be conservative—certainly *National*

Review never has, even recently—ignoring as it does the density and intractability of culture and people's high valuation of a *modus vivendi*. Wilsonianism derives from the Lockean and Rousseauian belief in the fundamental goodness of mankind and hence in a convergence of interests: "The human heart desires the same good things everywhere on earth," as George W. Bush decelared in February 2003. Welcome to Iraq. Whereas realism counsels great prudence in complex cultural situations, Wilsonianism rushes optimistically ahead. Not every country is Denmark.

At this writing, the fighting in Iraq has gone on for more than two years, and the ultimate result of "democratization" in that fractured nation remains very much in doubt, as does the long-range influence of the Iraq invasion on conditions in the Middle East as a whole. In general, Wilsonianism is a snare and a delusion as a guide to policy, and far from conservative.

11. *The Republican Party. National Review* has assumed since its founding in 1955 that this political party is by and large conservative. But this party has stood for many and various things in the course of its history. The nation at the present time exhibits a strange configuration. A recent analysis in the *Economist* showed the American polity to be polarized, with support for the Democratic Party at 31 percent, the Republican Party at 30 percent, and independents at 39 percent. On the issues, this analysis found that "most Americans have fairly centrist views on everything from multilateralism to abortion. They like to think of themselves as 'moderate' and 'nonjudgmental.'" Then why does moderation not rule? Because, this analysis concludes, a growing proportion of Democrats comes from deep-blue congressional districts where it is more important to pander to the liberal base than to seek a moderate consensus. And Bush's electoral strategies depended upon consolidation of his base rather than upon a wide appeal, and in consequence it issued in narrow victories.

The Republican Party has changed in the past: for example, in 1912, when the party of William Howard Taft and the reform party of Theodore Roosevelt in effect rejected one another. The Republican Party changed again in 1964, when its center of gravity shifted to the South and the Sunbelt, now politically the solid base of "Republicanism." All the consequences of that shift could not have been foreseen in 1964, but they perhaps were already sensed inchoately in 1963–64, as we have seen here, by Burnham and Buckley. The implications of that profound cultural shift have now become evident, especially with respect to prudence, long views, education, intellect, and high culture. The seismic geographical-political shift of 1963–64 eventually produced an example of Machiavelli's observation that institutions can retain the same outward name and aspect while transforming their substance entirely.

12. *The Presidency*. In the relatively recent past, Franklin Roosevelt, Dwight Eisenhower, and Ronald Reagan have been consensus-building presidents, each winning reelection by large margins. Each was essentially prudent, and each achieved his goals. Each, in his time, was conservative. In 1955, *National Review* rebelled retrospectively against FDR's modest welfare state, but Eisenhower, against his personal inclination, accepted the New Deal reality. On that, Whittaker Chambers, Willmoore Kendall, and James Burnham essentially agreed. Roosevelt, fending off extremists from right and left, ameliorated the Depression with a center-left coalition and large injections of cash into the economy, and then orchestrated an international coalition to win the war.

Franklin Roosevelt seems secure in his standing among the top ten American presidents, and Eisenhower and Reagan more recently have been placed there by many historians. *National Review* in 1956 was mistaken about Eisenhower, as was the Kennedy campaign in 1960. Eisenhower, behind a deliberately created benign persona, contributed greatly to the development of U.S. weapons systems, was willing to threaten nuclear war with China when there was little risk in carrying out the threat, stayed out of Vietnam when implored by the French to intervene, and refused to bail out the British and French at Suez. In what he did *not* do abroad, as well as what he *did* do, Eisenhower demonstrated a prudential conservatism.

THAT COMPLETES THE PARADIGM that evolved through my reading of *National Review*, in the contexts of both history and conservative political theory, from the beginning of the magazine through the present. By its very adventures with ideology and utopianism, *National Review* has shown, by deviating yet correctable lunges, that the conservative mind is a work in progress. Its guides in self-correction have always consisted of prudence, reserved judgment as an operative principle, a healthy practical skepticism, and the requirement of historical knowledge as a guide to prudent policy. Without a deep knowledge of history, policy analysis is feckless.

And it follows that the teachings of books that have lasted are essential to the conservative mind, these books lasting because of their agreements, disagreements, and creative resolutions. It is not enough for conservatives to repeat formulae or party-line positions. The mind must possess the process that leads to conservative decisions. There is no substitute for Aristotle vs. Plato, Luther vs. Erasmus, Burke versus himself—as well as against the abstractionist *philosophes* of the Rights of Man.

One of the electrifying moments in the history of thought occurred toward the end of 1516, when Erasmus, then a predominant intellectual power in Europe and dominating through the new medium made possible by Gutenberg, received via diplomatic pouch a letter from an obscure German Augustinian monk named Martin Luther. Especially alert to the power of sin, Luther advised the most influential writer in Christendom to pay more attention to Paul's Epistle to the Romans, especially its implications for *justification*, and to study Saint Augustine. Erasmus's Catholic humanism was at stake. He advised everyone, including Pope Julius II, to forbear and have patience with Luther; but when Luther denied free will, Erasmus attacked him philosophically. Luther and Erasmus were to contest the future of Christianity at that great juncture, a future that today remains far from settled, as traditional Christianity, while possessing a strong metaphysics and ways of expressing it, has been helpless to achieve similar success in its recommendations within a changing social reality where people make their ethical decisions based on experience.

As a guide, the books, and the results of experience, may be the more difficult way—much more difficult in a given moment than the recommendations of precooked dogma or a party line, which are always irresistible to the uneducated. Learning guards against having to reinvent the wheel in political theory from one generation to the next.

National Review has been a great model, vigorous always, through mistakes and self-corrections, from November 1955 forward. If read as a single book, all of those bound volumes from 1955 forward constitute one of the great works of conservative thought and experience. For the things of this world, the philosophy of William James, so distinctively American, might be the best guide, a philosophy always open to experience and judging by experience within given conditions—the experience pleasurable or, more often, painful, but utopia always a distant and destructive mirage. The ship of *National Review* sails on, taking on water sometimes, but never smashing to bits on the rocks.

Notes

Introduction to Paperback Edition

1. Richard Lowry, "Reaganites and Neoreaganites," *National Interest* (Spring 2005).
2. Jon Eisenberg, *Using Terri* (Harper: San Francisco, 2005.) This provides an excellent account of the medical, legal, and political aspects of the case.
3. David Frum, *The Right Man* (New York: Random House, 2003), 26. During a job interview, White House chief speechwriter Michael Gerson told Frum that Bush would overthrow Saddam. Frum called this prophetic. See *The Making of the American Conservative Mind*, 352.
4. *The Constitution in Crisis* can be obtained online from the office of Rep. John Conyers. Pages 53 ff. deal with Bush's WMD claims.
5. The conclusions of the Democratic staff of the House Judiciary Committee are supported by an accumulating body of evidence, for example:

    a. James Risen, *State of War: The Secret History of the CIA and the Bush Administration* (New York: Free Press, 2006). Chapter 4 deals with WMD and the supposed evidence.

    b. Thomas Powers's review of Risen's book (*New York Review of Books*, February 23, 2006). Powers is a recognized intelligence expert and has written a biography of Richard Helms as well as *Heisenberg's War* (New York: Knopf, 1993), about Germany's nuclear effort, and a history of modern intelligence. In this long review-essay, part 3 deals with Risen's fifth chapter. Regarding WMD, Powers uses the word "fabricated."

    c. Paul Pillar, "Unheeded Intelligence" (*Foreign Affairs*, March-April 2006) Editorial summary: "During the run-up to the invasion of Iraq, writes the intelligence community's former senior analyst for the Middle East, the Bush administration disregarded the community's expertise, politicized the intelligence process, and selected unrepresentative raw intelligence to make its public case."

    d. John W. Dean, *Worse Than Watergate* (New York: Little, Brown, 2004). This book is thoroughly documented, footnoted, and irrefutable about the falsity of WMD claims. I think the book probably lost some credibility because of Dean's connection with Watergate and Nixon. Because of the book's exploitative title, I myself would have disregarded it had I not read Dean's *Warren Harding,* also published in 2004 in the series on presidents edited by Arthur Schlesinger. Dean is a good historian and calls himself a "Goldwater Republican."

    e. Other intelligence agencies did *not* agree with the Bush WMD claims. The *Los Angeles Times* reported that the Germans had "Curveball," a former Iraqi engineer, in custody and considered him not only unreliable but probably a mental case.

    f. Con Coughlin, *American Ally: Tony Blair and the War on Terrorism* (New York: Echo, 2006). Blair hoped to make a documented case to the public for war with Iraq. But, "The difficulty he faced was underlined when he had to abandon plans to publish a dossier on Saddam's WMD, because it did not contain sufficient evidence to support military action." (218). Blair stuck with Bush for political reasons. He conceived of Britain as a "bridge" between the Continent and the United States, and did not want England to be alone with a Continent dominated by Germany and France.

    g. Mark Danner, *The Secret Way to War: The Downing Street Memo and the Iraq War's Buried History* (New York: New York Review Books, 2006). "C," the head of British intelligence, reported to Blair after a visit to Washington that "intelligence and facts were being fixed around policy" as early as July 2002.

Chapter 1: William F. Buckley Jr.: Present at the Creation

1. George H. Nash, *The Conservative Intellectual Movement in America since 1945* (New York: Basic Books, 1976), 153.
2. Neils Bjerre-Poulsen, *Right Face: Organizing the American Conservative Movement, 1945–65.* (Copenhagen: University of Copenhagen Press, 2002), 116.
3. Ibid., 124.
4. Letter of Whittaker Chambers to William F. Buckley Jr., April 6, 1954, in *Odyssey of a Friend* (Washington, DC: Regnery, 1987).
5. William F. Buckley Jr., "A Distinctive Gentility," in *Miles Gone By: A Literary Autobiography* (Washington, DC: Regnery, 2004).

Chapter 2: James Burnham: Power

1. Daniel Kelly, *James Burnham and the Struggle for the World: A Life* (Wilmington, DE: ISI Books, 2002), 227. Throughout I am dependent on Kelly's definitive biography of James Burnham, which supplements information I have

had from Burnham himself and from mutual acquaintances.
2. Ibid., 205.
3. Ibid.

Chapter 3: Willmoore Kendall: Perhaps Too, Too . . .

1. "Kendall-Strauss Correspondence," in *Willmoore Kendall: Maverick of American Conservatives,* eds. John A. Murley and John E. Alvis (Lanham, MD: Lexington, 2002), 218.
2. Ibid., 201.
3. Buckley conversation with Jeffrey Hart.
4. Buckley, *Miles Gone By*, 286.

Chapter 4: Russell Kirk vs. Frank Meyer

1. For some details of Meyer's biography, especially of these early years and through his break with the Communist Party, I have drawn on Kevin Smant, *Principles and Heresies: Frank S. Meyer and the Shaping of the American Conservative Movement* (Wilmington: ISI Books, 2002), ch. 1.
2. For my discussion of the reception of *The Conservative Mind* I draw on Nash, *The Conservative Intellectual Movement in America*, 74–76.
3. The discussion of Kirk's early biography is based on Nash, *The Conservative Intellectual Movement in America*, 69–77.

Chapter 5: Arriving Talent

1. *The Joys of National Review, 1955–1980*, compiled by Priscilla Buckley (New York: National Review Books, 1995), xv–xvi.
2. William F. Buckley Jr., *Getting It Right* (Washington, D.C.: Regnery, 2003), 201–203.
3. Nash, *The Conservative Intellectual Movement in America*, 37–41.
4. William F. Buckley Jr., "Life with a Meticulous Colleague," *Let Us Talk of Many Things* (Roseville, Calif.: Forum, 2003), 123–126.

Chapter 6: 1956: *NR*'s Education Begins

1. Stephen Ambrose, *Eisenhower: Soldier and President* (New York: Simon & Schuster, 1990), 334.
2. Kelly, *James Burnham and the Struggle for the World*, 232.
3. Fred I. Greenstein, *The Hidden-Hand Presidency: Eisenhower as Leader* (New York: Basic Books, 1982), viii.

4. Ibid., 9.
5. Ibid., 99.
6. Ibid., 44.
7. Ibid., 49.
8. Ibid., 49.
9. Ibid., 49–50.
10. Ibid., 50.
11. Ibid., 66.
12. Ambrose, *Eisenhower: Soldier and President*, 553–54.

Chapter 7: McCarthy: *National Review*'s Populist Agon

1. Kelly, *James Burnham and the Struggle for the World*, 184–92.
2. Bjere-Poulsen, *Right Face*, 59.
3. Willmoore Kendall, "Do We Want an Open Society?" *National Review* (January 31, 1959); *The Conservative Affirmation* (Chicago: Regnery, 1963), chaps. 3, 4, and 6.
4. The McCarthy history here draws from Thomas C. Reeves, *The Life and Times of Joe McCarthy: A Biography* (New York: Stein and Day, 1972) and David M. Oshinsky, *A Conspiracy So Immense* (New York: Free Press, 1983). The judgments made of McCarthy here are my own.
5. Thomas Powers, "Spy Fever," *New York Review of Books* (February 12, 2004).
6. I made a thorough analysis of the report as an independent project while in Naval Intelligence from 1953 to 1956. Many congressional investigations were sloppy. But that takes nothing away from this one; and indeed the questioning throughout was careful, even polite, and the documentation was ample. It should be read as a window on the period.
7. In *Acheson: The Secretary of State Who Created the American World* (New York: Simon & Schuster, 1998), James Chase says that asked about his reaction to the firing of MacArthur, Acheson replied with an anecdote: A man, with his wife and daughter, were obliged to buy a house near an army base because of his business with the army. The man and wife worried incessantly about the daughter's chastity. One day she came home in tears, saying that she was pregnant. The man commented, "Well, I'm glad that's over."
8. William F. Buckley Jr. and L. Brent Bozell, *McCarthy and His Enemies* (Chicago: Regnery, 1954), 388.
9. See Oshinsky, *A Conspiracy So Immense*, 200.
10. For an excellent reportorial account of the disarray, incompetence, and corruption of Chiang's operation in Chunking see Joseph Alsop, *I've Seen the Best of It* (New York: Putnam, 1992). Numerous reliable scholarly histories are available.

11. An enormous amount of historical scholarship exists regarding George Marshall, but I recommend the summarizing work that I have followed here: Mark A. Stoler, *George C. Marshall: Soldier-Statesman of the American Century* (Boston: Twayne, 1989).

Chapter 8: *National Review* and the Black Revolution

1. Paul D. Carrington, *Steward of Democracy: Law as a Public Profession* (Boulder, Colorado: Westview, 1999), 155.
2. Ibid., 156.
3. Ibid., 162.
4. Ibid., 162.
5. Ibid., 147.
6. John B. Judis, *William F. Buckley, Jr.: Patron Saint of Conservatives* (New York: Simon & Schuster, 1988), 322.

Chapter 9: *National Review* and Religion

1. See Jeffrey Hart, "The Great Narrative," in *Smiling through the Cultural Catastrophe* (New Haven, Conn.: Yale University Press, 2002), especially ch. 4, "Socrates and Jesus: Internalizing the Heroic." Socrates and Plato internalize the Homeric heroic as heroic philosophy; Jesus internalizes Moses and the Prophets as heroic holiness.
2. Robert Jastrow, *God and the Astronomers* (New York: Norton, 1978), 12–16. Here, Jastrow uses the figure 20 billion years for the age of the universe; in conversation, he has said that it is 17.5, according to recent scientific work. Arno Penzias and Robert Wilson made the earlier measurements in 1965 at the Bell Laboratories.
3. George Gilder, "The Message from the Microcosm," in *Microcosm* (New York: Simon & Schuster, 1989).
4. Hart, *Smiling through the Cultural Catastrophe*, 4–7.
5. That the Apostles Creed evolved over a long period of time, beginning very early, is clear enough, though the earliest indication of the existence of the creed as we know it appears in a treatise *Scarapius* by the monk Priminius (d. 753). It is, however mentioned by Ambrose in a letter (Ep. 42:5) written in approximately 390. This refers to a creed that developed out of the old Roman creed that developed by the end of the second century. Evidence for this exists in the interrogatory creed for baptism found in Hypolytus's *Apostolic Tradition* (ca. 215); in the creed given by Marcellus, the Bishop of Ancyra to Emperor Julius I (340); and the commentary on the Apostles Creed (ca. 404) by the monk Tyrannius Rufinius (345–410). In this commentary,

Rufinius includes the earliest continuous Latin text of the Apostles Creed as confessed at the Church of Aquileia. The earliest authorization of the creed appears to have been by the Emperor Charlemagne (742–814). The history of the creed in some form thus dates back to the earliest years of the church in the second century, and there is no reason not to connect it with the Apostles themselves, or at least the mind of the group concerning what it had experienced. See *The Harper Collins Encyclopedia of Catholicism* (San Francisco: Harper Collins, 1995).

Garry Wills, a former seminarian, adds considerably to this in *Why I Am a Catholic* (Boston: Houghton Mifflin, 2002), 299–302. The profession of faith during the time of the Apostles soon developed into an accepted form of the Apostles Creed, agreed upon before the Apostles left Jerusalem on separate missions. Each clause supposedly was contributed by a different Apostle. The tale of the contribution of each appeared in writing in 404. But modern scholarship traces the creed's core to a basic form used in baptism before 100. It was used as an interrogatory at baptism—"Do you believe, etc."—and is clearly connected with Matthew 28:19. Additions were made during the second century in order to combat the heresy of Gnosticism. Augustine required that it be memorized by those being baptized, though he helped those who stumbled, and also considered daily recitation a form of re-baptism. Aquinas was disturbed because his transcription had fourteen articles instead of twelve. He apparently resolved this to his satisfaction. The Apostles Creed is used here as an example of verbal representation of Things Unseen; the Nicene Creed could have been used to the same purpose.

6. Richard Hooker (1554–1600), *The Laws of Ecclesiastical Polity*. One of the great works of the Church of England, and of English prose, this work includes few variations from traditional Christian theology, though the Book of Common Prayer in Elizabethan times, for obvious reasons, added the queen to its liturgy. Unfortunately, Hooker's church lacked the central authority to preserve its (correct) doctrine of Things Unseen over the centuries.

Chapter 10: JFK: The Nightingale's Song

1. Judis, *William F. Buckley, Jr.*, 234.
2. Robert Dallek, *An Unfinished Life: John F. Kennedy, 1917–1963* (Boston: Little Brown, 2000). Dallek was the first historian to examine all of the John F. Kennedy health records at the Kennedy Library, and his list is the most comprehensive available. Thomas C. Reeves, in *A Question of Character: A Life of John F. Kennedy* (New York: Free Press, 1991), 294–295, also discusses Kennedy's illnesses. See also Michael Beschloss, *The Crisis Years: Kennedy and Khrushchev, 1960–1963* (New York: Harper Collins, 1991), 187–191.

3. Reeves, 273.
4. Stephen Ambrose, *Eisenhower: Soldier and President* (New York: Simon & Schuster, 1999), 453–454.
5. Beschloss, *The Crisis Years,* 575.
6. Reeves, *A Question of Character,* 278.

Chapter 12: The John Birch Society: A Menace

1. Judis, *William F. Buckley, Jr.,* 193–194. I have found Mr. Judis valuable throughout this chapter. Buckley's novel *Getting It Right* has also been valuable, especially for its portraits of Welch, Oliver, and other top Birchers.

Chapter 13: Farewell, Willmoore

1. I have mentioned the importance of his edition of Rousseau's *Government of Poland* (Indianapolis: Bobbs-Merrill, 1972). Its great importance lies in the fact that it shows in a new light a very important writer. Ordinarily we consider Rousseau's politics, as in his *Social Contract*, to consist of a radical republicanism that declares all existing European governments illegitimate. This is the radicalism that Burke and Samuel Johnson loathed and that inspired many French revolutionaries, such as Robespierre and St. Just. But *Government of Poland*, little known, severely qualifies, if it does not contradict, the views of many regarding Rousseau. And, as Kendall says in his long and intricately argued introduction, it is "certainly shrewd and sharp as anything Rousseau has bequeathed to us." Tantalizingly, Kendall wonders whether Burke, "had he read the *Poland*, would have hailed Rousseau as the other great Tory of the century." In his complex reading, things may be more complicated than that. But this is an important consideration of a major text by a major writer, and Kendall has performed a great service in bringing it forward.

   As Harvey Mansfield Jr. says in his preface to the 1985 edition, "Rousseau says on his first page that 'one must know thoroughly the nation for which one is building,' and he proceeds to prescribe for Poland's politics and constitution with a view always to the character of the Polish nation. Rousseau was the first political philosopher to prescribe in this manner by taking the nation as a given fact, to which the politics must adjust, rather than as a product of politics, which legislators can remake. . . . Rousseau's legislator must 'move men's hearts.' . . ." With that, Mansfield of course notices a problem. "How can Rousseau's prudent advice to Poland be consistent with his insistence (in *The Social Contract*) that only the best state is legitimate?"

   To this looming question, Kendall provides a brilliant double answer.

First, he argues that in the *Republic* Plato provides a theoretical model of the best polis, a model based on pure theory and the priority of the soul, whereas in the *Laws* he prescribes for the actual Athens. Rousseau's *Social Contract*, writes Kendall, stands to the *Poland* in exactly the same relationship as the *Republic* to the *Laws*.

While one is enjoying that solution, Kendall has something else up his sleeve, based on a very close reading of the text of the *Poland*. Rousseau also advises for Poland, and universally, always with conditions and prudence governing, a "republic in the heart" as a guiding model to which Poland and other nations should bend their efforts. This renders the famous opening of the *Social Contract*, that "Man is born free but is everywhere in chains," not a radical injunction to return to a state of nature, but an invitation to make the "chains," that is, civilization, legitimate.

In Kendall's reading, the *Poland* becomes a major document in the history of political theory, and his reading itself a major achievement. His is not the understanding of Rousseau that we find in Burke, Johnson, Babbitt, Kirk, or other demonizers of Rousseau, who had never heard of the *Poland*. But it now must be taken into account.

Chapter 14: *Not* All the Way with LBJ

1. Robert Dallek, *Lyndon B. Johnson: Portrait of a President* (New York: 2004), 168–70.
2. Stanley Karnow, *Vietnam: A History* (New York: Penguin, 1997), 558. On this subject a great deal of controversy exists. This book seems to me to make a strenuous effort to achieve objectivity.
3. Jules Witcover, *The Year the Dream Died: Revisiting 1968 in America* (New York: Warner, 1977), 153.
4. Ibid., 223.
5. Ibid., 219.

Chapter 16: Nixon: In the Arena

1. Richard Whalen, *Catch the Falling Flag* (Boston: Houghton Mifflin, 1972), 138.
2. Tom Wicker, *One of Us: Richard Nixon and the American Dream* (New York: Random House, 1991), 597. Tom Wicker is widely known as a *New York Times* columnist of liberal views. This book is a scholarly effort free from preconceptions, a mild surprise to those familiar with his column, but writing history does introduce an element of salutary professional responsibility.
3. Ibid., 599.

4. John Ehrlichman, *Witness to Power* (New York: Simon and Schuster, 1982), 316.

Chapter 17: Watergate: Nixon X-Rayed

1. An amusing incident happened with regard to those tapes. Early in 1971, if memory serves me, I was working on an article about the 1968 campaign and had an appointment to see Nixon in the Oval Office. Due to something happening in the Middle East, Dean Acheson and Tom Dewey were waiting on the bench across from me in that small room or corridor outside, and I had to wait for half an hour while they went in and conferred with Nixon; they looked exactly like Dean Acheson and Tom Dewey, a generic phenomenon that always surprises me. When I finally went in, I took a seat alongside Nixon's (Wilson's) desk and put my tape recorder on it. At that point, Bob Haldeman, who had stayed in the room, rushed over and exclaimed, "The President is never recorded in the Oval Office." I suppose that admonition is somewhere on the miles of tape. At the time, I felt like a crude know-nothing—Washington, Lincoln, all of them looking at me as if to wonder how I could have been so foolish.

Chapter 19: Ford Transition: Populism Growls at *NR*

1. Richard Reeves, *A Ford, Not a Lincoln* (New York: Harcourt Brace Jovanovich, 1975), 69. For details of Ford's career prior to the presidency I am indebted to Reeves.

Chapter 20: Reagan to Ford to Carter: Bouncing Ball

1. Kelly, *James Burnham and the Struggle for the World*. Details regarding Burnham's final illness and other matters may be found in this excellent biography.

Chapter 21: What We All Worked For

1. Peter Robinson, "Morning Again in America," Hoover Digest (no. 3, 2004), 23.

Chapter 22: Reagan: The World Transformed

1. Peter Robinson, *How Ronald Reagan Changed My Life* (New York: Harper Collins, 2003). My discussion of the four key Reagan speeches depends on Robinson. Overall, Robinson's book is a remarkable firsthand response to Reagan.

2. Edmund Morris, *Dutch* (New York: Modern Library, 1999). When this book appeared considerable dismay was aroused by Morris's introduction of fictional characters. But this aberration stops with chapter 28 and the Reagan presidency. The firsthand and documented material thereafter has been useful in this chapter. Footnotes have not been necessary because the procession of Morris's narrative is strictly chronological.
3. Donald T. Regan, *For the Record: From Wall Street to Washington* (New York: Harcourt Brace Jovanovich, 1988), 359–65.

Chapter 23: Bush One: Train Wreck

1. John Podhoretz, *Hell of a Ride: Backstage at the White House Follies 1989–1993* (New York: Simon and Schuster, 1993), 55.

Chapter 24: Bill Clinton: Was It Better Than It Looked?

1. I heard this during a conversation among reporters during the 1992 New Hampshire primary.
2. John F. Harris, *The Survivor* (New York: Random House, 2005), 223.
3. Harris, *The Survivor,* 329.
4. Harris, *The Survivor,* 263.
5. Edmund Burke, *Thoughts on French Affairs* (1791). While not at all withdrawing his criticism of the ideology of the "rights of man," Burke recognizes here that the multiple forces dooming the *ancien regime* were too powerful to be resisted successfully. Here Burke, who had analyzed the complexity of structure in society, sees complexity in social process. This was a moment of enormous importance in the history of conservative thought. To an increasing extent today, conservative thought must understand change. Unless it does, conservative rhetoric is irrelevant. For Arnold's great appreciation of this turn in Burke, see his "The Function of Criticism at the Present Time," available in many selected and collected editions. This passage in Arnold deserves prolonged consideration by conservatives. The edition I have been using is *Essays by Matthew Arnold* (London: Oxford University Press, 1914). Burke is a hero for Arnold because he brings ideas to bear in politics and is responsible to them. My copy is full of annotations from courses I took at Columbia with Lionel Trilling, some of the annotations of an undergraduate quality and painfully embarrassing.

Index